Child Studies Titles from Zed Books

Too little attention is still given in the Social Sciences to children. Zed Books has a small list of titles devoted to this extremely important social group.

Jo Boyden, *Children of the Cities*

Judith Ennew and Brian Milne, *The Next Generation: Lives of Third World Children*

William E. Myers (ed.), *Protecting Working Children*

Bernard Schlemmer (ed.), *The Exploited Child*

Jeremy Seabrook, *No Hiding Place: Child Sex Tourism: The Role of Extra-territorial Legislation*

For full details about these titles and Zed's general and subject catalogues, please write to: The Marketing Department, Zed Books, 7 Cynthia Street, London N1 9JF, UK or e-mail:

sales@zedbooks.demon.co.uk

Visit our website at: http://www.zedbooks.demon.co.uk

THE EXPLOITED CHILD

edited by
Bernard Schlemmer

translated by Philip Dresner

Zed Books
LONDON · NEW YORK

in association with

l'Institut de Recherche pour
le Développement
PARIS

The Exploited Child was first published in 2000 by Zed Books Ltd, 7 Cynthia Street, London N1 9JF, UK and Room 400, 175 Fifth Avenue, New York, NY 10010, USA in association with l'Institut de Recherche pour le Développement, 213 rue La Fayette, 75480 Paris Cedex 10, France.

Originally published as *L'enfant exploité: oppression, mise au travail, prolétarisation*, Editions Karthala-ORSTOM, Paris, in 1996 (522 pp.) (Diffusion: Karthala, 22–24 Boulevard Arago, 75013 Paris).

Distributed in the USA exclusively by St Martin's Press, Inc., 175 Fifth Avenue, New York, NY 10010, USA.

Cover designed by Lee Robinson/Ad Lib Design, London N19
Set in Monotype Garamond by Ewan Smith
Printed and bound in Malaysia

Grateful acknowledgement is made to the International Programme for the Eradication of Child Labour (IPEC-ILO) and the Swiss magazine, *Page 2* (Lausanne) for their financial support.

The views expressed in this book are the sole responsibility of their respective authors. Under no circumstances may they be ascribed to the institutions to which they belong or which have financed their work.

A catalogue record for this book is available from the British Library

US CIP has been applied for.

ISBN 1 85649 720 8 cased
ISBN 1 85649 721 6 limp

Contents

About the Contributors

ROSILENE ALVIM is a sociology lecturer at Rio de Janeiro Federal University, involved in ground-breaking studies on the working children of Brazil and author of, among other work, *Constituçao da Familia e Trabalho Industrial* (1985).

CHANTANA BANPASIRICHOTE is the author of research reports and an adviser to NGOs and government projects on child labour in Thailand. She currently teaches at Chulalongkorn University in Bangkok.

MICHEL BONNET is currently an official representative at the ILO where he has long worked as an expert, chiefly with the IPEC programme, and is recognized internationally as one of his field's top specialists. He has recently published *Regards sur les enfants travailleurs* (1997) which is currently being translated into English.

ROBERT CABANES is a director of research at IRD, specializing in the sociology of industry and work in the developing world.

BÉATRIZ S. CÉSPEDES SASTRE has led a number of UNICEF surveys on working children in her native Colombia.

ABDOU SALAM FALL is a researcher and lecturer in sociology at the Dakar Institut fondamental d'Afrique Noir (Senegal).

LIA FUKUI is a sociologist working, among others, for the Brazilian Ministry of Childhood, Family and Social Welfare (São Paulo). She has headed several surveys and for more than twenty years was the editor of numerous publications on child labour in Brazil.

BERNARD GARET is a former French teacher dismissed for his criticisms of the professional training establishment. He currently chairs the Maine et Loire regional branch of the League of Human Rights.

FRANCIS GENDREAU is a demographer and a director of research at IRD, specializing in developing world population studies. Currently, he is president of the Committee for International Cooperation in National Research in Demography.

MOHINI GULRAJANI is a lecturer at Delhi Unversity and pursues extensive research on the socio-economic aspects of child labour in India.

MARIE-FRANCE LANGE is a researcher at IRD, and a renowned expert in the sociology of education in Africa (see, among others, *L'école et les filles en Afrique*, 1998).

MICHAËL LAVALETTE has published widely on child labour: *Child Labour in the Capitalist Labour Market*, 1994; *A Thing of the Past? Child Labour in Britain 1800–Present*, 1999; with Sandy Hobbs and Jim McKechnie, *The ABC-CLIO World History Companion to Child Labour*, 1999.

YVES MARGUERAT is a sociologist at IRD where he is working on African youth issues, and co-founder of MARJUVIA (Juvenile Marginality in African Towns).

SERIGNE MOR MBAYE is a psychologist working with deprived children at the Centre of Child Guidance in Dakar (Senegal).

CLAUDE MEILLASSOUX is internationally renowned for the pioneering work which sparked what came to be known as the French school of economic anthropology. He is a CNRS silver medal winner and author of, among others, *Femmes, greniers et capitaux* (1975).

ALAIN MORICE is an anthropologist at the CNRS (France). His publication, *The Exploitation of Children in the 'Informal Sector': Proposals for Research*, is a classic reference work in this field.

OLGA NIEUWENHUYS teaches at the University of Amsterdam, the Netherlands. She is one of the all too few anthropologists to work on the issue of the exploitation of children and is the author of, among other works, *Children's Lifeworlds: Gender, Welfare and Labour in the Developing World* (1994).

USHA RAMANATHAN is a well-known specialist in labour law who teaches at Delhi University (India).

BODO RAVOLOLOMANGA is a Madagascan researcher and author of, among other works, *Être femme et mère à Madagascar* (1992). She now works at the Institut de Civilisations, Musée d'Art et d'Archéologie, Antananarivo, Madagascar.

BERNARD SCHLEMMER is a director of research at IRD and head of the 'Savoirs et Développement' programme, which includes his personal research on child labour and scholarship in Morocco.

ALESSANDRO STELLA is an historian at the CNRS, a specialist in labour and slavery issues in Western Europe, one of the very few in the world to have worked on the exploitation of children.

CHARLES-ÉDOUARD DE SUREMAIN is an anthropologist at IRD. He spent nine years in the field in Guatemala, studying the social organization of large coffee plantations (see *Jours ordinaires à la finca*, 1996).

ELVIRA TARACENA teaches at the Mexican Independent National University and has led several teams investigating the lives of street children in Mexico.

MARIA-LUISA TAVERA is a researcher and lecturer at ENEP-Iztacala, the National School of Education (UNAM, Universidad Autonoma de Mexico). She is also a psychotherapist and works in institutions for abandoned children.

MARTIN VERLET is a sociologist at IRD and a renowned Ghana specialist. He is now working on education in Ghana.

MARÍA-ISABEL ZARAMA V. MEYER has worked in Colombia with Bogota shanty-town children and their mothers (as part of the 'Casas Vecinales' programme) and has carried out surveys on the working children of Boyaca (Topaga).

CHAPTER I

General Introduction

Bernard Schlemmer

Although it has not yet reached the top of the agenda, the issue of child labour is occupying a growing place in the public consciousness. In the last few years, thanks to the work of the concerned international authorities – the International Labour Organization (ILO), the United Nations Children's Fund (UNICEF)[1] – and NGOs, there have been demonstrations, conferences and debates, television and radio programmes on the subject as well as newspaper articles and special reports in periodicals. Some may well deplore the weakness and limited scope of the means made available; others might feel that the media reports (much less the world of scientific and academic research, to which I shall return later) have not always been equal to their specific responsibilities; but it cannot be denied that the issue is now far more visible, and that in itself is no mean achievement. Grounds for pessimism, though, are hardly in short supply and many await the reader within the pages of this book; all the more reason to rejoice, then, as *awareness-raising* remains the key requirement to making any progress in this matter. The United Nations has already passed a 'Convention on the Rights of the Child'. Its results are barely visible, but the French Revolution's 'Declaration of the Rights of Man and the Citizen' – a time-bomb planted in the old world – did not change the political landscape overnight; yet nobody today would dream of denying the part it played in gradually shaping the system of values now governing our lives. If, with the help of the United Nations, we fight for the values, the corresponding legal systems may be extended to cover the entire planet.

The Absence of Theoretical Research

Despite having, to its credit, established the principles, and possessing the authority to impose them upon the international community, the Convention remains at a level of generality that betrays a lack of maturity in the thinking being done on the subject. It may well address the problem of child labour, but it gives no clear idea as to either *who* should be regarded as a child, working or otherwise, or *what* should be regarded as the work to which he

I

or she must not be subjected. Practising child labour specialists are now beginning to realize that this field requires a backbone of theoretical thought specific to this very issue and not one merely derived from the general work carried out on adult populations: 'When we confront a problem we often say "Don't just stand there, do something!" Now we are saying: "Don't just do something, stand there first!"'[2]

So one cannot help but conclude that all the policies drawn up, the efforts agreed upon and the means invested over so many years if not actually to eliminate the phenomenon – the originally declared intention when all is said and done – then simply to improve the situation of working children, have been about as effective as watering the sand to stop desertification. The reasons for such powerlessness are many and varied; nor should we believe that once the world of research finally deigns to look into the matter, it will, in one fell swoop, come up with the answers. But the theoretical vacuum really does exist. Not that nothing has been achieved; on the contrary, the past few years have seen substantial progress in the thinking, thanks to the efforts of specialized associations confronting the problem and the work of a handful of researchers who work in the service of such organizations or as university academics with an interest in the issue. Several authors have shown child labour to be a structural phenomenon stemming from present-day capitalism (even though, of course, nobody needed to wait for capitalism before putting children to work!).[3]

If that is true, then child labour cannot realistically be ignored by anyone hoping to produce a serious analysis of developments as momentous as those occurring in working relations, international migration or economic relations at regional, national and world level – not to mention in the collective strategies of the poverty-stricken populations of both deprived rural areas and dehumanized conurbations; in short, the great social and economic changes being witnessed today.

The fact is, however, that except for a fringe minority, child labour may not even enter the frame as a recognized basic factor, even though social scientists and, moreover, economists (the first concerned when all is said and done) may eventually have to take it into consideration. Child labour would appear to be regarded as a problem whose current magnitude is a mere epiphenomenon of a passing economic crisis, something about which little can be done and which, although naturally worth the odd burst of moral outrage – a job best left to the activists and NGOs – warrants no special attention from the theoretical point of view (supposedly that of the researcher).

It is on this subject that we wish to make a contribution through collective theoretical thought.

Exploited Children: Child Labour and Proletarianization

The present book is composed of papers discussed during an international symposium staged in Paris, on 24–26 November 1994, under the title 'Exploited Children – Child Labour and Proletarianization'.[4] As far as we know, it was the first event of its kind on this subject organized solely by researchers for researchers, i.e. with the strictly scientific goal of collating and enhancing theoretical and concrete analyses rather than debating which policies to promote. Needless to say, we were not setting out to produce definitive (theoretical, not to mention practical) answers to the difficult questions raised by child labour; and we take the liberty of criticizing the appalling degree to which the world of research underrates the phenomenon only because we see ourselves as our first target;[5] apart from Alain Morice, none of us had ever previously worked on the question, even though we had all been confronted by it at one stage or another.

Since we were not experts in the matter, we were therefore hardly expecting to penetrate what was if not an untouched, then a virtually uncharted, field of science. Once again, that does not mean to say the world of research had previously been absent from the debate; on the contrary, only a dozen or so of the fifty authors of thirty-eight papers were found to belong to institutions specializing in a child- or child-labour-specific work project and campaign of action (and many of them regarded themselves first and foremost as researchers).[6] But if we were to count, on the one hand, the number of researchers (about thirty) for whom child labour did not constitute their main focus of investigation and who were simply taking advantage of the opportunity the symposium offered to discuss a subject encountered in the course of other work, and, on the other hand, those who had genuinely made it the focus of ongoing research, then the conclusion would be that the majority of the conference speakers were not (strictly speaking) specialists.

As a matter of fact, only a handful of researchers around the world[7] are actually working full-time, and as researchers, on this issue.[8] It is generally regarded as belonging to the field of action and of idealism: and hence is seen to constitute a social problem rather than a problem for the social sciences, a 'problem of society' rather than subject matter for research.[9] We, however, believe it to be an outstandingly fertile topic from the scientific – epistemological and methodological – standpoint; and we hope the reader will agree. Active involvement has never stood in the way of thoroughgoing analysis, as we shall see in the course of the following contributions where, if the highly varied observations providing the bases of analysis do not contradict each other, the tone adopted by their authors, the insights they offer and their suggested solutions clearly convey the full complexity of the phenomenon.

The Prevailing Ideology: An Effective Mask

It is true to say that the image of childhood masks the reality experienced by children. The world of childhood is regarded as a time of innocence to be protected from the brutal aggression of the real world; a period of latency during which a child needs shelter while growing up until he or she is finally ready to confront reality. Even less than the labourer, the peasant, the immigrant, pauper or exploited person – already more often considered as the objects of social policies, development, integration, support and consciousness-raising rather than the subjects of their own history – the child is never perceived as an actor but always as the 'target' (according to international institutions' current term, whose cruelty and cynicism one would prefer to believe was unintended), the passive recipient of measures taken to protect him or her, i.e. to hold him/her 'outside' the world he/she is going to have to face on reaching adulthood. Reality, however, does not correspond to that image, not by a long shot: far from behaving as irresponsible in-dividuals, there are many working children who have become their families' de facto breadwinners, and who are perfectly well aware of and derive legitimate pride from this fact; but also, far from being innocent, there are many children whose moral sense teaches them stand up for themselves and their families, and who would dare blame them? These two patterns of behaviour, by the way, are by no means mutually exclusive; both raise doubts about the general model.

Also, in order not to destroy the comforting ('natural' and 'universal') image of innocent and protected childhood, the gap separating it from that other 'unjustifiable' side of reality is narrowed by reducing the latter to a marginal reality that can be isolated and eliminated. This results in those not conforming to the ideal model being seen solely as victims and, ultimately, objects: objects of pity, compassion and charity for well-to-do people turning their attention to their predicament; objects of shame and guilt for their parents, their families and communities.[10]

This practice is further boosted by the fact that the vast majority of the most outrageous cases of exploited child labour are to be found in regions outside the richer and more industrialized countries. The authors of one particularly lucid book on child labour in Peru make the following argument:

> Ethnical and racial discrimination is in our opinion an essential part of any definition of the specifically Peruvian version of children's work. It is not normally taken into account [...] perhaps because it is so common that it almost goes unnoticed [...] Children's work is only found among the Indian and mestizo races, never among white Peruvians. While this may seem to be self-evident, and a tautology, it is important to indicate its implications. What does it mean to make this mass and almost exclusive identification of children's work with a racial majority which is subordinate and looked down on by the dominant culture? First of all it leads to a common belief that children's work

is the remnant of a custom of a primitive race which has still not been completely modernized and civilized. It makes it possible to cover up class contradictions by disguising them as the backwardness of one culture in comparison with another. Second, racism in our culture and social relations serves as a unconscious, ideological sedative in the face of the evident contradiction between the dominant image of childhood and children's work. In other words, it is true that according to this image, children should not work, but those who work are 'cholitos' (Indians and mestizos) or children from the poor sectors, and they do not represent 'modern Peru'. Finally, racism in children's work helps to reproduce and assimilate the more extreme forms of exploitation of children, which would be unlikely to be accepted or tolerated were the children white.[11]

Can we not extend their line of reasoning beyond the Peruvian context they were studying? All we would need to do would be to paraphrase their remarks, replacing 'Peru' and 'Peruvian' with terms like 'in the world' and 'world situation'; and 'mestizos' and 'Indians' with 'Third World countries' and 'underdeveloped populations'. Is not the same brand of racism practised by the West, likewise allowing us to maintain that child labour, like poverty in the Third World, is but a passing phase likely to last only as long as it takes for everyone to get their share of the fruits of economic growth? Until then, so the argument goes, we could, and of course should, lend as much support as possible to the organizations whose job it is to come to the assistance of those poverty-stricken people. But there is no reason to cast doubt on the rich countries' economic system, the only one to produce economic growth and protected children and, in so doing, prove its superiority: *quod erat demonstrandum!*

Paternalism: An Ambivalent Concept?

The very nature of child labour works to the advantage of that corrupt line of reasoning. Indeed, putting children to work only rarely, if ever, corresponds to conventional employment practices consisting of a contractual exchange between an employer needing such and such a job done and an employee able to supply him with the necessary services, in return for a predetermined fee. That, in theory at least, is how things are supposed to happen; it is known in the literature as 'the labour market'.[12] However, even less than in the adult world (where the term is largely fallacious and obscures otherwise complex social relations), there is strictly speaking no such thing as a 'market' for child labour. In the vast majority of cases where a child is put to work, there is not the slightest resemblance to the so-called 'free-bargaining-based exchange'; as a rule, the decision, taken above all by the family, brings a whole raft of extra-economic factors into play. Naturally, the expected earnings and estimated work load will be taken into account and looked at in relation to the child's age, gender, rank (e.g. senior, junior) and place in the family (e.g. direct descendant, collateral) (Poirier).[13] In addition to that, the type of relationship with the employer prior to recruitment will also be considered: kinship, friendship, relations based on trust, dependence, submissiveness, or even a chance or formal encounter, albeit in the company of parents.[14] The type of relationship is what will determine the benefits expected from the employment which, much more than in monetary terms, are often calculated in terms of training, upbringing, care, protection and *future* employment. In this way, the fact that the child has actually been hired on the spot – for what is at times very hard work – is masked by the illusion that he or she is guaranteed both protection for the time being and a job on reaching adulthood.[15]

This – and several papers stress the point – accounts for the fact that the children often have no precisely defined tasks to perform; like any child in the family home, they are there to satisfy the demand, to contend with the thousand and one needs of their employer: housework, keeping watch, running errands; labour is transformed into service.

> The fact that a child enters employment via kinship channels ultimately ends up lending a domestic feel to working relations, which assume the vocabulary and ideology of kinship. The master and mistress can then adopt a pseudo-parental role on the grounds that they were originally granted authority by the parents [...] This domestication of working relations, and the use made of it, will be one of the masks of exploitation. (Verlet)

Plainly, the mask works all the better for having been amply reinforced by the traditional image of the child as an evolving being, someone incomplete, not fully responsible and requiring guidance and protection, training and control.

This, by the way, is why the employer, and even the family, do not regard the money working children receive under such conditions as a 'wage', a payment calculated precisely for the task carried out; instead it is seen rather as a bonus, a reward to encourage them in their efforts. Anyway, it never matches an adult's earnings, even for an equal amount of work, because the employer needs his own rewards for all the effort he has agreed to put into guiding and protecting, forming and controlling the child entrusted to his care. It is not necessarily a fundamentally cynical attitude; it is much more of an interiorization of the prevailing ideology by each and every actor in this warped game. The parents are grateful to the person who will relieve them of a share of their responsibilities by becoming their children's guardian, keeping them close and preventing them from wandering the streets and falling into delinquency or high-risk sexual behaviour. And they are all the more willing to accept such a transfer because, apart from anything else, the employer will (or at least they want to persuade themselves he will) give their children an apprenticeship in a trade, turn them into responsible adults and equip them to contend with life's hardships.

In the most directly productive sphere itself, the bosses (or, as they prefer to think of themselves, 'mentors'), 'convinced that they have a bona fide mission to civilize children from a humble background' (Suremain), are more often than not quite conscious of their duty, since the role of mentor and their economic interests, far from being mutually exclusive, logically lend each other support. Ultimately, the children are still the ones least fooled by the allegedly balanced exchange binding them to their employer, which is not hard to imagine considering how they are in the best position to grasp the realities of the work they do, and what they receive in return: but this further underscores the paradox whereby they, and they alone, are deprived of the status of responsible subjects because, as minors, they have no right to express themselves and are expected to submit without a word.

That is how, as Alain Morice recalled during one of the conference debates, the paternalism governing virtually all working relations involving children consists above all in the dialectic of protection and threats. We shall define it as being either an exploitative relationship which, under cover of biological or fictitious kinship ties, conceals itself (consciously or otherwise) beneath a more or less genuinely granted protective relationship; or a protective relationship stemming from biological or fictitious kinship ties that transforms itself into a more or less severe exploitative relationship. However, if the collective consciousness regards paternalism in connection with the defining of employer–employee working relations as a negative term, that is because it suggests that the employer abusively treats his employees as his children, as minors. The 'protection' is the particular aspect the public has in mind; it is this aspect that is being challenged in the name of respect for, and the dignity of, the worker. 'It's for your own good!' is not an easy argument for an adult to stomach. But why take umbrage as soon as the employees in fact *are* children? During the same debate, Marie Anderfuhren stressed the fundamental ambiguity of paternalism applied to the child, whereby the employer sees that child as both a source of labour *and* the son or daughter for whom he is responsible; such ambiguity serves as a safety mechanism against over-exploitation but also as a means of masking and refining the exploitation.

This brings us back to the difficulty of defining child labour. How can we regard as 'labour' the housework a young girl does to help her own family, or the helping hand a young boy gives in his father's shop, not to mention the compulsory participation in a guard of honour to welcome a visiting dignitary (Lange); or even the housework a young girl does to help the family that has agreed to take her in, or the helping hand given by the young boy placed in an apprenticeship?

To add to that, the matter of defining child labour is hindered by the international institutions' and specialized agencies' passion for bookkeeping. 'Child labour,' they all seem to think, 'is whatever we can measure it to be.'

How Many Children are Working? What Does the Question Mean?

The sheer scale of child employment has, as we have said, given it a place of growing importance among the crucial problems troubling public opinion as the twentieth century becomes the twenty-first. But how big a problem is it exactly? Even the most casual reader of the literature on the topic cannot help being struck by the fact that the vast majority of authors open with an estimate of the number of children working in the world, or in their particular region of interest. They either quote figures released by the ILO – over 100 million children under the age of fifteen worldwide – or put forward their own counting methods which, as a rule, take ILO estimates as a lower limit and set the upper limit at more or less double that amount.[16] Each and every one of them points out how hard it is to calculate exact numbers of working children, for quite obvious reasons. To begin with, the bulk of the work done by children can be considered, practically 'by definition', as evading any form of inventory. This is at best because it is done in what we have agreed to call the 'informal sector' (petty street trading, domestic services, agricultural labour, etc.), where it is visible yet unrecorded, not always legal but quite often tolerated; and where the situation is extremely changeable: a child may, for instance, be working in the fields during harvest season, but not the following month. Greater secrecy surrounds the work done in a climate of illegality, though only illegal because an age limit fixed by law is not being respected and the employer is careful not to brag about it. Even harder to estimate is the work that is not only illegal but also regarded as unacceptable by society at large: children recruited as thieves, drug pushers, prostitutes, fighters in armed struggles or henchmen for organized crime.

Given these conditions, the main criterion the ILO now uses is that of schooling: rather than actually being 'added up', the number of children put to work is 'deducted' from that of children not benefiting from a primary school education. For an under-fifteen-year-old child, this is as good as saying that school activities cannot coexist with money-making activities, which is obviously untrue; all the more so because if it is detrimental to their schooling for children to have to divide their time between schoolwork and outside work and if it is often the start of a process which, in more or less the long run, will lead to their dropping out of the education system, for just as many other children it can, on the contrary, be the only way for them to obtain the money they need to continue their studies.

This is where we find one of the aspects that may perhaps explain the reluctance to see child labour as just as important a problem as malnutrition, population growth or (to stay close to our theme) abandoned children ('street children', as they are commonly known). It is not so much the shortage of reliable figures that is the problem – for we do know that the phenomenon is of such importance that regardless of the precise numbers of children affected it still warrants serious attention; rather it is the vague feeling that we do not really know what we are talking about, that vastly different situations are being placed 'in the same basket', and that nobody can effectively fight such an ill-defined phenomenon. After all, in the countries where economic conditions are difficult, is it not normal to find children working, helping their parents in the fields, lending a hand around the workshop, starting to learn their trade alongside their parents or parents' friends?

> Where 'education' in the form of training for future adult life is provided in and around the home by parents, 'work' in the form of household and farming chores often begins as soon as the child can work, increasing with the growth of the child's physical strength, knowledge and capacity to handle the small hurdles of daily living. Millions of children today are still raised in an environment where the distinctions between 'helping parents', 'education and preparation for future adult life', and 'child labor' are blurred.[17]

Extreme cases of children aged ten or under working a ten- to twelve-hour day, twelve months a year, in appalling hygiene and safety conditions, for example, are bound to infuriate people. But where exactly does the scandal begin?[18] If the whole world cannot be guaranteed the same level of development as the richer countries, how can we accurately define what amounts to an intolerable degree of exploitation?

Several authors stress the pride felt by certain children, and endorsed by their social milieu, at having accomplished work which is especially hard (and degrading in the light of the values we defend as universal). Does this mean that they are therefore colluding in the exploitation of children?

Thinking on the matter has made great progress over the past few years. ILO involvement dates back as far as 1919; but how many internal revisions have occurred since the days when it was hoped that passing international conventions would bring an end to the employment of children throughout the entire world. Nowadays, the ILO, not to mention UNICEF and the majority of interested NGOs, would, off the record at least, agree that the issue here is not the fact of whether or not the child is working but the nature of the work performed, his or her burden, we might say, assessed in both qualitative and quantitative terms, given that putting a child to work might very well amount to a positive option, both for him/herself and the family – a fitting and timely assumption of responsibility.

> ILO has tried to make a clear distinction between children working in socially and personally useful ways – working for pocket money, doing household chores, helping in the family business during the school holidays – and children whose working conditions should be regulated or eliminated. Working children at risk, according to ILO, are: children who are prematurely leading adult lives and working long hours for low wages, under conditions which are damaging to their health and to their physical or mental development.[19]

Plainly then, the question as yet remains unresolved.[20]

What is Child Labour?

When we think of child labour, the tendency is to regard *labour* as referring solely to a *paid* job, done *outside the family unit*. Scientific literature on sexual divisions of labour, however, has shown us the true extent, and burden, of domestic labour. But the domestic labour done by children – as a number of the conference papers powerfully pointed out – can be just as heavy, if not heavier, than that done by women. For the work performed in, and on behalf of, the household can assume even worse forms than in the industries exploiting this type of labour force and rightly condemned as inhuman; and yet those industries are generally the only ones we would think of blaming because they are located outside the household. It has to be said that the small girls working late into the night at the shrimp-curing yards north of Kerala (India) and sleeping in huge sheds without beds, for example, are actually doing so out of choice and find it much easier – and, above all, far better for their self-esteem – than what they are required to do by the prevailing traditional economic system in their home villages (Nieuwenhuys). Another example, not drawn from industry but no less eloquent, is that not one of the young girls who have left the Brazilian Nordeste and moved to the city to be employed as housemaids – not the kind of post guaranteed to foster a great deal of self-respect – misses the work they previously used to do in the fields with and on behalf of their families (Anderfuhren).

So the nature of the social working relations does not necessarily create exploitation, any more than the real or fictitious kinship ties with the employer will provide protection from it. The brutality of exploitation may be found within as much as outside the domestic environment. And the work performed by a child is not inevitably bound to be subject to unacceptable conditions, outside as much as within the domestic environment.

> Abuse, violence, aggression, exploitation and relations of servitude masked by family ties, the use of cheap, weak labour with no social representation or legal protection, physical risk and danger, tiredness, fatigue, the constant temptation to go beyond the bounds of the law and join in criminal activity, the existence of established mafias which trap young workers: all this exists [...] But not all informal children's work is like that. On the contrary, most children work under the care and protection of their relatives. Many of them work independently and have great freedom in deciding when and how hard to work.[21]

Work can just as easily provide children with an opportunity to escape the violence of a broken home; or at least to stand up for their right to choose, their independence and sense of personal responsibility within the family group.

So child labour is hard to define because it falls within the province of specific forms of social relations – paternalism, in the strict sense of the term as described above – and forms of exploitation rightly judged incompatible with a social relationship claiming to be rooted in kinship. The labour itself is not what is in question here; rather the fact that it is done by a minor, a dependant, a child. People will either refuse to call it *labour*, as is almost always the case with work done inside the family unit, or be appalled that such work is forced upon children who should not even be working. As Olga Nieuwenhuys usefully points out, 'the way common wisdom conceptualizes the exploitation of children betrays a greater concern with the threat posed to society by deviations from what are seen as acceptable forms of socialization, than with the welfare of working children'. A genuine conceptual revolution needs to occur before people accept that the child really is a subject and not just the object of specific measures, a responsible social actor perfectly capable of exercising rights which are, or should be, the rights of every human being and, in particular, every worker (not just those specific rights designed to protect physical and/or psychological incompleteness).

The Question of Schooling

The question of schooling is, of course, inseparable from that of child labour; and few papers did not broach it. It helps to confuse the matter of arriving at a definition. In the words of Lia Fukui: 'School activities do not exclude children from employment, but employment can exclude them from school.' Accordingly, several papers remind us that children, especially young girls, often work in order to be able to pay their school fees (or those of their brothers, or cousins living under the same roof). On the one hand, 'combining school work and a paid job leaves them constantly exhausted, overworked and unable to cope properly with either' (Mathur); and we are not even talking here about certain disconcertingly extreme situations.[22] On the other hand, there is the recurring theme of parental disinvestment *vis-à-vis* schools, which parents accuse of teaching their children things of no useful value. Besides, they say, look how many qualified young people there are out of work and loitering idly on the verge of delinquency. What is more, there are not necessarily any qualifications at the end, the teaching hardly seems relevant to real life, and the pupils do not even learn what they are being taught.[23] Our child would be better off learning a trade, having a skill that will always be useful when he really has to go out and earn a living. What is important, they think – with some justification – is to equip the child for later life and, in the meantime, keep him/her off the streets. Hence the factory, in contrast to the streets, may 'take over the protective role, replacing the family while also serving as a "school" [...] Even if the working classes and society at large do not regard work as "good" for children, it appears, alongside school, as a means of protecting them from a life of crime' (Alvim).

Actually, this is a largely artificial opposition and the debate is built on false premises. No matter what the parents' background, they are very well aware of the fact that education, despite its failure to adapt, still remains a guarantee of professional success for anyone capable of successfully seeing it through. Which implies that unless the child is exceptionally gifted, the parents have to provide all the required cultural grounding, or enough money to pay for private schooling – both conditions being mutually enhancing, of course. When weighing the advantages against the costs in an attempt to decide whether or not to withdraw a child from school, what they measure is not the school's ability to foster future social mobility 'for one and all', but for *their* child and for them as parents; otherwise, being denied the opportunity to escape the social status into which they are born, it would indeed be wiser immediately to set about acquiring the skills that their environment requires. In short, 'school represents a value in the eyes of the working classes, but the education system does not help them to attain that value, since it automatically excludes anyone who does not conform to its own established model pupil' (Fukui).[24]

All Children Work

These thoughts on schooling bring us back to the problem of defining child 'labour'. Would it not be more heuristic to consider that *all* children work, be it in the factory, the fields, the home, the streets or at school? Historically speaking, this is an obvious fact: since the beginning of time children have always undergone socialization by being progressively introduced into the 'world of work' and, as they grow up, being given an increasingly important role in the collective work of the community; not even free, secular and compulsory schooling – still a relatively recent revolution – has been able to curb the use of children in productive tasks.[25]

For a child whose labour is directly productive, and when the person profiting from it has no bond of kinship with him or her, the question poses no problem. The child's activity is labour because it will be exploited in every sense of the word 'exploitation'. We have seen that exploitation can just as easily occur within the household framework; conversely, however, labour can exist without exploitation. In the Moyen-Mono district of Togo, for example, children 'are directly responsible for increasing the wealth of the head of the family', writes Marie-France Lange. 'But,' she goes on, 'since this wealth will eventually be left to them in their father's will, it is something of a *return on investment* for the work put in during childhood or adolescence.' Is it not the same case with apprentices who invest the share of their total working hours confiscated for productive labour, but recover that investment later when they have acquired the skills of a trade? The objection may be made that the apprenticeship master is rarely a philanthropist: if the apprentice in his keeping costs him more than he earns, the system will have neither such reach, nor such a sense of continuity. An apprentice is a worker who contributes directly, through his labour, to his employer's earnings in return for the time the latter devotes to teaching him or her a trade – this being in no way equal to the time the apprentice devotes to his employer.[26] Often, however, the apprentice also contributes indirectly to the master's income by making a cash or kind *payment* (Marguerat). This is actually a payment agreed because the young person's labour in the workshop is not judged economically viable enough to compensate for the working time lost by the employer in having to supervise or pass on his know-how.

Let us take the point a stage further: how then can we tell, by looking at the nature of the occupation alone, what should and should not be regarded as labour? Apprentices, like children working in factories or fields, school-children or students, devote a share of their time to restricting, non-leisure activities, 'socially useful production', either immediately or later when the work consists of an investment (studies) for future productive work. So all children are working, but not under the same conditions. What makes the difference is not the fact of whether or not an individual's activity deserves to be considered as 'labour', but whether that work is to some extent exploited by another party, or an investment for his/her future good. Some children start out with better opportunities than others. Only students are in the privileged position of not being required immediately to take part in production in exchange for their intellectual work. Meanwhile, students and apprentices share the same (privileged) position of receiving a training which prepares them for adult life. But apprentices will generally have fewer oppor-tunities of finding interesting and properly paid work.[27] Similarly, it is better to be an apprentice and learn a trade, even if you have to pay for it, than to be recruited to work in a factory and condemned to the same, unskilled drudgery all day long. At worst, if we go to the extreme limits of the social relations continuum, it is better, even under conditions that are more than difficult, to be free – that is, your own master – than inextricably bound to an employer, as is the case of the children in 'bonded labour' that Michel Bonnet talks about later in this book.

The problem is therefore not that children are working, but the con-ditions under which they are doing the work, the degree to which their work is exploited.

Oppression and Exploitation

So the question then becomes: where does the *exploitation* of child labour begin?

We ought to differentiate here between 'exploitation' and 'oppression'. Oppression binds children to their *minority status* which – as is often the case with women, although to a far more severe degree – denies them the status of individuals or responsibility for their acts; exploitation confiscates their *surplus labour*, that unpaid share of their working hours, a necessary pre-requisite for the employer to produce *surplus value*.[28] The two situations are not mutually exclusive; on the contrary, when combined they reinforce one another: pure economic exploitation adds to the oppression linked to minority status.

The fundamental difference is therefore as follows: employment in the domestic economy works within a system which also assumes responsibility for the worker's social reproduction (reproduction of life and living conditions), while in the capitalist economy a large share of that responsibility is delegated to other systems (family solidarity) or institutions (the welfare state), if any such institutions exist at all and are equal to the task. Wages merely contribute to the costs necessary for the upkeep and renewal of the labour force, the former being by no means calculated in relation to the latter; they even fall well below the poverty line. The myth that wages should provide for the worker's family's needs – already crude enough in the case of adult workers, especially if they happen to be women – vanishes when the worker in question is a child; children's earnings are not even *supposed* to be sufficient for their needs, but rather to serve as secondary income for their families.

However, that does not mean to say that the poor price of labour necessarily represents a source of excess profit for the employer. In a world where the free movement of capital and goods (but not labour) is now globally speaking guaranteed, the industries of the South can only maintain their position on the market by making the most of the sole area in which they remain well and truly competitive: cheap labour. But the burden of debt forces those countries to do all they can to increase their exports.[29] Without putting children to work – and paying them far lower wages than adults – countries such as India and Pakistan would see a dramatic fall in their foreign currency earnings (Gulrajani).

Children can indeed be regarded as the final links in a 'chain of exploitation' (Morice) whose dynamics may be outlined as follows: to begin with, by taking over the housework, the children leave their mothers free for paid work to supplement (or provide the whole of) the family's income. Women's wages, which the employer regards as secondary income, are set at a lower rate than men's, which is how the employer manages to keep his head above water in a competitive market dominated largely at the end of the chain by industrialized country buyers. The latter for their part impose tougher terms of payment, forcing every level of the chain to cut labour costs still further; at the end of the line, many children are in turn made to work for the market in order to add to the family income; from then onwards they, like their mothers, perform both paid work and domestic labour, for even lower financial rewards. So the exploitation of domestic labour and child labour would seem to be inherent to a system whose international policy-making bodies (the International Monetary Fund and World Bank) aim, notably through their structural adjustment plans, to 'rationalize' economic policy, in particular via the cutting of production costs.

Let us leave the conclusion to Michel Bonnet, International Labour Organization expert, and one of the best specialists in the field: 'the workers of tomorrow – born of the child labour of today – [...] are ready for anything, open to any sort of work [...] and all sorts of exploitation. It is here, perhaps, in this transformation of a skilled worker into a subservient jack of all trades, that we should seek the greatest threat posed by child labour' (M. Bonnet).

But we should also add that the process has two sides to it: first there is a whole growing population of unskilled workers who have never been trained for anything other than obeying orders and 'sorting things out for themselves'; then there is the growing population of workers who have had a training but have been deskilled because of the employment shortage.

A labour market where, having learnt a trade, skilled workers take up posts they will occupy all their working lives with a steady income enabling them to earn a living for themselves and their families, is a picture which has more or less corresponded to a certain reality in richer countries since the end of the Second World War. But it has imposed itself as the normal model to which the employment situation ought to conform, except at times of crisis. However, not only are the historical roots of such a 'model' hardly a guarantee of its durability and not only is its geographical scope highly limited, but it no longer even conveys a true picture of the real-life situation today; job insecurity is increasingly becoming the norm, and workers experience sporadic periods of being unable meet their own needs, never mind stand as the sole breadwinner of the household. First the women then the children go out to work, and 'odd jobs', unsteady, underpaid and unskilled work on the fringes of the law proliferate right across the board. One understands why child labour is developing along with what we generally call the 'informal sector'.

If there is one feature specific to child labour it is that when such labour does nothing to prepare the children for their future as adults, then – and Michel Bonnet is right to insist on this point – the exploitation of their present goes hand in hand with the privation of their future. Incidentally, and this is not so far removed from what has just been said, it is clearly not a matter of child labour beginning to resemble adult labour (even in the countries where no-holds-barred capitalism is spreading, children very rarely find themselves in a situation comparable to nineteenth-century Europe's treatment of the children of the working classes) but, on the contrary, of the labour of a growing number of adults becoming 'infantilized'.

Notes

1. On its own admission, UNICEF has only very recently begun taking a real interest in the question of child labour. Its first official statement was released in 1986: a paper entitled *Exploitation of Working Children and Street Children* (Document E/ICEF/1986/CRP.3).

2. William Myers, ILO child labour expert, quoted in Black (1993: 15).

3. Cf. the remarkable historical introduction to Part I of this book.

4. Jointly organized by ORSTOM (the French Institute of Scientific Research for Overseas Development now IRD), CEPED (the Population and Development Centre) and CEA (the Centre for African Studies – a body run by the National Centre for Scientific Research [CNRS] and the School for Advanced Studies in Social Sciences [EHESS], with the financial backing of the International Labour Organization and the French Ministry of Cooperation. A volume entitled *Colloque international: L'enfant exploité - oppression, mise au travail et prolétarisation* contains the five synthesis reports compiling the full corpus of the symposium papers; it has been distributed to the main specialized documentation centres (BIT, UNICEF, IRD-CEDID, CEPED, BICE, DEI).

5. The conference organizing committee was comprised of R. Cabanes, F. Gendreau, C. Meillassoux, A. Morice, D. Poitou, B. Schlemmer and M. Verlet.

6. NGOs, on the other hand, were very much present among the audience.

7. The symposium can definitely be said to have reached the vast majority of institutions likely to be interested.

8. This lack of interest, or low level of interest at the least, is particularly noticeable in France. If our information is correct, not a single ORSTOM research programme was ever conducted specifically on this theme; the same goes for the CNRS (apart from the work of historian Alessandro Stella, one of the conference speakers), and as far as university research is concerned, there is but a handful of student dissertations and theses. The situation is obviously different in the countries of the South that have managed to develop a strong scientific community, e.g. Brazil, India or even Peru. But it is not quite so bad in all countries in the North either: Great Britain, in particular, holds an important place with regard to scientific literature on child labour.

9. It was for pedagogical reasons that we therefore chose not to publish the full 'Proceedings' containing all the papers delivered, but to write four articles on four basic themes, presenting a synthesis of what had been brought forward during the symposium, each illustrated by the papers we felt to be the most representative. We sincerely hope that the authors whose work does not appear here will have the goodness to forgive us. And the reader can always consult the volume containing the full corpus of papers (see above, note 4).

10. This also leads to a refusal to regard as victims those people whose exploitation occurs in forms considered acceptable by the ruling culture. Both standpoints were illustrated during the symposium by two symmetrical absences: nothing on child prostitution and next to nothing on domestic child labour, as if subconsciously we considered the former form of occupation to be located beyond child labour and the latter, short of it.

11. G. Schibotto and A. Cussianovich (1994: 31–2). (English translation of four chapters from *Niños Trabajadores, Construyendo una Identidad*, IPEC, 1990, Hipolito Unánue 335, Lince, Lima, Peru.)

12. One paper (Uribe) describes the contracts offered by recruiting agents dispatched by landlords to 'round up' employees, children or adults:

- the workers shall be transported to the work site free of charge, but they must pay for the return trip;
- workers [...] shall receive bed and board, payable by the mine owners;
- at the end of 3 months' work, the mine owner shall give the workers their pay, minus any sums spent during that period on provisions purchased from his stores (the owner sells food, clothing, medicine, alcohol, etc.).

Although apparently fair, the 'exchange' is in fact fictitious: forced to accept the job in order to have the accommodation and advanced payment he is offered on the spot, the worker is never able to settle a 'debt' which has been carefully calculated to exceed his wages. On the theoretical consequences of these types of social relations, see C. Geffray (1995).

13. A name in brackets but no date refers to the paper delivered at the symposium by the person in question (in the case of joint authorship, only the first author's name is printed) and published in the unabridged volume of symposium papers (see above, note 4).

14. Cf. M. Anderfuhren: 'In all likelihood it is quite different for parents to leave their children in the hands of somebody they will have seen, with whom they will have conversed, to whom they can put a face. For all that, though, there is something fictitious about such a bond because, on both sides, it is basically a matter of convincing oneself that the relationship has been personalized, hence humanized.'

15. M. Bonnet stresses the enormous importance of this personal relationship between employer and child by showing how, even in its worst form, it may constitute the only possible solution: to safeguard the child from unemployment, he says, 'the only way to create a solid bond (with an employer) is often by incurring a debt and pledging a child as bonded labour in order to pay it off'.

16. Ninety-five per cent live in developing countries, half of them in Asia. As a percentage of total population, however, it is in Africa that we find the highest proportion of child labour – a third of all African children, according to ILO criteria.

17. Black (1993: 15).

18. The ambivalence here is not too dissimilar from what we find with regard to feminist struggles. All women undoubtedly face a situation where they are unfairly disadvantaged on account of the fact that they are women; but the living conditions in which a French woman will find herself are so very different from those of, say, an Algerian woman that, unfortunately for both, the theme of 'Dominated Women' fails to mobilize, interest or concern.

19. Black (1993: 16).

20. The report continues thus: 'This clarification helped to define for the Seminar participants the "at-risk" street and working child on whom attention should focus; they recognized, however, that in practice this distinction is not always easy to make' (ibid., p. 17).

21. Schibotto and Cussianovitch (1994: 67–9).

22. 'If they want to be able to go to school [...] the day divides up as follows for the majority of children: minework from 1 to 7 a.m.; school from 8 till noon; domestic or farm work from 2 to 6 p.m. This means they do 10 hours of labouring for every 4 hours of school' (Céspedes).

23. During the debates, Elvira Taracena showed how the children were actually *selecting* what to learn at school, retaining nothing but the knowledge they felt would be of material use to their parents and, hence, to themselves for later on in life.

24. Having said that, continues Lia Fukui, 'despite all the criticisms levelled at school, no other institution capable of giving children a minimum of training to prepare them for employment and life in adult society has yet been invented to take its place'.

25. Even if, by introducing a certain degree of autonomy to the personality-building process, school has contributed greatly to the enhanced value, at community level, of this aspect of education.

26. There is no fixed ratio between the two (no more than there is between the wage

rate and the real cost of reproducing the work force), even if both sides are perfectly well aware that a balance must be struck, and that the more it weighs in favour of the actual work time to the detriment of the time invested, the more the apprentice can claim s/he is being exploited.

27. This is not always the case, especially in countries gripped by strong graduate un-employment; similarly, the position of being an apprentice does not always actually allow a person to acquire useful skills; but we are arguing here on a very broad level, with the simple reminder that, as popular wisdom puts it, 'You're better off rich and healthy than poor and sick!'

28. It is interesting to note that, to my knowledge, the concept of exploitation is never defined anywhere in economic literature which more often than not, when embracing the subject of the exploitation of labour, uses it with the moral undertones given by the dictionary definition, 'to utilize or take abusive advantage of (esp. a person)', and not the more neutral definition (and the only one to which a scientific approach ought to refer), 'to bring out the value of a resource (in this case, labour) by rendering it productive'. According to Marx, the concept has to be rebuilt upon the basis of its definition of 'surplus value'.

29. Michel Bonnet's chapter describes the extreme form of work contract known as bonded labour: the debtor pledges the labour power of one or more of his children as collateral. But the mechanics of it are such that the debt can never be repaid, as every penny spent on behalf of the child serves to preserve it. Many people are appalled by this system because it is so obvious that the debt becomes a pure fiction. What difference is there, however, between this and the process whereby the same chain of exploitation allows the richer countries to keep the Third World permanently in debt? Here, too, the debt quickly becomes a fiction and every indebted state in the South is forced at all costs – i.e. at lowest cost – to put some of its children to work.

References

Black, M. (1993) *Street and Working Children*, Summary Report of the Innocenti Global Seminar, 15–25 February 1995, Florence, UNICEF, International Child Development Centre.

Geffray, C. (1995) *Les maîtres hors la loi*, Paris, Karthala.

Schibotto, G. and A. Cussianovich (1994) *Working Children – Building an Identity*, Lima, MANTHOC.

PART I

The Economic and Social Context of Child Labour

CHAPTER 2

Introduction: A History of Exploited Children in Europe

Alessandro Stella

'Every city is composed of families [...] and perfect is the family composed of slaves and the free [...] and the fundamental constituents of the family are the master and the slave, the husband and the spouse, the father and the sons.'

(Aristotle, *Politics*, I, II-3)

'Let women submit to their husbands as they would unto the Lord [...] Sons, obey your parents within the Lord. [...] Slaves, obey your earthly masters with fear, respect and a sincere heart, as you would the Lord.'

(St Paul, Epistles to the Ephesians, 5–6)

'Each type of government enacts laws that are in its own interests [...] and in enacting these laws they make it quite plain that what is "right" for their subjects is what is in the interests of themselves, the rulers.'

(Plato, *The Republic*, Part One, Introduction, 333–7)

The Industrial Revolution and Children in the Factories

Child labour was first singled out as being a problem in the nineteenth century by doctors, political activists and industrial philanthropists. Field surveys, particularly in the 1830s, highlighted how physically, mentally and morally damaging certain working conditions could be for children (Le Grand 1831; Villermé 1840; Dupin 1840; Ducpetiaux 1843). Simultaneously describing and condemning a certain number of harmful industrial environments, these surveys were used to support parliamentary debates which culminated in legislation for the protection of working children. Beginning with laws passed in England (in 1802), then France (in 1841), this legislation aimed at establishing a fixed minimum employment age, daily and weekly working hours, age-related restrictions on working nights and on public holidays, a ban on children's work in what were judged to be hazardous occupations, and a compulsory schooling age. The principles differ in detail depending on the year and the country: in 1819, English law barred the cotton mills from hiring children under the age of nine; in 1841, France set a minimum legal age of eight years and a twelve-hour maximum working day. in 1874, the former was raised to twelve while the latter remained unchanged (Fohlen 1973; Service éducatif de l'Yonne 1991: 71–7).[1]

The industrial surveys first of all exposed the magnitude of the phenom-enon. Although children are sometimes found to represent a sizeable proportion of the work force in nineteenth-century mines, foundries, brick-works, tile yards and sugar houses,[2] by far the period's biggest employer of child labour was the textiles industry. Around the turn of the nineteenth century, the percentage of under-sixteen-year-old workers at forty-three Manchester cotton mills stood at 22.8 per cent; 2693 (that is 35.4 per cent) of the 7614 mill-workers in Lancashire belonged to that age group; as did 4220 (34.9 per cent) of the 12,076 people working at the twenty-nine mills in Glasgow (Villermé 1840: 371–3). By 1835, Great Britain's textile factories were employing a total labour force of 355,373 people; nearly 6 per cent of them were aged between eight and twelve, 10 per cent between twelve and thirteen and 30 per cent between thirteen and eighteen: practically half of all textile workers had not yet reached their eighteenth birthday (Ducpetiaux 1843: I, 15).

Children in England, as in France (Rouen, Mulhouse, Lille), were chiefly hired as knotters and spoolers for the cotton trade and as combers and carders for wool; theirs were the simplest tasks demanding no real training (Villermé 1840: 107, 140, 172, 192). Almost all of the six- to fifteen-year-olds working at the Jouy-en-Josas Oberkampf calico works – 10 per cent of the labour force in 1804 – belonged to the category of unskilled day labourers (Dewerpe and Gaulupeau 1990: table 10). As for the wages, Louis-René Villermé concluded that adult men in the textile factories were earning an average of about 2 francs a day, while adult women were on 1 franc, thirteen-to sixteen-year-old children on 75 centimes, and the eights to twelves on 45 centimes (Villermé 1840: 370; Service éducatif ... de la Côte d'Or 1979: 34–5).

The nineteenth-century factory surveys also brought to light another distinctive aspect of child workers: their socio-familial backgrounds. At the Maison Neuve ironworks (Lower Burgundy) in 1837, 'two-thirds of the children belong to the workers employed at the factory, and the remaining third are mostly foundlings'; at the Vitteaux merino wool factory in Auxois, 'a third of the children are either the brothers, sisters, sons or daughters of the adult workers' (Service éducatif ... de la Côte d'Or 1979: 47). Villermé observed that 'those who are employed in the factories with their fathers or mothers constitute between a tenth and a half of the young workers, the mean being a third' (Villermé 1840: 426). So the supply source of young hands for the factories appears linked to the willingness of parents or family friends to send children – and, to a large extent, take them with them – to work; and at the same time, to the willingness of homes to place the orphans in their keeping in work: poorhouses and workhouses were among the most significant purveyors of children to English factories (Fohlen 1973: 320–2). As a result of the massive influx of children into factories in England, we find far fewer children being placed in service outside their homes from as early as the mid-eighteenth century (Laslett 1973: 316).

Progress and Status Quo

Two centuries on from the first English laws for the protection of working children, what is the position to date?

Certainly in the rich countries of the West we find hardly any children in the factories any more; it would be interesting to know whether this progress has been more to do with a growing humanistic awareness in society, the effectiveness of the laws, the effects of greater wealth on family behaviour patterns or technological innovation. In the countries undergoing industrial revolution today, however, the employment of children in factories remains commonplace. A quarter of Cairo tannery workers are under fifteen years of age; they are mainly assigned to do maintenance, cleaning and carrying work and their wages correspond to about a quarter or a third of what an adult might earn. Whether in the brickyards of Bogota, carpet-weaving shops in Varanesi (India) or the Filipino cottage clothing industry, the employer's ability to give certain kinds of work to children goes with drudgery and low wages (Bequele and Boyden 1990: 65–91, 100–6, 161–87, 141–60). And we can see in the present-day cottage clothing industry of Manila, another feature in common with the western model of last century: 'nearly 73 per cent of mothers are working at home for the same employer as their children' (Bequele and Boyden 1988: 149).

Nowadays, most of the world's nations regard twelve as the minimum age for employment in what is judged to be *light* work (BIT 1987: 69–80). But as if harking back to nineteenth-century thinking on big industry, the majority of child labour laws 'almost always exclude work in family firms, schools and training colleges from their field of application. Many countries go even further by excluding domestic and farm labour too' (Bequele and Boyden 1990: 34). Yet in rich and poor countries alike, agriculture and domestic service are the very fields where we find the majority of child workers today (BIT 1992: 14–17).

Looking at the laws themselves, not how they are applied on the ground, it would seem as though a concerned society which likes to think it is humane and enlightened were able to attack nothing but the most blatant and shameful examples of abuse, the aspects with the most devastating effects on the individual, without striking at the root causes of child labour usage.

Industrial surveys from the nineteenth and twentieth centuries bring out a number of common denominators: certain sectors prefer to employ children for certain tasks; these are without exception unskilled and mundane; children's wages fall well short of what an adult might earn. Exposures, investigations, laws and international conventions have been built up around the employment of children in large-scale concentrated manufacturing – that is to say tied to a specific historical phase and production model. Whereas child labour has in fact been exploited since much earlier times and some aspects of the industrial revolution ironically give it the appearance of a liberation.

Definition of Working Age

Before the advent of the concerned law-maker, customary practice and nature had already done much to settle an age for admission to employment. Nineteenth- and twentieth-century protective legislation has effectively ratified the most widely prevailing custom. Let us consider the use of slaves, workers by definition, in the Middle Ages and modern times. A 1778 inventory of slave work on the Pimelle sugar plantation of Santo Domingo counted thirteen young Negro boys and girls from six months to eight years old, 'not yet of working age' (Foubert 1981: 82). In 1774, the Mauger sugar refineries on the Artibonite river in Haiti had a work force of 101 adult men, 71 adult women and 42 children under the age of thirteen; if seven six- to ten-year-olds were found at the plantation's indigo works that year, three years later there were none younger than ten (Debien 1981: 230). For there is a minimum age at which a child is able to do even the simplest of tasks and before which children, not to mention slave children, are nothing more than mouths to feed; non-profit-yielding and a burden on their owners. That is certainly why, apart from the low slave population growth rate, purchasing fresh slaves on the market would long remain the policy adopted in preference to a pro-fertility approach of rearing their offspring (Moreno Fraginals 1983: 31 et seq.; Gautier 1985: 223 et seq; Debien 1981: 238).

Here are some other examples. The ages of the slaves sold on occidental markets towards the end of the Middle Ages clearly show the buyers' lack of interest in any not yet fit for work; and we should stress that those slaves were being bought for domestic purposes and the vast majority of them were female. Of the 357 slaves sold in Florence between 1366 and 1397, only ten (2.8 per cent) were younger than ten, while forty-eight (23.8 per cent) were ten to fifteen years old; under-sixteens were priced at lower-than-average rates (Livi 1928: x). On the Genoa market, 491 slaves were sold between 1400 and 1450; only five were aged less than ten as opposed to 125 (i.e. 25.4 per cent) tens to fifteens. Of the 939 slaves sold in the second half of the century, fourteen were under ten years of age and eighty-one (8.6 per cent) between ten and fifteen. Here too under-sixteen-year-olds fetched a lower-than-average price (Gioffre 1971: 117–37). Meanwhile, traders in Spain were importing male slaves averaging eighteen years for the hardest work of all, i.e. in the mines (Stella 1992).

All in all, if caretaking, vegetable picking and peeling, minor housework, assisting artisans and the like could be done by children younger than ten or twelve, it was only starting at that age that the majority of sectors of activity looked upon them as profit-yielding sources of child labour. Consider this final point: in many Genoa guild statutes from around the end of the Middle Ages, members of the Arts were obliged to attend the funerals of their colleagues and familiars, except if it were a matter of children under the age of ten (Casarino 1982: 102). I am therefore of the belief that child exploitation basically concerns the ten-to-fifteen age group; upwards of fifteen it becomes juvenile exploitation.

A Practice as Old as the Hills, a New History Subject

While child labour in the days of Dickens and Zola has attracted attention, compassion and a range of interventions, for earlier periods it remains a subject if not completely ignored by historiography, then only surfacing here and there in the shape of apprenticeship or domestic service. The *Annales de démographie historique* journal's 'Child and Society' monograph contains but a single article on child labour, focusing (as it happens) on children's work during the industrial revolution (cf. Fohlen 1973). Even on the nineteenth century, the historian still needs to resort to the research of contemporaries because the existing bibliography is too poor to offer much information. For periods before then, it is even poorer. The special issue of the journal *Histoire de l'éducation* devoted to 'Education in Medieval Times' looks into the education and emotions of children, the lives of students, but touches only lightly upon child labour in a mechanical reminder (Histoire de l'éducation 1991). Even Philippe Ariès, who looked into childhood at length and played a decisive role in getting it on the agenda as a recognized history subject, skimmed over the matter. The XIIth Congress of the Society of State Higher Education Medieval Historians[3] heard papers on teaching methods, educational tracts, schools and universities – the only exception being F. Michaud-Fréjaville's paper which deals with indentures from the district of Orléanais (Les Entrées 1982).

Over the past two decades, labour history, which long used to be seen as the history of adult working men, has made room for working women; the history of working children remains largely untold.

Apprentices Learning or Children and Juveniles Working?

When considering child labour in past centuries, our first thoughts tend to be of apprentices and the documents allowing us to apprehend them: indentures. Apprentices are seen as young men training under a master, producing a masterpiece of their own before they in turn become masters. A true picture or make-believe about the 'good old days'? It would rather appear that most apprentices, on completing their indentures, joined the ranks of the Parisian *valets* or Genoa *lavoranti*; and that being the son of a master and having sound finances were by far the most decisive criteria for access to mastership (Geremek 1968: 51 et seq.; Didier 1984: 208; Casarino 1984: 459). What then was apprenticeship and, moreover, what purpose and whom did it serve?

Carola Ghiara has studied the fate of the apprentice silk-spinners of Genoa. 'Of the 258 *garzoni* recruited between 1461 and 1530, only 24 appear in the records for subsequent years with a trade: 3 as *textor pannorum lane*, *tinctor lane* or *lanerius*, 21 as *filatore sete*. Only nine of the *filatore sete* later contracted apprentices of their own – indicating that they had gained tenure of a spinning business, which means they had become *magistri* in every sense' (Ghiara 1991: 90). So apprenticeships only very rarely produced masters, with apprentices more often than not ending up as menials in the same trade or in another.

The picture of apprentices striving to learn a trade does not withstand close examination of the indentures. In his studies of the fourteenth- and fifteenth-century indentures of Dijon, Philippe Didier notes with some surprise that 'the duration of apprenticeships sometimes seems to vary conversely to the difficulty of the trade. It will be one year for a moneychanger, for example, and sixteen with a wine grower or eighteen with a hatter' (Didier 1976: 36). Françoise Michaud-Fréjaville makes the same observation about the Orléanais district where pewter potters, for instance, could expect between five and eight years of apprenticeship (Michaud-Fréjaville 1991: 203). The same goes for medieval Rouerge (Landes-Mallet 1988). In Montpellier, the vast majority of apprentice moneychangers or gold- and silversmiths were recruited for one to three years, while apprentice bakers or cobblers faced periods of four to eight or even ten years (Reyerson 1992: 356).

If the aim of apprenticeship were to learn a trade, we might have expected to see aspiring youngsters hurrying to draw up a contract with the master of a prestigious one; whereas the trades most frequently mentioned in the indentures are, on the contrary, the most large-scale: textiles in Genoa (wool and cotton), the vineyards of Orléanais (Gatti 1980: 18; Casarino 1982: 91; Michaud-Fréjaville 1991: 274). Apprentices' ages could vary greatly from one trade to the next and between towns. The seventeenth- and eighteenth-century guilds of Venice had a fixed minimum age (in extreme cases eight to ten years) and maximum age (eighteen to twenty) for hiring an apprentice. As a matter of fact, serial analysis of guild indentures shows fourteen years to be the average right across the board, with an average employment span of three to six years (Beltrami 1954: 198). In fifteenth-century Genoa, the average age rose to fifteen, with a modal value of fourteen (Casarino 1982: 103). In Orléans, it was even a little higher, at fifteen and a half (Michaud-Fréjaville 1982: 193). There are equivalent findings for the apprentice silk-workers of eighteenth-century Lyon (Garden 1975: 99). As a rule, apprentices were therefore of an age that made them profitable for use as labour.

What exactly was an indenture? Be it in Latin or in everyday language, in medieval times or modern, the notarial form from the North Sea to the Mediterranean was virtually identical. Usually settled between the parents (or other adults with parental authority) and master, it would stipulate that the child would go to live in the master's house, that the latter would be bound to supply bed and board, the occasional laundry or even a pair of shoes; in return the child would become his apprentice, assist him in his work and (according to the customary wording) 'in all his honest and lawful chores'. Substantially, then, an exchange of upkeep for labour supply. And the remuneration? Contrary to expectations, the master was often the one paid for his services, in cash or kind – gifts of geese, capons, lamb, cereals etc. (Greci 1988: 227; Didier 1984: 238; Garden 1975: 99). This would continue up to a given age beyond which the master (saving money by not having to hire a servant) would be contractually bound to pay the apprentice a small wage (Michaud-Fréjaville 1982: 206).

For here is the crux of the matter: many of the edicts and articles in the statutes of medieval and modern guilds stipulated a maximum number of apprentices a master could employ. By hiring an apprentice in place of a servant or journeyman he would be making savings in labour costs while enjoying the availability of a meek and obedient labour force. This fundamental issue is illustrated in the uprising of the printing journeymen of Lyon and Paris during the mid-1500s. The fact that workshop masters were granted the facility of being able to employ as many apprentices as they wished for any tasks that pleased them had disastrous effects on the employment and pay of journeymen, which sparked off strikes, assemblies and turmoil (Hauser 1899: 184 et seq.).

Work and Family

Who were the apprentices? In the first place the vast majority were boys, except in certain occupations traditionally regarded as being feminine 'by nature', e.g. dress-making and spinning. Another essential characteristic is illustrated in a term often found in the indentures: the master is bound to treat the apprentice 'as if he were his own son' (Bernardi 1993a: 71; Didier 1984: 217). Indeed, an indenture appeared to be the transfer of a child or young man from one family to another for a given period of time. Very often, however, it was more a matter of a family lodging orphaned children. An examination of apprentices' family backgrounds shows that in fifteenth-century Orléans, 60 per cent of child apprentices were fatherless or motherless orphans; and in Genoa, those who had lost their fathers made up 30 per cent of the 7000 hired apprentices (Michaud-Fréjaville 1982: 188; Casarino 1982: 106).

Abandoned children taken in by charitable institutions, fatherless children whose mothers could no longer provide for their needs, or younger children who were simply too much of a burden on a deprived family: such seems to be the profile of those being apprenticed.

The role the charities played in early exploitation of child labour is clear to see in their archives and makes their true vocation look somewhat (euphemistically speaking) suspect. First founded in the thirteenth to fifteenth centuries and proliferating through the modern era on the back of a great many private donations and annuities bequeathed by wealthy parishioners, the public hospitals and homes for abandoned children in particular were keen to attend to the social scourge of infanticide and neglect. Infants were either weaned at the home or put out to nurse. But the few (very few) surviving the frightening levels of infant mortality soon became a burden on the mothering institution. From about the age of six or seven, they would therefore be apprenticed to craftsmen or put to work directly in the factories the institutions themselves had set up for the very purpose (Sandri 1991: 1010; Raffaele 1991: 928; Pollet 1991: 902; Schiavoni 1991: 1039). The fact is that abandoned children were seen not so much as a matter of conscience by 'honest people' and 'noble souls', but as a potential threat to public order and social discipline: steps had to be taken to prevent orphaned children from becoming beggars and delinquents. This is fully spelt out in the deeds founding the Hôpital de Langres in 1599 (Garnier 1955: 201) or the Hôpital de Saragosse in 1543 (San Vicente 1988: I, 189). Homes also imposed rules and regulations that were strict and geared to a blend of moral discipline and hard work, as in the 1772 deeds of the Orphelins de Sens home for orphaned girls, for example: 'Following morning prayers, they shall be given breakfast and then, as far as may be possible, taken to mass; following mass they shall each be made to work according to her individual strengths and talents, but mainly in all the work of the home such as sweeping out the chambers and the dormitory where they sleep, cleaning them, making bread, doing the laundry, the cooking, etc.' Employed from the age of six or seven, those orphans were altogether profitable sources of labour; indeed, the institution's accounts for the years 1682–1711 show that sales of embroidery work or garments made by the young girls more than compensated for the cost of their upkeep (ADY, 6E4). According to the books of the Hôpital de Dijon, the allowances and work of those in its care kept income well in excess of expenditure from the sixteenth to the eighteenth centuries (Bolotte 1968: 47); the economically and socially viable 'charity workshops', which were mainly textile mills in the seventeenth century, became extremely popular in the eighteenth century under the impetus of royal decrees, and were extended particularly to highway maintenance where they employed not only women and children but able-bodied beggars too (Bolotte 1968: 24). The employment of abandoned children, paupers and vagabonds, together with the building of establishments in which to shut them away, certainly contributed to the emergence of the large-scale concentrated manufacturing of the industrial revolution.

Food Lease, Care Lease and Other Forms of 'Child Rental'

It must be understood that for certain children being apprenticed was just one of the many ways in which they were put to work/placed with a family. In eighteenth-century Paris, a 'placement contract' was developed with all the basic features of an indenture (average age of around fifteen years, average duration of four years) except for one major difference: it stipulated that the placed person had no right of access to mastership. In fact, this just gave the masters a way of circumventing the guild laws governing the maximum number of apprentices in service (Kaplan 1993: 461). We should remember that 'labour rentals' in medieval and modern times alike concerned not just children and juveniles, but adults too. Contracting oneself out to a craftsman, merchant or farmer and going to live with them for an agreed period of time was a very common practice. But for rented adult workers, on the one hand the contract would be short-term (a season, a year or two), and on the other the pay included not only bed and board – and occasionally other supplies – but a wage as well (Druot 1889–1902; Forestier 1936–77).

Other contracts of a similar ilk included the 'food lease' and 'care lease'; but in such cases the 'put to work/placed with a family' equation ought to be reversed: children were first placed with a family and then put to work. Contracts like these began appearing as soon as notarial deeds had become current practice, that is to say in the thirteenth century. Once again they concerned orphans placed by a surviving parent, a collateral or guardian with a foster family until adulthood (eighteen to twenty years). The differences between these and other types of child rental contract, especially indentures, lay in the (often very long) duration, as well as in the fact that together with the child, the lessee would also gain access to his or her inheritance in usufruct until he or she had come of age. The lessee would be bound to pay the parent or rightful guardian some sum of money; in which case 'fostering' actually turned into a veritable child auction (Fagniez 1877: 61; Frappier-Bigras 1989; Couturier 1984; Desaive 1986).

Where did the 'food lease' come from? There are striking similarities to a Merovingian custom found in the notarial archives of the cities of Angers and Tours: children found abandoned on the steps of churches or monasteries would be sold to the highest bidders and kept by them as slaves (Verlinden 1976: 111). Analogies between the contracts establishing familial and working dependency between free subjects and those ratifying servile dependency are more numerous and disturbing. Was it by chance, for example, that some late medieval guild statutes talk not about renting but of an actual 'sale of apprentices' (Fagniez 1877: 72; Geremek 1968: 32)? And what of the 'escape clause' contained in indentures up until the last century of the Ancien Régime, whereby the apprentice giver would be obliged to pay the lessee a pecuniary fine if ever the apprentice ran away from the workshop/home and avoided being captured and returned to his master (Fagniez 1877: 73; Hauser 1899: 29; Forestier 1938: 301)? Why should an apprentice run away? Here is an illustration from testimony delivered in a small Burgundy town in the year 1727:

Claude Langin quit the house of Nicolas Rolan only because the said Rolan, in place of instructing the said Langin in the skills of his trade of cobbler, employed him each day solely to carry earth to the vineyards, to labour there and do all manner of summer and winter work, solely to serve at his tavern and deliver wine to the houses, pick and sift the hemp, launder and do all manner of chores within and outside the house, not to mention the fact that Rolan in no way involved him in his trade of making shoes, did not treat him humanely, fed him very poorly on bran and barley bread, made him sleep on the floor and abused him with insults, kicks and beatings with a stick. (ADY, 15B 299)

One can equally contemplate the ten-year-old *anime* (souls) of fifteenth-century Venice. In 1386, moved by the plight of the children imported from Albania and sold as slaves outside town even though they were Christians (not soulless infidels!), the Venetian authorities prohibited their re-exportation and ordered their emancipation – to take effect after a period of four years. The deferral applied because it was considered that the children should nevertheless work for a certain length of time until their owners had recovered the money they had spent; they therefore moved to the status of 'temporary slaves'. It was extended to ten years in 1388 at the masters' request: 'these souls are so rustic and crude of intellect', four years of their labour would not suffice to cover their purchase price (Verlinden 1977: 674 et seq.).

Entry into Service

Using the example of Venice and its cousin town of Raguse, we can glimpse the progression from being a lifelong to a temporary slave and, ultimately, entering into 'free' service. In a case study of Raguse, Susan Mosher Stuard (1986) illustrates well the historical development and continuity of content. Indeed, the town's notarial contracts show that if in the thirteenth century good families purchased Bosnian slaves for domestic service, in the fourteenth century employment contracts were being drawn up for the purpose: in return for a certain sum of money, parents themselves were putting their daughters into service for periods that could sometimes stretch to as many as twenty years. *A contrario*, in Florence during the first half of the fifteenth century, the shift was towards the employment of girls of servile status (Klapish-Zuber 1986). The status may change, but the population involved in domestic service remains substantially the same: women, young girls, even infant girls.

It might also be said that being put into domestic service was the female equivalent of being apprenticed, with some common features and some gender-related differences. Slave or free, maidservants, apprentices and fostered children were all given bed and board by a master (or mistress); in return for their keep, the girls would take care of household chores while the boys worked in the workshop or store. The main gender-related difference is found at the end: the boys would, if possible, have learnt a trade; the girls would have saved up a modest dowry for their marriage. In theory, very young and juvenile girls went into service with that very life-cycle-related goal in mind (Klapish-Zuber 1986; Goldberg 1992). Like apprenticeship leading to mastership, domestic service as a prelude to marriage was often a figment of the imagination; when young maidservants became adults, they would continue their life of service in the state expected of domestics, i.e. unmarried. This did not prevent them, be they slaves or free, from having children – often the fruit of the sexual services required by the master (Livi 1928: 218 et seq.; Gutton 1981: 209 et seq.).

Children born from 'amorous adventures with the servants' or, to put it more bluntly, domestic rape, had a good chance of being abandoned, reproducing the infernal cycle experienced by their parents. In late medieval Venice, 30 per cent of the young girls recruited as maidservants had been contracted out by the 'prosecutor of orphans' (Iradiel 1986: 248).

Underage and Underpaid

What fate did former societies reserve for children and juveniles, apart from those fostered out to other families? It should first of all be pointed out that not all children worked. In urban societies, a relatively large number went to school and escaped premature labour, some for good and others only temporarily or partially. This was of course a male privilege: in Florence *circa* 1338 or Lisbon in 1552, probably one small boy out of every two had had schooling (Herlihy and Klapisch-Zuber 1978: 563; Buarcos 1923: 204).

Working conditions for children who worked while living at home with their parents corresponded on the one hand to the status of minors and on the other to the type of pay in the activities in which they were employed. On a *métayage* system farm (Pastor 1990), in a domestic craft or a widely distributed industry employing casual labourers or pieceworkers, sons and daughters worked alongside their parents, and the agricultural yield or wages paid to parents therefore represented not personal but family earnings. Similarly, in late Middle Ages Florentine wool production, combers' sons combed with their fathers and spinners' daughters span with their mothers; and on the building sites of Provence, masons would turn up for work accompanied by their sons and daughters (Bernardi 1993b: 277). In such cases children were supplying 'free' labour to parents who were looking after them.

So the use of children's work as much in agriculture as in textiles dates back to the dark ages. Significant numbers of small girls were spinning and weaving in the *gynaecia* of ancient Greece, in Roman and Carolingian villas and the workshops of medieval monasteries (Herlihy 1990). They were concurrently in servile dependency, sexual dependency and minority-related dependency. Their condition did of course evolve, but not until very much later: not until the seventeenth century and the first concentrated textile factories do we find girls earning a wage (Neveux-Maisonneuve 1933). Before that, in the late medieval textiles sector, the only child wage-earners were boys. The *ragazzi* (ten- to thirteen-year-old boys) employed in the wool mills of Florence earned little over half the wages of the lowest paid adult workers (Franceschi 1993: 251). For here is the heart of the matter: when they are paid anything other than their keep, children are underpaid.

This is a permanent feature found in every area of activity from the late Middle Ages through to the twentieth century. According to the oldest existing building site account books, the *pueri* (children) on the payroll are system-atically paid far less than the adults. Such was the case with the construction of the Augustinian monastery in Paris in 1299–1301 (Fagniez 1877: 359–65), as with the Domes of Florence, Siena and Milan at the end of the fourteenth century (Pinto 1984: 78). And the same went for agricultural work. The accounts of the Hôpital de Tonnerre (northern Burgundy) reveal that in the fourteenth and fifteenth centuries children were consistently employed in the vineyards as assistants to the vine tenders, grape-pickers and weeders; and just as consistently paid half as much as adult wine-workers and, signifi-cantly, a rate equal to that earned by the women hired to plant shoots or pick grapes (ADY, 1Mi 650, E1–E98). In 1480, in an attempt to stem the incessant wrangling between vineyard-workers and owners, the Bailiff of Auxerre imposed a maximum pay limit for vineyard labour according to which young boys could earn no more than 60 per cent of an adult man's wage, and women no more than 40 per cent (AMA, HH-27). For the fact is that when it is a matter of underpaying workers, we automatically think of women and children.

The Vocabulary of Dependency

Children were made to work in order to secure free or low-cost labour. A review of the facts will confirm this, as will the vocabulary of real or symbolic dependency.

Indeed, there is a whole range of terminology referring back to the equation: child = inferior, child = submissive. Let us take the most complete term used to denote personal dependency, *mancipium*, the classical Latin word for 'slave'. With *servi* having come to designate 'serfs' in the mid-Middle Ages and 'slave' used in the twentieth century with reference to the late medieval occidental slave trade, *mancipium* therefore served to connote the state of inferiority due to age and gender. Granting that its entry into usage was of course gradual, it is none the less symptomatic to note that in some cases medieval Latin employed *mancipium* in place of *discipulus* ('apprentice') (Du Cange 1883). In Spanish, Portuguese and Provençal French, the word *mancebo* gradually went from meaning 'servant' to 'boy' to 'bachelor'. The feminine form, *manceba*, came to mean 'prostitute', with a brothel being a *mancebia* and the brothel manager a *padre de mancebia* (*Enciclopedia Universal*; *Dictionnaire étymologique* 1985; *Diccionario* 1956). The erudite seventeenth-century Spanish scholar Sebastian de Covarrubias explains such a terminological shift thus: 'one is still in the power of one's father, as if one were a slave' (Covarrubias 1611). Everyone knows, by the way, that emancipation is used solely to describe the end to submissiveness for a social group (emancipation of the working classes), gender (female emancipation) or those regarded as minors by law (emancipation of minors).

In the Middle Ages and in modern history, the word *moço*, which originally meant 'child', came to be used in Spanish and Portuguese for a young servant, domestics in particular (*moços/as de soldada*), and later appears in French as *mousse* or 'ship's boy' (*Diccionario Critico* 1981). In Spain, the term was used as an alternative to *criado/a* (literally: 'raised in the house') in reference to domestic servants. And when the slaves were set free, the many who chose to stay on and serve the same household were reclassified as *criados*. Applied to adults, adolescents and children alike, the shifts in terminology convey the confusion that has arisen between dependency relating to age, membership of a household and, in short, personal dependency. An example of this confusion may be seen in a fifteenth-century notarial form where a young girl's domestic service contract is registered under the title of *affirmacio ancille* (*Formularium* 1986, 52), the classical Latin feminine equivalent of *mancipium*; similarly, the words used for indentures in thirteenth-century Piacenza were *dedit* and *locavit* (Greci 1988: 227).

In Italian, the term *fante* served practically the same purpose. Derived from *infante* (child), it applied to the domestic servant and military servant (*fantassin* in French) with no indication of age difference. Popular usage created a situation whereby terms such as *fantina* and *fanticello/a* were invented to describe young servants. The domestic servant was also called *famiglio* ('familiar'), derived from the classical Latin *famulus* – a slave belonging to the family. Semantic confusion reached its peak in a Venetian law of 1402 addressing the City Guilds; its aim was to sort out the working contracts made with 'boys and girls (*pueros* and *puellas*) big and small, domestics (*famuli*), servants, maids, workers and familiars' (Lazzarini 1960: 70). Finally, the French word *garçon* ('boy'), which in modern Venice could be taken to mean 'apprentice', has been used in a wide variety of ways according to the type of work: from the factory boy, errand boy, farm hand, kitchen boy etc. If not a young dependant, it can mean a small one.

Conclusions

From the *padre-padrone* of a medieval house, workshop or farm to the *patron-père* of nineteenth-century French factories, what changed and what remained constant? The first thing to do would obviously be to associate labour and family for every scenario. Far from being a modern invention, the employment of children was commonplace until the latter half of the twentieth century, mechanized agriculture, increased life expectancy, social enrichment and mass education. Children worked, first of all for the parents who were feeding them. Making themselves useful and then, when old enough, profitable for the family housekeeping, did not necessarily mean that working children were exploited children. But the exploitation of children as workers is indeed rooted in this nurturing-based relationship; for the first characteristic feature of child labour is when children are paid in bed and board. What was regarded as 'normal' pay for children living with their own flesh and blood, would also be normal for those in a surrogate family. Why should a child sent into apprenticeship or service expect to be treated any differently by the new 'family' than would have been the case in the parental home? And the situation would be still more prohibitive for orphans who had lost or never known their families. The fifteenth-century Florentine writer, Leon Battista Alberti, put it in rather a neat nutshell with the following dialogue: 'What do you call family?' 'Giannozzo: the children, wife and other domestics, servants and slaves' (Alberti 1960: I, 186). For the assimilation was easily made with the other family 'members' who were given their keep in payment for their work.

This could only continue because the child's dependent status was regarded as 'natural'. Children are, by definition, dependent upon their parents; up until a certain age they cannot survive without them, but why should the natural dependency persist beyond the age at which they start work? To justify exploitation.

That being the case, it is no surprise to find that children's work had basically been domestic labour, which is to say attached to the family, the house, home economics. For domestic labour is the work of subordinates; the woman (in a couple), the children and adolescents (in the parental home), 'familiarized' servants (in extended families). And personal service bears the marks of servile dependency. Hence, ironically enough, if the changing forms of production engendered by the industrial revolution undoubtedly caused working conditions to deteriorate for children (environmental pollution in the big factories, the stressful rhythms of automatic machinery, etc.), those same changes may also have been somewhat liberating: children were after all earning a wage in the concentrated factory and, being lost in a crowd of workers also meant they were released from the constant control and authority of a father/master; they were to some extent less 'minor'.

Having said that, even at the stage of 'waged liberty', they remain grossly underpaid; which is why they have always been employed.

Notes

1. Yonne District Education Authority.

2. In 1874, the work force at the Schneider ironworks in the Creusot (Central France) comprised 4882 adults and 323 under-sixteen-year-old children (Service éducatif de la Côte d'Or 1979). Service éducatif de la Côte d'Or = the Côte d'Or regional education authority.

3. XIIth Congrès de la Société des historiens médiévistes de l'enseignement supérieur public on the theme '*Les entrées dans la vie. Initiations et apprentissages*' (The ways in to life. Initiations and apprenticeships).

References

ADY = Archives Départementales de l'Yonne.

Alberti, L. B. (1960) *Opere volgari*, Bari, Grayson.

AMA = Archives Municipales d'Auxerre.

Aries, P. (1973) *L'enfant et la vie familiale sous l'Ancien Régime*, Paris, Seuil (1st edn, 1960).

Beltrami, D. (1954) *Storia della popolazione di Venezia dalla fine del secolo XVI° alla caduta della Republica*, Padua.

Bequele, A. and J. Boyden (1988) *L'enfant au travail*, Etude du Bureau International du Travail, Paris, Fayard (1st edn, Geneva, 1988).

Bernardi, P. (1993a) 'Apprentissage et transmission du savoir dans les métiers du bâtiment à Aix-en-Provence à la fin du Moyen Âge (1400–1550)', *Les Cahiers du CRISIMA*, 1, 69–79.

— (1993b) 'Pour une étude du rôle des femmes dans le bâtiment au Moyen Age', *Provence historique*, XLIII: *techniques et travail*, 267–78.

BIT (1987) *Le travail des enfants: manuel d'information*, Geneva, ILO.

— (1992) *Le travail dans le monde*, Geneva, ILO.

Bolotte, M. (1968) *Les Hôpitaux et l'assistance dans la Province de Bourgogne au dernier siècle de l'Ancien Régime*, Dijon.

Buarcos, B.(1923) *Tratado da majestade, grandeza e abastança de Lisboa na 2a metade do seculo XVI*, ed. Gomes de brito, Lisbon.

Casarino, G. (1982) *I giovani e l'apprendistato. Iniziazione e addestramento, Maestri e garzoni nella società genovese fra XV° e XVI° secolo*, IV, Quaderni del CSST du CNR, Genoa.

— (1984) 'Mondo del lavoro e immigrazione a Genova tra XV e XVI secolo', in R. Comba, G. Piccinni and G. Pinto (eds), *Strutture familiari, epidemie, migrazioni nell'Italia medievale*, Naples, ESI, 451–72.

Couturier, M. (1984) 'Entre famille et service. La mise aux enchères de personnes', *Bulletin de la Société archéologique d'Eure-et-Loire*, 103, 233–61.

Covarrubias, S. (1611) *Tesoro de la lengua castellana o española*, Madrid.

Debien, G. (1981) 'Sur les plantations Mauger à l'Artibonite (Saint-Domingue, 1763–1803)', *Enquêtes et documents*, VI, Université de Nantes, 219–314.

Desaive, J. P. (1986) 'Le bail à nourriture et le statut de l'enfant sous l'Ancien Régime en Basse-Bourgogne', *Bulletin de la Société des Sciences historiques et naturelles de l'Yonne*, 118, 11–21.

Dewerpe, A. and Y. Gaulupeau (1990) *La fabrique des prolétaires. Les ouvriers de la manufacture d'Oberkampf à Jouy-en-Josas (1760–1815)*, Paris, Presses de l'ENS.

Diccionario critico etimologico castellano e hispanico (1981), ed. J. Corominas, Madrid.

Diccionario de la lengua española (1956), Madrid.

Dictionnaire etymologique de la langue latine (1985) ed. J. André, Paris.

Didier, P. (1976) 'Le contrat d'apprentissage en Bourgogne aux XIVe et XVe siècles', *Revue historique de droit français et étranger*, 54, 35–57.

— (1984) 'L'apprentissage médiéval en France: formation professionnelle, entretien ou emploi de la main-d'œuvre juvénile?', *Zeitschrift der Savigny-Stiftung für Rechtsgeschichte, Germanistische Abteilung*, 200–55.

Druot, E. (1899–1902) 'Recueil de documents tirés des anciennes minutes de notaires déposées aux Archives de l'Yonne', *Bulletin de la Société des Sciences historiques et naturelles de l'Yonne*.

Du Cange (1883–87) *Glossarium mediae et infimae latinitatis*, Graz.

Ducpetiaux, E. (1843) *De la condition physique et morale des jeunes ouvriers et des moyens de l'améliorer*, 2 vols, Brussels (new edn, Paris, EDHIS, 1979).

Dupin, C. (1840–47) *Du travail des enfants qu'employent les ateliers, les usines, les manufactures, considéré dans les intérêts mutuels de la société, des familles et de l'industrie*, Paris.

Enciclopedia universal Ilustrada Europeo-Americana, Barcelona.

Fagniez, G. (1877) *Études sur l'industrie et la classe industrielle à Paris aux XIIIe et XIVe siècle*, Paris.

Fohlen, C. (1973) 'Révolution industrielle et travail des enfants', *Annales de démographie historique*, 319–25.

Forestier, H. (1936–77) *Extraits analytiques des minutes déposées aux Archives de l'Yonne*, Auxerre.

— (1938) 'Rupture de contrat d'apprentissage et droit de fuite au XVIIIe siècle', *Annales de Bourgogne*, 301–3.

Formularium diversorum instrumentorum (1986) ed. J. Cortés, Sueca.

Foubert, B. (1981) 'Une habitation à Saint-Domingue à la veille de la guerre d'Amérique (1777)', *Enquêtes et documents*, VI, Université de Nantes, 31–84.

Franceschi, F. (1993) *Oltre il 'Tumulto'. I lavoratori fiorentini dell'Arte della Lana fra Tre e Quattrocento*, Florence, Olschki.

Frappier-Bigras, D. (1989) 'La famille dans l'artisanat parisien du XIIIe siècle', *Le Moyen Âge*, 1, 47–74.

Garden, M. (1970) *Lyon et les Lyonnais au XVIIIe siècle*, Paris, Flammarion (1st edn, Lyon, 1970).

Garnier, A. (1955) 'La fondation Charmolue et autres fondations charitables pour la mise en apprentissage des orphelins et des enfants pauvres', *Bulletin de la Société historique et archéologique de Langres*, 159, 197–232.

Gatti, L. (1980) *Un catalogo di mestieri, Maestri e garzoni nella società genovese fra XV° e XVI° secolo*, II, Quaderni del CSST du CNR, Genoa.

Gautier, A. (1985) 'Traite et politique démographique esclavagistes', *De la traite à l'esclavage, Actes du Colloque international sur la traite des Noirs*, 2 vols, Nantes (Nantes-Paris 1988), II, 223–41.

Geremek, B. (1968) *Le salariat dans l'artisanat parisien aux XIII-XVe siècles*, Paris, EHESS.

Ghiara, C. (1991) *Famiglie e carriere artigiane: il caso dei filatori di seta, Maestri e garzoni nella società genovese tra XV° et XVI° secolo*, VI, Quaderni del CSST du CNR, Genoa, 90.

Gioffre, D. (1971) *Il mercato degli schiavi a Genova nel secolo XV*, Genoa.

Goldberg, J. (1992) *Women, Work, and Life Cycle in a Medieval Economy. Women in York and Yorkshire, c.1300–1500*, Oxford, Clarendon Press.

Greci, R. (1988) *Corporazioni e mondo del lavoro nell'Italia padana medievale*, Bologne, CLUEB.

Gutton, J. (1981) *Domestiques et serviteurs dans la France de l'Ancien Régime*, Paris, Aubier Montaigne.

Hauser, H. (1899) *Ouvriers du temps passé (XVe–XVIe siècles)*, Paris.

Herlihy, D. (1990) *Opera muliebria. Women and Work in Medieval Europe*, Philadelphia, Temple University Press.

Herlihy, D. and C. Klapish-Zuber (1978) *Les Toscans et leurs familles. Une étude du Catasto florentin de 1427*, Paris, EHESS.

Histoire de l'éducation (1991) 'Éducations médiévales. L'enfance, l'école, l'Église en Occident (VIe–XVe siècles)', *Histoire de l'éducation*, 50, May.

Iradiel, P. (1986) 'Familia y funcion economica de la mujer en actividades no agrarias', in *La condicion de la mujer en la Edad media*, Madrid, Universidad Complutense, 223–59.

Kaplan, St L. (1993) 'L'apprentissage au XVIIIe siècle: le cas de Paris', *Revue d'histoire moderne et contemporaine*, 40–3, 436–79.

Klapish-Zuber, C. (1986) 'Women Servants in Florence (14th–15th Centuries)', in B. A. Hanawalt (ed.), *Women and Work in Preindustrial Europe*, Indiana University Press, 56–80.

Landes-Mallet, A. M. (1988) 'Travail et apprentissage en Rouergue médiévale', *Libertés locales et vie municipale en Rouergue, Languedoc et Roussillon*, Montpellier, 91–8.

Laslett, P. (1973) 'L'attitude à l'égard de l'enfant dans l'Angleterre du XIXe siècle', *Annales de démographie historique*, 313–18.

Lazzarini, V. (1960) *Proprietà e feudi, offizi, garzoni, carcerati in antiche leggi veneziane*, Rome.

Le Grand, D. (1831–54) *Sur le travail des enfants dans les manufactures*, Paris (new edn, Paris, EDHIS, 1979).

Les Entrées (1982) *Les entrées dans la vie. Initiations et apprentissages*, XIIe congrès de la SHMES, Nancy, PUN.

Livi, R. (1928) *La schiavitù domestica nei tempi di mezzo e nei moderni*, Padua.

Michaud-Fréjaville, F. (1982) 'Bons et loyaux services: les contrats d'apprentissage en Orléanais (1380–1480)', *Les entrées dans la vie. Initiations et apprentissages*, Nancy, PUN, 183–208.

— (1991) 'Apprentis et ouvriers vignerons. Les contrats à Orléans au XVe siècle', *Le vigneron, la viticulture et la vinification en Europe occidentale, au Moyen Âge et à l'époque moderne*, Auch, Flaran, 273–85.

Moreno Fraginals, M. (1983) *La historia como arma*, Barcelona, Critica.

Mosher Stuard, S. (1986) 'To Town to Serve: Urban Domestic Slavery in Medieval Ragusa', in B. A. Hanawalt (ed.), *Women and Work in Preindustrial Europe*, Indiana University Press, 39–55.

Neveux-Maisonneuve (1933) 'L'industrie dentellière à Auxerre au XVIIe siècle', *Bulletin de la Société des Sciences historiques et naturelles de l'Yonne*, 23–33.

Pastor, R. et al. (1990) *Poder monastico y grupos domesticos en la Galicia foral (Siglos XIII–XV)*, Madrid, CSIC.

Pinto, G. (1984) 'L'organizzazione del lavoro nei cantieri edili (Italia centro-settentrionale)', in *Artigiani e salariati: il mondo del lavoro nell'Italia dei secoli XII–XV*, Pistoia, 69–101.

Pollet, M. (1991) 'Les enfants abandonnés de Grasse au XVIIIe siècle', *Enfance abandonnée et société en Europe. XIVe–XXe siècle*, Rome, École Française de Rome, 897–903.

Raffaele, S. (1991) 'Il problema degli esposti in Sicilia (sec. XVIII–XIX). Normativa e risposta istituzionale: il caso di Catania', *Enfance abandonnée et société en Europe. XIVe–XXe siècle*, Rome, École Française de Rome, 905–36.

Reyerson, K. L. (1992) 'The Adolescent Apprentice/Worker in Medieval Montpellier', *Journal of Family History*, 17, 4, 353–70.

Sandri, L. (1991) 'Modalità dell'abbandono dei fanciulli in area urbana: gli esposti dell'ospedale di San Gallo di Firenze nella prima metà de XV secolo', *Enfance abandonnée et société en Europe. XIVe–XXe siècle*, Rome, École Française de Rome, 993–1015.

San Vicente, A. (1988) *Instrumentos para una historia social y economica del trabajo en Zaragoza en los siglos XV a XVIII*, I–II, Zaragoza.

Schiavoni, C. (1991) 'Gli infanti esposti del Santo Spirito in Saxia di Roma tra 500 e 800: numero, ricevimento, allevamento e destino', *Enfance abandonnée et société en Europe. XIVe–XXe siècle*, Rome, École Française de Rome, 1017–64.

Service Éducatif des Archives Départementales de la Côte d'Or (1979) *Le travail des enfants au XIXe siècle dans les industries de Bourgogne*, Dijon.

Service Éducatif des Archives Départementales de l'Yonne (1991) *La révolution industrielle dans l'Yonne. De la manufacture à l'industrie moderne*, Auxerre.

Stella, A. (1992) 'L'esclavage en Andalousie à l'époque moderne', *Annales ESC*, 1, 35–63.

Verlinden, C. (1976) 'L'enfant esclave dans l'Europe médiévale', *Recueils de la Société Jean Bodin*, XXXVI, Brussels, 107–25.

— (1977) *L'esclavage dans l'Europe médiévale*, II, Gand.

Villermé, L. R. (1840) *Tableau de l'état physique et moral des ouvriers employés dans les manufactures de coton, de laine et de soie*, Paris, J. Renouard et Cie (new edn, Paris, EDI, 1989).

PART 1a

Child Labour in the Current Economic System

CHAPTER 3

The Economy and Child Labour:
An Overview

Claude Meillassoux

The exploitation[1] of child labour[2] in the world harks back to a situation seen in Europe at the turn of the nineteenth century, by which time it had escalated to unprecedented levels and found itself at the centre of heated, now largely forgotten debates (Stella).

During the eighteenth- and nineteenth-century onslaught of capitalism, a social rift opened up between the workers in-migrating from the countryside and the wealthy middle classes of the towns. The latter at first regarded the rural exodus as a barbarian invasion. They greeted the reputedly 'dangerous' poorer classes with hatred and disgust. Sending their miserable children down coal mines or to the mill was not just good business, it was an act of charity. Child labour spread.[3]

When, however, labour is recruited and housed in one and the same region, as is the case within the framework of national capitalism, it is not long before the middle classes are feeling uneasy about the social and sanitary side-effects of overly close exploitation – crime and epidemics. Then, when international competition leaves the marketplace for the battlefield, the workers and their children suddenly regain recognition as citizens whom the army will go to great lengths to render physically and ideologically fit for service, to 'die for the homeland' or 'defend the Empire' (Lavalette). School provides another indispensable means of equipping them with the civic virtues of patriotic citizens, on top of the minimum skills required for industrial work. All in all, regulating the employment of children is imperative if they are to contribute, as civilly as possible, to the welfare and security of the ruling classes. To turn-of-the-century national (and republican) middle-class society, guranteeing the future of those children was considered essential in order to guarantee the future of the nation as a whole. The ideal at that time was to have a large population, educated and occasionally cared for by the state.

Owing to the global expansion of capitalism, the position of children today is of far greater concern. It is not just that child exploitation is spreading; the short-termism of the market economy is no longer counterbalanced by thoughts for the future. We are no longer living in an age when the political and social entities (the nation, the family) define the common heritage and impose civic concerns. Nowadays, with labour exploited way beyond the borders of the great capitalist nations, Third World children do not represent the future of wealthy countries. What happens to Brazilian or Indian children does not directly affect the fate of the businessmen and women of the richer countries; they are just their profits in-the-making. Seen as a swarming menace in foreign and proletarianized populations whose sole purpose it is to die anonymously at their station, they are victims, therefore, of a resurgence in the cruellest forms of exploitation. From such a distanced vantage point, the well-intended arguments which, in an attempt to address the business community in what one assumes to be its own terms, present children as an investment in need of protection, are no longer tenable (D. Bonnet). Even in the European countries where child labour is resurfacing (e.g. Great Britain), business people and politicians remain insensitive to the warning signals.[4] Hence the pointlessness of trying to advocate long-term interests in an effort to persuade wealthy capitalists to ease their pressure on the Third World. The fact that children are being exploited to death in the gold mines of Peru means nothing to the affluent classes speculating on the napoléon or adorning themselves with jewellery.

Contrary to what we have been led to expect, the impact of economic globalization on social development has been negative, especially in the lesser developed countries. International competition, foreign investment and the tutelage of the international funding agencies go hand in hand with social breakdown in the developing world and one of the most unbearable and morally least justifiable manifestations of it all is the growing exploitation of children.

In order to understand why the exploitation of child labour is developing at world level, we must try to analyse the political and economic context in which it comes to pass.[5]

Market Theory, or How Can We Enforce Natural Laws?

Producing for the market is not part of human nature. Prior to their penetration by trading countries, many peoples used to supply themselves with goods produced by the family unit without needing to resort to trade. 'Economic development' has above all meant inducing the millions of individuals belonging to these self-supporting domestic societies to produce for the market, whether they like it or not. Slavery and then colonization figure among the major stages of such 'development'. Since the end of World War II and the setbacks of bureaucratic centralism, 'development' has been placed under the general heading of the market economy, which the ruling political classes now view as the only possible form of organization for the production and distribution of wealth.[6] This now very advanced global evolution has undoubtedly done more than any other to favour the growth of production. But it has gone hand in hand with tremendously widespread misery. It cannot be ignored that wherever it spreads, the market economy goes together with the exploitation of children.

When a domestic economy encounters the market, the result is always profound and painful changes which reoccur as the process spreads to new regions of the world. What is most striking is the massive exodus of rural populations towards the towns. This large-scale movement is still ongoing. Millions of impoverished rural families around the world still constitute significant reserves of people – and thus labour. Slow to start, the rural exodus picked up speed in the Third World when the private appropriation of land as a factor of production helped drive families from their villages; and also when, after World War II, country people realized that their labour would be better remunerated if applied to the more efficient production of the cities or richer countries, than if it were kept confined to stagnating manual agriculture. Entry into the market economy, the urgent need for cash in order to gain access to the most vital, as well as the most attractive, goods and, hence, the resulting demand for paid work all led to accelerated urban growth. Much to the liking of the (mostly foreign) investors, rural exodus fuels, unemployment as it always exceeds the amount of jobs megalopolis-based firms are able to offer. Separated from the land, newly urbanized households (men, women and children) thus constitute an overabundant proletariat that is prey to the fluctuating labour market and the daily demand for subsistence commodities.

Unable to produce their own food as they used to back on the land, urbanized labourers need to acquire money in the shape of wages. None of the classical economists, not even Malthus, use the ideas of a minimum living wage or social reproduction to support their notion of wages, when such ideas could provide the moorings for the theory of basic requirements. Their reasoning seems to assume that the 'laws of value' have similar effects when acting on the wages of living beings as with the prices of lifeless commodities. To contemporary free-marketeers, as well as employers, the worker is nothing but a 'human resource'(!), existing for only as long as it remains within the firm and only while there is an ongoing exchange of labour for wages. The firm is not responsible for what happens outside. This doctrine makes no allowance for a human being's vital everyday organic needs, meaning that the deleterious effects of austerity measures on the health and survival of the reified beings they target can go by the board.[7] For, as the monetarists always tend to forget, the proletarian is no ordinary supplier: selling his wares, that is his labour, is a matter of life or death for himself and his family.

In market economics, with all production ultimately bound for monetary exchange, a division of labour is established between all the components of the economy, keeping them mutually dependent. For more than two centuries, classical economists have been maintaining that this universal complementarity is (or soon will be) achieved in a harmonious and natural way and that because of it, everybody enjoys (or will enjoy) an equal share of the fruits of his or her labour. Competition is presented as the system's big regulator: the best producers prevail over lesser ones. This idealistic argument, however, remains hypothetical for it cannot take into account the influence of the power struggles which actually generate the competition in economic relations. But these power struggles play a decisive role in a world which openly declares itself capitalist and where initiative and decision-making belong to those who hold the capital. Upon this basis is established the economic hierarchy of individuals, firms, social classes, nations. Contrary to its theoretical precepts, 'free competition' enduringly and cumulatively favours the firms with the most abundant capital. The resulting concentrations bring great pressure to bear on other firms, the markets and governments. These power struggles are so present that the United States, for whom the 'free-enterprise system' is the unwritten doctrine, has equipped itself with a legal arsenal (the anti-trust laws) to try and thwart the pressure of the monopolies operating, however logically, in this type of economy. But if capitalist entrepreneurs seek to defend themselves from each other *vis-à-vis* such practices (even via state intervention), they all individually employ them at the first available opportunity.

Similarly, at international level, power struggles are the rule between strong states and weak. But because these struggles are presumed to be 'non-economic', they are ignored by the doctrine of free enterprise and its followers. Yet these forces operate out in the open. The world today is shared between, on the one hand, the big industrial and financial powers (the G7) and, on the other, a multitude of nations regarded, to varying degrees, as politically inferior. The former own the largest part of the industrial and financial capital and govern the international funding agencies, both public (IMF, WB) and private (GATT). The G7 are the de facto rulers as much at the political and military level as the technological.[8] Competition between the so-called 'advanced' countries and the others is rooted in the former's decisive historical advantage, which is still being consolidated by the monetarist agencies today. Restructuring is possible only with their assistance, such as in the case of Japan (on post-war aid from the United States, anxious at the time to hold the USSR in check). Soviet or Indian attempts at economic independence, looking likely to undermine the supremacy of the major powers, were attacked and defused; the emergence of the 'dragons' turns out to have been initiated and assisted by already established interests. Countries like North Korea or Iraq, which have attempted to industrialize without international tutelage, have been ravaged by war. As for China, with all its considerable potential, the general view is that its development as an economically competitive power would create extreme global tension. But China's appeal to the IMF does not smack of a genuine desire for economic independence. Today, almost every country outside the G7 is subject to an economic tutelage which reaches right into the heart of government, where there is usually a post occupied by a WB or

IMF 'creature', sometimes even at the very top. The power struggle between these agencies – with their colossal financial resources – and the countries in debt – deprived of capital – works to the advantage of the major powers who maintain statutory rule over the agencies.[9]

Dependence on the big powers is therefore another effect of *structured* adjustments. Attempts by the dominated countries to construct an autonomous and coherent economy are not only hampered by the difficulty of amassing capital, but also condemned and sanctioned for being protectionist, hence generating financial and commercial retaliation. Meanwhile, international businesses secure world control over commodities such as hybrid seeds or basic pharmaceutical products, thereby increasing the technological or healthcare-related dependence of the weaker countries.

Through a paradoxical misappropriation of the theories of free-market economics, these power struggles take place in the name of the re-enactment of the so-called 'natural' laws of the market economy. The international funding agencies (IMF and WB), the instruments of the most powerful states, evoke the need for development as a means of justifying the imposition of great *natural* equilibria which, contrary to the beliefs of the free-enterprise system, are not established automatically of their own accord; so that the inaccuracy of the theory becomes a pretext for an arrogant interventionist policy, symptomatic of the economic pressures the strongest powers bring to bear upon the weakest.

The unprecedented levels of poverty that neo-free-market interventionism has been producing world-wide since 1950, particularly since the 1980s, leads one (barring acceptance that these institutions have failed and/or the unlikely possibility that their functionaries might be clueless) to believe that the ultimate aim of the policy is not development at all. Indeed, the International Labour Organization's 1992 employment report showed that national government support in some areas (loans, trade and investment incentives) has had more impact than the straight free-enterprise system, and that adjustment policies should include measures to counter the fall in living standards and investments and run-down machinery. It goes on to say that over and above an abundance of cheap labour, the key to success is the existence of a trained work force, human investment. This sort of talk has fallen on deaf ears at the IMF and WB. So we should not judge the results of their interventionism on the declared intentions, but on the de facto results, i.e. the constant lowering of raw materials and labour prices to the benefit of transnational industrial and financial circles. We have to admit that, on this score, it has been undeniably successful.

Between the Cost and the Price

According to market logic, a marketable commodity's price results from its confrontation with the buyers. Price levels therefore depend upon the prevailing economic climate at the time of sale and, more importantly, on the balance of power between buyers and sellers. These factors – climate, balance – are independent from those governing the determination of the commodity's cost (i.e. what the supplier must pay to acquire the necessary ingredients for its manufacture: raw materials, machinery, labour, etc.). So both sides strive to capitalize on their bargaining power in order to swing the price to their advantage.[10] So the market system does not include a relationship of causality linking the cost and the price of the same commodity; each is determined in its own, organically distinct, context: the former in the workshop, the latter on the market. While sellers for their part seek to recuperate the cost of making a product, buyers on the other hand are busily trying to force the price down, possibly even to below its cost. Equilibrium, according to the classical economists, implicitly means that there is either an absence of power struggles or a moral duty on the part of the buyers to keep the sellers alive by paying them enough for their products *at least* to guarantee reproduction. In practice, however, buyers are operating in the short term and cannot burden themselves with the kind of generosity that might place them in a weaker position than their competitors.

This is the situation in North–South trade in so far as the trading partners are unequal. Countries importing goods from the South seek to pay as little as possible. The structural adjustment policies imposed upon the countries supplying raw materials and labour by the IMF and WB are ultimately designed to cut prices. So-called austerity measures, wage freezes, the abolition of welfare, redundancies, etc. are all used to bring down labour prices. Depending on the economic climate, these agencies have on the other hand varied their policy as far as the labour cost is concerned (i.e. what it costs to keep wage-earners alive). Between 1950 and 1975 – a period of industrial growth and rising employment in the dependent countries – the Third World became the focus of a huge import drive of foodstuffs from high-output, food-producing nations, the intention being to reduce the cost, and price, of workers in the city.[11] From 1975–80 onwards, however, the technological revolution and mass redundancies caused wage cuts solely due to unemployment, and World Bank policy changed. The new, so-called 'true price' measures recommended by the WB are now applied to foodstuffs on the pretext that it would increase the incomes of farmers. Such a policy has helped to raise the price of food for wage-earners,[12] the cost of whose labour has increased at the same time as its price (wages) has fallen due to unemployment. The underlying reality of this 'true' pricing policy for foodstuffs is that it is intended to force the urban unemployed back to endure the recession in the countryside and rid the cities of potentially disruptive elements.

Meanwhile, workers in underdeveloped nations are all too often relatively unorganized and lack the means to do anything about the prices of life's basic necessities and, hence, the cost of their labour.[13] But 'arrangements like GATT provide for free trade in goods and capital without lifting the barriers blocking the free movement of labour. Third World countries are thus forced to export commodities whose comparative cost advantage rests solely on extremely low labour costs' (Gulrajani). In this respect, among others, the cost of labour – and its price: wages – depends on having the economic circumstances governed for their good by the major powers. The classical economists talk as if the wage a worker is paid for his labour cannot not fall below his cost. Here again, as with the price of commodities, the theory assumes that there is an inherent morality in the workings of capitalism. But when the labour force is plentiful and, above all, remote and easily disposable, capitalism is indifferent to whether or not people are starving to death. In today's situation of decline, wages can be cut to below their cost, i.e. below the 'bread-line', even below the survival threshold, not on account of some obscure economic laws, but because of a deliberate, if not planned, trade policy.

Competition and Dependence between Countries

Structural adjustment is therefore the manifestation of a power struggle aimed at bringing down the price of the labour force employed by firms and hence the cost of manufacturing their products.

These policies which claim to structure local economies in order that they might produce cheaply, are joined by another (global) one: making supplier countries compete with each other in order to lower their prices even further on the international market. The World Bank systematically encourages the simultaneous farming, development or manufacture of the same products in a lot of countries at the same time, so as to create chronic overproduction and hence keep prices at their lowest. And because of the difficult international relations between the many producers of the same products, speculators can easily capitalize upon tentative refusals to sell in order to push up the prices – as Houphouet-Boigny attempted, to his own cost, with Ivory Coast coffee. We also know how coffee prices, for instance, have been held very low even though raising them could have dissuaded Colombian peasants from cultivating cocaine. Meanwhile, the major powers only respect 'agreements' like GATT or Lomé, which put raw materials suppliers at a disadvantage from the outset, when it suits them to do so.

Another (less often raised) practice enters the frame to weaken the so-called developing countries: 'foreign investment'. Often presented as desirable 'aid', these investments are the fruit of relocation policies whose aim it is to find the least expensive labour force possible around the world, even if it means having quickly to shift investments from one region to another because of local labour prices. Some countries, such as so-called 'popular' China, cater to this by creating 'special zones' where particularly cheap workers are delivered to foreign firms, children included, naturally. Foreign investments increase the dependence of the countries into which they are channelled by not allowing capital to be amassed in the places where the commodities are produced and the work is done (which is why these countries are always appealing to the international financial authorities for assistance). Their contribution to the building of coherent national economies is incidental and mediocre, whereas a country's economic progress depends on its ability to accumulate, make use of and manage capital: i.e. its ability to constitute and reconstitute its human and material bases so that the nation can have its best configuration for development. Unable to keep the profits from capital, these countries are kept in a position of constant dependence upon foreign banks and funding agencies. But economic progress relies on their remaining independent of outside decision-making for it jeopardizes the stability of the industrial infrastructure, hence employment (Sancho). Foreign firms set up shop in a country not with a mind to building up its national economy, but to make profits from a specific activity. They send their profits back home, leaving just enough to pay their often very low wages, which is why they relocated in the first place. The wages[14] go solely towards paying the labour force; i.e. to be consumed entirely by wage-earners. The money may well fuel local demand for basic necessities; but not enough to contribute to any meaningful accumulation of national capital. Profits are supposed to do that. Yet they go back to the investor's homeland, often in return for some enticing tax exemptions, thus depriving the host country of the added value; i.e. the productive capital produced by the work of its nationals. Since foreign firms' profits leave the country and are not reinvested, only low-level state investment in the 'informal', infra-capitalist sector is possible. And the existing industrial infrastructures are in danger of stagnating, if not decaying. Finally, since the volume of productive capital is proportionally much lower than labour sector demand for basic necessities, wages, even when very low, act as a factor of inflation and serve to weaken the currency.

Countries that appeal for foreign capital are therefore placing themselves in a delicate situation where they have no control over their economies and are forced to export at the lowest price. To add to that, the more open they are to foreign capital, the more exposed they will be to international specula-tion and economic collapse in the event of sudden changes on the stock market.[15] Lacking an accumulation of national capital and, hence, modern means of production, longer working hours are needed in order to produce; and labour productivity stagnates. The cost of a labour force that uses low-productivity means of production is proportionally higher than in the countries enjoying strong capitalization. Therefore, while the cost of the labour force in undercapitalized sectors is higher in real terms, the international trade structures are at the same time striving to bring down the prices of export goods. These conditions combine to weaken the balance of trade and make it more difficult, if not impossible, to repay debt. Appealing to foreign investments is a stop-gap, not the expression of a development policy.[16]

In order to offset the relative costliness of the labour force (on account of its low productivity), to make direct or indirect inroads into the international market, to remain competitive no matter how scant the capital, labour has to be paid bottom rate wages and be exploited to the full. The presence and persistence of an infra-capitalist sector allows for severe wage cuts, thus enabling the best-equipped firms to profit from lower labour costs and, at the same time, better productivity. Thus begins a process whereby a handful of business people locally become richer, in contrast to the meagre profits of the intra-capitalist firms (Uribe) and the growing poverty of a work force whose resources are endlessly being reduced through structural adjustment. The gap between rich and poor is widening in virtually every country subjected to this policy. This is the most accurate indicator of underdevelopment. It makes the existence of a large undercapitalized sector beyond state control an 'expression not only of growing, maybe irreversible, impoverishment but also of destabilization' (Sari). It makes this infra-capitalist sector 'an integral part of the world capitalist system's process of surplus extraction; and super-exploitation, especially of child labour' (Gulrajani).

The global spread of the labour market via relocation, the division of wage-earners into competing groups, the so-called structural policy measures which hamper both the value enhancement and capitalization of local work, the programmed weakness of national capital accumulation; such are the circumstances creating the conditions for low-cost production of exportable commodities. In this way, the poorer countries – held in the stranglehold of an endlessly sustained international debt through the low prices of their export goods – are coerced into the service of the wealthier countries. And abandoned to the meagre profits of all the more demanding entrepreneurs are the least costly, the meekest and most perishable members of the proletariat: the children.

Notes

1. *Exploitation*: organic relationship between social classes, whereby the class owning the means of production, distribution and financing, takes all or part of the labour surplus from those deprived of such means and dependent upon paid work; this exchange sustains the reproduction of exploitative relations (*labour surplus* refers to the working hours available over and above the basic time required for the worker to earn a subsistence wage; *production surplus* refers to the quantity of goods the worker produces over and above his basic consumption needs).

2. *Child*: human being of either sex who has reached the stage of growth where s/he can understand and act but, due to the transient physical weakness of youth and the relative pusillanimity instilled by the family upbringing, who puts him/herself under the authority of adults.

3. L. R. Villermé (1840) *Tableau de l'état physique et moral des ouvriers* (Picture of the physical and moral condition of the workers), Vol. 2, Paris, J. Renouard et Cie (new edn, Paris, EDI, 1989); L. and M. Bonneff (1908) *La vie tragique des travailleurs* (The tragic lives of the workers), Paris, Rouff et Cie (new edn, Paris, EDI, 1984).

4. From 1989 to 1994, the number of children hurt in accidents at work in Great

Britain rose to 23,868 (*Monde du Travail Libre*, November 1994, 8). Conservative Party policy, which created deep inequalities in income, in many respects brought British social structures closer to those of the underdeveloped world.

5. We exclude the hypothesis of full employment, where child labour would become supplementary to that of adults under more worker-friendly conditions; that is not the prevailing climate in the present-day global market to which the articles in this book refer.

6. See the series of articles published in *Le Monde diplomatique* (winter 1995) on 'la pensée unique' or 'the single line of thought'.

7. For IMF managers, the social problems caused by their (they believe, strictly economic) structural adjustment policies are a matter for other international bodies, to which they anyway pay no heed.

8. Such dependence even exists among the G7 countries themselves, particularly *vis-à-vis* the United States.

9. A state's representation is based on the size of its contributions, i.e. on the 'wealth of nations'.

10. There are some international commodities markets that are theoretically designed to harmonize supply and demand. These mainly end up generating fluctuations in price which in turn attract speculation, more often than not at the expense of the sellers.

11. But at the expense of the development of local food production.

12. The rising price of basic necessities runs counter to economic development when, as is the case today (1995), there is no accompanying growth in food production productivity. Increased food production should be the starting point for development, as more workers can then be fed by fewer farmers, hence at minimum cost. From this point of view, however, guaranteed balanced and sustainable development would have required the gradual modernization of subsistence farming beginning at the moment of independence in order to control the impact of the inevitably ensuing rural migration.

13. The price and cost of labour can only ever concur if the wage-earners have bargaining powers allowing them to refuse to supply their labour below its cost. Strikes and other forms of industrial conflict testify to the ongoing power struggle at this level, not the harmonious application of market laws.

14. According to our definition, wages are described as a sum calculated *vis-à-vis* a precise measure of working time completed or quantities produced (as opposed to the 'salaries', 'stipends', 'emoluments', etc. paid to executives and other management collaborators).

15. Cf. the case of Mexico (February 1995) whose entry into the North American Free Trade Area (NAFTA) provoked a wave of speculative investment (rather than industrial investment) which was then suddenly withdrawn leaving the Mexican state with a US$ 50 billion debt that forced it into a position of aggravated dependence and left it with no choice but to hock its oil industry. The economic situation is being rehabilitated by means of harsher structural adjustment, wage cuts, redundancies, cheap sales of export goods, i.e. penalizing those who are least responsible for the situation with social hardship, yet not imposing a single sanction on the speculators who made themselves rich from the event. We should note here that, along the lines of the Stalinist model denounced by Orwell whereby the facts are concealed beneath an adulterating vocabulary, the international agencies grace speculators with honourable names such as 'investor' or 'saver'.

16. Hostility towards foreign investments fills the propaganda of nationalist or fascist parties or sects (cf. the Thakeray Shiv Shena of Bombay).

CHAPTER 4

Child Labour and the Export Sector in the Indian Carpet Industry

Mohini Gulrajani

India is the country with perhaps the largest population of working children in the world: now nearly a third of the world total and rising fast. Many are employed in hazardous industries such as match-making, fireworks, glass, carpet-weaving.

Child labour has become an issue of increasing importance in India due to pressure from the international community to have it regulated. The US Senate is considering the Harkins bill, which, if passed, will ban imports from Third World countries that use child labour. The European Parliament has a similar bill. The spectre of a consumer boycott looms large. Apart from these unilateral measures, it is expected that the developing countries which failed to incorporate the issues of environment, human rights and labour standards at the Uruguay round of GATT, will definitely be further pressed at the World Trade Organization (WTO).

The central theme of this chapter is that recent developments in the world capitalist system have increased the economic motivation of Third World countries to use the cheapest sources of labour. Arrangements like GATT provide for free trade in goods and capital without lifting the barriers blocking the free movement of labour. Third World countries are thus forced to export commodities whose comparative cost advantage rests solely on extremely low labour costs.

The policies of their governments, with their outward-looking growth strategies, aim for the integration of the domestic economy into the world economic system. Yet the IMF and World Bank often initiate stabilization and structural adjustment programmes that have the effect of reducing the bargaining power of the weakest segments of the labour market and increasing wage differentials in the organized and unorganized sectors of the economy. This, plus many other related causes, stimulates the informal sector of Third World economies. Unstructured as it may seem, the informal sector is not a relic from a pre-capitalist era. In fact, it is an integral part of the world capitalist system's process of surplus extraction; it is super-exploitation, especially of child labour.

This chapter tries to establish this with the help of the case study of the hand-woven, knitted woollen carpet industry in India, which produces almost exclusively for the export market and is perhaps the biggest employer of child labour in the manufacturing sector.

The Magnitude of the Problem

The state of information about the magnitude of child labour in the Indian economy is unsatisfactory. A variety of estimates exist, but they differ drastically from one another and do not lend themselves easily to comparison. The most conservative official sources place the total size of the child work force at about 20 million, while organizations like the South Asian Coalition on Child Servitude (SACCS) claim it is closer to 55 million. Some sources even say that India has more than 100 million children working in both the family and hired labour segments of various sectors. According to the 1981 census, 86.4 per cent of child workers were engaged in the agriculture sector, 8.6 per cent in manufacturing and about 5 per cent in the services sector.

The main employers of child labour in the manufacturing sector are the carpet industry, the fireworks and match-making industries, diamond polishing and glass. In spite of the ban imposed by the Child Labour Act of 1938 and the Child Labour Prohibition and Regulation Act (1986), the carpet industry in the Bhadohi/Mirzapur belt of Uttar Pradesh remains perhaps the biggest of them. According to the latest estimates of the Indian Social Institute, the bulk of the child labour force is employed in sixteen categories of small-scale industries operating in the unorganized sector.

Although it is not possible to put figures to child labour with any great accuracy, it can be said to have been galloping since the 1980s.[1] While the sectoral composition of the child labour force in the 1990s remains unknown, there are enough indications that its incidence, and the degree of its exploitation, has grown at a relatively faster rate in certain labour-intensive export industries. The next section discusses this point in detail. Almost all the growth in numbers of child labour in manufacturing and services has taken place in the informal sector. Its incidence in the factory sector, which stood at 48 per cent of the child labour force in 1948, had fallen to a mere 0.07 per cent by 1976 and must be negligible at present.

Economic Policy, Poverty and Child Labour

In 1991, India had a per capita annual income of US$ 330, i.e. one sixty-seventh that of the USA. Some 360 million people were living below the official poverty line of Rs 132 (US$ 4) per capita monthly expenditure for rural areas, and Rs 172 (US$ 5) for urban areas. Out of a total labour force of 331 million, 9.3 million (i.e. 2.8 per cent) were openly unemployed in 1987–88, up from 6 million (1.9 per cent) in 1983. The Indian economy, undergoing its first, milder, phase of liberalization in the 1980s, grew at an impressive average rate of 5.2 per cent per annum. Employment generation in both the organized manufacturing sector and agriculture was low – the former has in fact registered a decline since the mid-1980s. But employment in the informal manufacturing and services sectors grew at a fast rate. This resulted in an increase in per capita earnings, mainly due to longer working hours, while at the same time employment became increasingly informalized and casualized. Also, the government spent a considerable part of its expenditure on specific poverty-alleviation and employment-generation programmes.

All this led to a slow-down in the increase of poverty in relative terms during the 1980s, even though the absolute number of poor people went up. The hypothesis of this chapter is that in the 1990s, government policy initiatives on the one hand, and events like GATT and globalization on the other, must have had the combined effect of reversing the process. With the further impoverishment of the poorest segments of the labour force, this in turn must have created the conditions for an increase in the supply and demand of child labour.

THE REFORM The economic reform programme initiated in 1991 to meet the serious external debt and a high level of inflation was supposed to be implemented in two phases: short-term stabilization and medium-run structural adjustment.

The stabilization measures, such as compressed public expenditure, have induced industrial recession thereby reducing the level of employment. They have also resulted in cuts in public expenditure on anti-poverty/employment-generation programmes. Although the National Sample Survey Organization (NSSO) has not yet released the findings of its 1993 quinquennial survey, it can safely be said that while employment must have undergone very slow growth, the quality of employment has almost certainly deteriorated.[2]

If industrial recession persists, employment conditions will worsen in all sectors of the economy. And the condition of the poor is likely to deteriorate further if food grain prices continue rising at the over 20 per cent rate registered in 1991–92 and 1992–93. This will force many more children to drop out of school and enter the labour market, thus depressing wage rates and reducing the supply price of child labour.

Another important element of reform – the external sector reform, including the devaluation of the Indian rupee, its current account convertibility and a significant drop in tariffs – has increased the outward orientation of the economy, a process likely to be aided by events like the Uruguay round of GATT. The economy has been becoming increasingly export-driven during the early 1990s. What is more, there has been mounting pressure for good export performance.[3] Although exports have been picking up, it can be attributed to various policy interventions, including an artificially lowered exchange rate by the RBI. Fear of a reversal in the positive trend is likely to prompt the government to offer further incentives, including more relaxed labour laws. This is likely further to deteriorate the quality of employment.

In fact, there is already evidence that the accelerated export effort is actually causing such deterioration. Major industries (such as diamond polishing, ready-made garments, leather goods, hand-knotted carpets) have been fast increasing their share of total exports, mainly through their expansion in the unorganized sector. They all depend on very cheap and unprotected segments of the labour force. Many of them have been becoming increasingly dependent on either female or child labour. While the ready-made garments industry of Tamil Nadu and the seafood-processing industry of Goa have recently started using female migrant labour, the diamond polishing industry of Surat and hosiery industry of Tirpur have registered a fast rate of growth in child labour over the past few years, due to the linkages with the global economy. In fact, Tirpur is one of the newly emerging export enclaves where child labour is being introduced for the first time. Most of these industries have appalling and dangerous working conditions. In the glass industry of Firoza-bad (nicknamed Dante's Inferno), for example, children are made to carry rods of red-hot glass.

So child labour is no relic from pre-capitalist days and may, in fact, grow as poor economies build up their links with the world capitalist system.

Child Labour in the Carpet Industry

The hand-knotted woollen carpet industry of India is one of the several labour-intensive, low-skill, low-technology industries that have grown rapidly in recent years due to the impetus of the international market. The industry produces almost exclusively for the international market, and imports more than 50 per cent of its crucial raw material, wool, from abroad. So it has very few linkages with the rest of the economy. Almost all its production is 'programmed' by the advance orders of the carpet importers, who not only specify the quality, colours and the type and number of knots per square inch, but in many cases also supply the designs. The industry manufactures a very large variety of carpets of all sizes. They include high quality Persian carpets, with a knot density of 180 to 300 per square inch, druggets, loosers and Indo-Nepali carpets.

In recent years, India has emerged as one of the most important players in the international hand-knotted carpet market. Standing at only Rs 30 million at the time of independence and less than Rs 1 billion as late as 1977–78, the value of exports rose to Rs 13.9 billion or US$ 443.16 million, by 1993–94, the main importers being Germany and the USA. And the industry's share of total exports has been growing steadily: to 1.9 per cent in 1993–94, as against 0.53 per cent in 1980–81.

THE CARPET BELT Although the hand-knotted carpets are produced in the states of Rajasthan and Jammu as well as Kashmir, the Mirzapur/Bhadohi carpet belt of Uttar Pradesh (UP) accounts for more than 80 per cent of total exports. The belt actually comprises five districts of the impoverished region of Eastern UP – Mirzapur, Bhadohi, Varanasi, Sonbhadra and Jaipur – and spreads over a roughly 4500 km² area, with about 1500 villages. The belt's labour supply comes from a very large area including other districts of UP as well as Bihar and, to a lesser extent, Madhya Pradesh, West Bengal and even Nepal.

The child labour problem in the carpet belt cannot be understood without knowing some crucial facts about UP and Bihar, the poorest states of the Indian union. Bihar has long been at the bottom of the ladder, where it remains with an annual per capita income of Rs 2330 in 1990–91, less than half the meagre national level of Rs 4964. Uttar Pradesh was fifth from the bottom in the 1980s and has since slipped to second poorest state with a per capita income of Rs 3557. Not surprisingly, the two states together had as many as 111.7 million people living below the poverty line in 1987–88.

The number of poor must have gone up since then, and the percentage of children joining the labour market must have grown, especially in the rural areas where poverty is much worse. The fast-growing carpet industry is the only important industry in those areas, so it comes as no surprise to find it able to carry out extreme exploitation of its child labourers, especially migrant children.

International concern has been focusing on the brutal exploitation of child labour in the carpet belt for several years now, but the problem has been around for a lot longer. It came to national attention in 1984 when the press began to highlight the plight of carpet children from the Palamua district of Bihar. Some of them were reported to have been kidnapped, kept in captivity, beaten with iron rods, hanged from tree tops and even branded with red-hot iron rods.[4] Since then, the number of child labourers in the carpet belt has grown at a fast rate, with an important rise in the use of migrant children, especially in the last four years. This is borne out by, among others, a study by the National Council of Applied Economic Research (NCAER), according to which 87.6 per cent of the working children migrated into the carpet belt only after 1989 (Vijayagopalan 1993).

THE NUMBERS OF CARPET CHILDREN The informal structure of the industry, the vast area it covers and the secrecy due to its 'hazardous' nature make it very difficult to obtain reliable information about the numbers of children it employs. Various estimates have been made at various points in time, but they all use different sample sizes and methodologies and, hence, produce different results. At one end of the spectrum is the claim made by the Carpet Export Promotion Corporation (CEPC) that child labour no longer exists in the carpet industry. At the other is the study Professor B. N. Juyal conducted in 1991 for the Child Labour Action and Support Project of the

International Labour Organization, which puts the figure at anywhere between 300,000 and 450,000 (Juyal 1993). The latter took only three months to complete and looked at a very small sample of three village clusters: one from the core of the belt and the other two from its outer and peripheral zones. It was confined to 2666 out of an estimated total of 168,000 looms, and found that children represented as much as 70 per cent of the total working population, with 76.09 per cent of them belonging to the hired labour segment and the rest to the family labour segment.

These results contrast sharply with those of the study conducted in 1992 by NCAER, commissioned by the Handicrafts Development Commissioner (Vijayagopalan 1993). That one examined a cross-section survey of 500 children drawn from fifty villages in the districts of Mirzapur and Bhadohi. Its main finding, which is extensively quoted by both the industry and the government, was that child labour accounted for only 8 per cent of the total work force in the hand-knotted carpet-weaving industry; 4.4 per cent belonged to the family labour segment while the rest was reported to be hired labour. If we were to go by the industry and government-accepted estimates that the population of carpet workers totals 1.5 million, this would put the total number of carpet children at 120,000. In its foreword, though, the report says that the actual incidence may be higher, because the sample survey was conducted at a time when the industry had been advised of the penalties of employing child labour.

Thus it can be said that anywhere between 100,000 and 300,000 children were employed in the carpet industry as recently as 1992. Due to the mounting national and international pressure to put an end to the exploitation of child labour, these figures might have come down marginally. In any case, the CEPC claim about having eliminated child labour cannot be taken seriously. The basis of the claim is a registration drive carried out by the CEPC, whereby every single loom has to be registered and every loom-holder has to make a declaration saying they will not use labour in contravention to the Child Labour Prevention and Regulation Act (1986). Not only does the CEPC lack both the necessary financial and human resources to monitor the more than 200,000 looms spread over an area of 4500 km^2; even if it *did* have the funds, the prohibitive cost of foolproof monitoring, if borne by the industry, would soon result in its closure.

In the meantime, the government, alarmed at the prospect of losing an important export market, has tightened up its law-enforcement machinery. On the guidance or instructions of central government, the state government has stepped up the number of inspections considerably over the last three years. All this may well have yielded results, especially with regard to the organized sector of the industry in urban areas, yet to imagine that far-flung rural areas are now child-labour-free can only be wishful thinking.[5] According to Kailash Satyarthi of Bachpen Bachoa Andolan, even today the carpet industry employs 250,000 children, 200,000 of whom belong to Koshi and the Palamua district of Bihar.

THE EXPLOITATION OF CHILDREN   Although there may be no consensus about the exact numbers of child labourers in the industry, all sources agree that almost every child labourer, especially in the hired labour segment, belongs to the most vulnerable section of the society and is subjected to the most brutal forms of exploitation.

Children in the carpet industry are mainly employed in three stages of production: (1) *Kabli*, or making balls from the wool; (2) knotting and cutting; (3) *Berai*, or packing the knots in the right position.

Carpet-weaving has been listed as a hazardous process under the Child Labour Prohibition and Regulation Act (CLPR) 1986, and is reported to be harmful to the lungs because of the wool-fluff that floats in the atmosphere in the weaving place. To add to that, acute concentration on design and the uncomfortable posture in which the children sit for long hours in low pit-looms is reported to injure their eyesight and fingers. Some of the dyes and chemicals used can cause skin problems.

Carpet children who come from the weakest segments of the society have no vocational or even physical mobility, because most of them are pledged against small loans that their parents may have taken. Not only are they grossly underpaid and made to work for long hours in sub-human conditions, but they are often subjected to severe coercive violence. Here are some of the facts about carpet children as brought out by the NCAER study:

- The study showed that a majority of the children in the hired labour segment belonged either to the schedule caste or schedule tribe (50.3 per cent in Bhadohi and 51.9 per cent in Mirzapur). In addition, 22 per cent of children in Mirzapur belonged to the weaker section of the Muslim community.
- Most carpet children came from families of landless labourers or very poor farmers. The average size of holding owned by the child's family in the self-employed segment was 0.28 hectares, even lower in the hired labour segment.
- The degree of indebtedness of families was found to be high, even in the family labour segment. Even though 62.5 per cent of the self-employed households did not report any debt, the remaining households owed an average of Rs 6940 (US$ 213).

Families whose children have gone into hired labour must have been suffering a far worse plight. About 97 per cent of the children in this segment reported that their parents had received lump-sum payments from the pro-spective employers through their agents. Normally the payment ranged from Rs 2500 to Rs 2800 (US$ 73–9). The children were signed up to work for a specified number of years: between one and ten years. Most of them – 100 per cent in Mirzapur and 47 per cent in Bhadohi – had migrated without their families, making them more vulnerable.

All the children get a wage rate which is considerably lower than that of adults. One way of keeping it low is the apprenticeship system. According to the report, 44.4 per cent of the child labourers in Mirzapur worked as *Chela* or apprentices. The fact that all the children in Bhadohi were reported to be on full-time wages shows the spurious nature of apprenticeship. As stated earlier, carpet-making is a low-skill industry, with a typically short learning curve.

Whereas the average wage reported by the NCAER study was Rs 12.2 (US\$ 0.38) per day, the ILO study showed much lower rates, with as many as thirteen out of a sample of seventy-two children being paid nothing at all and a very large number receiving between Rs 1 and Rs 5 a day. Earlier, the Prembhai's report had claimed that in 1984 the adult daily wage ranged between Rs 2 and Rs 5 and that children were being paid even less.

Most of the children reported very long working hours. While some of them worked fifteen hours or more a day, an overwhelming majority of 84 per cent worked at least nine to ten hours. Most of them enjoyed no weekly holiday: 95 per cent of the children in the hired labour segment worked seven days a week and 77.3 per cent for all twelve months of the year.

A majority of the children were subjected to coercive violence and other forms of punishment, such as wage cuts, late nights, no food and oral abuse. As mentioned earlier, horror stories of extreme physical violence on children – beatings, branding, hanging from tree tops and even mutilation – have been reported in the Prembhai's (1984) report and the newspapers. Most of the children, according to the NCAEP report, appeared to be suffering from starvation and stunted growth. The numbers suffering various diseases was reported to be abnormally high.

COST SAVING AND COMPETITIVENESS The underpayment of child workers, along with other forms of exploitation, results in considerable savings in production costs. The question is how much and how critical they are for the industry if it is to maintain its comparative cost advantage on the international market. We shall look at this in two stages. The first examines the competitiveness of the Indian carpet industry of today. The second discusses the probable impact on the industry's global competitiveness of cost increases due to the removal of child labour.

How Competitive is the Indian Carpet Industry?

The Indian carpet industry is the world's biggest producer of hand-knotted carpets in volume terms, accounting for about a quarter of the total world market (the rest being shared by Iran, Pakistan, China, Nepal and Morocco). India gained prominence here as a result of a decline in the 'mother country', Iran. In recent years, however, intense competition from China and Nepal, along with a revival in Iran, have combined to narrow the profit margins. The competition is severe in terms of both price and quality.[6] The result is an increase in the percentage share of loosers or Indo-Nepali carpets, which cater to the lower end of the market and fetch an average price of US$ 20 to US$ 30 per m², as against Persian carpets, which fetch a price of US$ 200 and more per m². As a result, while India accounted for about 26 per cent of world export volumes of hand-knotted carpets in 1992, its share in value terms was under 12 per cent. The degree of the Indian industry's competitiveness has been decreasing in recent years. The president of the All India Carpet Manufacturers' Association (AICMA), Kailash Nath Baranwal, claimed that there has been a 20–25 per cent fall in the international price of Persian carpets in the past year. A similar fall in prices of all types of carpets was reported by the honorary secretary of AICMA, Mr Hadi.

Meanwhile, costs have been steadily on the rise. The cost of wool imported from New Zealand, which accounts for about 50 per cent of the total used, has gone up sharply over the past year. The price of 32-micron wool has risen from US$ 1.8 per kg in 1993 to US$ 2.65 per kg. Domestic Bikaneri wool, a less than perfect substitute for the imported material, is not available in sufficient quantities, thus forcing many to produce carpets with low-quality Panipat wool, which fetches a much lower price.

The exporters claim that the labour costs have also increased sharply in recent years. While the manager of India's biggest export house, Obeetee Carpets, believes the devaluation of the rupee was helpful, he says it has been offset by the withdrawal of the cash compensation scheme under which exporters used to receive cash incentives amounting to Rs 200–250 million per annum and a reduction in duties from 17 per cent to 3 per cent (now revised to 4.5 per cent). The captains of industry thus claim that their ship is in serious trouble. There is severe competition from rival countries on the one hand as well as the damage caused by adverse publicity about child labour on the other. Competition has become all the keener recently, with the Iranian and Chinese governments devaluing their currencies and offering extra incentives to exporters. Indeed, Indian exporters claim that China is virtually dumping carpets on the international market by charging prices which just cover raw material costs. It is able to do this because carpets are produced in the state-owned factory sector and the government fixes artificially low prices. Nepal is able to charge low prices thanks to its extremely low wage rates and child labour. (The decline of the Iranian carpet industry in 1970s, by the way, was not entirely unrelated to the withdrawal of child and female labour.)

The Indian carpet industry therefore seems and claims to be in troubled waters, so much so that many exporters have said there is no future in carpets, and some have already started diversifying their product ranges. Their declared profit levels range between 5 and 10 per cent. Only one has said it may be higher for some exporters, i.e. 15–20 per cent. Is the Indian carpet industry really in trouble? Will the elimination of child labour be the straw to breaks the camel's back? Today the captains of industry vehemently deny that child labour is crucial to their survival. This is in sharp contrast to their earlier stance. In a 1985 memorandum to the Indian government, the president of AICMA claimed that 'the child labourers, with their soft and nimble fingers, are very important for the hand-knotted carpet industry'. Indeed, the government was warned that any interference on the pretext of regulating bonded child workers would prove fatal to the industry's development.

Any meaningful discussion on both the short- and long-term impact of the possible withdrawal of child labour from the industry must be carried out in terms of its implications for the costs of production.

STRUCTURE OF THE INDUSTRY   The Indian carpet industry works on a three-tier system. At the top of the ladder are some 2000 exporters/manufacturers who are engaged in cut-throat competition with each other. They are responsible for meeting all the export orders and organizing production which is, by and large, 'programmed'. The exporters operate through a whole range of intermediaries, such as contractors and sub-contractors, who constitute the middle tier and are mainly responsible for various production processes. The contractors normally work on the basis of a 25 per cent commission. At the bottom of the ladder are the loom-owners, master-weavers and weavers.

The production of carpets involves some thirteen stages, ranging from cleaning and dyeing the wool to knotting, clipping, washing, sizing, binding and packing. The most significant point to note is that virtually all these processes are carried out in the unorganized sector, in a decentralized manner. The premises of the so-called manufacturer/exporter merely constitute a coordinating unit where they may carry out minor processes such as final clipping, packing and so on. Weaving, which accounts for 80–90 per cent of all activities, is mostly done in the 'cottage' sector or in weaving sheds. Production of this kind is decentralized not for technical reasons but in an attempt to circumvent the labour laws. Such was the avowal of Mr Ravi Patodia of Universal Exports, who claimed that some composite units were ruined because of the enforcement of the labour laws and trade union activities. The manager of Obeetee also agreed that many would have to close shop if they were to pay benefits like the provident fund to every worker, including weavers.

So the industry, which used to produce a significant part of its output in the factory sector in 1960s, has metamorphosed into a 'cottage industry' and now carries out almost all its processes in the unregistered, informal sector, mainly to avoid labour laws and to keep down the wage component of its costs.

This decentralization of various processes entails the cost of the repeated transportation of bulky carpets from processing plants to the exporters' premises. The cost is mostly borne by the worker/craftsman who is responsible for arranging the transport. So the overriding considerations of avoiding labour laws are responsible for producing an industry structure involving considerable wastage. Information about detailed cost structures for the various varieties of carpets is not available from the AICMA office of CEPC. However, numerous discussions with the manufacturers have suggested that labour costs are the most important cost component. Most of them have said that the wage bill accounts for about 50 per cent of the total value of carpets, although it may vary for differing types of carpets.

Roughly speaking, the breakdown of costs that emerged was as follows:

Wages	50%
Raw material cost	35%
Overheads	5%
Profits	10%

These are crude and highly aggregated estimates. But they may suffice to make the point that labour costs which account for at least 50 per cent of total revenues and 55 per cent of total costs, at a 10 per cent profit margin, is the crucial determining factor in the comparative cost advantage the industry enjoys. If the profit margin figures provided by the exporters are to be believed, even a slight increase in labour costs may be enough to force many of them out of business.

CHILD LABOUR AND COST SAVINGS   The crucial question is: what cost savings in percentage terms can be made through the use of child labour? Or, in other words, what would the percentage increase in cost be if child labour were withdrawn? This obviously depends on two highly important parameters: (1) child labour as a percentage of the total work force; (2) child wages in proportion to those of adults.

No single figure can suffice for either of these parameters. There is no unique wage rate in the carpet industry either for adults or children; instead, there is a hierarchy of rates which keep decreasing the further you move away from the urban core of the industry towards the periphery and interior rural areas. Some exporters have claimed the daily wage rate to be as high as Rs 50 to Rs 60. This, it has emerged, is based on the assumption that a weaver can complete two *deharis* a day (one *dehari* is comprised of 6000 knots). In reality, most are able to complete no more than one *dehari* or even less. So the Obeetee manager's figure of Rs 35 per day for adult workers seems more reasonable. If you deduct the contractor's 25 per cent commission, along with the various other commissions (sub-contractors, loom-holders, master-weavers) the average adult daily wage can be assumed to be about Rs 20–25.

Otherwise, if we were to use the figure of 1.5 million workers in the carpet industry, and taking the 1993–94 export figures of Rs 13.9 billion as a proxy for output value, the exporters' wage bill would (as estimated, i.e. at 50 per cent) come to Rs 6.95 billion. Total earnings made by the carpet-workers – not counting the 25 per cent commission – would stand at Rs 5.2

billion. On the basis of 300 working days a year, we arrive at a wage of Rs 11.6 (about US$ 0.34) a day.

This figure of Rs 11.6 must be taken to be a weighted average of the adult and child wage rates. Sticking to our adult wage rate figure of Rs 25 (US$ 0.64) would suggest either or both of the following: (1) child labour must represent an extremely high percentage of the total work force; (2) the wage differential between adults and children must be very high to have pulled the average wage down from Rs 25 to Rs 11.6.

If, by the way, all 1.5 million carpet-workers were adults, as is claimed by the industry, and if they had a daily wage of Rs 25 (which is much lower than the exporters say), the total wage bill would work out at Rs 11.25 billion, exceeding the above-estimated sum of Rs 6.95 billion by Rs 4.3 billion! Compared to the approximately Rs 1.4 billion annual profits earned by the industry, this is enough to explain why very low wage rates are necessary for its survival.

The Rs 4.3 billion figure as an estimate of cost savings made through child labour may be contested on several grounds, for example: (1) the figure of 1.5 million carpet-workers may be an exaggeration; (2) some of the workers are only part-time/seasonal workers; (3) the actual average adult wage rate is less than Rs 25.

In fact, the exact cost savings due to use of child labour are very difficult to calculate, given the nature of the data. Even if we accepted the lower ends of the scale, however, its withdrawal would be enough considerably to reduce the industry's competitiveness, if not to make it non-viable. Based on the conservative estimates of the NCAER, the number of hired carpet children works out at 54,000 (3.6 per cent of the 1.5 million total). According to this study (Vijayagopalan 1993), average monthly underpayment per child is between Rs 404 and Rs 474. This means a total annual underpayment of children in the hired labour segment of between Rs 260 and 317 million. This would be much higher were the cost savings made by the employment of the 66,000 children (4.4 per cent) in the family segment to be taken into account.

Having said that, Juyal's (1993) estimate that there are at least 300,000 carpet children, about 228,000 of whom (76 per cent) work in the hired labour segment, leads us to believe that total annual underpayment stands at an astonishing Rs 11.63 billion.

Some may argue that the extent to which the carpet children are underpaid does not represent savings in the manufacturers' wage bill, but merely a transfer payment, for it is appropriated by intermediaries (loom-holders, weavers) and the removal of child labour would have no significant effect on the total costs. This argument is erroneous on at least two counts: (1) the elimination of child labour is bound to increase the adult wage rate; and (2) the network of intermediaries provides the manufacturers and exporters with the means to be able to keep the wage bill low by having weaving take place in the decentralized or unorganized sector. A massive cut in their share may make this structure unsustainable and eventually cause a considerable increase in costs.

To repeat, the carpet industry, like many Indian export industries, gets its cutting edge from very low labour costs. Without making any precise claims about the increase in labour costs that may result from the elimination of child labour, it is possible to say that it would be enough, by all accounts, considerably to reduce the (already low) degree of competitiveness of the carpet industry, and may indeed present a serious threat to its very survival.

Import Bans and Child Labour

In the light of the above analysis, it must be clear that if the developed countries were to impose import bans on developing-country goods made using child labour, it could in many cases result in the elimination of the industry itself, thereby worsening the overall employment scene and increasing, rather than decreasing, the need for working children. Second, since such a ban is brought to bear only on the export sector, it may merely shift child workers from this sector (which represents about 5 per cent of the Indian economy as a whole) to others where their plight may be no better, if not worse. To borrow the jargon of standard trade theory, if the distortion is domestic, then the optimal policy has to be domestic. In this case, it is Indian government policy simultaneously to remove child labour from all sectors of the economy. A ban or a boycott by external agents is no panacea for the problem of child labour in Third World countries.

An attempt by the developed nations to introduce the issue of child labour (and other labour laws) along with those of human rights and the environment on to the trade agenda, either unilaterally or through GATT/ WTO, is viewed with a huge amount of scepticism by a majority of Indians. Left-wing opinion sees these attempts (and in fact the entire GATT agreement, including its 'social dumping' clause and provisions about TRIMS and TRIPS) as yet another way of perpetuating the dominance of the developed countries, while the free-market economists see them as non-tariff trade barriers aimed at undoing the gains of the Uruguay round of GATT.[7] Thus, an attempt to bring social issues on to the trade agenda is widely seen as neo-protectionism on the part of developed countries, rather than an expression of concern for developing countries' social problems. Bringing the issue to multinational fora like GATT/WTO is not likely to help and will be opposed by developing countries as a neo-protectionist device.

The problem of child labour in India calls for massive policy intervention on the part of the Indian government. Tackling it cannot wait for a time when the trickle-down effects of growth make it possible to dispense with child labour. Growth alone does not do away with the problem of child labour, as is shown in the case of Latin American countries as well as the 'Asian Tiger'. Second, some have argued that the existing levels of poverty do not justify the elimination of child labour. This is erroneous. According to Gary Rodgers and Guy Standing (1981; 1986), as well as Myron Weiner (1991) and many others, child labour increases poverty by depressing wage rates and reducing employment opportunities for adult labour. This is particularly valid for the Indian economy, given its widespread under- and unemployment. It must be recognized right away that any employment clashing with the child's right to an education is hazardous for his or her growth and has to be eliminated. Furthermore, the outstanding constitutional obligation to provide all children with at least six years' compulsory free education within a formal framework has to be met without any further delay.

However, the two measures – i.e. a ban on child labour, and compulsory primary education – can do very little on their own to help eliminate child labour. As some studies have shown, including one conducted by UNICEF in the Sivakasi region (see Kothari 1983), the existence of an educational infrastructure is not enough to keep down the percentage of drop-outs from school.

The necessary condition for the elimination of child labour is to tackle effectively the problems of parental poverty and the inter-generational transmission of poverty. This, at the very least, requires a minimum guarantee of employment to all families and their access to assets such as land. Special attention has to be paid to the most vulnerable segments of the labour market, such as the members of Scheduled Castes, Scheduled Tribes, etc. Labour market segmentation must be reduced and the weakest segments have to be brought under the protective cover of, for example, modern labour institutions like trade unions, receive a minimum wage and be protected by job security laws. In the meantime, their meagre market entitlements have to be supplemented with non-market entitlements such as subsidized food from the public distribution system and adequate health and education facilities. Only then will it be possible to implement the policy of compulsory primary education in a meaningful way and progressively to move towards the elimination of child labour within a reasonable time-frame.

All this calls for a rethink on the present development strategies in addition to a major effort directed specifically at the elimination of child labour in India by the government and non-governmental organizations. A developed-country import ban or boycott on products made by child labour is no solution to the problem.

Notes

1. Using the official sources: the 1971 census gave the number of workers in the fourteen and under age group at 10.74 million (4.4 per cent of the total child population and 5.95 per cent of the total labour force); the 1981 census put the figure at 11.17 million (the percentages being somewhat lower, i.e. 4.23 per cent of the total child population and 5.03 per cent of the total labour force). Even though the results of the 1991 census are still pending, a National Sample Survey Study has estimated the number of child labourers

for 1985 at 17.58 million. This shows an astounding increase of 6.41 million in four years, sharply contrasting with the increase of less than one million in the 1970s. On the basis of this information, as well as inferences drawn from the recent events in the economy, it can be said that the incidence of child labour has grown rapidly since the 1980s and the official figure of 20 million is an underestimation.

2. The average annual rate of growth of GDP, more than 5 per cent in the 1980s, rose by 1.5 per cent, 4.2 per cent and 3.8 per cent in 1991–92, 1992–93 and 1993–94 respectively. More importantly, manufacturing sector performance has been worse, the average annual rate of growth in three years of reform being just over 1 per cent. As per Planning Commission estimates, recent total employment generation was of the order of 3 million in 1991–92, 6.2 million in 1992–93 and 5.6 million in 1993–94. This suggests that the target of creating 43 million jobs during the eighth five-year plan is not likely to be met without a sharp improvement on the 4 million registered in 1987–88. The medium-term outlook appears to be as follows: even if growth were to revive in the immediate future, employment in the organized sector of the economy (a mere 8 per cent of total employment) is likely to stagnate, it is unlikely to pick up in agriculture and the dynamism in the rural non-agriculture sector observed in the 1980s is likely to be missing in the 1990s. All this may mean accelerated rural to urban migration. As a result, conditions in the urban informal sector may worsen and the incidence of poverty may well rise.

3. Exports rose by 20 per cent in 1993–94 (the target having been 25 per cent) but have already shown signs of deceleration. Exports must go up in order to pay an import bill which is likely to be considerably heavier as a result of proposed (further) tariff reductions and other restrictions. A pick-up in the economy will also increase an import bill which reached Rs 104,120 million in 1993–94 as against Rs 89,480 million in 1992–93. To add to that, although the short-run debt situation has been managed by the reform, the total external debt has undergone a considerable rise in absolute terms as a percentage of GDP and also as a percentage of exports. Moreover, many, including the policy-makers, believe India must increase its share in world trade from its present 0.5 per cent to 1.5 per cent if it is to emerge as a great Asian Tiger. All this calls for a rapid growth of exports in value terms. The effort with regard to volume has to be even higher, due to the probability of deterioration in India's terms of trade. The competition between China and India, for instance, is most likely to accentuate the process of falling international prices of their exports. Thus, the so-called New International Division of Labour, coupled with the provisions of GATT, like TRIMS, which allow for the free movement of capital without the free movement of labour, are likely to strengthen the process of unequal exchange between the North and South. Instead of factor price equalization taking place, the wages in developing countries will continue to be only a fraction of wages in the developed countries, even though their skills and productivity in some lines may be no less. The low wages in Third World countries in turn keep the international prices of their exportables low, forcing them to export ever larger volumes of goods.

4. At that time, the Supreme Court ordered the release of 800 children as well as an inquiry by the Prembhai of Seva Ashram.

5. A newspaper report dated 19 September 1994 related the story of an underage carpet-worker from the Darbhanga district of Bihar who was hacked to pieces when he tried to break free.

6. While India has never been able to equal the finest quality of Persian carpets, China and Nepal are now providing stiff competition too.

7. Similar sentiments are also echoed in official circles. At a recent ESCAP (Economic and Social Commission on Asia and the Pacific) meeting, the prime minister observed that

a move to introduce social issues onto the trade agenda was intended to nullify the comparative advantage of developing countries. At the same forum, the commerce minister said: 'We are not at all convinced that the motive force compelling such moves is humanitarianism, or that a trade body is competent to consider issues of social policy.' The finance minister also voiced his objection to such a move recently at the fiftieth meeting of the IMF.

References

Bequele, A. and J. Boyden (eds) (1988) *Combating Child Labour*, Geneva, ILO.

Burra, N. (1986) 'Glass Factories in Firozabad', *Economic and Political Weekly*, 15 and 22 November.

— (1988) 'Exploitation of Children in Gem Polishing Industry in Jaipur', *Economic and Political Weekly*, 6, 13 June.

Chaterjee, S. and R. Mohan (1993) 'India's Garment Exports', *Economic and Political Weekly*, 28 August.

Elson, D. (1982) 'Differentiation of Child Labour in Capitalist Labour Market', *Development and Change*, October.

Ilo Artep (1993) *India: Employment Poverty and Economic Policy*, New Delhi.

Juyal, B. (1993) *Child Labour in the Carpet Industry in Mirzapur–Bhadohi*, New Delhi, ILO.

Kanbargi, R. (ed.) (1991) *Child Labour in the Indian Subcontinent: Dimensions and Implications*, New Delhi, Sage.

Kannan, K. (1994) 'Levelling Up and Levelling Down – Labour Institution and Economic Development in India', *Economic and Political Weekly*, 23 July.

Kothari, S. (1983) 'There is Blood on those Match Sticks: Child Labour in Sivakasi', *Economic and Political Weekly*, 17 October.

Kundu, A. (1993) 'Trouble Lies Ahead: Update/Child Labour', *Economic Times*, 13 September.

Lee, E. (1984) *Export Processinq Zones and Industrial Employment in Asia*, Bangkok, ILO-ARTEP.

Nayyar, D. (1993) *Economic Report on India: A Critical Assessment*, New Delhi, ILO-ARTEP.

Prembhai (1984) 'The Working Condition of the Child Weavers in the Carpet Units of Mirzapur', Interim Report.

Rodgers, G. and G. Standing (eds) (1981) *Child Work, Poverty and Underdevelopment*, Geneva, ILO.

— (1986) *Economic Role of Children in Low-Income Countries*, Geneva, ILO.

Tendulkar, S., K. Sundaram and L. Jain (1993) *Labour Policy in India: 1970–71 to 1988–89*, New Delhi, ILO-ARTEP.

Tylor, L. (1988) *Varieties of Stabilisation Experiences: Towards Sensible Economics in the Third World*, Oxford, Claredon Press.

Singh, M. (1990) *The Political Economy of Unorganised Industry: A Study of Labour Processes*, New Delhi, Sage.

Vijayagopalan, S. (1993) *Child Labour in the Carpet Industry: A Status Report*, New Delhi, NCAER.

Weiner, M. (1991) *Children and the State in India*, New Delhi, Oxford University Press.

CHAPTER 5

Growing Up in Ghana: Deregulation and the Employment of Children

Martin Verlet

Nima, a run-down district of the city of Accra, was where we chose to conduct fieldwork for our analysis of the correlation between the crisis currently afflicting families and households in Ghana and the increasingly intensive use of child labour in the country's urban centres.[1] The crisis in question has grown over nearly a decade of structural adjustment policies inspired and managed by the international financial institutions, in particular the IMF and World Bank. Deregulation of the labour market, of social legislation and institutional control over the economy ties in with social deregulation, a process having such an effect on social reproduction patterns that the customary capacities of the family and household to protect and socialize are being eroded.

'Household' here is understood to mean a relatively stable community of permanent residents and consumers. More often than not, family groups primarily structured on bonds of kinship and marriage have been falling apart in urban environments largely owing to labour migration, redundancies, changing patterns of social behaviour and changing internal roles. It follows that while households and family units may occasionally coincide, they are rarely ever one and the same. Most households are shifting assemblies cobbled together from divided and conflicting bonds of kinship, marriage, neighbourhood, membership and friendship (Dwyer 1988).

By 'domestic deregulation' we are referring to the break-up of family units combined with the increasing fragility and destabilization of households which has been gathering pace and becoming more serious under the impact of the policies of liberalization through structural adjustment. A connection exists between the deregulation of the labour market and what we call domestic deregulation. Clearer still is the correlation between both these processes and the general spread of child labour. Until recently, critical diagnosis of adjustment policies was mainly based on global, macro-economic or sector-based analyses. Yet those policies are deeply rooted within the very social fabric they claim to be reshaping (Nash 1983). To examine the crisis to which the household is subjected as a result, we have chosen to focus on the troubled interface between the macro-economic and micro-social, between world level and local level (Verlet 1992). If the changes generated in the social and economic role of women in domestic life by the outside world's mandatory free-market strategies have been receiving a lot of attention of late, the attention given to the revived forms of child employment and exploitation stimulated by household deregulation seems to have been rather more discreet and less systematic.

From this point of view, a case study of Ghana is particularly illustrative. Ghana first became embroiled in adjustment policies in April 1983 (Rothchild 1991) and they have since been pursued with greater verve and perseverance here than anywhere else (World Bank 1994). International institutions are quick to present it as the outstanding example of an African nation miraculously cured by adjustment. It stands as the IMF and World Bank showcase model for the rest of the continent to emulate (Campbell and Loxley 1989). Since 1986, the World Bank has found itself having to provide remedies that are ultimately more symbolic than effective for the social groups directly suffering the most negative and disastrous social effects of the macro-economic adjustment strategies (Pamscad 1990).

Nima is an equally useful case study for our focal subject of domestic deregulation and the proletarianization of children in working-class areas of Ghanaian cities. Nima is a shanty town, a hinterland suburb historically reputed to be a melting pot for the Ghanaian labouring classes. During the colonial and post-colonial periods, it attracted migrants coming from the north in search of work. Within the space of a few years, its masses of largely untrained and unskilled country people had been transformed into a stable, disciplined and hard-working force of urbanite labour. This swift conversion caused the Accra working classes to swell. Nima men were largely recruited as manual labourers, security guards and domestic servants or joined the lower ranks of the police force and army. Two to three generations of migrants were proletarianized in this way (Sandbrook 1977). Yet they were to be the first casualties of the state's public sector restructuring and privatization programmes. Formerly established men suddenly found themselves out of work, feeling irretrievably worthless and incapable of retraining. Redundancy not only stripped them of their social status and income, but left them petrified, marginalized, no longer the family protector, chief and guide. Women then took over as breadwinners and saw their domestic role grow broader and more complex (Pellow 1977). Nearly 40 per cent of Nima households are now headed by a woman. But their activities alone have ceased to suffice. Hence the introduction and growth of child labour as a necessary means of supplementing, if not the sole source of, household incomes (Unicef 1990).

Our definition of a 'child' is primarily sociological and generational. We are looking at a whole generation of children tossed around on the waves of liberalization, having grown up under adjustment with no vision of the future other than that mapped out and muddied by international macro-economic constraints (Verlet 1993). This generation of 'child labourers' is quite unlike any of its predecessors. The conditions, the degree of exploitation, the functions and fruits of underage labour differ greatly. It is the generation of the 'adjusted child', whose work has lost its value in terms of domestic use and become a unit of exchange, a negotiable labour-market good instantly convertible into cash. The children in question are aged from six to sixteen years (Government of Ghana 1992).

Before going any further, let us draw a distinction between 'child labour' and 'domestic work'. The latter refers to the everyday tasks children have always done for the general maintenance of the family unit and as part of the normal run of socialization. The former differs in that it oversteps the bounds of socially acceptable norms and uses (Hammond 1993). Furthermore, its end purpose is monetary gain. Between these two opposite and opposing poles, children are open to a wide range of varying degrees and conditions of domestic work or exploitation which all lead to widespread premature proletarianization. It is not a matter of gradation but degradation; domestic work progressively slips into tougher forms of exploitation that tend to remove children from their family milieu, from the lands and life-paths of childhood, and cast them on to the labour market. Domestic ideology serves to mask and legitimize such changes (Avorti 1990; de Souza 1990). In the vast majority of cases, the child's access to the labour market will be brokered by a family friend, parent or relative (mother, maternal aunt, elder brother). Channels of recruitment and exploitation techniques all capitalize on bonds of kinship and friendship, even if the former are often fictitious and the latter dubious.

Nima: From Melting Pot to Scrap-heap

Nima, once a melting pot where thousands of northern migrants were shaped into a working class, a proletariat, has become a dumping ground for a brutally depreciated labour force. It has happened in little over a decade (1983–94) alongside the successive structural adjustment plans applied in Ghana. Nima's history has above all been that of stratum after stratum of northern migrants, strangers to the town yet attracted to it by the prospect of waged work (Frimbong-Yeboah 1975, Chambas 1977).

With World War II, the setting up of army bases and a growing labour market, the town's population grew considerably in size. That was when it began gaining a reputation as the gateway from labour migration to wage-earner status, the training ground then residence for an urban labouring class. During Ghana's twenty-year transition from colonialism to independence, the population of Nima more than doubled (Annorbah-Sarpei 1969) as the state structures expanded and a vast industrial and commercial public sector developed, capable of absorbing a large number of the newcomers to the town via the area's network of recruitment channels. In addition to openings in neighbouring residential districts for domestic servants, people could otherwise try their hand in (sometimes self-employed) services or trading activities. The town's labour force at the time was chiefly composed of young, single men.

Nima was then officially incorporated into Accra, but the move was not followed by any immediate redevelopment and amenities work (Wellington 1968). Conditions had begun becoming difficult with the deepening economic slump of the 1970s. Overpopulated and congested, the town's growth gradually slowed down. A number of urban planning projects were drawn up (Darmstadt University 1972); at one point the authorities were even toying with the idea of simply tearing down the whole of what they saw to be an unhealthy and dangerous shanty town and moving the population to Madina, north-east of Accra (MWH 1973). The project was eventually scrapped due to staunch opposition, not to mention its sheer cost. Soon after that, the Nima Highway was laid, cutting through the agglomeration from north to south, opening it up to the outside world and abruptly ending its insularity. It stimulated a flurry of trading activity: wealthier members of the community opened shops along the roadside and, with the markets of Accra within easier reach, the women went into retailing (80 per cent of them today work in the informal sector).

The deteriorating economic climate complicated access to waged work. Yet the people of Nima managed to adapt: black market, smuggling, buying political influence (for the better-off), accumulating jobs, secondary activity (for some wage-earners) or becoming self-employed and acquiring professional qualifications. Many chose to migrate, attracted by the powerful illusion of the Nigerian economic 'boom' which began in 1975. The most constantly adopted means of coping, however, was a more systematic and intensive use of female labour in a wider range of activities. Some of the effects of the economic chaos, which was to continue deepening until 1984–85, taking a heavy toll on daily life, were dampened or delayed.

The structural adjustment strategies launched in 1983 undermined precisely what had until then been the social and economic lifeblood of Nima: stable, low-skilled, waged employment for adult men. One constantly recurring and much-feared term summed up this change of perspective: 'redeployment'. To the worker it meant losing his post, having to learn a new trade and being cast from the position of wage-earner into the condition of a redundant person, hunting for work in a clogged-up labour market.[2]

The private sector did not compensate for the slow erosion of public sector employment – too slow according to the international financial institutions. In many cases, the subsequent second phase of Ghanaian adjustment – i.e. the accelerated privatization of publicly owned companies (Kambur 1994) – amounted to pure liquidation and cuts in the numbers of state sector employees.

A team of University of Ghana geographers, sketching a profile of population changes in Accra, classified Nima-Mamobi as a 'low income – old migrant residential area' (University of Ghana 1990). So Nima has found itself justifiably branded as a centre for labour migration and poverty. True enough, the vast majority of inhabitants are poor, but it does have a narrow band of residents (just under 10 per cent of the population) who are relatively well-off after having prospered from commerce, crafts, monetary speculation and real estate. What appears to have shaped Nima most profoundly and given it its patent originality is the (unevenly accomplished) passage from village to town, from 'zongo' to shanty town, from migrant to wage-earner.

Nima is unlikely ever again to be the accommodating place it once was for migrants. Its image as a prototype proletarian suburb is fading and the wage-earner is no longer the sole model of worker. Now superimposed on that is the spectacle of informal sector workers, female traders, child rag-and-bone merchants.

Meanwhile, Nima's history of in-migration, wage-earning classes and poverty provides an excellent backdrop for assessing the impact of 'redeployment' and its traumatic effects on the lives of households. Redeployment may not be the only critical factor to have sparked off domestic destabilization (even though a third of families and households have directly suffered its consequences over the past ten years), but it is both the symbol and the symptom of the decline which has seen Nima the proletarian melting pot become Nima the scrap-heap, where public policies simply dump whole generations of wage-earners.

The Household Crisis

Analysis here focuses on the crisis currently besetting the households of Nima after Ghana's decade of structural adjustment. It does not mean to say that all the factors contributing to this crisis stem directly from the adjustment policies themselves; simply that the liberalization process has permeated social relations and now seriously affects the ways in which households attempt to cope with the multiple hardships they are having to endure.

This present critical sequence seems marked by a double paradox. First of all it began just as domestic groups were starting to resemble family units more closely. The migrant had settled in Nima. The unmarried worker had founded a family: he had his wife or wives living with him; his children were born there. And the town's population was gradually settling into a certain normality. Yet becoming the head of a family meant greater responsibilities and, hence, a greater burden to bear, posing a threat to the relative stability of the family unit. Second, the town was just beginning to see the installation of previously lacking public utilities such as water and electricity. The shanty town was edging its way towards urbanization (Aboagye-Atta 1990). Yet the germs of modernization had a downside in these impoverished districts.

Responding to everyday needs and making life easier entails heavier costs. This double paradox reveals the link between the household crisis and financial constraints.

One of the fundamental factors here is the working man's loss of position as the family breadwinner, the protector, the cornerstone of the household. The case of the worker hit by 'redeployment' may appear extreme, even though it is an experience widely shared in Nima. Yet it is just one excessive manifestation of the erosion undermining the organization of most households. The term 'redeployee' has extended from referring to the public sector worker made redundant to embrace private sector employees hit by company restructuring. The term 'redeployment' suggests vocational retraining, a mapped-out passage from one type of activity to another, from the public to the private sector, from wage-earning class to the informal economy.

'Redeployment' has obviously had a less disastrous impact on people losing only one of two jobs or reaching retirement age. And the impact may also have been cushioned for those receiving generous severance pay linked to rank and long service.[3] Mostly, though, restructuring has left the lower strata of the labouring classes in an impasse. Many exits remain sealed. They cannot face the shame of returning to their place of birth without outward (ostentatious) proof of success. Exile is out of the question because of their age and lack of qualifications. And waiting around for a hypothetical paid job to turn up in the private sector is simply draining. Some manage to find a way out: those who have acquired occupational skills (builders, plumbers, electricians, drivers, mechanics); or those who have established a strong support and solidarity network through their work or social circles. Yet these are the exceptions.

The most common path leads into decline. A redundant wage-earner is left without resources. He sees himself as an outcast and becomes withdrawn, isolated. When the protector becomes the protected and dependent upon his household, he will go absent. Waiting, aimlessness and idleness make him lose his bearings formerly instilled in him as a worker. Sometimes he will take the initiative of splitting the family unit and seeking a relative to take care of one or more of the children; he may send the younger ones back to the home village with his wife (or one of his wives). In other cases the man leaves the family and goes to live alone or with a friend, only returning for the odd brief visit, getting by on the occasional job or handout, existing on meagre resources while awaiting an opening on the waged labour market.

Women are often the ones who choose to leave, taking the rest of the family with them. Some decide to return home to their parents. Others take in a sister, relative, friend or even, if the marriage has ended, a protector, and eventual sexual partner, enabling the household to increase its working capacity and bring in more income. In some cases, unemployed men are marginalized in their own homes, becoming outcasts or, more rarely, being thrown out. Prospects are less grim for households whose women have previously managed to build up a prospering business. They are then in a position to loan the man a sum of money to start up a business of his own. An already well-established relative may take him on as a casual assistant, use his services or help him open a small business. This narrows the otherwise materially and psychologically impossible gap he has to cross between regulated, stable, waged work and insecure, fluctuating work in the informal sector. In any event, the redeployee most commonly experiences a depreciation of his position within a household over which he once had total or shared responsibility, as well as the loss of his role as guarantor and protector. Then, in subsequent efforts to cobble the household back together again, the woman will play the prime role in mustering working capacities and resources.

This erosion of the man's social and economic role – rendered extreme by the experience of redeployment – is most widespread among the poorest families, even those not suffering the direct impact of lost earnings or whose family head is engaged in unwaged work. The income generated by the men is rarely enough to satisfy the daily needs of the family and home,[4] so women's work is first necessary and then vital as a growing share of daily consumption progressively comes to depend upon it. Women's work thus takes a central position in the organization of relations within the remodelled household group, but, as it becomes more widespread, it encounters some of the same constraints as male labour. Most households feel that their condition is deteriorating and financial pressures are growing increasingly burdensome. A series of particularly heavy expenses are perceived as playing a decisive role in that deterioration.

First of all there are the expenses linked to the home. Only 10 per cent of families are actually home-owners. The majority (70 per cent) are tenants. This proportion is growing as a share of the 20 per cent who claim to have been living rent-free ten years ago become tenants. Demand for housing is on the increase but little land remains for building new homes and public works projects such as the Nima Highway or Kanda Road have reduced the amount of inhabitable space available. To add to that, soaring rents in other parts of Accra are driving ever larger numbers of young, single people into Nima in search of cheaper accommodation.

Then there is the pressure exerted by the tax department. Taxation has become tougher over the last decade and now targets even the smallest-scale informal trading activity. Income tax is deducted straight from wages. And for unwaged labour, the tax department sets a lump sum amount according to the activity, payable at relatively short, regular intervals. Furthermore, the Accra Municipal Assembly (AMA) collects local taxes daily from the market-places, streets and in city districts. As soon as tax collectors spot an informal activity, it is tolerated as long as it is registered, which will mean levies and various forms of extortion.

Another burden is education. There are several contributing factors here. First of all, Accra parents are keener these days to send their children to school. Far from waning, its attraction is ever stronger. But school education does not come cheap and the education system reforms initiated in 1986 have served only to push the costs even higher. Many regard the school fees parents have to pay every quarter as the chief obstacle preventing children from being sent to and kept at school. School fees vary greatly depending on the school and grades. On average, they range from between 10,000 and 30,000 Cedi per quarter. Added to that, however, are the related expenses: purchasing a school uniform (around C 10,000), exercise books, textbooks, stationery as well as the child's daily travel expenses (C 100–C 150) and food (C 100–C 200). This means an accumulation of costs – some periodic, others daily – multiplied by the number of children (most Nima women have an average of six children to raise). Professional apprenticeship gives rise to even greater difficulties. Parents or tutors face an entrance fee of C 30,000 to C 120,000, plus a range of customary gifts. The same sum will be demanded as an 'exit fee' at the end of the course. The child also needs to buy his or her basic tools or instruments. An apprentice in the garments trade, for instance, has to own a sewing machine. A new one can cost anything from C 60,000 to C 130,000, and that is for a manually-operated machine. Second-hand, they sell for 10–30 per cent less. Apart from that, there are the same sundry outlays on daily necessities, travel and food as with school pupils.

Travel costs also add to the strain on the household budget. When Nima was still isolated from the rest of Accra, working men used to walk to work and back. Most still do. However, the women with business interests outside Nima have no choice but to take the minibus (or '*trotro*'), which usually means spending between C 200 and C 400 a day.

Less predictable are the healthcare costs. Disease, especially malaria, is common in environments as insalubrious as that of Nima (Larbi 1989). Medicine for a normal bout comes to around C 1000. A more serious attack will require a hospital visit (C 1500 a time) plus more costly treatment (C 4000 to C 5000). Alternatively there is the option of a herbalist (around C 800). Special attention will be paid to children's health. Routine visits, compulsory tests, infant vaccinations will entail monthly outlays to the tune of C 500. A serious illness calling for hospitalization or even surgery amounts to a real domestic disaster, forcing the household to raise a large sum of outside money.

New needs emerge when people settle in an urban environment. The men take up smoking and gambling. These needs, exacerbated by the wave of liberalization and the temptation of imported consumer goods – more popular, say seniors, among the younger generations – generate much spending, especially on leisure-time activities. This goes hand in hand with the phenomenon of individualization with regard to income, expenditure and consumption. The woman earning her own income is expected to take care of most everyday expenses such as food and clothing. And the man, while paying occasional bills (rent, school fees), has come to play a supporting role in the household's daily expenses for which the woman is now responsible. The latter's absence during the day means costly individualized food consumption whereby each individual buys his or her own portion, while evening meals are by and large prepared for the whole group.

Coping with this financial adversity pushes people to opt for a combination of various solutions. Working men attempt to diversify their income sources, either through a second job (doing piecework in their spare time, chiefly at weekends) or by seeking to make extra earnings from their main job (bonuses, fiddles). Some may be forced into debt, although borrowing is becoming harder and more expensive in Nima. Alternatively, more and more of them are sending their women out to work. They encourage them to do so largely by procuring the capital to help them start up and run a small business. Female labour is no longer confined to run-of-the-mill vending at market or on the streets; it is becoming diversified, specialized, professionalized.

Female labour, though, is subject to a number of limitations: taxes, harassment of vendors on roadsides or along railway tracks, rental costs for an authorized fixed sales point, stall, shelter or shop. Other constraints tie in with their child-bearing role and routine domestic responsibilities. Faced with the greater competition and shrinking markets of Nima, women are driven to sales points ever further afield, thus incurring heavier travel expenses and longer hours outside the home. Meanwhile they have to contend with an even more fundamental problem: shortage of capital which steadily dwindles due to the daily costs of consumption. In organizing their time and work, working women soon come to depend on their daughters either to take care of a large share of domestic chores or to help them with their businesses.

Gradually, domestic poverty-line economics become the norm. Food consumption is first to be rationed: there is less to eat, of a lower quality. Social interaction then suffers as the sharing of food and drink is restricted to ever tighter circles, as if it were some sort of clandestine activity. Next come cuts in spending on the home and adult healthcare. Financial hardship eventually leads to one or more children being removed from school, which may in turn incite parents to place their children in the keeping of a relative in Accra or the home village, or else, more rarely, to work as an assistant to a friend or acquaintance.

One crucial aspect of such poverty-line economics is that the struggling household will mobilize all able-bodied members in order to generate extra income. The most common symptom of this in Nima today is child labour.

Domestic Deregulation and Putting Children to Work

There are two hybrid, intermediary situations between children's domestic work on the one hand and child labour on the other. The first is that of schoolchildren, especially young girls, involved in part-time retail sales. It is often an extension of their mother's, maternal aunt's or elder sister's work as hawkers or vendors in the marketplace or streets, in order to raise more money for the housekeeping or to contribute towards school fees. Rather than pushing children away from the home environment, it gives them an active role helping the household contend with its financial difficulties. Their work is sporadic and encourages them to take partial charge of building themselves a future. It is nothing like putting a child prematurely to work as a domestic servant in another person's house.

The second situation is where elderly relatives (for the most part grand-parents) ask for a child to be sent to stay with them, often in rural areas, to assist them around the house or in the fields. Although it may help to consolidate family ties and relations by marriage while establishing the child's place in the family network, it also plays a role in the splitting of the family unit. Once again, though, there is no question here of their being *put to work* in the strictest sense of the term.

Having said that, the best-known forms of child labour are a manifestation of the household crisis. Some children may of course decide to look for work of their own accord: to escape a restrictive school education system or conflict in the home; or else, in more exceptional cases, with a very precise, personal career plan in mind. They may take the decision without their parents' prior knowledge, against their will; and it involves a variable degree of distancing, or breaking away, from the family unit. Such cases are extremely rare, though. Most children admit to having been driven to become child workers because they absolutely had to earn enough to provide for both their own needs and, more generally, to diversify the household's sources of income.

More often than not, the parents encourage and broker the admission into the world of work. A father or his brother might arrange and pay for an apprenticeship, standing surety with an employer. Or else he may place his child with a relative, friend or acquaintance to work as a servant or assistant until times change for the better. But the women are the ones who play the key role in putting young children to work. This generally applies first to the girls, as they are easier to remove from school than boys. Young girls are frequently left in charge of the day-to-day running of the household while their mothers are out at work. They are more systematically and consistently drawn into a money-making activity where they increase the labour power of their mothers or female relatives, usually in petty retailing or street vending. As a rule, girls are kept close to the household, within its protection. Boys, on the other hand, are more likely to find themselves in a work environment separated from the home. The woman's action and influ-ence are once again decisive factors in their admission to employment. As soon as a boy leaves school, she will watch over him, often putting up the capital he needs to start a lucrative business of his own. Children's earnings help to boost the housekeeping; the money is regularly handed over to the woman who then decides how it will be used and distributed once she has deducted the child's daily expenses (transport, food) and the amount needing to be put back into the business.

The household's role in the mechanics of premature employment is not to be ignored. First of all it shows how a share of economic exploitation is rooted in, if not initiated by, the household. And the fact that a child enters employment via family channels ultimately ends up lending a domestic feel to working relations, giving them a veneer of kinship. An employer can then adopt a pseudo-parental role on the grounds that his authority comes from the parents, from the child's own home environment. The domestication of working relations and the ways in which it is used serve as a mask for exploitation.

Analysis of 'working environments' reveals the complicated, varied and shifting relationship between working environment and home environment and between family relations and exploitation-based relations. From this point of view, a number of major sets of working environment can be differentiated.

The first corresponds to that which has strong connections with the household. These chiefly include:

- the residence, when an adult member of the household uses it as a work base for sales, repairs, processing or services and the child helps with the work itself or, more commonly, concentrates on selling the goods outside
- the point of sales in the retailing trade
- the route in street vending

In this set, the children (mostly small girls) work together with other members of the household, which continues to provide them with their moorings and their main bearings.

A second set suggests clearer divisions between the household and working life. It chiefly includes:

- shops, hairdressing salons
- workshops (clothing, repairs, garages)
- chop bars
- apprenticeships

In the majority of these cases, a family member plays a fundamental role in a child's recruitment or apprenticeship. These environments in particular are where working and exploitation-based relationships are contrived to appear domestic.

Another set also making use of domestication and featuring a clean break from the household is represented by what we call 'factories' and 'building sites'. Large numbers of children can be found working in such places: forty at a furniture factory, sixty at an industrial bakery. In both cases, the employer will have hired them in his home town or neighbouring villages, with their parents' consent. They live full-time on the premises and can therefore be made to work nights if need be. They may spend five to seven years at the factory before the employer decides to send them back home. Although temporary, for the time they are there they are totally cut off from the home environment.

Yet another set is comprised of the working environments created away from and independently of the household, where the networks of connections leading to recruitment are based not on kinship but on acquaintanceship, social relations, affinities, peer groups. The relationship between older and younger children plays an important role here, provided it falls within that narrow age group where childhood is blending into adolescence. Each environment has its own hierarchy, its own rules, code of conduct, forms of protection and social interaction. They are largely male-dominated and chiefly include:

- the queue: attracting hordes of child street vendors on the busiest thoroughfares
- the team: a specialized working environment with strong affinities and children monopolizing recruitment
- the gang: the *kaya kaya* (porters), for instance, living full time in certain marketplaces
- vagrancy: totally autonomous children of no fixed abode, with no ties
- exile: especially the girls who migrate to the Ivory Coast and Nigeria, often totally losing touch with their families

Far from always resolving the household crisis, the vast range of child labour seen in the above-listed working environments can, in some extreme cases, even serve to deepen it. Far from offsetting domestic deregulation, child labour can actually fuel it.

'Ruthlessly Serviceable': A Generalized System of Supply and Demand

Whenever the issue of child labour crops up in Ghana, it is instantly plastered with images of street children. Yet the street child is merely the visible side of a more far-reaching phenomenon. There are other, more common, more excessive forms of exploitation. Those linked to apprenticeships are well known. Those at the core of the household crisis are more difficult to recognize. Some working environments (the factory, building site, gang) are purely and simply ignored. At this stage of our analysis, however, perhaps we should look beyond the notion of the 'domestication' of exploitative relations as it contaminates only one segment of the spectrum of working environments. Let us also describe two complementary yet possibly more crucial aspects of the working relationship and its conversion into exploitation: the dialectics of good-will and willingness; 'serviceability', the state of being 'ruthlessly serviceable'.

The exploitative relationship builds within a constant tension between two poles: good-will and willingness. The dialectics between the two are, of course, rooted in and cultivated by the domestication of the working relationship. They demonstrate the asymmetry between the position of the master and the condition of the working child. The master's good-will gives him the power to do what he will. His desires, his needs and moods govern the wages, set the working hours, assign the tasks and influence the quality of the relationship. Willingness means the availability, the obedience expected of a child. Vulnerable children seeking protection and support see themselves bound over to remain meek, ever-present, ever-willing. Their labour power is malleable, flexible. This polarization of good-will and willingness is both line of force and field of live current. Although rarely breaking into open confrontation, the children have several forms of resistance, evasion and retaliation simmering below the surface.

An inventory of the types of work being done by children reveals it to be highly concentrated in the services sector. And even when it is a matter of production work, the form of working relationship will disguise them as services. As such, we therefore see a sort of slide from the legal to the prohibited, from the licit to the illicit, more commonly from one job to another. One job can cover another, can lead to another. There is nothing to prevent the employer from shifting the boundaries of the required work as he sees fit. But this extension to the demands stemming from the good-will of the master or client may be echoed in a greater willingness to serve; a good-will and a willingness whose limits are established neither by contract nor by job description. For instance, an apprentice may sometimes be required to satisfy other demands, perform other tasks or services than originally agreed (household chores or prostitution for girls; building-site labouring for boys). Child labour puts children in the position of general service suppliers. With the small groups of *kaya kayas* living in the marketplaces, for example, supply and demand of general services can range from carrying parcels to sexual intercourse. Sometimes the same sort of crossover can be observed in certain hairdressing salons, sewing shops or, more commonly, in the chop bars.

Child workers 'enter service' – formerly a term applying to domestic servants – and become dependent and available. It may be tempting to describe it as 'servile labour'. But 'servile' has the drawback of being too directly linked to the state of slavery and serfdom. So we have chosen to use 'serviceability' as a means of describing a personal, transitory condition of dependence and submissiveness which in many cases forces children into a generalized system of service supply and demand.

It can therefore be said that the children prematurely sucked into working and exploitative relations are fated to become 'ruthlessly serviceable'. Such is their lot.

Conclusion

Two brief comments to conclude this analysis. The first concerns making children subservient or autonomous; the second, how they see the future.

Children sent to work for the sake of their much-needed earnings are placed in the position of household protectors, breadwinners. They are primarily cast in the role – lessening the effects of the domestic poverty-line economy – by the women, their mothers in particular. Now that they are partially responsible for the reproduction and survival of the household, their bonds with their mothers are deeper. At the same time, the children made to work in an environment away from home are likely to take their distance and gain a more often than not illusory autonomy.

Entrepreneurs without an enterprise, proletarians without wages and, 'ruthlessly serviceable', all Nima boys harbour the same dream for the future: exile.

Notes

1. The fieldwork was undertaken in collaboration with Bugri Nachinaba, senior research assistant at the Institute of African Studies, University of Ghana, Legon.

2. One analysis of employment fluctuations in Ghana which includes companies employing ten or more wage-earners gives an idea of the scale of the collapse of the wage-earning classes affecting Nima today (source: Ghana Statistical Service). In 1960, a total of 332,900 wage-earners were found to be working across the board in all sectors of activity. The figures peaked in 1979 at 482,100. They then began to slide in 1986, dropping to 166,300 by 1991. During the decade of adjustment, the industrial sector crumbled with the exception of ore extraction. Waged employment in the services sector was no stop-gap. Public sector employment figures stood at 184,300 in 1960. They peaked at 359,300 in 1978 and began to slide in 1986, falling to 155,700 by 1991. The decline began earlier in the private sector: in 1960, employee figures stood at 148,500, then fell and languished before climbing back to 143,900 by 1977. By 1991, they had plummeted to 30,600.

3. 'Redeployees' receive severance pay whose amount depends on length of service at the establishment, qualifications, grade, the establishment's status and specific collective redundancy plans. They also receive a lump sum payment to cover travelling expenses for themselves and their families. This settlement – large or small, depending on the case – may well be paid some time, often several months, after dismissal and in instalments, thus considerably reducing its incentive power. It is supposed to provide for a range of options: unemployed people can either move back to their home villages, invest it as start-up capital in a retailing or services business, or even use it to pay for technical training to improve their bargaining power on a troubled labour market.

4. In November 1994, the statutory minimum daily wage in the public sector stood at 790 Cedi, the national currency of Ghana. It was then raised to 1200 Cedi in January 1995 (at which time US$ 1 = C 1080 on the foreign exchange market).

References

Aboagye-Atta, K. (1990) 'East Maamobi Slum Upgrading Scheme. An Evaluative Study', BA Dissertation, Department of Geography, University of Ghana, Legon.

Acolatse, J. S. (1974) 'Urban Renewal in Accra. The Example of Nima', BA Dissertation, Department of Geography, University of Ghana, Legon.

Afum-Ansah, G. (1993) 'A Case Study of Street Children at Nima. A Slum Suburb of Accra', BA Dissertation, Department of Sociology, University of Ghana, Legon.

Agye-Mensah, S. (1986) 'Slums and Health Problems in Urban Centers. A Case Study of Nima-Mamobi Area in Accra', BA Dissertation, Department of Geography, University of Ghana, Legon.

Annorbah-Sarpei, J. (1969) *Letters from Nima*, Accra, Asempa.

— (1974) *Operation Help Nima. Five Years of Christian Involvement in Urban Renewal*, Accra, Asempa.

Apt Van Ham, N. (ed.) (1992) 'Street Children in Accra. A Survey Report', Department of Sociology, University of Ghana, Legon.

Avorti, J. Y. (1990) 'Children at Work. A Study in Sociology', BA Dissertation, Department of Sociology, University of Ghana, Legon.

Campell, B. K. and J. Loxley (eds) (1989) *Structural Adjustment in Africa*, London, Macmillan.

Chambas, M. (1977) 'The Political Economy of Urbanization. A Study of Leaders and Development in Nima, a Slum in Accra', MA Thesis, Department of Political Science, University of Ghana, Legon.

Darmstadt University (1972) *Nima*, Institut Tropisches Bauen, Fakultät für Architektur, Darmstadt.

de Souza, G., 1990 – '"Child Labour" , "Child Work", a Sociological Reconsideration', BA Dissertation, Department of Sociology, University of Ghana, Legon.

Dwyer, D. (ed.) (1988) *A Home Divided. Women and Income in the Third World*. Stanford, CA, Stanford University Press.

Frimpong-Ansah, J. H. (1991) *The Vampire State in Africa. The Political Economy of Decline in Ghana*, London, James Currey.

Frimpong-Yeboah, F. (1975) 'The Role of Urban-Rural Migration in the Evolution of Slums. The Case of Nima', BA Disssertation, Department of Geography, University of Ghana, Legon.

Government of Ghana (1992) 'The Child Cannot Wait. A National Programme for Action on the Follow-up to the World Summit for Children', Accra, Multisectoral Task Force.

Hammond, D. K. (1993) 'Working Children in Madina', BA Dissertation, Department of Sociology, University of Ghana, Legon.

Isser (1994) 'The State of the Ghanaian Economy in 1993', Institute of Statistical, Social and Economic Research (ISSER), University of Ghana, Legon.

Kambur, R. (1994) 'Welfare Economics, Political Economy and Policy Reform in Ghana', Accra, World Bank.

Larbi, A. K. (1989) 'An Appraisal of Health Care Delivery Systems in Nima', BA Dissertation, Department of Geography, University of Ghana, Legon.

MWH (Ministry of Works and Housing) (1973) 'Nima-Maamobi Redevelopment Sheme', Accra.

Nash, J. (ed.) (1983) *Women, Men and the International Division of Labor*, Albany, NY, New York State University.

Okaiteye-Blessyn, D. (1993) 'Street Children. A Growing Social Canker in the City of Accra', BA Dissertation, Department of Geography, University of Ghana, Legon.

Pamscad (1990) 'An Evaluation Report on PAMSCAD (27 Oct. 1988–31 March 1990)', Accra, World Bank.

Pellow, D. (1977) *Women in Accra: Options for Autonomy*, Algonac, MI, Reference Publications.

Rothchild, D. (ed.) (1991) *Ghana. The Political Economy of Recovery*, Boulder and London, Westview Press.

Sandbrook R. and J. Arn (1977) *The Labouring Poor and Urban Class Formation: The Case of Greater Accra*, Montreal, Centre for Developing Area Studies, McGill University.

Stephens, C. et al. (1994) 'Collaborative Studies in Accra, Ghana, and Sao Paulo, Brazil, and Analysis of Four Demographic and Health Surveys', Accra, Planning and Development Programme.

Twumasi, P. A. (ed.) (1987) 'Problems and Aspirations of Ghanaian Children: Implications for Policy and Action', Accra, Ghana National Commission on Children.

Unicef (1990) 'Children and Women of Ghana. A Situation Analysis. 1989–90', Accra, UNICEF.

University of Ghana (Department of Geography) (1990) 'Demographic Studies and Projections for Accra Metropolitan Area (AMA)', University of Ghana, Legon.

Verlet, M. (1992) 'Du local au mondial. Lieux et parcours du politique', *Revue Tiers Monde*.

— (1993) 'Jeunesses sous influence. Le Ghana ajusté', in E. Le Bris and F. Chauveau (eds), *Jeunes, villes, emploi. Quel avenir pour la jeunesse africaine?* Paris, Ministère de la Coopération et du Développement.

Wayoe, P. A. (1980) 'Housing Quality as an Index of Slum Creation. Case Study of the Nima Residential Area, Accra', BA Dissertation, Department of Geography, University of Ghana, Legon.

Wellington, A. (1968) 'Nima. Spontaneous Urban Growth', MSc Thesis, University of Science and Technology, Kumasi.

World Bank (1984) 'Ghana. Policies and Program for Adjustment', Washington, DC, World Bank.

— (1992) 'Ghana – 2000 and Beyond: Setting the Stage and Equitable Growth', Washington, DC, West Africa Department, World Bank.

— (1994) 'L'ajustement en Afrique: réformes, résultats et chemin à parcourir', Washington, DC, World Bank.

CHAPTER 6

Living and Working Conditions: Child Labour in the Coal Mines of Colombia

Béatriz S. Céspedes Sastre and
María-Isabel Zarama V. Meyer

This research was motivated by stirrings in the European Community after the BBC (London) broadcast a documentary on the exploitation of child labour in the coal mines of the Angelópolis and Amaga districts of north-west Colombia. With pit closures pending, the British Parliament tabled a motion to veto Colombian coal which would have meant a 20 per cent drop in sales, i.e. losses of US\$ 90 million. The employment of children in Colombian mines provided the grounds for such a veto by British mining unions faced with the prospect of mass redundancies. Yet the argument has little substance because although small-scale collieries – mainly family concerns supplying coal for domestic consumption – may well use children for labour at various stages of the production process, exported coal comes from the Cerrejo Complex (where Intercor, a subsidiary of the foreign Exxon group, has invested half of its resources) which does not use any child labour at all.

Child Labour in Colombia

It is not easy to gauge exactly how much of the nation's total activity is performed by child workers because of the very nature of their work: 'invisible' work within the family and jobs in the 'informal' sector are marginal, illegal and hard for statistical measuring devices to detect. There are studies, however, which confirm that large numbers of children are working in cities and rural areas alike, and that there is a world of difference between what the law provides and the real-life situation.

With regard to the city (73.8 per cent of the population inhabit urban areas), the State Department of Statistics (DANE) found that in 1991 there were 36,500 children aged between twelve and fourteen working in the country's seven biggest cities as street-hawkers (39 per cent), domestic servants (38 per cent), in manufacturing (17 per cent) and construction, transport and

83

others (6 per cent). DANE also counted 433,839 twelve- to nineteen-year-olds working in the country's nine most important cities.

Meanwhile, large numbers of children participate in economic activity in rural areas (26.2 per cent of the population). They begin from a very early age, joining in with domestic labour and farming. According to the findings of a 1988 DANE survey, 24 per cent of the working population in rural areas at the time were aged between six and eighteen; and 6 per cent of the total were between six and nine years old (UNICEF 1994). The numbers of children at work fluctuated between 1,259,730 (those whose job was their main activity – basic definition) and 1,725,057 (those whose job was just one of a number of other activities – extended definition). Agriculture was found to be the biggest employer, followed by domestic service in the case of girls.

Colombia is a signatory of the International Convention on the Rights of the Child and its Colombian Institute of Family Welfare (ICBF) has been in existence for more than twenty years; a Minors' Code was drafted and then written into the constitution in 1991, but the protective measures seem to have had little effect and there are apparently no fewer underage children at work. When governments with neo-free-market leanings open up their economies, it tends to go hand in hand with a rise in child labour as the informal sector develops, rural and urban incomes fall and the quality of employment deteriorates. Some studies have shown that part-time employment rose from 14.8 per cent in 1989 to 21.2 per cent in 1992 while underemployment over the same period progressed from 13.5 per cent to 16.8 per cent (Estrada 1993). The informal sector has developed into an alternative means of survival, generally involving work in which the whole family takes part.

Colombia, like many other industrialized or developing countries, has introduced child labour laws in keeping with the guidelines laid down by the International Convention on the Rights of the Child passed by the United Nations Assembly in 1989; although it has not yet ratified ILO Agreement no. 138 which requires governments to implement policies to eradicate child labour and set a standard minimum working age, it has at least established a specific set of child labour regulations.

The Minors' Code (enacted in 1989) sets out the basic rights for minors and the action and measures the authorities should take to deal with irregularities. It classifies unauthorized child workers – i.e. any child under the age of twelve in any way active in production and any child between the ages of twelve and eighteen performing activities banned by law – as *minors in an illegal situation*. All work under the age of fourteen is without exception strictly forbidden (ICBF 1992).

The code lists twenty-two types of work from which minors are prohibited because of the severe risks they pose to the health. Yet children over the age of fourteen are allowed to do some such work as long it offers proper training and safety facilities. One of the areas of activity expressly forbidden is mining work.

Protection of working children is the responsibility of the Ministry of Employment and Social Security whose job it is to monitor the application of child labour protection standards. According to figures released by DANE in 1992, however, the ministry monitored only 2 per cent of the children working in the country's nine biggest cities. It takes care of their legal guidance, issues work permits, deals with claims and complaints, pays visits to the companies and holds hearings. Yet there are far too few specialized government agents to cope with such complicated matters.

Colombian Coal Mining

Recent economic analyses have shown the mining and energy sector to have become an increasingly important contributor to the national economy over the past few years, a fact reflected in its rising share of GNP: from 1.27 per cent in 1980 to 4.17 per cent in 1988 and 4.37 per cent in 1990. According to the Ministry of Mining and Energy, Colombia possesses some of the largest coal reserves in Latin America: in 1990 the annual output came to 20,000 tonnes.

A mining industry survey conducted in 1988 found that 76 per cent of Colombian mines were being run on an 'informal' basis (without ministry authorization) employing 90,278 people in 764 of the country's 1029 districts. Meanwhile, there were only 28,322 people working the mines operating within the law, 12 per cent of whom were the owners.

Mineral excavation is regulated by the Mining Code, a legal tool designed to promote rational exploitation and standard employment conditions. Depending on their annual output capacity, mines are classified as small-, medium- or large-scale. Small-scale mines are the ones producing under 30,000 tonnes a year; medium-scale, from 30,000 to 50,000 tonnes; large-scale, 50,000 tonnes and over.

Coal mining is an area of considerable contrast. Large-scale concerns (like the open-cast Cerrejo complex in Guajira) are equipped with the latest technology, modern machinery and a skilled work force that enjoys the full protection of the law.

Medium-scale or semi-mechanized mines are characterized by the use of machinery offering maximum output at the least possible risk. Coal is generally mined underground, with an electricity-powered ventilation system preventing the build-up of gases; it is extracted with explosives or pneumatic drills, transported on conveyor belts and there is technical assistance on hand at every stage of the work. Workers have metal hard-hats, boots and emergency equipment. They are covered by the social security.

Small-scale developments are characterized by production units owned by individual operators who possess, or have applied for, a mining permit. Although they lack any clear organization and accounts books are unreliable, they do benefit from a minimum of technical control. Coal is extracted manually with pneumatic drills and explosives, loaded by hand and transported on the backs of men or beasts or in waggons running along steel rails. Galleries are lit by battery-operated lamps and water is pumped out by electric pumps or by force of gravity; tunnels and shafts are ventilated by air ducts. Miners have hard-hats, overalls and may sometimes use charts and count on a minimum of technical assistance.

Traditional collieries are the most common, and they employ children. They are subsistence concerns, working with rudimentary techniques and no safety measures for the miners. As a rule, the coal is manually mined and loaded underground in chambers shored up with pillars; mine-workers transport it either on their backs or in waggons pushed along wooden tracks; tunnels and shafts are carbide-lit; walls are protected with wooden beams to minimize risk of a cave-in. Shafts and tunnels are dug into the mountain and galleries can stretch to lengths of 150m or more, with diameters of between 1 and 1.5m. Miners work leaning at an angle, extracting coal with a pick. Extracted coal is dragged to the main entrance and brought out either by the *terciador* (see p. 88) or in a waggon. The miners have no training whatsoever. Most of these collieries are illegal; their proprietors have no official Ministry of Mining and Energy permits.

Child and Adolescent Participation in Coal Mining

Traditional small-scale collieries are the ones generally employing children, as they used to employ women. The work is done by the family, with the mother doing subsidiary tasks such as preparing meals or sewing coal-sacks. Miners are given no apprenticeship; they learn from childhood by observing their elders and through experience.

Children have been working in the mines for a long time. According to the old-timers, mining first started in Tópaga in the district of Boyacá in around 1941. One pioneer, Saul Hurtado, says that before a German prospecting team arrived in search of fresh coalfields, agriculture used to be the main activity there and on-the-job training was given during visits conducted by members of the team.

> Smallholders started excavating plots of their land and then the first tunnels where whole families would go to work began to appear. In the beginning we worked by candlelight, oil lamps or home-made gaslights; the women and children carried the coal in cowskin sacks on their backs. Around 1945, we started using metal-wheeled trolleys and the women stopped actually working down the mines; but the children stayed. Later, things slowly began to improve technically with the introduction of pneumatic drills. It was only from 1970 that we started using electric lights and pumps to extract water.[1]

Modernizing the process has not stopped mine-owners from continuing to hire children, a situation probably set to endure for as long as traditional small-scale collieries remain in family hands. As in any other economic sector, child labour would dwindle and die out altogether if the work could only be modernized and made more technically advanced, with specialized jobs done by more skilled workers.

As most studies demonstrate, child labour is not exclusively confined to a single activity. On the contrary, it is frequently combined with other tasks: looking after younger siblings, doing a variety of household chores and working in the fields or the mines. Some also go to school.

In the district of Boyacá, for instance, a schools survey conducted in 1980 showed that all of the 1200 five- to fifteen-year-olds questioned worked in the fields and half of them in mining (Gutierrez 1989). Boyacá's mining and agricultural industries are developed on small properties where the labour force is comprised of a close-knit family. The development of subsistence farming is so weak that not all available hands are able to find work. So they resort either to migration or mining. Migration levels are very high, made worse by the country's political violence. Some regions are therefore left with relatively little adult labour and the available workers go into agriculture and mining. While subsistence farming is not necessarily linked to the market, mining on the other hand allows small mine-owners to enter market channels and hence make money, although their situation is not that advantageous as the marketing conditions subject them to the rules laid down by middle-men.

In the district of Antioquía, the vast majority of mine-workers come from rural areas. They combine mine-work with other activities: coffee-picking or ranch work. Children in the district start working in the mines from a very early age because poor families see it as a way of increasing their meagre incomes (Ortiz and Roa 1994).

A survey conducted by the People's Counsel Office found an average of three thirteen- to fifteen-year-olds working in the mines visited. In fifty-five of them, 142 children were found performing several sorts of different activities (Defensoria 1994).

Working Conditions for Underage Children

The People's Counsel has issued a report showing that children are preferred for ore extraction in the deepest, narrowest parts of the gallery because they are so small and agile. They work in hot, humid, contaminated spaces with no ventilation and constant exposure to lung-damaging toxic gases and dust. The government agents assigned to visit the collieries went down only to a depth of 200m, even though some galleries are known to be more than 300m underground; there is no light down there, little air and real danger of death due to cave-ins or fireball explosions – caused when a spark strikes a pocket of methane. Flooding is another equally common hazard.

Some children start down the mines from as young as six years old. They are said to be ready to work as soon as they can pick up objects and drag them along.

The smallest children work at the pithead: sorting coal, carrying wood, tools, water and food. Older ones do jobs that demand a greater degree of resistance. Although underground work is largely done by children between the ages of twelve and fourteen, they can, as mentioned, be of any age. Recent surveys by the municipal committees for the protection of working children in the regions of Amaga and Angelópolis show that between 50 and 60 per cent of children work as *arrastradores*. The classification below relates the kind work done by child mine-workers; it was produced in Angelópolis and revised by us after we had studied it alongside observations made in other parts of the country:

Achicador	drains water from pit to prevent flooding
Arrastrador	transports coal up to pit-head on a metal blade strapped to the shoulders
Arriero	leads the mule used to transport packaged coal
Asoleador	washes, dries and repairs coal-sacks
Barretero	extracts coal from seam with a pick; also known as *piquero*
Carretillero	transports coal in handcarts full from the depths of the mine up to the entrance; they work in pairs, one child pulling the cart, one pushing and lifting
Cochero	drives an electric cart transporting packaged coal to the pit-head
Empacador	wraps coal in large rope or fibre sacks at pit-head
Garitero	carries food to miners
Paleador	shovels fallen lumps of coal up from floor and loads them into the carts or sacks
Piquero	extracts coal from seam with a pick; also known as a *barretero*
Terciador	carries fibre sacks of coal on back with straps attached to head or chest

Working hours usually extend from 1 or 2 a.m. through to 8 or 9 a.m. when the children are released for school before later going to work in the fields. These hours are chosen because air conditions and temperatures are more bearable down the mine at daybreak.

One study of the Boyacá district found that 55 per cent of the children were working night-shifts down the mines and 45 per cent were doing pit-head work during the day (Gutierrez 1989). It shows that the day was divided as follows for the majority of children: minework from 1 to 7 a.m.; school from 8 till noon; domestic or farm work from 2 to 6 p.m. This means they do ten hours of labouring for every four hours of school.

There may be variations depending on the region and a child's personal circumstances. Another study carried out in Antioquiá contains the following statement: 'I used to leave for work at 4 in the morning and stop at 11. We worked at dawn so we could get some rest in the afternoon and be able to get up at dawn the next day' (Ortiz and Roa 1994).

The following passage taken from the above-mentioned Boyacá study reveals a young miner's feelings about school and mine-work: 'I'm up at midnight, I gulp down a coffee and then I'm off to the pit where I work till 7 a.m. In the afternoon I'm at school from 2 till 6. After that, I help out at home till 8 at night. I wish I could work longer down the pit, for the money. School's useless' (Gutierrez 1989).

When children are paid a wage, it is on the basis of an unwritten contract whose conditions are dictated by the pit-owner. They are generally paid by the amounts of coal extracted per day. Most children do not even earn a minimum wage (i.e. $US 120). On average they are taking home around 50,000 pesos ($US 60). In Boyacá and Cundinamarca, regions featuring a good many small-scale properties, children usually work with their parents for no pay at all.

Because the state exercises no control over recruitment and the majority of the collieries that employ children are illegal, the youngsters are obviously deprived of any welfare: no holidays, no travel or food allowances, not even any medical treatment. As in almost every case of child labour, legislation goes unheeded.

Health and Education

The child workers' state of health in these regions is marked by parasites, calorie and protein deficiencies, anaemia, avitaminosis and rotting teeth. Mine-work causes infectious diseases: pharyngitis, tonsillitis, sinusitis, influenza, pulmonary ailments and silicosis. Skin diseases and injuries to the hands and the face are common as are bone deformations in those who have been working for a number of years.

We should also analyse the problem of school attendance, education standards and the attitudes of parents and the state towards education. Entering employment at an early age makes a child apathetic or indifferent towards school as there are no opportunities locally to make progress and education is seen as a waste of time rather than an investment. 'You've got to work if you want to be a man; otherwise you won't know how to do anything by the time you grow up and it'll be really hard to survive.'[2] Although the constitution provides for compulsory free education, there are not the means to apply the law, nor any programmes tailored to the various different milieus. Drop-out rates in these areas are therefore very high and nobody stays on beyond primary school.

Tópaga: A Project for Eliminating Child Labour

Tópaga is a four-hour drive from Bogotá. It is a small Boyacá district town of 5000 inhabitants where coal has been mined by traditional means for about the last sixty years. In 1992, there were still 150 to 200 children – some under the age of twelve – working in conditions such as those described above; most also had farm-work and domestic chores and a few were attending school, but all were working down the mines to earn extra money to buy clothes and help towards the family's housekeeping.

Although, objectively speaking, the children's contributions may well be useful, what we find above all here is a general community attitude in favour of child labour: a work culture, a view of life which puts work before school with an obvious disregard for the notion of children's rights as acknowledged in modern democratic societies.

Having recognized the lack of safety measures and the physical and mental health risks to which child mine-workers are exposed and established the illegal nature of the work, a community leader striving do something for the good of his town launched an initiative with the firm support of a young miner. A programme was gradually pieced together drawing on the participation of every institution directly or indirectly concerned by the situation: the town hall, Ecocarbón, the Ministry of Labour, the Colombian Institute of Family Welfare and UNICEF. The programme essentially aimed at improving standards of living, reforming hazardous conditions and stimulating thought on the matter of child labour and its consequences (Ortiz 1993). It was rooted in principles such as the child's right of access to healthcare, education, recreation and culture, the involvement of different sectors of the community, the gradual involvement of parents, the possibility of bringing pressure to bear on politicians and child labour legislation and the prioritizing of teaching and training over production.

Guided by these principles and adopting a participatory and self-management style approach, the programme set out to organize the children and young workers to promote education, vocational training, production and income-earning by creating a multi-functional cooperative of which they themselves would be the members. Training courses are provided, for example, on cooperatives, on associations, on making overalls or souvenirs carved from lumps of coal. Alongside traditional schools, children are given the chance to learn techniques which will make them more resourceful and, in the medium term, provide them with an alternative activity to labour. At the same time, organized women's groups offer courses in bakery, needlework, community work and management.

The project has been underway for a couple of years now and the results have been promising, despite the many difficulties. The cooperative's member children are involved in activities in production zones, in education, healthcare, social development and management for a peasants' association – all with the backing of additional institutions to those involved in the project at the start. In the district's schools and colleges, a campaign has been launched to encourage eleven- to thirteen-year-old children to join the cooperative: the very age group that is working in the mines. Teachers, government agents and parents all approve of the project, although the parents have expressed some reservations. At project assessment meetings, the children have stressed that financial and family pressures are the biggest obstacles they have to overcome. When we interviewed the children belonging to the cooperative, we were surprised at their maturity, their lively minds, their powers of analysis and intellectual development.

Although the project has many facets, emphasis has above all been placed on the work with the children. Work with women and the construction of a community-oriented perspective have been somewhat neglected. At present, there are nearly thirty children taking part in the project making carved coal souvenirs. A few participants have dropped out and some children combine their work at the cooperative with a colliery job because it earns them a weekly wage, whereas the cooperative pays only according to sales.

By Way of Conclusion

Child labour is inevitably linked with poverty, and as long as the state fails to regard the phenomenon as a structural fact within the economy which requires new social policies to improve conditions in the most disadvantaged quarters, then eradicating child labour will never amount to anything other than a pious wish.

One of the chief obstacles to eradicating child labour is the attitude of certain sections of the population that regard work as the most effective means of training new generations, seeing education as having scarcely any merit whatsoever and remaining ignorant as to the basic conditions a child requires in order to develop: the need, among other things, for rest, a balanced diet, recreation, education. In some rural sectors and marginalized urban areas, living conditions reproduce a climate of apathy. It is a difficult situation, one that requires a real break from the culture of the past in order to bring about change. From that point of view, the case of Tópaga, where economic conditions and cultural characteristics are not exactly ideal for getting rid of child labour, is an interesting one; projects for improving family incomes could scale down the use of child labour. The participation of women in educational and productive activities appears to be an interesting initiative in so far as they are helping to raise the family income and modify the norms as regards education and family relations, thus providing for cultural change.

Education is particularly important for eradicating child labour. The more children there are at school, the fewer there will be at work. But it is not enough simply to declare that education is a compulsory duty; it must also be made clear that it is a right. These two conditions require action with a view to guaranteeing access to school for children and improving the standards of schools so that they become a genuine social asset. Having programmes flexible enough to adapt to the characteristic features of different regions would add much weight to declarations on the importance of education. In our particular area of interest, emphasis will have to be placed on technical training which would in turn produce better levels of education and better conditions in coal mining.

The existence of legal standards on child labour seems to have had no real influence whatsoever. As long as the control mechanisms are defective and no precise forms of intervention are being put forward, the situation, in all its guises, will persist with impunity.

Finally, we would like to underline the importance of the pressure being brought to bear through censure and intervention on the part of national and international agencies responding to concrete cases such as that of child labour in the coal mines of Colombia.

Notes

1. S. Hurtado, from a speech delivered in Tópaga, Boyacá (1994).
2. F. Alvarez, from a speech delivered in Tópaga, Boyacá (1994).

References

DANE (Departamento administrativo nacional de estadística) (1994) 'XVI Censo Nacional de Población y Vivienda: Resumen Ejecutivo', Santafé de Bogotá.

Defensoria del pueblo (1994) 'Legislación de protección al menor trabajador violada en su totalidad', Santafé de Bogotá.

Estrada, J. (1993) 'Informe de trabajo', Bogotá.

Gutierrez, R. (1989) *Drama y tragedia del menor trabajador*, Bogotá, Ed. Beneficencia de Cundinamraca.

ICBF (Instituto Colombiano de Bienestar familiar) (1992) Código del menor, *Diaro Oficial* 39,080, Santafé de Bogotá.

Ortiz, F. and T. Roa (1994) 'Informe sobre la situación de los niños y jóvenes mineros en Angelópolis y Amaga', Agua Viva, Centro National de Salud, Ambiente y Trabajo.

Ortiz, N. (1993) 'Erradicación del trabajo infantil, Mito o realidad? Una experiencia específica de la mina a la escuela Ponencia', communication au Seminario Interinstitucional Sobre el Menor Trabajador en Colombia, Santafé de Bogotá.

Ramirez, L. F. (1992) 'Hacia un mejoramiento de las condiciones laborales y de seguridad del menor trabajador en Colombia', Santafé de Bogotá, Ministerio de Trabajo y Seguridad Social.

Umaña, E. (1991) *El menor de Edad*, Santafé de Bogotá, Corporación Colectivo de Abogados.

UNICEF, Departamento Nacional de Planeación (1994) 'Niños y jóvenes en circunstancias especialmente difíciles y en situación de alto riesgo', Análisis de situación 12, Santafé de Bogotá.

CHAPTER 7

Stigmatization versus Identity: Child Street-workers in Mexico

Elvira Taracena and Maria-Luisa Tavera

This chapter is the outcome of a research project we have been running on the child street-workers of Mexico with a team of researchers and students specializing in social minorities. Children working on such a huge scale is a relatively recent phenomenon in Mexico. Apart from the actual existence of child labour, the most disturbing thing about it is the degrading way in which society as a whole pictures the children in question. It gives them a double dilemma to contend with: the work itself plus stigmatization.

Organizations such as UNICEF are beginning to realize that a total blanket ban on all Latin American child labour would only serve to deepen poverty; and that notwithstanding the many cases of unprotected children exposed to exploitation and abuse, work may under the right conditions be formative for young people. They have therefore developed a method of intervention through 'street educators', whose work it is to accompany the children in their everyday lives on the streets and try to reduce the risks they run. One such example is the MESE (Minors in Distress) programme conducted in Mexico with the help of the state agency DIF (Total Family Development). Other street child agencies have adopted the technique to establish first contact with the children before eventually offering them a place in a children's home (see, for instance, the work of Casa Alianza).

Different sources tend to report quite different figures. Some journalists talk about there being 5.7 million children on the nation's streets, with 1.5 million in Mexico City alone (Bárcenas et al. 1992); UNICEF estimates put it at 5 million and 1 million respectively (MESE programme report); the Labor Congress claims there are 8 million children on Mexican streets and the ARDF (Federal Assembly of District Representatives) maintains that 3 million are working there (Sanchez 1992). According to CEDEMIN (the Mexican Center for the Right to Childhood), the figure is more likely to be 12 million.

They differ because these are estimates based on the percentage of children in Mexico and people in extreme poverty; and there is not a lot of clarity as to the criteria for determining which categories of children to include and which to omit. Children working on the streets who still have links with their families? Children for whom the street is their only home?

UNICEF and the DIF have tried to draw a distinction between 'children *of* the street' and 'children *in* the street'; the former referring to those living full-time on the streets with no family ties whatsoever and the latter those who spend a large amount of time in the street, often working, but who still have family ties. An important distinction indeed, but a little too subtle for the mass media to absorb as can be seen in headlines such as '54,000 abandoned children scrape a living on the streets' (*Metropoli*, 1989); 'Emergency: 6 million child drug addicts must be saved' (*El Dia*, 1989); '8 million kids working in Mexico without legal protection' (*El Dia*, 1990).

Because of this, we set about producing a more accurate diagnosis of the issue of child labour on the streets of Mexico. Determined to steer clear of another quantitative-type diagnosis based on percentages,[1] our study focused on the problems experienced by the children. We found that we needed to become acquainted with their characteristic features, the work they perform, the risks they run and, above all, with the children themselves in order to put a face to them and remove the stigma. Because it is essential to produce proposals for different methods of intervention and aid tailored to the children's characteristics, we chose to adopt a qualitative approach using clinical-type interviews and build case studies of specific children; although not representative of all working children, they allowed us to read deeper into the children's life stories and experiences and establish how they relate to their social position and its attendant constraints (as well as to identify and analyse the role of the researcher). With this in mind, we set out to correlate our findings with those from studies using more representative samples regarding the percentages of children employed in given occupations.

In the course of an earlier study of ours (Taracena and Tavera 1992), we interviewed forty-five children found working on the streets of Mexico City as well as sixty-seven adult residents; we also analysed thirty-seven newspaper and magazine articles with a view to ascertaining how street child labour was being portrayed and its image in the eyes of public opinion.

The interviews were semi-directed with an accent on the relationship between interviewers and interviewees, the process of transfer and counter-transfer. Processing the data gathered during these sessions and from the press cuttings was done by means of content analysis.

In interviewing the child street-workers and residents of Mexico City, our purpose was to explore the following areas:

- interviewee's attitude during interview
- image of children's work
- public attitude towards the child
- child's attitude towards the public
- perceived root causes of the phenomenon
- work-related risks run by children

- opportunities for apprenticeship and self-improvement via the experience of street work
- child's family relations (structure, quality of relationship)
- child's health
- child's working relations
- child's relations with institutions (police, protection agencies)
- child's religion

Interviews were sorted for analysis according to the following categories of child labour:

- sales: selling chewing-gum, food, drinks, toys, flowers, cassettes, etc.
- services: shoeshine, car-wash, windscreen-cleaning, porter
- performance: singers, musicians, fire-eaters, etc.

Analysis results of the interviews with the children and residents were compared to those from our analysis of the press. We thought it would be interesting to compare the images projected by each of the three population types.

We found not a single child under the age of seven. This is confirmed by press claims that the majority of children are aged between seven and sixteen. Nines to fourteens constituted the largest age group.

The press says – and our data largely confirm this – that there are practically no young girls on the streets. Among the children working there, however, two out of every three in the *sales* category are girls.

Levels of schooling vary with the type of work: school attendance rates are highest among the sales children, with most reaching the end of primary school and one in three going on to secondary school or an apprenticeship. *Services* children tend to drop out during the third year of primary school and *performance* children are often illiterate. This diversity is in stark contrast to the picture unanimously painted by the press which maintains that children working in the street are virtually uneducated.

The views of the residents, the children and the press converge on the subject of working hours and the working week for most types of work: six to ten hours a day; six or seven days a week. One in three sales children, it should be said, work only weekends – undoubtedly those still attending school.

City residents and children see sales to be the biggest category. This is further confirmed by a recent COESNICA census which found it covered over 70 per cent of the children.

The children say that people accept them when their services are needed; residents confirm this. The press on the other hand describes them as socially useless individuals, as beggars. The children see themselves in no such light.

As for the nature of the work itself, all the children say it is easy. Windscreen cleaners and other services children add that it is tiring. Residents reckon children's work is tiring and dangerous; the children themselves do not see the danger.

Windscreen cleaners and performance children sense hostility or, at best, indifference on the part of the general public; residents agree about people's hostile attitude towards the children and the press even describes it as aggressive.

With regard to the children's attitude towards the public – the press, residents and children unanimously agree that it depends on how people behave towards them; the press, however, goes on to add that because people very often treat them badly, the children answer back in an aggressive manner; one in three sales children say they are friendly towards the public.

As for the root causes of child labour, everybody points first to poverty, then to broken homes. The press and residents add that another important factor is rural-to-urban migration.

Among the risks cited by both children and residents the biggest is disease, followed by police violence; one in four services and performance category children mention drug-related risks, as do the residents. When the press picks up on addiction to inhaled substances it presents it as a fact rather than a risk, claiming that 80 to 90 per cent of children take drugs and emphasizing the dangers of delinquency and homosexuality. This, by the way, is echoed in how easily city residents associate life on the streets with delinquency, but it is the press that talks about child homosexuality, often to a rather exaggerated degree.

On the matter of training and self-improvement – the children associate apprenticeship with learning how to manage time and money, make decisions, assess risks and, above all else, gain independence and self-sufficiency; they see it as a means of discovering how to make money for themselves and their families. The press takes the same view, adding that they also learn to organize themselves into groups and cultivate solidarity and collusion among peers.

As for family relations, nearly half the sales children claim to have a normal family, with only one in five admitting to deep conflict with parents; but among services children, two in three windscreen cleaners (67 per cent) admit to coming from broken homes; nearly two-thirds of the other services children have normal families. The press nevertheless tends to project a picture of street children living free with peer groups, protecting one another. It also talks about them seeking protection in a relationship with an adult. Residents believe the children all come from broken homes or belong to peer groups. They associate this picture with that of exploitation.

The most commonly cited health problems are respiratory and gastro-enteric ailments followed by accidents and drug-related illnesses (with attend-ant physical and psychological damage). Both the press and residents are in agreement about that, although the press does no doubt exaggerate the extent of the drug abuse: only seven of the forty-five children we met were found to be taking drugs; none of these was a sales child, several of whom were suffering from respiratory diseases.

The press, residents and children all believe that relationships among street children are primarily based on mutual assistance and collusion, but that there are some based on violence too. This is seen particularly among performance and services children. Reference is also made to cases of physical abuse and financial exploitation, at times perpetrated by the police.

It is with the police that the children have their most serious problems. Relations with the institutions are not, as a rule, very good; apart from the police, many talk about the bad experiences they have had at the hands of the state's so-called 'child protection' agencies. Most residents appear to know little about these agencies or how they operate. The press for its part criticizes the inefficiency of the state institutions, depicting them as schools for delinquency and vice; on the other hand, it speaks very well of non-governmental organizations.

Religion-wise, most of the children claim to be devout Catholics and a good number say they regularly attend mass. The residents suspect that they do believe in God, but do not go to church regularly. There is not a word on the matter in the press.

Despite this having been the first study of its kind, and much of our data remain to be confirmed, we can still draw a number of conclusions.

1. The risk of stigmatizing the street child. The press, even those sections of it which claim to have a committed interest in social matters, tends to be too quick to associate child street-workers with delinquency and drugs.

2. The children fall into a variety of different categories; and the majority have preserved their links with families.

3. A majority of children work in sales activities; they have kept up their links with school and are the least exposed to risks of illness (including drug-related).

4. Windscreen cleaners and performers, meanwhile, are the children exposed to the greatest risks. Performers constitute a case apart; in our opinion, they are the ones closest to being beggars; they also have the highest incidence of illiteracy and addiction to inhaled substances. We should point out that they are the most uncommunicative subjects during interviews, the most mistrustful.

In a second study (Taracena et al. 1993), again using semi-directed techniques, we interviewed thirty-six children with a mind to finding out how they perceive their work situation. Our earlier study had shown us that it was highly influenced by family situations, especially when it was a matter of the work being formative or, on the contrary, risky. Because of this, we decided to observe more deeply how the children relate to their families. The material to which our earlier interviews had given us access had been rather discursive and we felt that by adding an exercise whereby children would be asked to draw pictures of their families – according to Corman's suggested guidelines (Corman 1990) – we would obtain material of a more projective kind (Meredieu 1992). The pictures would give us an opening into the subjects' mental representations: how they live their family situations, the nature of their conflicts and desires and, hence, how the situation affects apprenticeship and the relations they are able to establish at work.

A fresh category of child worker was introduced for this study: *supermarket* children: the thirteen- to sixteen-year-olds helping shoppers pack up their goods and carry them to the car park in return for a tip. Most work four to five hours a day on top of their school studies. They receive no wages as such, only whatever sums of money people are willing to give. Having said that, it is so deeply entrenched in Mexican customs that tipping is a widely accepted practice and everyone knows the going rate. So the children are guaranteed a certain income every day. The shops for their part insist on a number of basic requirements: youngsters, for example, must have their parents' permission and prove that they are enrolled at a school; they must purchase their own uniforms, always remain clean and punctual and organize their work in a disciplined manner. Although they are not really in the street as such and therefore run fewer risks, we nevertheless thought it would be interesting to include this category of child worker in order to find out how they integrate the experience into their everyday lives.

Our second study therefore focuses on four activity groups:

1. Supermarkets   (assistants)
2. Sales   (hawkers)
3. Services   (cleaners, porters)
4. Performance   (busking and odd jobs)

Tables 7.1, 7.2 and 7.3 (below) show the children's working conditions and family characteristics. We have indicated that the work was formative for them, going by the interviews, whether the work was compatible with school-ing and whether it offered opportunities for apprenticeship and improvement.

Supermarket children are better educated – most are at secondary school; sales and services children have not completed primary schooling; performance children are the least educated (two years of primary school). The latter are exposed to the biggest risks, while supermarket work is virtually risk-free.

All four categories of children interviewed claimed to be earning approx-imately the same amount per day: between 25 and 30 new pesos – equal to one and a half times the Mexican minimum wage (no family can survive on the minimum wage; hence the need for more wage-earners, more sources of income). Most supermarket children spend their earnings on personal items (clothing and leisure-time activities); performance children all use their money for their own ends as well, but that is because they are fending for themselves; in sales and services most hand over their wages to their parents for the housekeeping.

Category 1 (supermarket) youngsters are the ones with the most ambitious social plans and siblings with the highest levels of schooling. They have better qualified parents with apparently more stable careers. And a large number of their mothers stay at home, which can be taken to suggest that

TABLE 7.1 Description of the sample

	Supermarkets	Sales	Services	Performance
Number of interviewees	12	14	4	6
Age	14–15	8–15	12–15	9–14
Sex	m: 9 f: 3	m: 11 f: 3	m: 4	m: 6
Schooling*	secondary: 2–3	primary: 3 secondary: 1	primary: 5 secondary: 1	primary: 1–3 (not completed)
Daily earnings	N$ 30	N$ 25	N$ 25	N$ 30
Risks	none	pollution: 3/14 accident: 8/14	pollution: 2/4 accident: 1/4 violence: 4/4	pollution: 6/6 accident: 6/6 violence: 6/6 drugs: 6/6

Note Primary: 1 = 1st year infants; 2 = 1st year primary; 3 = 2nd year primary; 4 = 3rd year primary; 5 = 4th year primary.
Secondary: 1 = 1st year secondary etc.
Table figures indicate lowest level/highest level.

TABLE 7.2 Type of work

	Supermarkets	Sales	Services	Performance
Number of interviewees	12	14	4	6
Formative work	yes: 12/12	yes: 9/14	yes: 4/4	yes: 5/6
Reasons for work	pers. expenses: 4/12 pers. + fam.: 8/12	pers. exp.: 1/14 pers. + fam.: 3/14 fam.: 10/14	pers. exp.: 1/4 pers. + fam.: 2/4 fam.: 1/4	pers. exp.: 6/6
Future plans	none: 3/12 university: 5/12 tech. college: 3/12 employee: 1/12	none: 2/14 university: 5/14 commerce: 3/14 musician: 2/14	none: 2/4 university: 1/4 employee: 1/4	none: 6/6

TABLE 7.3 Work and scholarship

	Supermarkets	Sales	Services	Performance
Number of interviewees	12	14	4	6
Siblings' schooling	primary: 4/12 secondary: 7/12 tech.: 2/12 6th form: 4/12 univ.: 2/12 working (or other studies): : 3/12	prim.: 2/14 sec.: 1/14 tech.: 1/4 working (or other studies): 8/14	prim.: 2/4 sec.: 1/4 tech.: 1/14 working (or other studies): 2/4	
Number of sibs	4 to 7: 7/12	5 to 8: 9/14	5 to 9: 3/4	7: 1/6
Father's occupation	commerce: 4/12 employee: 4/12 craftsman: 2/12 labourer: 2/12	salesman: 10/14	salesman: 1/4 cleaner: 2/14	driver: 1/6
Mother's occupation	housewife: 9/12 employee: 2/12 commerce: 1/12	saleswoman: 10/14 cleaner: 2/14 housewife: 2/14	saleswoman: 1/4 housewife: 1/14	

their families are financially better-off. This contrasts with the case of the mothers of sales children (10 out of 14 of whom also work in sales). It further confirms Bourdieu and Passeron's (1970) hypotheses on the education of children and reproduction of the parents' social situation. This is particularly clear with the children from category 2 (sales), among whom we found high levels of consistency between current work, ambitions regarding future careers and the parents' situation.

On the whole, families of category 2 and category 3 (services) children face greater material hardship; a larger number of siblings are working and there is a greater incidence of father absenteeism, leaving more mothers thrust into the role of head of the household and having to attend to the family's financial as well as relational affairs. In our view, the conditions created by instability or poverty are not directly responsible for the family's relational problems, but can act as a catalyst and magnify the scale of those problems. A larger number of category 2 children find their parents to be not too available.

We were struck by the consistency between the children's discourse during interviews, the projective material gleaned from their pictures and the stories they told when asked to describe their family situation: those whose homes were free from major conflict were only too pleased to talk; those living alone were highly reluctant to do so.

Three types of connection emerged between the child's family situation and work situation:

The first type is represented by category 1: family conditions are generally more favourable; conflicts here resemble those normally experienced by most adolescents. The work is more formative and agreeable for children with supermarket jobs. Most importantly, the majority of these children have decided to work of their own accord and have, of course, obtained their parents' permission; older than the other children, they have reached the age at which youngsters begin to seek independence; their work is also more structured, with a larger number of rules to respect and clearer limits.

The second type corresponds to what we call a 'risk situation'. It is typified by the case of the children from categories 2 and 3 (sales and services). Working conditions are tougher and the work itself is less structured. The children are younger (an average of twelve years) and many have already been working for several years. A good number appear worn out and disheartened. They generally earn relatively large sums of money but it is needed to keep the family alive; this introduces a degree of tension into the child–parent relationship, particularly if the former's earnings should fall. Being constantly required to bring in a steady revenue increases the pressure they have to bear and the work can become incompatible with school.

Compared to supermarket children, those in sales and services often work longer hours; despite which, these categories were also found to include children whose parents pay close attention to school timetables. Sales and services children generally appear to come from less structured families that have greater difficulty fulfilling their duties as providers of shelter and support. The children in these categories are the ones with the most severe insecurity problems.

At the same time, however, we also encountered families with very strong internal bonding, especially where they have a shared activity serving as additional cement. Such is the case of one of the families with whom we had the opportunity to spend six months for the purposes of carrying out more in-depth work; it was a five-member family: the father (thirty-five years), mother (thirty-two) and three children (eight, twelve and fifteen). All are Mexican-born. Neither parent had completed primary education, but all three children still attend school (the eldest at secondary level): every morning and afternoon the children go to school and every evening they are out on the streets with their parents selling sweets, toys, flowers, drinks and so on until 8 or 9 p.m. The father purchases the merchandise in the morning while the mother is doing the housework; she takes the children to join the father at work after dinner. He is responsible for negotiating the sales pitch and 'permit' with the police. At the end of the day, they all go home together and the children then try to do their homework, although they are often too tired. The children feel a certain tension in their filial relations because of the money and because they do not always enjoy being 'made' to work; yet they are proud to be helping their parents. The eldest child has been working for nine years and the other two have been brought in little by little. The eldest and second eldest complain about how little work the youngest does. But despite the difficulties, they have a relatively harmonious relationship and the children feel protected.

The third type of correlation is found among category 4 (performance) children. They have totally broken away from their families and live full-time on the streets. Five of the category's six interviewees sleep in an air vent or subway exit where it is relatively warm or shelter under a bridge. They live with their peers and often take drugs, especially inhaled substances. They are sexually promiscuous, some are highly active homosexuals. They work on an irregular basis: cleaning windscreens, helping out in the marketplace, performing as fire-eaters. They claim to have little trouble raising the 20 to 30 pesos required daily to meet their needs, the most important, they say, being slot machines and glue to sniff. Although irregular, the work seems to represent the only activity where they find themselves confronted with rules and limits.

Category 4 children had great difficulty depicting a family in their drawings; they often drew a peer group, a couple of friends or brothers. When asked about their families in interviews, most flatly refused to talk. These children evidently have trouble establishing affective links in their self-representations. Our interviews, observations and analyses of drawings agree with the comments of Taboada-Leonneti: some youngsters tend to play up to other people's stigmatizing image of them.

We find that the situation of these children has several points in common with Angel, Botbol and Facy's analysis of adolescent drug-inhalers (Angel et al. 1987). Within a social problematic (in this case marginality, poverty, neglect), abuse of inhaled substances is in fact a symptom of a troubled mind. The children taking drugs are not yet mentally mature and drug-induced euphoria can often fill them with a feeling of physical omnipotence. In the case of the category 4 children, we see it in the important place sexual activity occupies in their lives and in their real taste for dicing with death: an accident, violence or a narrow escape leave them feeling all the more powerful.

General reflections

There are many points where data from our two studies matched those of COESNICA. We both found the majority of child street-workers to be hawkers and that they have largely kept ties with the family. Those without families and actually living on the streets represent 9.13 per cent of the COESNICA study sample and 13.18 per cent of ours.

As for education, 39 per cent of our survey and 38 per cent of COES-NICA's had passed primary and moved up to secondary school education. COESNICA found 17.6 per cent of its sample to be illiterate; we found 13.8 per cent of ours to be functional illiterates who could produce and recognize a handful of words but did not really know how to read and write.

Our studies found 14 per cent using inhaled drugs. COESNICA found 14.7 per cent (with 8.5 per cent smoking marijuana and 8.7 per cent using other unspecified drugs).

These data confirm our belief that the press is rather partial to over-sensationalizing the issue of working children: projecting a generalized picture of children in the street as delinquents-in-the-making, beggars, ultimately doomed to total exclusion. Little is said about the vast numbers who, notwithstanding difficulties, arrange with their families to have a job to enable them to contribute to the family budget; who still go to school; who are ambitious to master a trade; who learn how to make a living on the streets, with its rules, its culture and demands; who are prepared to struggle there day in day out to survive. It should be clear by now that press sensationalism counter-productively serves only to stigmatize.

There has, however, been greater awareness at government level; new, ideologically more humane programmes are now underway, marking a departure from the old lock-them-up approach aimed at keeping these children hidden from view; the root causes of the problem are now under scrutiny. NGOs for their part are running outreach programmes and children's homes. This has perhaps been spurred in part by the numerous press articles criticizing society's indifference.[2] In any event, most programmes still tend overly to narrow their focus to street children (living on the streets, no family ties);

nothing has yet been done for families whose children, because they have to work, are in danger of finding themselves exposed to high-risk situations.

Notes

We wish to thank the United Mexican States government for the grant given within the framework of its SEIE programme.

1. A COESNICA (Commission for the Study of Street Children) survey observing 11,172 children in the city districts most frequented by child street-workers found that 28 per cent were girls, and only 9 per cent had no contact with their families. Regarding their activities: 72.8 per cent were pedlars, 20.3 per cent service providers (coolies, shoe-blacks, car cleaners etc.), 3.6 per cent performers (singers, clowns, fire-eaters etc.), 3.3 per cent beggars. This study, among the first to focus on the children's characteristic features, nevertheless remains rather descriptive.

2. During the time we were working with the children at risk as consultants to government and non-governmental organizations, we were able to provide more preventative solutions for some families, more therapeutic ones for others.

References

Angel, P., M. Botbol and F. Facy (1987) *Adolescence et solvants*, Paris, Echo-Centurion.

Bárcenas, A., W. Guzman and L. C. Rodríguez (1992) 'Niños callejeros, árboles para los que no quieren ver el bosque', *La Jornada*, Mexico, June.

Bourdieu, P. and J. C. Passeron (1970) *La reproduction – éléments pour une théorie du système d'enseignement*, Paris, Minuit.

Cemedln (1992) *Informe del Centro Mexicano para los derechos de la infancia*, Mexico.

COESNICA (1992) *Estudio de los niños callejeros*, Mexico.

Corman, L. (1961) *Le test du dessin de famille*, Paris, PUF (new edn, 1990).

Meredieu, F. de (1992) *Le dessin d'enfant*, Paris, Blusson Éditeur.

Sanchez, F. (1992) 'Los niños: los seres más sufrientes de este planeta empobrecido', *Revista Metropoli*, Mexico, April.

Taboada-Leonneti, I. (1990) 'Stratégies identitaires et minorités: le point de vue du sociologue', in C. Camilleri et al., *Stratégies identitaires*, Paris, Presses Universitaires de France.

Taracena, E. and M. L. Tavera (1992) *La imágen social del niño que trabaja en la calle*, ENEP, Iztacala, Sous Presse.

— (1993) 'Le travail des enfants au Mexique, La représentation du problème par les différents partenaires sociaux', in V. de Gaulejac and S. Roy (eds) *Sociologies cliniques*, Marseille, Hommes et Perspectives.

Taracena, E., M. L. Tavera and G. Castillo (1993) 'La représentation de la famille chez les enfants qui travaillent dans les rues de Mexico', paper presented at symposium, 'L'approche clinique dans les sciences humaines: possibilités et limites', Montréal.

Vaylon, E. (1989) 'Urge rescatar a 6 millones de menores adictos a las drogas', *El Día*, Mexico, July.

— (1990) 'En el pais, ocho millones de pequeños trabajan sin ninguna protección legal', *El Día*, Mexico, August.

Child Labour in Society

CHAPTER 8

Public Policy, Society and Child Labour

Francis Gendreau

The exact scale of child labour in the world is difficult to gauge because definitions of the phenomenon are liable to vary and existing statistics systems are particularly bad at apprehending it. Even in this book, different articles refer to different definitions. They all basically take account of two criteria: whether or not the child belongs to his or her home environment and, whether s/he is employed in or outside the family. Crossing these criteria produces a number of quite distinct categories.

1. Children living and working within the family unit: a common means of socialization in all rural societies and also found in the urban informal sector; it does not necessarily mean an *a priori* exploitation of the child, but neither does it rule out the possibility; this category can also include children placed in other people's (collaterals') keeping, as is frequently the case in West Africa.

2. Children put to work outside the family unit: a lucrative form of labour more likely to expose children to exploitation; they may be living with their families or 'fostered out', living and working away from home with which links can remain more or less well intact; this category can harbour high levels of exploitation of child labour and, in more extreme cases, even situations bordering on slavery, e.g. 'bonded labour' (M. Bonnet).

3. Children without a family: abandoned children or runaways working to survive within or on the fringes of the law, street children.

Forms of exploitation affect working hours (up to twelve or even sixteen a day), pay (very poor, sometimes zero) and working conditions (unhealthy, hazardous, authoritarian or brutal). But the chief characteristic common to all working children is their age.

When is a Child a Child?

National laws often set a 'minimum age for admission to employment'. The international community has produced legislation aimed at encouraging each country to adopt rules to protect children from premature employment and, 'in the long term, to abolish child labour and gradually raise the minimum age' (Bequele; see Myers 1992: 219). The chief examples are the Declaration of the Rights of the Child adopted by the United Nations in 1959, the ILO's 1973 Convention Concerning Minimum Age for Admission to Employment (Convention no. 138) and the 1990 UN Convention on the Rights of the Child.

These laws lay down a number of major principles and guidelines, e.g.: 'This Convention understands children to be any human beings aged less than eighteen years, except in countries where majority is reached earlier by virtue of the prevailing legislation' (UN Convention, 1990).

This is intended to represent the international community's definition of a 'child', whereas in actual fact, alongside a clear-cut age limit of eighteen years, it already provides potential loopholes based on individual notions of majority. So 'international law' is not normative on objective criteria.

The 1959 and 1990 laws broach the matter of child labour:

> Children must be protected from any form of negligence, cruelty or exploita-tion. They must never be subjected to any form of trade whatsoever. Children must not be admitted to employment before a suitable minimum age; they must never be compelled or authorized to take up an occupation or job which is harmful to their health or education or which hinders their physical, mental or moral development. (UN Declaration, 1959)

> The Member States recognize the rights of children to protection from economic exploitation, or from being compelled to any work involving risk or liable to jeopardize their education or harm their physical, mental, spiritual, moral or social development. The Member States shall take legislative, adminis-trative, social and educational measures [...] in particular: specify a minimum age or ages for admission to employment; provide suitable regulation of working hours and conditions of employment. (UN Convention, 1990)

These very broad laws are theoretically clarified in Convention no. 138 on the minimum age for admission to employment: 'The minimum age [...] shall not be less than the age of completion of compulsory schooling and, in any case, shall not be less than 15 years.' For countries 'whose economy and educational facilities are insufficiently developed', this may be lowered to fourteen years. So-called 'light' work is admissible for children from thirteen to fifteen years of age (twelve to fourteen for the aforementioned countries) as long as it does not prejudice their health, development or attendance at school. Work 'likely to jeopardize the health, safety or morals of young persons' is inadmissible before the age of eighteen or, with special dispen-sation, sixteen years. Ultimately, then, we are left with an age range stretching from twelve to eighteen years, as summarized in the table below:

TABLE 8.1 Minimum age for admission to employment according to Convention no. 138

Type of work	Basic minimum age	Exceptional cases
Normal	15	14
Light	3 to 15	12 to 14
Hazardous	18	16

The Convention's 'flexibility' is even further accentuated by the fact that it does not have to be applied for certain 'limited categories of employment or work'.

Its content is astonishing: although supposedly designed to bring about 'the effective abolition of child labour', it actually authorizes such labour by means of flexible provisions and a range of special dispensations. It is unfortunately typical of the paralysis of international institutions yielding to the interests of the strong and the cynicism of states which should be working for the good of their populations, yet propose or ratify laws allowing the exploitation of children to persist. It makes one wonder what purpose a convention like this might serve: perhaps it is intended to do no more than mark another stage in the very slow development of international thinking. Let us leave this point with a reminder that after coming into force on 19 June 1976, the Convention was ratified on 31 October 1994 by only seventy-six states (BIT 1995: 133).

An examination of national laws (ILO 1991: 224) shows that only 59 of the 140 countries documented have set the basic minimum age for normal work at fifteen or over. For the other 81, it varies between twelve and fourteen years; six have set it at twelve (Egypt, Morocco, Qatar, Sudan, Thailand, Yemen).

The authors of the various chapters in this book, by the way, refer to a rather scattered range of age groups. At the bottom of the scale are children aged between four and twelve, while the top end extends from twelve to nineteen; nineteen-year-olds enter the frame only when the limited availability of statistics has forced authors to work with the fifteen to nineteen age group.

The Imprecision of Statistics

The statistics published by the various different countries can hardly be said to paint an accurate picture of the scale of the phenomenon of child labour: 'an erratic representation in statistics carefully conceals their true number' (Ramanathan). Indeed, they are based on censuses, surveys and administrative sources whose focus is all too often narrowed down to persons over a particular age (fifteen years, sometimes ten or twelve). Even when the field researchers or census-takers opt for a low starting age for the question of working activities (e.g. six, ten or twelve years), they do not necessarily go to the trouble of properly completing their questionnaires on this point; perhaps because they consider it to be of secondary importance, or because they have not been well enough briefed.

There are many reasons for this: a general problem of statistical definition of work-types; the difficulty in detecting illegal work-types (i.e. which employ children below the minimum age); low awareness of the phenomenon on the part of the statisticians, even those undertaking employment surveys.

Table 8.2 shows the percentages of ten- to fourteen-year-old children[1] at work in eighty-five countries, as compiled by the ILO from various national sources during the 1980s. The figures presented are not intended for general use. Quite the contrary. The intention is to put potential users on their guard, for the inconsistencies are plain to see.

TABLE 8.2 Work rates of children aged ten to fourteen years in various countries (per cent)

Region, country	Boys	Girls	Region, country	Boys	Girls
Africa			**Latin America**		
Algeria	0.6	0.1	Argentina	8.8	4.4
Angola	1.9	0.8	Bolivia	10.8	6.9
Benin	36.6	27.2	Brazil	25.0	11.6
Burkina-Faso*	–	–	Chile	–	–
Cameroon	10.4	9.6	Colombia	5.6	3.5
Chad	59.2	18.7	Costa Rica	11.9	2.2
Egypt	12.4	1.4	Cuba	–	–
Ethiopia	47.8	43.1	Dominican Republic	19.9	11.0
Guinea	35.9	28.4	Ecuador	–	–
Malawi	10.9	10.8	El Salvador	30.7	12.4
Mauritius	11.2	3.4	Guatemala	27.8	8.2
Morocco	16.5	11.9	Haiti	26.0	22.0
Nigeria	4.0	1.8	Honduras	26.8	2.7
Senegal	61.0	38.5	Jamaica	0.6	0.2
South Africa	–	–	Mexico	11.1	3.4
Sudan	39.0	25.3	Nicaragua	25.9	6.9
Togo	12.7	12.7	Panama	6.5	2.5
Tunisia	2.7	4.0	Paraguay	19.7	4.0
Zimbabwe	–	–	Peru	3.1	2.5
			Trinidad and Tobago	–	–
			Venezuela	–	–

TABLE 8.2 continued

Region, country	Boys	Girls	Region, country	Boys	Girls
Asia, Oceania			**North America**		
Australia	–	–	Canada	–	–
Bangladesh	39.4	30.4	United States	–	–
China	–	–			
Hong Kong	–	–	**Europe**		
India	13.5	10.3	Austria	–	–
Indonesia	12.4	9.2	Bulgaria	0.1	0.1
Iran	5.5	2.5	Czech Republic	–	–
Iraq	6.2	1.1	Denmark	–	–
Japan	–	–	Finland	–	–
Jordan	3.2	0.2	France	–	–
Kuwait	–	–	Greece	–	
Malaysia	8.8	6.5	Hungary	0.2	0.3
Mongolia	0.4	0.2	Ireland	–	–
Myanmar	10.2	11.5	Latvia	–	–
Nepal	–	–	Netherlands	–	–
New Zealand	–	–	Poland	–	–
Pakistan	19.2	6.9	Portugal	5.2	5.2
Philippines	–	–	Romania	–	–
Singapore	–	–	Slovakia	–	–
South Korea	0.3	0.4	Sweden	–	–
Sri Lanka	5.3	4.6	Switzerland	–	–
Syria	6.2	4.2	Turkey	–	–
United Arab Emirates	–	–	United Kingdom	–	–
Vietnam	–	–			

Note * – means zero or less than 0.05 per cent.
Source: BIT 1995

Let us take the thirty-seven countries claiming a zero rate of working children (including twenty-one of the twenty-four developed countries); considering some of their social realities and how they compare to one another, this appears surprising to say the least. In Africa, for instance, South Africa, Burkina Faso and Zimbabwe are all on zero, while very high rates are registered for Benin, Chad, Ethiopia (43 per cent of girls), Guinea, Senegal (61 per cent of boys), Sudan and Chad. Similar remarks can just as easily be made of the other continents. There is a very low rate in twenty countries for boys (less than 10 per cent) and in thirty-two countries for girls. Once again it is astonishing to find such low figures for Nigeria, Iran, Jamaica or Peru.

There does appear to be one common denominator nevertheless: with the exception of four countries (Myanmar, South Korea, Hungary and Tunisia), rates for boys are mostly higher than for girls. The main reason for this is without doubt the fact that the various sources fail to take account of housework.

In Europe, Portugal is the only country showing anything other than a zero rating, which makes one wonder about the reliability of figures from the other countries of southern Europe (e.g. Greece or Turkey).

Despite the great uncertainty surrounding the statistics, however, a recent ILO study (Ashagrie 1993: xi–xxvi) estimated that percentages of ten- to fourteen-year-old children working at world level in 1990 (or in the 124 countries monitored, at least) stood at 15.7 per cent of all boys belonging to that age group and 11.5 per cent of girls. Taking the developing countries of the sample in isolation, corresponding percentages come to 19.1 and 14.1 respectively. Notwithstanding the doubts about the decimal points, this still means that the phenomenon must be affecting between 100 and 200 million children world-wide.

Perceptions of Child Labour

Whatever the scale of the phenomenon, it is perceived in a wide variety of differing ways depending on the times, the countries and the group in question.

Rosilene Alvim demonstrates this very clearly when she talks about childhood in Brazil gradually becoming a 'social problem', leading to the 1990 Children and Adolescents Act passed thanks to the influence of the new actors (educators, NGOs) emerging to work alongside the more traditional ones (journalists, lawyers etc.). These new actors have managed to gain children and adolescents recognition as 'subjects of law' (Fukui). However, Lia Fukui uses studies of the press of the 1970s and early 1980s to point out how 'the popular press does not consider child labour to be a topic for public debate'. When newspapers do actually talk about it, they and public opinion largely tend to regard poverty as the chief cause: putting children to work is part of family survival strategies. So there is no systematic campaign to combat child labour as such. Some see it as a means of introducing children to the world of work. Others take the analysis further and seek to root out the causes of poverty, which may be regarded as the product of the capitalist system and/or the inequalities between North and South (in the shape of structural adjustment programmes, for example).

Other suggestions as to the causes of child labour include the breakdown of the family (leading to the emergence of street children) or, very often, the lack of schools (or the mediocrity and cost of those that do exist). But there are also children who work *and* attend school: they, then, are working in order to be able to afford to go to school.

Finally, child labour is often regarded as a lesser evil than marginality, delinquency and crime (Alvim).

The debates focus above all on street children. Street children seem to be accepted by the inhabitants of Mexico City in so far as they provide services; and yet 'the press presents them as individuals who are worthless to society, beggars' and is 'naturally too quick to associate child street-workers with delinquency and drugs' (Taracena). Indeed, 'the media portrayal of street children consists of stereotypical pictures of dirty kids in rags, for ever sniffing glue, loitering and sleeping on the streets. Despite being nowhere near true, it is none the less an image that sticks' (Mérienne).

The authorities for their part often turn a blind eye to child labour (Anwar). This can result in a number of objective constraints (poor means of intervention, red tape). They choose to ignore it either because they are corrupt or because child labour is quite simply part of a widely accepted 'system' underpinning the power and survival of the ruling classes and the upper ranks of the civil service, and the source of numerous advantages: 'It is a manifestation of the logic and rationality of the (capitalist) system' (Schibotto and Cussianovitch 1994: 223). When the authorities do take an interest in tackling child labour, it is ultimately above all through measures of a legislative order.

Child Labour Legislation

The above-mentioned laws on the minimum age for admission to employment are based on the idea that no one is seeking to eradicate child labour (not for the time being, at least), but to improve legislation in such a way as to make it 'more humane' via special regulations covering medical examinations, night work, mine work, working hours, weekly rest periods, annual holidays etc. and to have them enforced (a problem of general underadministration, particularly the shortage of inspectors). This means 'an implicit acceptance of the inevitability of child labour' (Ramanathan).

As Michel Bonnet recalls in his work on Africa, however, it often happens that 'legislation benefits industry in a country that is essentially agricultural; focuses on the structured sector whereas it is relatively rare to find children working there; and excludes from its field of application so-called family firms and domestic or farming work, i.e. the very areas where child labour is at its most widespread' (Bonnet 1993: 411–30). What is more, many people, sometimes including the children themselves, believe that 'the appealing to and application of the law may well assume more froward than educational aspects', with the danger that 'those practices will be driven further underground and therefore rendered more dangerous' (D. Bonnet).

Finally, if it certainly is necessary to draft and progressively improve the laws, three types of approaches can be adopted (Ramanathan): realism (accepting reality), pragmatism (the art of the possible) and idealism (imagination). Yet legislative intervention alone is not enough. Other action needs to be taken.

Action to Combat Child Labour

It is not enough simply to denounce child labour and call for its immediate eradication. Action may be taken according to a reformist approach. Experience acquired in the matter allows one to suggest two lines of thought:

- there has been a lot of indirect action which, in addressing specific population groups (refugees, migrants, abandoned children, etc.), inevitably takes account of child labour but has done little to tackle it head-on
- the diversity of situations faced by working children makes them a highly complex group which is difficult to cater to in a single, all-purpose policy (Banpasirichote)

So direct action must be planned within the framework of a global approach, with diversified measures applied at central and local levels addressing high-risk environments as a priority (the most hazardous occupations and branches of industry), and backed up with on-the-ground initiatives (organizing the children, street educators, NGOs). The programmes to be put in place certainly ought to include two important aspects in particular: awareness-raising to awaken public opinion to the problem and services for the children themselves (information, hygiene and health, nutrition; school support etc).

What really needs to be done, however, is to clarify perceptions of working children. All too often, as 'children they are not really workers and as workers they are not really children'. And 'the child continues to be perceived as a social object which, because of the supposed nature of its condition, is incapable of asserting itself and contributing to the community', rather than as a social actor or subject. As a result, NGO action is increasingly becoming geared towards 'restoring children's true identity' and relying upon them to assume a responsible role in bringing about the necessary changes to their working and living conditions. This new identity must be 'not just individual, but also collective, social and political', so that the children become the actors of social change (Schibotto and Cussianovitch 1994: 223).

Finally, percentages of children in education must be raised because 'unschooled children form a reserve army for the world of labour' (Bonnet 1993), even if 'school activities do not (necessarily) prevent children from working' (Fukui). Education sometimes comes up against 'a child labour-friendly attitude on the part of the community: i.e. a work ethic, an outlook on life that puts work before school' (Céspedes Sastre et al.). And even if the education systems come in for a good deal of criticism and are subjected to in-depth reform, Lia Fukui sees school as the only 'institution able to give children a minimum of training and allow them to prepare for employment and life in adult society'. Having said that, many countries are making no headway with regard to schooling and one even observes a trend of children 'dropping out' as structural adjustment programmes are implemented and state support is withdrawn as a result (Lange, Ravololomanga, Toto).

These are just some of the difficulties faced in the struggle to protect working children, to combat and abolish child labour, and quite simply to allow them access to 'childhood rights'.

References

Ashagrie, K. (1993) 'Statistics on Child Labour. A Brief Report', *Bulletin of Labour Statistics*, 3.

BIT (1992) *Le travail dans le monde*, Geneva, ILO.

— (1995) *Le travail dans le monde*, Geneva, ILO.

Bonnet, M (1993) 'Le travail des enfants en Afrique', *Revue internationale du travail*, 132, 3, pp. 411–30.

ILO (1991) 'Child Labour: Law and Practice', *Conditions of Work Digest*, 10, 1, Geneva, ILO.

Myers, W. E. (ed.) (1992) *Protéger les enfants au travail*, New York, UNICEF.

Schibotto, G. and A. Cussianovich (1994) *Working Children. Building an Identity*, Lima, MAN-THOC.

INTERNATIONAL TEXTS

1959 – Declaration of the Rights of the Child, UN.

1973 – Convention Concerning the Minimum Age for Admission to Employment, ILO.

1990 – Convention on the Rights of the Child, UN.

CHAPTER 9

Why is Child Labour Tolerated?
The Case of Brazil

Lia Fukui

Crianças de fibra (Courageous Children) is the title of a photographic book offering an unadulterated picture of the exploitation of ten- to thirteen-year-old child labourers in Brazil. The accompanying text presents extracts from interviews where the children talk about their working day, the physical effort demanded of them, the dangers, the unhealthy conditions and poor wages. Published in 1994 with the backing of the ILO, a number of trade unions and an institution defending the rights of children, the book marks a moment of raised awareness in areas of society other than academia and the usual champions of human rights.

This chapter sets out to underscore the disparity between legislation and the real-life facts, as well as the indifference and ambiguity of the media.

To begin with, a definition of the notion of *labour* in the broadest and most general sense of the term: *any activity aimed directly or indirectly at earning a living.* When the responsibility is shouldered by a child, it becomes child labour. Tasks done within the home to meet the most basic needs – food, clothing, shelter, rest – are also regarded as labour and mostly performed by adults. Children can assist in such tasks and, when they do so under adult guidance, it moves into the realms of apprenticeship or informal, socialization-oriented education. Considering the wide range of activities children under-take, however, it is hard to tell what share of it is assisting and exchange, and what share 'the collective daily labour of the poor', inside the home or out. In any event, the rights of children to care and protection, and school and leisure-time activities have become the norm for contemporary society.

In the majority of working-class households, a child does the domestic chores to leave an adult free to find paid work and attend to the family's needs. When the children themselves are the ones going out to secure their own subsistence or that of an adult, we see a situation of extreme exploitation taking shape. Hence, the first sign to suggest that a family is successfully managing to secure the minimum needed for survival is when children are left free to attend school.

In Brazil, according to data from PNAD (National Domiciliary Sample Survey), the families with children at school are the ones where per capita income is twice the minimum working wage (some 12.8 per cent of the total PNAD sample population for 1990). The same ratio was found by an earlier empirical survey carried out at the beginning of the 1980s (Fukui et al. 1980).

Let us begin with the assumption that any child not attending school is in one way or another obliged to work for its living. Having said that, it is worth remembering that although school activities do not exclude children from employment, employment can exclude them from school.

What is a child? Societies generally develop their own defining criteria according to age, duties and responsibilities. Like most other western countries, Brazil adheres to the following age divisions: six years, pre-school; seven years, reading and writing; twelve years, vocational apprenticeship; fourteen years, compulsory schooling and, with some restrictions and specific protective measures, access to the labour market; sixteen years, the right to vote; eighteen years, civil majority. Although simple enough at first sight, there are a number of ambiguities. For example, the twelve to fourteen years bracket is simultaneously classed as a time for schooling and for vocational apprenticeship. There is no strictly regulated minimum apprenticeship age.

In this article, we tackle the issue of under fourteen-year-old labour in the light of three parameters: acquired knowledge, legislation on children and adolescents and information as relayed by the media, particularly the popular press. The hypothesis is that these authorities have parallel, not to say divided, lines of discourse. How come child labour is tolerated in Brazil?[1] We shall attempt to draft the terms of a policy proposal for furthering the effective protection of the child in the workplace, according to the law and justice principles advocated by the recent Children and Adolescents Act.

Acquired Knowledge: Exposure

The 1970 census and the 1977 PNAD regard the lower age limit of the active population to be ten years. This gives us our starting point for measuring the extent of child labour in Brazilian society. The quantitative data highlighted by the censuses have bestowed greater legitimacy on the few empirical research projects previously conducted in rural areas (Antuniassi 1981; Ribeiro 1982). It has also been possible to evaluate the amount of child labour in the big cities and begin constructing a problematic on the topic. Alvim and Valladares (1988) ran an inventory of existing literature on the theme of childhood and found forty-one publications (19 per cent) on child labour. Rizzini (1989) says there have been forty-five such items since the beginning of the 1970s. Although the lion's share of these surveys concentrate on the over-fourteens, the large number of publications suggests that it is a topic of growing academic importance. Not all of the surveys on child and adolescent labour categorize subjects according to age. Hence the first major difficulty: working children under the age of ten years are excluded from the data and it is hard to establish the differences and particularities of the work of apprentices according to their age (short of postulating that the amount of labour among the under-twelves is negligible, a fact largely refuted by a certain number of empirical publications, as we shall see).

CHILD LABOUR AMONG THE TENS TO FOURTEENS AS CHARACTER-IZED BY THESE PUBLICATIONS   During the 1970s and 1980s, child labour, associated with survival strategies, was thought to reproduce poverty. Calsing et al. (1986) define poverty as 'inadequate access to goods and services and non-satisfaction of the vital requirements of food, housing, health, etc.'. In agreement with Zylberstajn et al. (1985), they declare it to be highly trans-missible, with recourse to child labour constituting the link between 'old and new poverty, thus perpetuating the instability of the means needed to secure a living'. From the same point of view, and taking the PNAD surveys as reference, Zylberstajn et al. (1985) studied households with a per capita income of under a quarter of the minimum wage per person and found that between 1970 and 1980 the percentage of working children in the hired labour force belonging to this income bracket grew by 36 per cent. They show that:

- many children are forced to begin work from the ages of eight or nine
- the younger the child, the greater the job insecurity
- the younger the child, the lower the pay
- children work as long as adults: 62 per cent are on an average of forty-eight hours a week
- the money they earn contributes wholly or in part to the income of a third of all households

Calsing et al. (1986) add that there are twice as many male children and adolescents in this population and that half (under the age of seventeen) belong to a rural environment.

Juarez (1991) lists three different ways in which children help with the family expenses, the first being the most prevalent: producing a pay packet, providing for the whole family and giving unpaid labour.

In a recent study of the census, Ribeiro and Sabòia (1993) show that 73 per cent of ten- to fourteen-year-olds study, 9.8 per cent study and work, and 8.3 per cent just work. Of the ones who work, 46.5 per cent are on forty hours a week and 9.2 per cent receive more than a minimum wage per month.

CHARACTERISTIC FEATURES OF CHILD LABOUR IN RURAL AREAS AND IN THE METROPOLIS   It is worth recalling the scale of Brazilian society: 140 million people inhabit 8 million km²; economic and social groups are tremendously heterogeneous. Meanwhile, widespread poverty goes hand in hand with economic development and the concentration of income, leaving a large part of the population on the sidelines of economic progress; and judging by school attendance figures, we can safely say that child labour among them has become rife.

In the primary sector (agricultural production, mining), children are recruited either within the family or as waged labourers. The family unit is where we find the widest variety of circumstances, from those of the *posseiros* (tenant farmers selling surplus produce in order to obtain manufactured goods) through to the most sophisticated forms of capitalist agriculture. However they may be recruited, children will be released from having to work only when adult earnings are sufficient for family needs.

Most *posseiros* are based in areas of intensive agriculture and capital development and, for some time already, there has been a noticeable need for waged work on the part of some family group members. The men go out in search of work down the mines or road-building and leave subsistence production in the hands of the women, children and elderly. Division of labour is organized in such a way as to leave the adults free for the heavier work, with the children gradually joining in then taking over. Starting at the age of three or four years, they are first given lighter jobs such as carrying water from the well, gathering twigs for tinder or looking after younger siblings, until the day they replace the adult in the housework and, later, in the fields (Fukui 1979). These *posseiros* (literally 'occupiers') are prone to eviction by the landlord; eviction and violence are the fruits of capital development in pioneer districts (Martins 1992). In these regions of already capitalist production units (small-scale landowners commercially cultivating rice, tobacco and tea), the family is being reinstated as a production unit and counts on every available hand for production (Martins 1992).

Among seasonal wage-earners (*volantes*, *boias-frias*, in the high technology areas) child labour is used on a clandestine yet perfectly well organized basis. Capitalizing on the absence of public labour inspectors in country regions, *turmeiros* (freelance labour agents) recruit child workers and hire out their services to the proprietors of large farming concerns, without putting the employers under the least obligation towards their employees. These children work in secret for low wages and with no protection whatsoever. Gnacarini maintains that

> child labour is in steady and continuous growth in São Paulo state agriculture and accounts for 15 to 20 per cent of the labour force depending on the sector and type of work. Percentages are higher still among peanut, bean and corn pickers and egg collectors: rising, at certain times of the year, to over 50 per cent. The most brutal forms of exploitation hold sway, abusing the children's utter powerlessness. Employers can act with even greater impunity thanks to the complete absence of state regulations. They refuse to have anything to do with contracts and the unions see themselves barred from interfering in the field of labour. (Gnacarini 1992)

The picture in the state capitals is more heterogeneous and corresponds to the distinctive features of the regional markets. Regional differences aside, however, there are a number of common denominators. Spindel (1985, 1989), surveying eight of Brazil's district capitals, examines the conditions under which waged labour came to be legalized for ten- to eighteen-year-olds. His survey may well have included only a small number of working apprentices (twelve to fourteen years), but he gleans enough information to be able to show that these youngsters work harder and are more punctual than adults; their working day is over nine hours long and some 70 per cent of them have by rights adult duties to perform – above all when they belong to the female labour force of the clothing industry. Two-thirds of all the young workers studied are exposed to noise, fumes, chemicals or other health-threatening conditions. Sometimes responsible for a large part of the family income, they receive lower wages than adults. Legally regarded as minors, they are represented by their families in the signing and cancelling of contracts, the retrieval of service-linked guarantee funds, and it is therefore their families who benefit from the fruits of their labour. Trade unions accept them as members, but refuse them the right to vote and to be elected; without institutional protection, they can neither organize nor make demands.

Working children find themselves employed, in descending order: as paid domestics in a private household or domestic helps at home; in the services sector or small workshops with no fixed working hours or, in most cases, as freelance earners; as sellers, wrappers and so on, for established firms. Only a fraction of them, therefore, are street-workers. Actually, the latter are generally hidden away in places where they feel sheltered, which makes them harder to detect.

A government agency has conducted a sector-by-sector census of children and adolescents on the streets of São Paulo city (population 12 million). Thirty six per cent of the 4520 children and adolescents counted on 16 September 1993 were found to be wandering around, 36 per cent were working, 12 per cent playing games and 9 per cent begging; with the remainder distributing leaflets, sleeping etc. It then counted 895 children or adolescents on Friday 1 October 1993 at dawn: 42 per cent drifting, 35 per cent sleeping, 15 per cent working and the rest begging or playing. One sees how difficult it is to gauge the expansion of labour among the children.

Pires (1988) interviewed ten- to fourteen-year-old freelance and hired workers performing a variety of different activities on the streets of São Paulo: car attendants, marketplace porters, shoeshiners, pedlars etc. He demonstrates that there are no major differences between the various sectors from the point of view of 'qualifications' and working hours (the informal sector is not necessarily any worse than the formal). Work in the informal sector is more spasmodic: it is common to see a child in charge of more than one activity at a time, e.g. market porters selling snacks, icecream-sellers watching cars, collecting litter etc. The main difference is seen with regard to income: up to one and a half times the minimum wage in the formal sector and between three-quarters and double in the informal. Wages are directly linked to working hours: top earnings corresponding to forty hours a week, lower ones to twenty-five hours. For the best-paid jobs, children have to compete with adult labour. Alves (1991) has similar things to say in a comparison of children working in the city-centre and the residential districts of Rio de Janeiro as car attendants, litter collectors, shoeshine boys and girls and so on.

Taken as a whole, these surveys allow for the following conclusions:

1. Children's labour is an integral part of day-to-day family life for its important contribution to household revenues or in the housework, which goes against the argument that their contribution might not be indispensable.

2. It is on account of survival needs that work is sought outside the home. On average, children start from the age of nine years, mainly close to familiars or acquaintances at places in the neighbourhood such as small workshops or services; little by little, their working hours grow longer and they acquire abilities that allow them to compete for an adult's post.

3. The situation of child wage-earners is rarely legalized in the formal sector of the economy (7 per cent of the total according to Spindel), while their jobs and working hours are identical to those of adult workers.

4. We must distinguish between the working conditions of ten- to fourteen-year-olds and those of the fourteens to eighteens. The former enter the labour market not only stripped of any advantages, but with no legal protection whatsoever, in activities regarded as marginal: illicit work (in rural areas) and the informal market for merchandise salvaged from dumping grounds, marketplace refuse etc.

5. Paid labour and schooling are, of course, interrelated. Practising the former can easily lead to falling behind with the latter; many children will subsequently stop school altogether because they are unable to reconcile it with a long day's work. Recent data, however, show that, in the south-east of the country at least, every child goes to school. Barros (1991) draws attention to the fact that girls have a far higher level of schooling than boys. Madeira (1993) observes that there is no systematic link between poverty, child labour and dropping out of school. It would therefore be more accurate to say that, in urban centres at least, school attendance can be seen going hand in hand with work; we see a considerable backwardness in the age–education level ratio, attendances lasting five to eight years, failure and exclusion from the education system when school cannot be adapted to reality. School represents a value in eyes of the working classes, but the education system does not help them to attain that value, since it automatically excludes anyone who does not conform to its own established model pupil (Demartini 1988; Madeira 1993). So much so that, contrary to conservative opinion, child labour is linked more to poverty and the absence of public policies than to working-class misgivings about school (for needy families,

school actually represents expenses – uniforms, stationery – which they cannot really afford).

HOW THE YOUNG PEOPLE VIEW THEIR WORK The workers under the greatest pressure from the family group are the tens to fourteens. Almost all contribute their whole pay packet to the family housekeeping; very few keep any of it to spend as they please. The situation is different for older children in the countryside and city alike. Fukui (1979), Madeira (1993), Spindel (1989) show that their labour puts them in a position of autonomy; while a share of their income goes towards the family housekeeping, the remainder is for personal expenses.

Interviewing nine- to seventeen-year-old São Paulo boys and girls working in a variety of different activities, Gouveia (1983) found: great mobility in the jobs performed; no opportunities for acquiring skills; school pupils dropping out because of a need to work; personal responsibility for the use of earnings; and, most importantly, these children 'expressed a feeling of self-achievement, even pride, because they were working and thus doing their bit for the family's upkeep'. This, the author concludes, transforms the need to work 'into a virtue'. It matches the views of Rizzini (1991): in the eyes of working children, work is seen as a resolute duty and, at the same time, as a legitimate means of gaining a place in society.

Overall, the surveys show a certain unanimity (or complementarity) which makes it possible to establish a relatively coherent body of knowledge about child labour. The most frequently cited causes for child labour are: poverty, the breaking up of the family and Brazil's own special brand of capitalist production.

Three Theories about Child Labour

1. CHILD LABOUR IS CAUSED BY POVERTY This theory enjoys the unanimous support of the authors who have studied the problem. However, a number of differences in the way they formulate their arguments allows us to clarify this stance further. The theory that poverty is transmitted from one generation to the next, with the premature labour of children acting as 'the link between old poverty and new' was put forth by Zylberstajn et al. (1985). It is partly refuted by Barros (1991): there is 'no direct evidence to prove that precocious labour entails lower future revenues and constitutes a medium of poverty transmission from generation to generation'. The data from the various surveys and censuses have helped to produce a contrasted picture of poverty. A study by the SEADE Foundation (1993) takes in housing, instruction, employment and revenue in order to characterize the needs as well as how juvenile labour is integrated into work.

The complementary theory which considers that poverty stems from urbanization and rural–urban migration is firmly refuted by census data demonstrating that there are no major differences in terms of either sectors of activity, earnings or living conditions, between migrant and non-migrant workers. Even more important data concern the fact that in most metropolitan areas of Brazil activity rates are higher in the migrant than the non-migrant population (Pires 1988, referring to the work of Campino).

2. CHILD LABOUR IS CAUSED BY THE BREAKING UP OF THE FAMILY
This theory is refuted by the census data and qualitative empirical work alike. Parents resort to child labour because of poverty. Families comprised of single mothers with very young children are the ones most likely to find themselves on the poverty line. Child labour will then become a must for the livelihood of the family group. Studies performed among the child street-workers of Rio de Janeiro showed virtually all these children to be living with their families (Fausto and Cervini 1991).

One of the survival strategies highlighted by Fonseca (1993) consists of the to and fro of children between friends and neighbours for given periods, or while their fathers and/or mothers face a situation of great hardship. Such survival strategies point to values and priorities which diverge from those of the middle classes. We therefore have forms of structure and organization and not necessarily a situation of break-up and abandonment as has been presented in the literature.

3. CHILD LABOUR IS AN 'INTRINSIC POTENTIALITY IN THE CAPITAL-IST MODE OF PRODUCTION' The notion of childhood – based on Aries' work, now regarded as a classic – stems from fundamental changes in the division of labour: the emergence of a private domestic sphere wherein women, domestic employees and children are kept out of the world of individualized labour and public life, now the prerogative of men. Women find themselves confined to bringing up children, who undergo preparation for life and employment on the fringes of society, in a field restricted solely to the home and school.

The bourgeois model extends throughout the western world, taking in working-class children, sheltering them from the exploitation of their labour through the institutionalization and universalization of school, as well as legislation banning child labour and regulating that of adolescents. Despite all the criticisms levelled at school, no other institution capable of giving children a minimum of training to prepare them for employment and life in adult society has yet been invented to take its place.

The forms of child labour specific to Brazilian capitalism concern, 'the fraction of the agricultural labour force composed of children and the [urban] working activities geared solely to survival needs and unaccompanied by the proletarianization process seen in the advanced capitalist countries during the early stages of industrialization' (Ribeiro 1982).

This process leads the excluded population – particularly children and adolescents – to transform public places (the streets) 'into an arena for survival struggles, private spaces for producing the resources, cash or kind, needed to support the family' (Ribeiro and Sabòia 1993). Martins (1991) goes on to say that in Brazil, as in the other countries of the Third World, one encounters 'children without a childhood'. Adorno talks about their 'unfinished socialization'.

> What we have here is a perverse form of integration which teaches children and adolescents to confront the adult worker in an unfair situation. As children, they retain their childish nature in the adult world. They find it hard to understand such a world via any other medium than *face-to-face* relationships, hard to contend with the urgency of everyday problems and, to confront others in any other language than that of violence. (Adorno 1991)

The knowledge produced in the course of the 1980s allows one to draw a more diversified picture of Brazilian realities describing and measuring the various forms of poverty, the survival strategies, the multiplicity of working-class family structures and patterns of organization and characterizing Brazilian capitalism's own specific forms of child employment as labour. If, however, depicting the problem in such a way justifies its public condemnation, it does not encourage thought as to which paths to follow and proposals to tender in order to resolve it: e.g. by drawing up public policies to defend the 'childhood rights'.

The notion of childhood gives rise to an important affirmation which, curiously enough, only one young researcher (Pires 1988) has unearthed in Brazilian literature: child labour is not inherent to capitalism, but the outcome of specific, concrete forms of that mode of production. This affirmation allows one to accept denunciations of child labour within Brazilian society, while at the same time looking into the possibility of responding to them. If capitalism can do without child labour, it is up to society, the political parties, trades unions and social movements to interrupt the process, to give children the chance to leave the labour market and secure protection and access to school.

The Law: A Two-tiered Concept of Justice

Anti-child labour laws in Brazil are similar in almost every respect to those of the other Latin American countries who all, at virtually the same time, adopted the same ideas, institutions and references, albeit tailored to individual national specificities (Mendez 1992). Brazilian law remained attached to its Minors' Code until 1990, when the Children and Adolescents Act came into force.

THE MINORS' CODE Promulgated in 1927 and based on the principle of the right to protection, the Minors' Code established minors as a legally recognized group, allowing legal action to be brought *vis-à-vis* children and adolescents in an irregular situation. 'Irregular situation' referred to any situation not conforming to the accepted labour and education norms of the day; the minors in question were regarded as members of supposedly broken families associated with poverty and moral neglect. Poor children had to be protected from their families and, if in an irregular situation, withdrawn from their social milieu for re-education. Consequently, a new legal category – civil minority – and an ensemble of institutions were devised to take charge of the re-education of the alleged 'lost sheep'. So the state decided the matter of civil minority by bringing in special standards, as if there were two sets of weights and measures: one for poor children and another for the rest of society (Alvim and Valladares 1988).

The sixty years during which the Minors' Code was in force saw jurists fighting tooth and nail over proposals relating to child labour. Sometimes the proposals they were defending advocated a combination of work and school attendance for twelve- to fourteen-year-olds (the 1946 constitution); sometimes they assumed a more conservative stance in the name of realism. An example: having neither requested the judge's consent nor considered the right to welfare, jurists suggested that underage labour be paid 50 to 75 per cent of the basic minimum wage (the 1967 constitution; the 1989 'Courageous Boy' programme).

Legislative changes have always been based on two relatively contradictory presuppositions: that the minor needs to be given protection at work and, that work is a lesser evil than the dangers of marginality and delinquency.

THE CHILDREN AND ADOLESCENTS ACT The Children and Adolescents Act, which came into force in 1990, is the outcome of a major social movement to redemocratize the country. The general underlying principles of the Act – based on the United Nations tenet of full protection – were defined when the constitution was reformed in 1988. Since children are still developing as individuals, it regards them as having their own rights and requiring differentiated, specific and complete protection. Chapter 5 of the Children and Adolescents Act deals with the right to work and employment; the prohibition of labour under the age of fourteen, except in apprenticeship; vocational apprenticeship in line with the guidelines and basic principles of the education laws; guaranteed apprenticeship grants for children and adolescents up to the age of fourteen; guaranteed labour and welfare rights for apprentices under the age of fourteen; the banning of night work from 10 p.m. to 5 a.m.; overly heavy work, long hours or unhealthy conditions likely to jeopardize school attendance.

The law stipulates equal pay and recognizes the right to welfare as well as the special position of the working adolescent. It nevertheless has to be said that the definitions relating to apprentices, apprenticeship grants and socio-educational work are so imprecise that the law remains ambiguous and offers loopholes allowing for child recruitment. The jurists working together to produce the Children and Adolescents Act had been so concerned about removing the punitive aspects which marked the earlier Minors' Code, that they did not give enough thought to detail, leaving it open to interpretation and allowing children to be hired without a contract.[2] What is more, the ideological wrangling has not really been laid to rest either. Many people still consider child and adolescent labour as a lesser evil, a solution to delinquency.

So the Act attempts to adapt the legal machinery to the new legislation, by coming up against a number of different interpretations. Here, for example, is a transcript of the commentary relating to Chapter 4, 'For the Protection of the Work of Minors': 'The Constitution promulgated on October 5, 1988, fixed the minimum working age for minors at 14 years. It opens up a limited space targeting the apprentice. Everything leads one to believe that the legion of idle youths, a medium for juvenile delinquency, is tending towards growth' (SAAD 1990). An expert on the Act confirms that: 'in actual fact, the family (which is lacking in structure and neglecting its children), the father (who is failing in his paternal duties) and the state (which is not carrying through its most elementary social policies) are the ones who are in a situation of illegality; never the child or adolescent' (Liberati 1991). Despite exonerating the children from all responsibility, prejudice against the poor remains: they are regarded as incompetent; meanwhile, the research work which highlights the fact that different family models exist in the various different sectors of society goes unheeded.

However, apart from its ambiguity *vis-à-vis* work, with its omission of an outright ban on recruitment under the age of fourteen years during schooling, the Child and Adolescents Act – a victory on the part of a major social movement including progressive jurists – has allowed the old picture of minors in an 'irregular situation' to be replaced by that of children and adolescents as people with rights.

The Media: Omission or Ideology?

It is through the press that the public debate can be best grasped in its most spontaneous and immediate form. The press airs the various different versions and views and allows us to reconstruct the arguments. Child labour figured among the themes in a survey made of the São Paulo popular press during the 1970s (Fukui et al. 1984). It centred on the following dailies: *O Estado de São Paulo* (now OESP), a liberal paper whose readers identify with the ruling classes; the middle-class *Folha de São Paulo* (FSP); *Notícias Populares* (NP), a working-class tabloid. Here are its main findings.

Child labour provoked scarcely any interest in the popular press of the 1970s. Only 31 (6 per cent) of the 512 sample columns had anything to do with the labour of ten- to fourteen-year-olds. All three dailies published exposures of the exploitation of child labour, but analyses differed considerably.

O Estado de São Paulo highlighted the facts of child labour in industry, on the markets and among the *guardas-mirins* (literally: 'watch-kids'). It noted how the law was flouted and reminded its readers of the measures needing to be taken to legalize labour. Adopting a legalistic stance, it totally ignored any questions as to the nature of the work or the absence of apprenticeship. It stood up for equal pay and the regulation of the forms of integration for adolescents employed. Three per cent of all the sample articles dealt with child labour, 39 per cent with delinquency.

Folha de São Paulo for its part looked at the question of employment and its regulation for street-workers. The paper's position on the matter was, to say the least, ambiguous, shifting with the times, the circumstances, the support it was expected to give to whoever was in power. It remarked on the children's state of neglect and the risks to which they were exposed, and embarked on a campaign for the regulation of underage labour and changes in the law. Ultimately, however, this only made it easier for employers to hire minors without contract: the emphasis placed on the scale of child employment went hand in hand with a call for flexibility as far as both working contracts and wages were concerned. The actual work itself was given little attention, the main thrust being that any work done under institutional control was better than the freedom of the streets. Comment always centred on apprenticeship as either an opportunity for social mobility or a means of preventing marginality and delinquency.

Notícias Populares defended official positions depicting child employment as a means of preventing delinquency, leaving not the slightest room for any discussion. It stood up for anyone who hired children under the guise of apprenticeship and training: businesses, churches, local government. It backed every official initiative, as well as combined labour–schooling for the under-fourteens. And articles on child labour (5 per cent) were well outnumbered by those dealing with delinquency (59 per cent).

The papers very rarely tackled the various different forms of exploitation of child labour. When they did so, it was always through an individual case, thus exempting the institutions from liability in any law-breaking. An example: a case of fraud discovered in a *guardas-mirins* organization was put down to the improper attitude of an employee who subsequently lost his job; the *guarda-mirin*, which hired seven- to twelve-year-old children and acted as an intermediary for labour recruitment, remained completely blameless as an institution.

The press of the 1970s was not at all interested in the flood of ten- to fourteen-year-old youngsters joining the economically active population. It did of course call for greater control and specific regulations; but child labour was tolerated for its role in helping to prevent delinquency. In any event, it considered child labour to be no topic for public debate; one can even go so far as to say that in the 1970s the press committed it to silence. Has the situation changed since the adopting of the Children and Adolescents Act in the early 1990s?

A systematic, albeit non-sampled, survey was carried out from 1990 to 1992 on the same São Paulo papers, plus a selection of popular Rio de Janeiro papers chosen according to the same criteria (dailies with a target readership of employers, middle and working classes). It found a similarly pitiful number of articles on child labour.

For the São Paulo papers, the figures were as follows: *O Estado de São Paulo*, thirteen articles; *Folha de São Paulo*, twenty-one; *Notícias Populares*, two. There were a few new terms not seen in the 1980s, e.g. *meninos de rua, garotos de rua* ('street children', 'street kids'),[3] but they basically made the same points and came to the same conclusions. *O Estado de São Paulo* maintained its legalistic stance; *Folha de São Paulo* gave greater importance to delinquency than the exploitation of child labour; *Notícias Populares* purely and simply ignored the matter.

For the Rio de Janeiro papers, the surveys looked at the *Jornal do Brasil*, *O Globo* and *O Dia*, which correspond in every respect to those studied in São Paulo. During the analysis period, all three published a large number of articles on child labour. When the *Jornal do Brasil* broached the subject, it indiscriminately used the terms *criança, garoto, menino de rua* and *menor* ('child', 'kid', 'boy', 'street boy' and 'minor'), in a tone without a hint of negative criticism.[4] *Meninos de rua* was the term found cropping up most in *O Globa*, although it also used *menores*, especially when dealing with child labour.[5] Not many articles actually went into the work itself (only 3 per cent). *O Dia* chiefly used *meninos de rua* and *menores carentes* ('needy minors'). It devoted more column space to labour questions (fifteen, or 50 per cent, of the thirty-five items surveyed).[6]

The Rio de Janeiro papers devoted a little more coverage to child labour during this period than the São Paulo ones and terminology changed everywhere. Discussions leading up to the Children and Adolescents Act had served to lend the term *menor* legal status, for it did not suggest an *a priori* idea of transgression and delinquency, keeping the sense of fair treatment based on a notion of justice and citizenship. It can nevertheless be said that the popular press of Rio as much as São Paulo did not regard child labour as a major subject for public debate.[7]

When the popular press turned to thoughts about possible future perspectives for children in Brazil, it still remained attached to the idea of neglect, scarce resources and the incompetence of the working classes. We cannot help but notice the enormous rift between acquired knowledge and the information relayed by the media. The press rendered the facts uniform and boiled them down. Apparently equivalent terms such as 'slave children', 'working children under the age of ten', 'ten- to twelve-year-old working children' or 'working children aged twelve to fourteen', conceal a variety of situations which could, if well-defined, attract varying forms of action on the part of the law. The press should be spearheading the public debate on child labour; so far, however, it has declined to supply really accurate information. And it hardly ever makes reference to the United Nations tenet of 'total protection for children', which treats the child as a subject entitled to full rights.

Conclusions and Perspectives

In the wake of democratization, Brazilian society has become less tolerant towards social injustices. There may be the beginnings of awareness-raising, but the Acts and bills still stem from incoherent, scattered practices in the field of both governmental and non-governmental action alike. If child labour is to be abolished once and for all, the principles and priorities which will allow a policy to be adopted must first be established.

Put forward by the ILO and executed in Brazil by government agencies, businesses and trade unions since 1992, the International Program for the Eradication of Child Labor (IPEC) sets out first to provide a better understanding of the reality of the situation.[8]

Analysis of the knowledge, the legislation and media helps shed light on some of the difficulties and indicates what needs to be done to bring the issue to the forefront of Brazilian society. Until now, researchers have produced data used to mount a campaign to denounce child labour; yet they have done very little to defend the children's interests, in so far as they have thus far declined to play any part in the drawing up of public policies designed to eradicate child labour in favour of school.

As mentioned, the law is ambiguous: while prohibiting child labour and recognizing that adolescent labour should be compatible with physical development, it gives no precise details with regard to the concepts of apprenticeship and socio-educational work. Such vagueness can only lead to underage labour being tolerated. For Brazil, the idea that children are citizens with rights is still a fairly recent one; there has to be some extensive, in-depth discussion if it is to develop.

Caught between denunciation and the ambiguity of the law, the media – society's sounding board – cannot talk about deeds of citizenship which might steer them towards upholding the rights of children. In order to do away with such tolerance of child labour once and for all, there is an urgent need to establish connections between research and organized society (social movements, trade unions, National Congress, local government, the state).

It is a matter of clearly defining social policies for employers and the unions, of highlighting the principle of equal rights and wages for adults and children, *school being a compulsory activity* for all children, as compulsory as the *supervision and protection* of adolescent labour. It is also a matter of publicly debating the sense and scope of the Children and Adolescents Act which, despite its uncertainties and imperfections, needs across-the-board support in order to make it into a legal tool for action in Brazilian society.

Notes

1. The tolerance in question being taken to mean a lenient attitude whereby public opinion forgives failings and focuses on the positive rather than the negative aspects of the situation.

2. For example, the 'Courageous Boy' programme (whose goal is the recruitment of adolescent labour with neither contract nor guarantees) was submitted to the authorities a second time for approval (February 1991) in the shape of a bill entitled 'Provisional Scheme for the Integration of Adolescents on the Labour Market'.

3. Examples: 'Kids in Control of Sorocaba Streets' (OESP, 19 August 1990, p. 32); 'Boituva Employs Street Children' (OESP, 4 October 1990, p. 13); ' Slave Children ' (NP, 6 June 1992, p. 5). Only the odd article talks about the actual work: 'Street Children Nurse Lunatic Asylum "Patients"' (FSP, 17 May 1992, p. 6); or put child labour exploitation in the headlines: '50,000 6- to 13-year-olds Assist with Alagoas Sugarcane Harvest' (FSP, 23 October 1991, with the full story on page 10: 'Children Working Illegally on Sugarcane Plantations').

4. A couple of examples: 'Street Boys Want Employment and School' (6 November 1990); 'Street Children Sell Their Plants at the Museum' (11 April 1991); 'New Kiddy Tourist Guides' (1 April 1992). Thirty-three (i.e. a quarter) of the 131 articles surveyed during this period dealt directly with child labour.

5. 'Needy Children Become Tourist Guides' (2 April 1991); 'Street Children Help Clean Public Park' (10 April 1991); 'Underage Shoeshiners; Same Work, Different Pay' (30 November 1991).

6. 'Companies Guilty of Exploiting Minors' (25 February 1992); or else, from an article by Carlos Nobre: 'Working Minors Fear Penal Minority' (8 April 1990).

7. The Porto Alegre daily, *Zero Hora*, takes a clearly more critical stance: 'Minors Exploited in the Provinces' (3 January 1992); 'Enslaved Children in a Living Hell' (1 May 1992). Still, the number of items published on the topic remained low: 7, or 12.8 per cent, of the seventy-nine articles surveyed.

8. At present, the material gathered includes 5540 references (2074 periodicals, 1337 monographs, 236 films, videos, photos and posters). Publication is in progress. Together with the synthesis presented here, the above-mentioned book, *Crianças de fibra* (Courageous Children) by Huzak and Azevedo (1994), and the video *Profissao: Criança* (Profession: Child) by Sandra Werneck are the first products of a coordinated effort extending throughout Brazil.

References

Adorno, S. (1991) 'A experiência precoce da punição', in: J. S. Martins (ed.), *O massacre dos inocentes*, pp. 181–208.

Alvarez, M. C. (1989) 'A emergência do código de menores de 1927: uma análise do discurso jurídico e institucional da assistência e proteção aos menores', *Mestrado em Sociologia*, FFLCH USP, São Paulo, Cortez.

Alves, A. (1991) 'Meninos e meninas da rua: estrutura e dinâmica familiar', in A. Fausto and R. Cervini (eds), *O trabalho e a rua*.

Alvim, R. and L. P. Valladares (1988) 'Infância e Sociedade no Brasil: uma análise da literatura', *Boletim bibliográfico brasileiro*, 26, BIB, Rio de Janeiro, pp. 3–37.

Antuniassi, M. H. (1981) *O trabalhador-mirim na agricultura paulista*, São Paulo, FFLCH USP.

Barros, R. (1991), in M. Fausto and M. Cervini, *O trabalho e a rua : crianças e adolescentes no Brasil urbano dos anos 80*, São Paulo, Cortez.

Calsing, E. et al. (1986) *O menor e a pobreza*, Brasilia, IPLAN-IPEA-UNICEF.

Chaia, M. (1987) 'O menor no mercado de trabalho', *São Paulo em perspectiva*, São Paulo, 1, 1, April–June, pp. 9–16.

— (1988) 'O jovem no mercado de trabalho', *O jovem na grande São Paulo*, São Paulo, SEADE Foundation, pp. 231–47.

Demartini, Z. (1988) 'Desilgualdade, trabalho e educação: a população rural em questão', *Cadernos de pesquisa*, São Paulo, 64, February, pp. 24–37.

Fausto, A. and R. Cervini (1991) *O trabalho e a rua: crianças e adolescentes no Brasil urbano dos anos 80*, São Paulo, Cortez.

Fonseca, C. (1993) 'Criança, família e desigualdade social no Brasil', in I. Rizzini (ed.), *Levantmento bibliográfico*.

Fukui, L. (1979) *Sertão e bairro rural, a família entre sitiantes tradicionais*, São Paulo, Atica.

Fukui, L. et al. (1980) *Escolarização e sociedade: um estudo dos excluídos da escola*, São Paulo, INEP-CERU.

— (1984) 'A questão do trabalho infantil na grande imprensa paulista na década de 70', 14th Reunião Brasileira de Antropologia, 15–18 April 1984, Brasilia.

— (1987) *O escolar, o trabalhador infantil e o menor na grande imprensa paulista na decada de 70*, São Paulo, Centro de Estudos Rurais e Urbanos.

Gnacarini, J. C. (1991) 'O trabalho infantil agrícola na era da alta tecnologia', in J. S. Martins (ed.), *O massacre dos inocentes*.

Gouveia, A. J. (1983) 'O trabalho do menor: necessidade transfigurada em virtude', *Cadernos de pesquisa*, São Paulo, 44, February, pp. 55–62.

Huzak, I. and J. Azevedo (1994) *Crianças de fibra*, Rio de Janeiro, Paz e Terra.

Juarez, E. (1991), in M. Fausto and M. Cervini, *O trabalho e a rua : crianças e adolescentes no Brasil urbano dos anos 80*, São Paulo, Cortez.

Liberati, W. D. (1991) *'O estatuto da crianças e do adolescente', Comentários*. Brasilia, Instituto Brasileiro de Pedagogia Social.

Madeira, F. R. (1993) 'Pobreza, escola e trabalho: convicções virtuosas, conexões viciosas', *São Paulo em perspectiva*, 7, 1, January–March, pp. 70–83.

Malta Campos, M. (1982) *Escola e participação popular – A luta por educação elementar em dois bairros de São Paulo*, São Paulo, FFLCH-USP.

Martins, J. S. (ed.) (1991) *O massacre dos inocentes. A crianca sem infancia no Brasil*, São Paulo, Editoria Hucitec.

Mendez, E. G. (1992) *Legislação de 'menores' na américa latina: uma doutrina em situação irregular*, Brasilia.

Pires, J. M. (1988) 'Trabalho infantil: a necessidade e a persistência', São Paulo, Mestrado FEA-USP.

Ribeiro, I. 1982 – 'A multiplicação dos braços – Estudo sobre a utilização da fração infantil da força de trabalho entre famílias de trabalhadores do setor agrícola de uma agroindústria açucareira da Zona da Mata pernambucana', Rio de Janeiro, Instituto Universitário de Pesquisas do, Rio de Janeiro.

Ribeiro, I. and M. L. Barbosa (eds) (1987) *Menor e sociedade brasileira*, São Paulo, Edições Loyola.

Ribeiro, R. and A. L. Sabòia (1993) 'Crianças e adolescentes na década de 80: Condições de vida e perspectivas para o terceiro milênio', in I. Rizzini (ed.), *A crianças no Brasil hoje: Desafio para o terceiro milênio*, Rio de Janeiro, Editora Universidade Santa Úrsula.

Rizzini, I. (1989) *Levantamento bibliográfico da produção científica sobre a infância pobre no Brasil 1970–1988*, Rio de Janeiro, Editora Universidade Santa Úrsula.

Rizzini, I. (ed.) (1993) *A crianças no Brasil hoje: Desafio para o terceiro milênio*, Rio de Janeiro, Editora Universidade Santa Úrsula.

SAAD (1990) *Consolidation of the Labour Laws: Commentaries* (23rd edn), São Paulo, LTR.

SEADE Foundation, 1993 – *Crianças e adolescentes – pesquisa das condições de vida na região metropolitana de São Paulo.*

Secretaria da criança da família e bem estar social de São Paulo (SP) (1994) *Contagem de crianças e adolescentes em situação de rua na cidade de São Paulo* (2nd edn), São Paulo, Secretaria de Crianças.

Spindel, C. (1985) 'O menor trabalhador e a reprodução da pobreza', *Em aberto*, 4, 28, October–December.

— (1989) *Crianças e adolescentes no mercado de trabalho*, São Paulo, Brasiliense.

Zylberstajn, H. et al. (1985) *A mulher e o menor na força de Trabalho*, São Paulo, Nobel – Ministério do Trabalho.

CHAPTER 10

Rapid Economic Growth: The Social Exclusion of Children in Thailand

Chantana Banpasirichote

Over the last thirty years, since a number of country children began entering non-household employment, working children in Thailand have been perceived in different ways. The traditional role of children in the household economy has been changing together with national economic conditions. People's views on the issue throughout different periods have been influenced by factors such as how children are used in the labour market, how they are affected by it and the response of national social policy. Having started with the economic role of children in the labour force, the issue moved into the realm of social welfare, and today's debate is geared towards children's rights and the implications for social integration.

Studies on child labour appeared in 1968 when the Department of Labour, now the Ministry of Labour and Social Welfare, produced a report of a survey on child and female labour (Department of Labour 1968). At that time, children were found in the textile industry in the Bangkok area (Praisaengpech 1968). The early surveys and studies, however, did not focus on the working conditions of the young. With several years of economic stagnation during the 1970s, concern focused on the inclusion of the un- or underemployed on the labour market. Although children's working conditions were reported to be sub-standard, any real discussion about this was hindered by a lack of adequate information on the extent of the phenomenon, and a limited understanding of the workings of the child labour market.

Awareness of the Social Problems of the Disadvantaged

Towards the end of the 1970s, the issue of child labour was brought to the fore by a politically explosive series of in-depth documentaries and news reports showing cases of children exploited in the workplace. More studies followed, shedding light on the diversity of working children in various types of employment, their native communities and the process of job-seeking on the labour market. Bringing child labour on to the market had clearly become a business in itself, as was seen in the emergence of recruitment offices. Most studies indicated its highest concentration in metropolitan and industrial areas. Child labour has indeed grown alongside the industrial sector.

In the early 1980s, once job-seeking channels had been widely established, concern about child labour focused on economic abuse and exploitation. Analysis of the problem was summed up by the expression 'children in especially difficult situations' (Saisuree and Nisa 1984), reflecting the employment of young workers and sub-standard working conditions.

Revelation of the situation of working children in non-agricultural industries has altered the understanding of the traditional role of children in the household economy. This is because the elements of 'work' and 'working environment' have changed from being part of a process of work and community socialization to one of economic exploitation. It is especially true for migrant child workers. Yet the trade-off between economic gain and the social costs of child labour has not been balanced.

Discussions on child workers are directed more towards policy now that the phenomenon has been recognized by the state and accepted as a social problem. Concern has centred on social services needed by the children. By evaluating the availability and accessibility of services, working children are categorized as a disadvantaged group (CUSRI 1992). This classification has been used to explain the cause of the child labour phenomenon.

Children's Rights and Social Exclusion

By 1987 economic growth had reached its peak with a two-digit growth rate and it was expected that the increase in household income would reduce the number of children joining the labour market before an acceptable age. In fact, the situation went the opposite way. The labour force survey indicated a rising number of working children, from 20 to 25 per cent of the eleven-to-fourteen age group in the labour force in 1984 and 1988 respectively (Banpasirichote 1992: 11–12). The development of labour market segmentation has resulted in an expansion of the market for unskilled labour, including that of children. In the early 1990s, NGOs also reported finding working children from neighbouring countries, especially Laos and Burma. It can be observed that there is a diversity of working children and discrimination in labour protection.

Incidences of child labour exploitation and discrimination towards alien child labour have been addressed by human rights groups. Concern as to how children should be treated in the workplace raises the issue of the basic needs of children. To guide a social policy for different disadvantaged groups, including child workers, the National Youth Bureau presented an evaluation framework for children's development based on basic minimum needs and services (National Youth Bureau 1990). It is clear that child workers have been deprived of essential services.

The persistence of exploitation in the workplace and the low quality of life of working children have raised the question of how much those children enjoy the fruit of their hard work. This observation reflects upon the quality of economic integration through participation in the labour market. Economic gain is no longer sufficient to justify such participation on the part of children. The concept of 'social integration' (UNRISD 1994) is therefore brought into the analysis of child workers' development. Children who have to work for economic exchange have been classified as an 'excluded group' because they are cut off from other opportunities and services. It is said that child labour is a category of the 'forgotten children' in Thai society (Wallop 1988).

The Children's Background

An overview of working children (eleven to fourteen years) in Thailand shows that the majority of them are still in the agricultural sector. As mentioned earlier, the problem has intensified in the non-agricultural sector that now accounts for about 13 per cent of the total number of working children (Banpasirichote 1992: 11–12). The number involved in manufacturing industry is even smaller, about 3.4 per cent or 40,000 children. This number may be higher if we include children between the ages of fifteen and eighteen.

Data from the largest survey of child labour (1005 cases from 293 enterprises in four major provinces), conducted by Chulalongkorn University Social Research Institute in 1990–91, indicate that working children are migrant workers from agricultural households residing in the poorest region of the country, the north-east, and in slum areas in Bangkok (Banpasirichote 1992).

Fortunately, working children in the survey had obtained at least six years' compulsory education, although at this level it is hardly sufficient to get out of the unskilled group. The survey also found that around 65 per cent of working children are between the ages of thirteen and fifteen which, by law, is an acceptable age. There are children younger than thirteen years old, but no more than 3 per cent of the sample. Generally, very young working children will be those of the self-employed and still working with their family (Banpasirichote 1992; Orathai and Richter 1989).

The working children are scattered over seventy types of companies, with the majority working in small-scale enterprises with an average of ten to twenty employees. The types of work have changed over the past ten years from once popular domestic work and work in shop-houses to small companies and factories where children can seek more social interaction.

An overview of the characteristics of child labour might show some things in common, such as the family's economic background and their individual personal data. But in fact there is diversity within the group. From the policy-making point of view, the nature of the work divided child labour into different groups. There are children in fishing operations, self-employed, sub-contracted workers, or children working with their parents in some companies. Later on, child workers have been observed linking with other disadvantaged groups, namely street children and child prostitutes. They can also be divided according to industrial sector, not to mention the location of the workplace which determines if they are local or migrant child workers. The latest trend also indicates that there is more than one nationality of child labourer in Thailand. This diversity makes child labourers a complex group that is difficult to deal with in one general policy. Despite the complexity, those children identified as most needing action are, for instance, non-employee child labour, child prostitutes, migrant and alien child labour. These groups are not protected by labour law and are believed to be the most vulnerable.

Children's Attitudes and Perceptions

Although there is a limit to understanding children's attitudes, some answers from the survey indicate certain directions in their thinking (Banpasirichote 1992: 20). From their answers we can divide children into four different groups based on their motivation for leaving home for work:

1. children under direct economic pressure (51.3 per cent)
2. children seeking their own course in life or a separate income from their parents (44.9 per cent)
3. children with no specific goal (1.7 per cent)
4. children with a family problem and wanting to get away (0.8 per cent)

It is no surprise to find that half of the sample were aware of their household's insufficient income. More interesting, however, is the fact that there are a number of children looking for alternative income who have no regard for whether or not their households are facing severe poverty. This might indicate a trend away from poverty alleviation. The motivation becomes more diversified and most of them share the decision with their parents.

For most north-eastern people, going to work in Bangkok is a 'must'. This experience is passed from one generation to the next as if it were a certificate of life education.

At work, children said that they thought of home (35 per cent). Around a quarter of them said the work was heavy and they had too little rest (23 per cent). It is also interesting to find that around one out of every four children were aware of their low wage rate (26 per cent) and a large number had changed jobs because of it. Company owners also reported a high turnover of young workers.

The Extent of Exploitation

This chapter contends that the nature of child labour exploitation is common to many places, yet differs in degree. In Thailand, most studies point out similar findings on low wages (50 to 70 per cent of minimum wage), un-pleasant working conditions, long hours (an average of ten hours a day), absence of skill improvement (generally no training or education with work) and, minimal welfare (sleep in working areas or congested rooms, insufficient toilet facilities and lack of clean drinking water). One report indicates a concern only for minimum age, types of work and working hours (Ministry of Labour and Social Welfare 1992). There is a compromise on the issue of minimum wage and welfare provision because, according to officials, most companies provide children with accommodation and some meals. Officials have chosen to compromise with companies rather than strictly enforcing the law for fear that the children will lose their jobs.

Exploitation of child labour does not take place only in the workplace, but can begin from the day children leave home. Although the problem of child trafficking pertains mostly to the child prostitution and alien child labour groups, it still has an important impact *vis-à-vis* the violation of children's rights in society.

Social security law, under which three parties – companies, the government and workers – pay for employee insurance, covers companies only with at least ten employees. Also, the working compensation fund covering accidents at work does not include child labour in small enterprises. All in all, while the majority of child labour is found in small companies where children are not even classified as employees, existing social services are still in their early stages and cannot compensate for the impact of exploitation.

From Escaping Poverty to Industrial Dilemma

After some unsuccessful attempts to eliminate child labour, the issue has now moved from whether or not children should work to how to prevent them from being neglected by, or excluded from, their own society. Concern for improving the process of social integration is now uppermost, meaning that if children do have to work, they need to be treated fairly and can still have equal opportunities for personal development. Therefore, two questions need to be asked in order to understand the incidence of child labour: (1) Why does there have to be any child labour at all? (2) Why do working children ultimately become an excluded group despite their ability to earn a living?

Explanations for the incidence of child labour are directly drawn from the analytical framework of *demand and supply* in the labour market and the theory of *push and pull factors in labour migration*. This places the source of the child labour phenomenon within the interaction between household economic depression and cost-cutting in company investment. But an active ingredient in the acceleration of the use of child labour is the activities of job placement business. Child-brokers are important promoters as well as facilitators in extracting children from their communities. Nowadays, this role is diminishing but is still crucial for the recruitment of alien child labour. It has been observed that kinship networks are replacing the role of brokers in placing children in different jobs. These networks also, to a large extent, secure children's social connections in their new environments.

In viewing factors affecting the child labour phenomenon and the social exclusion of child workers, three topics need to be discussed.

THE POVERTY HYPOTHESIS A study of the original communities of child workers carried out in 1983 supported the hypothesis of poverty as the main factor behind child labour in the market. A comparative analysis of child workers' households and others in the same community indicates a situation of greater poverty in the former. The indicators are derived from household income, household subsistence level (having enough rice through the year), ownership of and accessibility of factors of production such as land, and household underemployment (Alternative Development Studies Programme 1983). Six years later, Orathai and Richter made another comparative study of the family background of children working in frozen-seafood factories and schoolchildren in the same area. The findings also show that working children come from already excluded families in terms of their parents' education, income levels, possession of property and assets (Orathai and Richter 1989: 68). It becomes clear that children inherit the status of being socially excluded from their parents.

In 1991–92, Chulalongkorn University Social Research Institute investigated children working in a number of factories and companies and found that only 50 per cent of children said that they were in poverty (Banpasirichote 1993: 20). If poverty still prevails in child workers' households, it was also found that more children *choose* to earn income than to pursue higher education. The fact of children entering the labour market is becoming more and more a pattern of occupational shift and not necessarily a poverty alleviation strategy of rural households. This has been one of the consequences of the expansion and segmentation of the labour market during the period of rapid growth.

ECONOMIC GROWTH AND DEVELOPMENT DISPARITIES Economic growth during the past five or six years resulted in an expansion and segmentation of the labour market. Employment opportunities and conditions are varied and this facilitates a better absorption of unskilled labour. For example, there is temporary employment, sub-contracting and work at home. The availability of all forms of employment provides rural households with a wider possibility of being integrated into the market but without questioning the quality of integration. The boom in employment in the industrial sector has gone hand in hand with stagnation in the agricultural sector. A trend of occupational shift in younger generations of farming households has become a clearer pattern.

The expansion of the labour market has not improved its quality; the trickle-down effect of growth has not been sufficiently effective. Adult workers cannot support their entire family, so it is still possible to find children working even in a high-growth economy. The widening economic gap intensifies the sense of 'relative poverty' in rural communities. Recently, there have been more and more children wanting to experience life in a big city like Bangkok. In village communities, people desire the same standard of living as in Bangkok. They adjust their consumption behaviour with the help of consumer promotion mechanisms such as advertising and credit services. The need to have one's own cash income is felt by the younger generation. Seasonal labour migration to Bangkok for survival is becoming more permanent. With profits from agriculture falling below expectations, abandoning farming is an important factor influencing a decision to allow children to go to work in town.

THE LAGGING SOCIAL SECURITY SYSTEM It is self-evident that being integrated into the labour market does not necessarily guarantee child labourers a better quality of life. On this point, child workers share the same fate as other sections of the working class, although the impact on them is much greater. The level of investment in the social security system has not kept up with economic progress and investment. Several surveys on the working conditions of children confirm that the same old problem of sub-standard conditions has not been resolved.

On the one hand, the government accepts that a complete elimination of child labour is not realistic for the near future. On the other hand, it is not capable of providing services and welfare for existing child labourers. The government's efforts in the past prioritized labour protection within the legal framework. An initiative to enhance the quality of life and personal development of child workers is still missing. The children and their families' quest to be a part of a larger economic system than household farming activities cannot prevent them from being excluded. Market-led human resource development has only ended up in a more complex situation which is more difficult to resolve. Existing social services only respond to certain groups that make themselves appealing in social policy planning, such as government officials, adult male workers and trade union members. In short, the current social security system is not ready to absorb more industrial sector labour, despite the influx of labour on to the market. So child labour is socially excluded for a second time when entering the labour market; and yet the trade-off of children's welfare for economic gain costs more than was expected.

Discussions have not yet touched on the value of children in Thai society, which appears to be a big gap in the study of child labour. Child labourers are in fact mistreated by adults in society. The moral issue has been raised particularly in the case of child prostitution, but there has not been much investigation into the perception of an important group such as parents and employers. The moral issue exemplifies a dilemma of a value conflict in relation to the role of children in economic development. On the one hand, children are supposed to show their gratitude to their parents; on the other hand, a sacrifice of their own welfare is not acceptable. Parents' moral responsibility for their children is one which is still a sensitive issue and and one which is difficult to circumvent.

Bottlenecks in Policies and Actions

We realize that fighting the child labour problem is an uphill battle. The problem is economic in nature but with concomitant social costs and impacts. Its causes stem from the social and economic structure of development imbalance. Therefore, to try and solve the problem simply by enforcing the law, which happens to be the key measure in Thailand, will not stop the tide of children seeking jobs and being exploited in the workplace. The most direct solution, often referred to in seminars and conferences, is to eradicate poverty and assume that this will solve all problems. But what children and their parents are trying to do is actually to cope with their poverty. Perhaps the solution is to establish a competitive alternative to child labour, or make it so that they are not harming themselves by working and have opportunities for personal development.

In Thailand, without considering the effectiveness and efficiency of implementation, the policy measures for child labour cover various stages of intervention.

- *prevention*: increasing the minimum age for employment from twelve to thirteen, expansion of compulsory education, skill development programmes, awareness-raising campaigns
- *preparing children who need to work*: work orientation, job-placement schemes, information dissemination
- *labour protection*: law enforcement focusing on minimum age, working hours, hazardous work and child trade, labour inspection
- *help*: reporting of incidents, rescue from captivity, emergency shelter, legal representation for child labour, home contact, rehabilitation
- *child labour development*: medical examination service, recreational and educational activities, non-formal education

These measures are intended to help meet the needs of the working child but in practice there are still a lot of problems. There is a lack of an adequate coordinating system and institutional arrangements, which results in inconsistency and discontinuity in activities. Other difficulties are caused by the diversity within the child labour group, a problem of identifying locations of child labour, of cooperation on the part of company owners, and insufficient awareness of the actors involved.

Suggestions for the elimination of child labour are not clear from the above measures, except for the increasing of the minimum age for admission to employment, which depends on the success of the expansion of compulsory education. The weakness is that those measures have shown no sense of proactive intervention. If child labour is not avoidable at this point, it is imperative to establish a better employment alternative and a support system. In this respect, the approach to tackling child labour should be based on a better understanding of the children's situation and include the missing elements in the policy and practice framework as suggested in the following:

1. Campaign on the child's rights and the responsibility of members of the society *vis-à-vis* all classes of children, i.e. employees, non-employees, disadvantaged and alien child labour.
2. Eliminate factors that would hinder the working child's ability to pursue personal development while fulfilling economic needs.
3. Develop educational and skill-development models to suit the conditions of working children, e.g. apprenticeship.
4. Develop and establish social and welfare services that will increase accessibility for diversified working children. This may require restructuring organizational networking and adjustment of the bureaucratic regulations obstructing utilization of government services.
5. Involve the business sector by applying regulations to secure the child's rights and enhance the development of working children.

From past experience in policy implementation, child labour can hardly use existing services or be a part of a larger society because of the unavailability or inaccessibility of services. A proactive approach could start with the debureaucratization of services and the decentralization of policymaking and implementation in order to involve more partners in the process. However, this will never be achieved without an increasing awareness of children's value and basic rights on the part of all groups: namely, politicians, officials, entrepreneurs, parents and ordinary citizens. Finally, economic growth has failed to improve the quality of life of the rural poor. To leave the problem of child labour in the hands of the labour market cannot guarantee a desirable social integration. Thailand might not enjoy its accelerated growth for much longer, unless there is a strong political will to achieve higher standards of human development and ensure better welfare for all children.

Conclusions: Some Analytical Observations

The special feature of Thailand is that the country is undergoing a change of course towards NIC status. It might have been expected that the impact of growth would reduce the number of children entering the market, but this does not seem to be the case. Although we might not be able to assess the number of children on the market, the complexity of the issue – including widespread child labour in a variety of activities, child labour linkages with street children and child prostitution, alien child workers – shows the persistence of the problem. It is interesting to see what is going on in this type of economy.

There are three points that should be highlighted: (1) poverty and its changing connotations; (2) value conflicts and the disappearance of the moral economy; and (3) the incomplete adjustment of traditional relations of production.

1. It was clear in the beginning that child labourers came from poor families. There is no doubt that poverty is a driving factor. However, recently, families and children have been developing a new attitude towards work and education. Before, children who had to work instead of continuing their education were those who had no choice. Today, there are more and more children and families who see that children *do* have a choice to earn cash earlier because the labour market opens up more employment opportunities. This trend is also seen as an occupational shift in the younger generation. It happens in parallel with the economic transition of agricultural decline. Allowing children into the labour market is a way of integrating into the mainstream economy because it could mean an improvement of their standards of living. For children, to work in a large city like Bangkok provides a kind of social experience which cannot be gained to such a degree from continuing education. The cost of trading children's welfare for cash income has not received enough attention.

2. While economic transition is taking place in Thailand, the question is raised as to why some children have to bear the burden as cheap labour. This question is more relevant to children who have to work outside their community environment and social norms, i.e. migrant child workers. It is customary in Thai society that children share some of the household work, including family economic activities. But allowing children out of the household to earn cash and the exploitation of children in the workplace are part of a new phenomenon. Child abuse is an issue about which we still do not have enough understanding. However, it is observed that there is a value conflict between children's welfare and a sense of economic achievement. This conflict stems from a misconception of the child's rights. Economic rationality boosted during the period of rapid growth overrides the fundamental values of social integration and solidarity. Social responsibility and care for children is obviously weakening at all levels: in the family, community, business and government sector. Parents are found to have traded their children; business exploits their labour; and the government invests less in the child's social security than in promoting economic growth.

This value conflict and misconception of children's rights will require a universal campaign of awareness-raising among all the adults concerned in order to soften the impact of economic rationality.

3. The employer–employee relationship, especially in small-scale companies, is a subject missing from the study of child labour despite its significance for policy formulation. It is observed that a large number of working children are caught in traditional relations of production where child labour depends on paternalistic relationships with employers. Unfortunately, the paternalistic relationship is now operating in the new environment of greater competitiveness. The pressure is then put upon employers, especially those recruiting from disadvantaged groups like child labour. Reciprocity between employers and employees is deteriorating and might not provide a guarantee of social security for young workers.

This area still needs further investigation, and obviously the existing labour protection cannot effectively interfere with this type of relationship. Law enforcement still continues to be an unresolved problem.

References

Alternative Development Studies Programme and Burirum Teacher College (1983) 'A Summary Report of the Workshop on Child Labour from Burirum: A Situation and Solutions', Bangkok, Chulalongkorn University Social Research Institute.

Banpasirichote, C. (1992) *A Situation Analysis and Policy Study for Disadvantaged Children: Child Labour*, Bangkok, Chulalongkorn University Social Research Institute.

— (1993) *Child Labour in Hazardous Work in Thailand*, Bangkok, Chulalongkorn University Social Research Institute.

CUSRI (Chulalongkorn University Social Research Institute) (1992) *A Situation Analysis and Policy Study for Disadvantaged Children*, Bangkok.

Department of Labour (Centre for Child and Woman Labour) (1968) *The Working Children in Thailand,* no. 1, Bangkok, Ministry of Interior.

Ministry of Labour and Social Welfare (1992) *Yearbook of Labour Statistics*, Bangkok.

National Youth Bureau (1990) *Basic Minimum Needs and Services for Children*, Bangkok.

Orathai, A. and K. Richter (1989) *Child Labour in Fishing Industries: A Case Study of Smutsakron Province*, Salaya, Nokornpratom, Institute of Population and Social Research, Mahidol University.

Praisaenpech, N. (1968) *Working Conditions of Women and Child Labour in Textile Factories in Bangkok-Dhonburi*, Masters Thesis, Bangkok, National Institute of Development Administration.

Saisuree, C. and X. Nisa (1984) *Children in Especially Difficult Situations* Vols 1–2 (Thailand), Bangkok, National Youth Bureau, Office of the Prime Minister.

UNRISD (1994) *Social Development News*, no. 10, Summer.

Wallop, T. (1988) *Forgotten Children in Thai Society*, Bangkok: Foundation for a Better Life for Children.

The Public Policy Problem: Child Labour and the Law in India

Usha Ramanathan

The child worker is no stranger to Indian statute law. The Employment of Children Act 1938 and the Children (Pledging of Labour) Act 1933 are testimony to the law's concern for child labour. With independence, the constitution outlawed the employment of children below the age of fourteen years in factories, mines and other hazardous work. In 1986, in an admission of defeat in the battle against the perpetuation of child labour, the Child Labour (Prohibition and Regulation) Act (CLPRA) was promulgated. That same year, the Juvenile Justice Act was passed, giving federal uniformity to the state's treatment of delinquent and neglected children. However, while their constituencies partly overlap, these two laws neither recognize nor draw support from each other; they inhabit isolated legal islands.

A multiplicity of labour legislation prescribes the age and physical condition of the child worker and sets minimum standards. The Factories Act 1948 requires certification before legitimating the employment of young persons, i.e. between fourteen and eighteen years; for young persons should not be allowed to work in any occupation unsuited to their health. The Mines Act 1952 prohibits anyone below eighteen from working in a mine, except for apprentices in training who may be as young as sixteen. The Plantations Labour Act 1951 sets the standard at twelve; yet with the CLPRA, the non-negotiable minimum age of employment is uniformly fourteen.

The debate on how expansive the definition of child labour should be is not addressed in this consideration of the legal context of the problem. The statement of position is confined to this: not all child work is child labour. It is the connection between waged labour and child labour which is relevant to the subject of this inquiry.

The Nature of Child Labour

A striking characteristic of child labour is its pervasiveness. Child workers are a familiar sight: as tea boys, porters, domestic servants, bootblacks, ragpickers, beggars, vendors, shop attendants, agricultural hands, cattle tenders, oarsmen's helpers and so on. They appear in industries and workplaces, particularly those not regulated by law, in houses, fields and on the streets. An erratic representation in statistics carefully conceals their true number.

It is the logic of poverty that condones child labour: the children of the poor supplement the earnings of the poor and hold out hope of survival; the right to subsistence should not be wrenched from them by an idealistic denial of the child's right to work. The 'poverty cycle' and the inevitability of impoverishment, which not merely keeps the poor poor but makes them poorer, cannot, according to this view, be realistically redressed. Poverty is sustained by inadequate attention to the wages of the adult population and often by a continuing concern for the survival of the employing agency. But if they were to be made to pay humane wages, the argument goes, profitability may sink into non-existence, while economic development needs to sustain, not allow the destruction of, such industry. The fact that cottage industries and small units are directly at the centre of the debate influences this reasoning.

Early entry on to the labour market ensures almost universal illiteracy among the child labour population. This illiteracy remains right through childhood and the adult years.

Poverty and illiteracy combine to make child workers vulnerable and easy subjects of exploitation. These traits naturally prevail throughout their working lives.

The minority status of child workers is integral to an understanding of the relationship between the child and the parent, the child and the state, and the child and the employer.

Minority status enhances their vulnerability. It imposes legal handicaps. A child cannot enter into a contract, not even for employment, yet he or she may work. A child cannot open a bank account. And any child not in the apparent custody of an adult can be picked up by the state agencies and treated as a 'neglected' juvenile, regardless of whether they are workers or not. The Children (Pledging of Labour) Act 1933 presumes the capacity of a parent to pledge a child's labour; so until majority (i.e. eighteen years), a child cannot even own his or her own labour. Poverty has been known to drive destitute parents to sell all rights over their children or simply confine the sale to their labour, which effectively may not be too dissimilar. Runaway children and street children who fend for themselves are further disempowered by the law of minority and become easy targets for exploitation. This is just a random sample of the impairing effects of minority.

Perceptions of Child Labour

The discourse, including its legal manifestations in the Children (Pledging of Labour) Act and the CLPRA, stands witness to certain perceptions that mould attitudes to the child worker. These attitudes influence the language of the law, the steps actually taken for its implementation and the popular sense of justice that has developed.

For one thing, the labour of the child worker is perceived as an 'asset'. The incapacity of minority puts this asset at the disposal of persons other than the children themselves.

Their labour is also seen, in justificatory terms, as standing between the survival and desolation of their impoverished families. By allowing children to work, the state relieves itself of some of the burden in its responsibility to deal with the sub-survival wage structures of the adult worker.

A link is also traced between population growth and poverty. Population growth is seen as synonymous with a population problem; and the poor as contributing directly, and in large numbers, to it. The blame for the population problem lies at the door of the poor. And, this view would have it, population growth is the reason why the poor continue to be poor and find subsistence difficult. It is a popular, though patently simplistic, appreciation of the issue of population growth which precludes empathy for the child worker: if the poor will have many children and find it difficult to make a living, it is solely their own responsibility when they send their children to find waged employment for survival. This view succeeds in benumbing societal conscience. The distancing of responsibility for child labour is further evidenced in another posture: if the poor are poor, it is their own fault and they have to solve the problems they have created for themselves. The child worker is consequently no longer seen as a 'child' but as a 'poor child'. Child labour is accordingly the price of self-inflicted poverty.

The population debate has been drawn into the child labour arena from another direction too. The relationship between poverty and child labour is axiomatic, as is the perception of the relationship between poverty and the population problem. One strand of opinion would accord priority to ending child labour in order to deter poor parents who find it profitable to have children. The 'profitability' factor comes from the earning potential of the child even when still a child. From this point of view, the low investment with relatively early returns cited are seen as being an incentive to having larger numbers of children. Doing away with the opportunities for waged child work would not merely deny the possibility of early returns, but would also make the child an expense. That child labour law has not contemplated abolition is not given serious consideration in this approach.

Where poverty persists, patterns of education have to be both imaginative and accommodating. The non-comprehension of the relevance of literacy coexists with the priority that is accorded to the child making him/herself economically useful. Planners view education as the cure for child labour; yet to move the children from the workplace to the school-room is an enterprise beset with hurdles. It is not emphatically clear if the years spent in a school represent a restoration of childhood, a protection from being prematurely inducted into the labour force, a training time for fending off exploitation, and time usefully spent in improving the quality of life. The stimulus for education remains weak.

The law ought to be the repository of this knowledge, and a response to it.

Legislation on Child Labour

The universe of the law relating to child labour could be seen as inhabiting two distinct, yet related, spheres. The first concerns itself with the object of the law:[1] is the intention to *abolish* child labour, or to *prohibit* the employment of child labour in specific processes and establishments, or to provide a scheme of *regulation* which will deal with the evils of child labour while not directly attempting to prevent its perpetuation? The related ambit leads on to consider whether the law relating to child labour is realistic, pragmatic or idealistic.

This is an appropriate juncture at which to explore the suggestion that the law on child labour is unacquainted with its abolition. 'Abolition' implies the absolute destruction of the practice of child labour. The law evinces an immediate concern for the lot of the child who may be a victim of the hazards that industry has brought with it. The law fears the victimization of the child from the factory, the mine or any other hazardous employment. This is the constitutionally voiced concern, and its attention is on the victim-creating potential and the need to protect the child. Safety is a key factor. The age of understanding, constitutionally fixed at fourteen, is the age of prescription of the child's capacity to cope with hazardous work. The protection is directed at the effects on health in childhood and of its extended effects into adulthood. The 'tender age' of children is not to be abused, and they are not to be forced by economic necessity to 'enter avocations unsuited to their age or strength'. This much can be gathered from the constitutional statement.

The CLPRA, too, is oblivious to the possibility of, or need for, the abolition of child labour. It is in fact a reiteration of a pre-constitutional statute – the Employment of Children Act 1938 – which it repealed. What it does effect is to 'clarify' what constitutes hazardous employment. This it does in its two schedules which are intended to be comprehensive lists of processes and establishments in which child labour is prohibited. While this list may be enlarged, it none the less constitutes the totality of the law's recognition of processes and workplaces from which children are to be excluded. The generality of the constitutional statement is interpreted and narrowed down to facilitate identification and implementation.

An exploration into the whys and wherefores of the non-consideration of abolition raises questions which are not readily answered from within the law. It is possible that the problem of defining child labour discouraged the constitution-maker and law-giver, for identifying its constituency is a primary requirement of such law.[2]

The economic poverty of the population into which child labour was born could have made child labour seem an unavoidable necessity. To abolish child labour would have then meant deepening the poverty of that population, adding to the economic imbalance which blights an iniquitous economy. This is an unconscionable act, that leaves the child to subsidize the state. Since cynicism is the escape route of the irresponsible, it must be presumed that this line of thought never really reached beyond the subconscious of the legislative mind.

Another possibility touched upon earlier suggests itself: that statute law addresses itself to areas it identifies as being the problem and leaves the rest well enough alone. The law-maker may have genuinely believed that the problem was only of the unsafe child in hazardous jobs. Or he may have been blinded by the obvious, leaving the other areas of the problem of child labour in its surrounding darkness.[3]

The stimulus for the abolition of child labour had to come from considerations beyond just the child's physical safety; this having been partially satisfied by outlawing children from hazardous workplace environments. It could have been provoked by a recognition of the exploitation of childhood, and its incidence – the innocence, the minority status, low bargaining power, ignorance and work concentration aided by a childlike unawareness of the future – which makes targets of the children of poverty.

Restoring the right to a childhood could have been the motivating force. It would inevitably have improved the quality of life, given a renewed meaning to human development and provided the spaces for the child to acquire the right equipment to avoid exploitation.

The continuance of child labour creates conditions for the perpetuation of adult poverty. Breaking the cycle of child labour is imperative to provide opportunities for them to extricate themselves from such a debilitating, impoverishing, humanity-degrading cycle.

Child labour, as understood in this effort at fathoming the law, is a problem whose only subjects are the poor. This constituency of the law puts children in a doubly disadvantaged position: as the vulnerable child and as the vulnerable poor. Abolition of child labour is not merely a question of freeing the child *from* a condition but also *for* developing beyond the oppression. Abolition thus means an onerous responsibility for the state. Abolition needs the law-maker not merely to see the ills of child labour but to believe that childhood has another purpose.

The objective of abolition would bring the law in tune with the constitutional mandate of equality before the law and of equal protection of the laws. It is the law's task to ensure that the inequality which sends the child worker on to the labour market is not endorsed and reinforced by legal prescription.

The language of prohibition could be misleading, for it refers not to a banishment of the practice but to the illegitimizing of the employment of child labour in specified occupations and processes. Prohibition, then, is not a general proscription of child labour, but forbids it by law within legislatively prescribed parameters.

Prohibition depends, for its legitimacy, on effective implementation. Consider particularly the fact that the 1938 law, which the CLPRA replaced, had found legislative salvation in prohibition keeping company with regulation; and that the CLPRA has essentially been reiterative. The occupations and processes which worried the law-maker in 1938 have continued to be the cause for concern, with some additions.[4]

With the enacting of the 1986 law, the law-maker's message needs no decoding: there is no legal energy being expended on abolishing child labour.

Every law has to seek its own legitimacy. The CLPRA, given its ineffective antecedents, has its work cut out for it. The assertion of the presence of child labour through statute was vociferously attacked when the legislation was debated in 1985–86; and the defence was that it was no longer wise or just or possible to neglect the use of law's instruments to deal with the severity of this spreading malaise. But the enactment of the law without invoking it, despite the obviousness of the problem, would itself delegitimize the law.

The dilemma of the law is palpable: the scope of the problem is vast. Having been in existence for decades, it has become institutionalized. The inter-dependencies between child labour and industry, wages, migration, development schemes, familial arrangements and education opportunities lend a complexity that no amount of law-making can wish away. Yet, the right of the child to be free from the threat of hazardous employment is, surely, non-negotiable.

The dilemma spills over into the question of the activation of prosecution under the law. There is little doubt as to the large numbers of people who would constitute offenders under the law: the child labour population is one obvious indicator. The law's efficacy is determined by the manner in which it detects, prosecutes and punishes offenders. The law must, through this process, acquire a deterrent value.[5]

Activation of the intent of the law may have to precede its punitive enforcement. Premature use of coercion could well prove counter-productive. The effective use of the distance between the enactment and its total adoption in action could determine the respect the law acquires. It could make the difference between the achievement of the purpose of the law and its failure. It is a solemn recognition that failure places more than merely the law in jeopardy; it would be a denial of basic protection to the child.

It is a stark truth about prohibition as envisioned in the law, that it is not concerned with reducing the incidence of child labour. Displaced children are at liberty to join the child labour market outside the zone of prohibition. They could thus find their way into the regulation regime outlined in the law. In the law's tame provision for regulation rests an implicit acceptance of the inevitability of child labour. Regulation is a gesture which could signify an acknowledgement of the problem, the benevolence of the paternalistic state, concern for the child, or a measure of protection for the child. It is within the law that the import of provisions intended to regulate the employment of child labour must be found, along with the conviction of the law-maker in providing for regulation too.

Labour laws have had a sorry regulatory history. The proliferation of workplaces to be monitored and policed is not in consonance with the inspecting staff. The variety of duties each empowered functionary is expected to perform is so vast as to paralyse the work. Not even minimum facilities for carrying out the work are available. The technical proficiency, stamina and regular upgrading of skills that it calls for are more than can be expected from ordinary mortals, particularly those who are in it for the job. The attitudinal inadequacies leave enacted aspirations unattended to. The causes are legion. The fact is inescapable. Yet the patterns of empowerment are unchanged, accountability of those responsible for regulation is untouched and there is no provision for appraisal which may provide the understanding required for meaningful change.

The scheme of regulation is sketchy: the hours and periods of work; a weekly holiday; procedure for settling disputes as to age; and a general authorization to the government to make provision for routine matters which conforms to the existing model of the Factories Act 1948. The lack of enthusiasm evident in the regulatory provisioning is heavy with the scent of defeat. It is almost as if the impossibility of regulation is admitted even in the statute. The tragedy is further deepened with the realization that the children are legally disentitled to speak for themselves because of their minority. Nor do they have any identified spokesperson other than the authority specified in this law.

It is perhaps possible to understand this defeatism even while rejecting it. The hope-denying experiences in implementing labour laws could account for it in part. What strikes us, however, is the complete absence of the child from this legislation; it is only the *problem* of child labour which haunts the law. And the inertia in even considering the inversion of accountability, empowerment and appraisal is a silent statement reinforcing the status quo.

Perhaps it was this premonition of defeat that lulled the law-making mind into settling for unimaginative repetition, for there are specific areas where the law could have made a difference. For instance, the question of paying the child worker a minimum wage. An exclusive legislation deals with the fixing of minimum rates of wages for a variety of jobs. Rates may be determined on a time-rated or a piece-rated basis. The computation of children's wages on the piece-rate system is not uncommon. In a bid to protect the child, the maximum permissible hours of work for the child is fixed at five, with no option of overtime. But there is no discernible concern for their affected earning potential. The danger of acting on empirical ignorance was witnessed when the court – acting in its compassionate jurisdiction in a public interest petition – actually ordered that child workers should be paid at least 60 per cent of adult wages, and this in an industry which is dominated by piece-rated payments. That it could be taken to mean a devaluation of the work of children, making it even more attractive, was lost upon the court! A provision in the law that a child has to be paid the minimum of what would constitute an adult's minimum daily wage might actually prevent the exploitation of the child, while it acts as a disincentive to the employing of children.

Let us consider another example: the question of the unionization of child labour. On the one hand is the perceived immaturity of the children, which casts doubts on the validity of their collectivity; on the other is a neglect of the need for an alternative process which can provide the children with the empowerment that unionization offers adults. The law is oblivious to its responsibility of enhancing protection.

These are merely instances of unconsidered neglect. In any case, regulation is at best a poor alternative to abolition which is, after all, the only way of restoring childhood to the child.

Realism, Pragmatism or Idealism?

Realism, pragmatism and idealism offer three possible approaches that the law-maker may adopt in fashioning a law to meet the child labour problem.

Realism implies an acceptance of reality in the making of the law. The law would then reassert the law-maker's vision of reality. The logic of the 'practical' informs a law which is, in this sense, realistic.

Pragmatism is used here in distinction from realism. Both pragmatism and realism acknowledge that which exists. Both are concerned with the practical, but pragmatism is the art of the possible. It understands reality, but does not endorse it. A pragmatic law would be cognisant of how far the law can change existing conditions to create an improved reality.

Idealism demands the most imagination. It exists in the realm of ideas and, even while envisaging the resolution of a problem, it may not evince concern for the possible. Idealism may inform the object of the law, even as it may be evidenced in the setting out of the processes by which the objective may be achieved. While unreal expectations may negate the value of prescribed processes, it is yet possible that the statement of the objective may itself lend it an acceptable morality.

The non-acceptance of child labour in the prohibited industries can be seen as a statement of the non-negotiability in the law's position. Yet there is a lack of ambition in the child labour law. The virtually unchanged treatment of the problems of regulation and prohibition is an indicator. There is continuity in the standards of definition, expectation and action in the law, which the law does not worry itself about. The 1938 law was therefore given a renewed lease of legitimacy in 1986 without any offer of explanation of how the failure of that law will be remedied in its re-enactment.

Is this perhaps the law-maker's admission of the law's inability to deal with the problem? Implicit in the law is the passive acceptance of the inequality of the child worker, poverty, processes of impoverishment, exploitation, powerlessness, hopelessness of implementation within the existing system, the low wages of the child which changes the content of profitability to profiteering and the temptation of innocent submission.

The low expectations of the law's performance are reflected in a court judgment. A major fire hazard in a fireworks industry had killed thirty-eight persons, including some children. The fireworks industry belongs on the prohibited list. The court ordered a commission to investigate and report on the accident. In its search for a means of dealing with such conscience-stirring incidents, the court practised its form of realism. No child should be employed in the prohibited industries, it said. If they are employed, however, an insurance scheme should be devised to compensate for their death or disability. The absoluteness of the prohibition was whittled away by this single endorsement of reality. Thus was born the age of the 'nameless' insurance policy. For children do not attain personhood in their workplaces, they are merely hands. Their unorganized status gives them no guarantee of regular employment, and no recognition of continuity where it exists. The insurance policy would have to cover a certain number of children, nameless as they are in their role as workers. There was no thought given to the effect that this blanket provision would have, if any, on victim-creation; nor to the dilution of responsibility of the offending employer and its public policy fall-out; nor to the distancing from responsibility that the offending employer experiences, for, once the premiums are paid, post-accident concern belongs to the insurance company alone.

The dehumanizing effect of realism on child labour law is demonstrated in this case. Yet it is realism that the law has adopted. Pragmatism would have called upon the legal imagination to improve the status of child labour, to pay serious attention to the problems of implementation, and to consider avenues of accountability which would warn both offenders and administrators of the uncompromising stand of the law.

The law's responsibility is aggravated by the legitimation it offers to the use of child labour. By specifying the prohibited employment, it commits itself only to limited matters of health and safety. Other premises which endorse child labour are not countered by the law. It does little to dispel the myths about child labour that, for instance, magnify the role of 'nimble hands' which are essential to the employing industry and which adult labour does not possess. It legitimizes the disappearance of guilt and prepares the ground for an unintended effect, that of actually creating a child labour market.

Conclusion

There is no denying that the issue of child labour is now firmly on the national agenda. It is education and literacy that are believed to hold the answer. The realism that the law practises is, however, not apparently complementary. Legal imagination has failed the law-maker, giving pragmatism no chance to succeed. A pretence of action through a law which lacks conviction may serve only to engender disrespect for the law.

Idealism need be no stranger to the law. The experience of the child labour law is a refutation of the meaningfulness of prohibition and, more so, of regulation. The experience is not encouraging on the implementing potential of the law either. The law may, perhaps, have to confine itself to taking an uncompromising moral stance. Unfettered by the need to attempt effectiveness, it may consider the possibility of advocating abolition. Idealism may restore to the law of child labour its legitimacy.

Appendix: Extracts from the Law

CONSTITUTION OF INDIA

Article 24. *Prohibition of employment of children in factories, etc.* No child below the age of fourteen years shall be employed to work in any factory or mine or engaged in any other hazardous employment.

Article 39. *Certain principles of policy to be followed by the State.* The State shall, in particular, direct its policy towards securing [...] that the health and strength of workers, men and women, and the tender age of children are not abused and that citizens are not forced by economic necessity to enter avocations unsuited to their age or strength.

THE CHILD LABOUR (PROHIBITION AND REGULATION) ACT, 1986

S.3. *Prohibition of employment of children in certain occupations and processes.* No child shall be employed or permitted to work in any of the occupations set forth in Part A of the Schedule or in any workshop wherein any of the processes set forth in Part B of the Schedule is carried on [...]

Provided nothing in this section shall apply to any workshop wherein any process is carried on by the occupier with the aid of his family or to any school established by, or receiving assistance or recognition from, Government.

S.5. *Child Labour Technical Advisory Committee.* (1) The Central Government may, by notification in the Official Gazette, constitute an advisory committee to be called the Child Labour Technical Advisory Committee [...] to advise the Central Government for the purpose of addition of occupations and processes to the Schedule.

Part III Regulation of Conditions of Work of Children

S.6. *Application of Part.* The provisions of this Part shall apply to an establishment or a class of establishments in which none of the occupations or processes referred to in S.3 is carried on:

S.7. *Hours and period of work* [...]

S.8. *Weekly holidays* [...]

S.9. *Notice to Inspector* [...]

S.10. *Disputes as to age* [...]

S.13. *Health and safety* [...] The appropriate government may, by notification in the Official Gazette, make rules for the health and safety of the children employed or permitted to work in any establishment or class of establishments.

The Schedule (see s.3)

Part A – Occupations. Any occupation connected with – (1) Transport of passengers, goods or mails by railway; (2) Cinder picking, clearing of an ash pit or building operation in the railway premises; (3) Work in a catering establishment at a railway station, involving the movement of a vendor or any other employee of the establishment from one platform to another or into or out of a moving train; (4) Work relating to the construction of a railway station or with any other work where such work is done in close proximity to or between the railway lines; (5) A port authority within the limits of any port.

Part B – Processes. (1) Bidi making (2) Carpet weaving (3) Cement manufacture, including bagging of cement (4) Cloth printing, dyeing and weaving (5) Manufacture of matches, explosives and fireworks (6) Mica cutting and splitting (7) Shellac manufacture (8) Soap manufacture (9) Tanning (10) Wool cleaning (11) Building and construction industry

Added by Notification

Zari making and embroidery [...] Delhi and U.P.
Precious stone polishing [...] Gujarat and Rajasthan
Slate and slate pencil manufacturing [...] Madhya Pradesh and U.P.

THE CHILDREN (PLEDGING OF LABOUR) ACT 1933

S.2. *Definitions.* In this Act, unless there is anything repugnant in the subject or context, 'an agreement to pledge a labour of a child' means an agreement, written or oral, express or implied, whereby the parent or guardian of a child, in return for any payment or benefit received or to be received by him, undertakes to cause or allow the services of the child to be utilized in any employment.

Provided that any agreement made without detriment to a child, and not made in consideration of any benefit other than reasonable wages to be paid for the child's services and terminable at not more than a week's notice, is not an agreement within the meaning of this definition.

'Child' means a person who is under the age of fifteen years ; and 'guardian' includes any person having legal custody of, or control over, a child.

S.3. *Agreements contrary to the Act to be void.*

S.4. *Penalty for parent or guardian making agreement to pledge the labour of a child.*

S.5. *Penalty for making with a parent or guardian an agreement to pledge the labour of a child.*

S.6. *Penalty for employing a child whose labour has been pledged.*

FACTORIES ACT 1948

S.67. *Prohibition of employment of young children.* No child who has not completed his fourteenth year shall be required or allowed to work in any factory.

MINES ACT 1952

S.40. *Employment of persons below eighteen years of age.*

S.45. *Prohibition of the presence of persons below eighteen years of age in a mine.*

Notes

1. A law is a composition of statements which, with the assistance of the draftsman's standardized pen, appears deceptively simple. Laws constructed to address a problem preambulatorily state the problem, define the constituency for protection, provide a procedure and append a sanction which will follow a breach of the law, while they identify the potential offender. The law would necessarily have to empower the agents of implementation, who are generally instruments of the state. It is of importance that these agents are presumed to act in good faith, and are not easy subjects to prosecution for wrongful application of the law, selective action under the law, or law-nullifying inaction. The path to the making of the law is often painful and complex. The way from the enacted law to its application shares these adjectival qualities, but could be textually completely different. That is, there is no certainty that the thinking, feeling, ratiocinating that go into the making of the law will be substantively and qualitatively identical, or even similar, to that which follows the making of the law. It is also in the nature of statute law that it may confine its reach to the extent of its comprehension at the time of the creation of the law. This may limit the dimensions of the legislatively acknowledged extent of the problem. This carries with it the danger of reductionism, i.e. the problem may itself be perceived as being of the shrunken magnitude and importance in which the law regards it. The larger problems which may be excluded from the statutory concern may remain in the active agenda of state policy, planning and programmatic action; yet the effect that the statutory statement has on the rigour of the state's activity cannot be discounted.

2. The omission in the law of addressing itself to the desirability of abolition leaves unanswered questions. It is left to the imagination to fathom the legal mind. The possibility

that there was a famine of meaningful alternatives cannot be discounted. To envision the erosion of child labour which would remove the child into an uncertain void of activity may have made it appear practical to leave the child where he/she was found.

3. Also, the law-maker is fettered by the fact of having to pronounce on issues at a certain point in time, and then the pronouncement is thereafter immutable by the law-maker without the expense of further legislative time, which is itself not readily available. This is unlike the judiciary which can refine its interpretation and response in each case it hears. Law-making, then, clearly needs identified problems capable of being provisioned in a statute.

4. Poverty of statistics may make it difficult to assess the extent of the problem with which the law is faced. Yet the unchanging language and concern of the law could be taken as evidence that the law-maker in 1986 had reason to believe that the 1938 law was ineffective in achieving its object. The dependence of the 1986 law-maker has to be presumed to be in a greater will to implement the law. The enactment of the old law in a barely revised form certainly brought the issue of child labour back on to the legal agenda. But beyond this, there appears to have been a failure of the legal imagination.

5. Acclimatization to the law, however, requires time and, earnest and effective communication. This is particularly so as the participants in this process have their experience under the earlier law to which they relate. Their presumption would naturally be of an unbridgeable chasm between the law and its operation. The prosecution of large numbers of offenders does not read like a realistic option within the executive, or judicial, framework. On the other hand, non-prosecution would run counter to the message of seriousness of purpose of the law. In any event, the purpose of the law is not the punishment of the offender so much as it is the prohibition and regulation of child labour; prosecution is only a device.

References

Gurupadaswamy, M. S. (1979) *Report of the Committee on Child Labour*, India, Ministry of Labour.

Hari Bhaskar, N. (1984) *Report of the Committee on Child Labour to Review the Present Working Conditions and Measures Taken to Mitigate Their Sufferings at Sivakasi in Tamilnadu.*

Ministry of Labour, Labour Bureau (1954) *Child Labour in India*, Delhi, Manager of Publications.

Myron, W. (1991) *The Child and the State in India*, Delhi, Oxford University Press.

National Child Labour Project (1991), 'Sivakasi at Virudhunagar', unpublished report.

Posner, R. A. (1977) *An Economic Analysis of Law* (2nd edn), Boston, Little-Brown.

Report of the Sub-Committee on Elimination of Child Labour in the Match and Fireworks Industries in Tamilnadu: A Proposed Strategy Framework (1993), unpublished.

Rorty, R. (1989) *Contingency, Irony and Solidarity*, Cambridge, Cambridge University Press.

Smitu, K. (1988) 'There's Blood on those Matchsticks', in U. Baxi (ed.), *Law and Poverty: Critical Essays*, Bombay, Tripathi.

Stuart, H. (1983) *Private Justice: Towards Integrated Theorising in the Sociology of Law*, London, Routledge and Kegan Paul.

Upendra, B. (1982) *Crisis of the Indian Legal System*, Delhi, Vikas Publishing House.

— (1988a) 'Introduction', in U. Baxi (ed.), *Law and Poverty: Critical Essays*, Bombay, Tripathi.

— (ed.) (1988b) 'Taking Suffering Seriously: Social Action Litigation in the Supreme Court of India', in U. Baxi (ed.), *Law and Poverty: Critical Essays*, Bombay, Tripathi, pp. 387–415.

Usha, S. N. and R. K. Kamini (eds) (1985) *Child Labour and Health: Problems and Prospects*, Bombay, Tata Institute of Social Sciences.

Vasant, G. (ed.) (1992) *Science, Population and Development*, Pune, Unmesh Communications.

CHAPTER 12

Debates on Poor Children in Brazil: Between Marginalization and Premature Labour

Rosilene Alvim

Making a Social Problem of Childhood in the Working Classes

THE TOPICALITY OF THE 'STREET CHILDREN' ISSUE Brazil is currently experiencing a phenomenon which, in everyday city life and in the media, seems to symbolize the country's many social ills: i.e. 'street children'. This new social grouping covers the poor children and adolescents seen on the streets of the big cities; over the past ten years they have progressively edged on to the front pages of the newspapers (and often fill the limited amount of column inches the international press devotes to Brazil).

'Street children' was established as a social category in the late 1980s by a group of agents from UNICEF, FUNABEM[1] and the Social Services Bureau of the Department of Health, the aim being to characterize the children and adolescents whose presence had been troubling the Brazilian population for a decade or so. They had previously been referred to as *menores*, but that legal term has acquired derogatory undertones since the 1950s. To Brazilians, the word *menor* conjures up images of poverty and, above all, delinquency – a fallacy reinforced by the press in its influential role of shaping public opinion (Alvim and Valladares 1988).

In actual fact, the agents were attempting to change society's negative view of street boys and girls by stressing the fact that these youngsters' experiences of life do not conform to our society's paradigm of childhood and adolescence; for they are deprived of a childhood. Poverty, economic recession aggravating family difficulties, rising unemployment and fewer opportunities for first-time job-seekers hit the younger members of the working classes first and plunge a larger number of families below the breadline.

According to the IBGE (Brazilian Institute of Geography and Statistics): 'in 1989 the Brazilian population included around 59 million children and adolescents (aged between 0 and 7 years), i.e. 41 percent of the total. The majority were living in extremely insecure conditions. That same year, just over half of all Brazilian children and adolescents (50.5 percent) came from families with a per capita monthly income of no more than half the national minimum wage' (Ribeiro and Sabòia 1993). Some commentators reckon that the fact that their parents are poor and out of work is the sole reason why children start work so young. At the end of the day, however, the Brazilian education system is also partly to blame for the empty classrooms.

In the late 1980s, social workers from government and non-governmental organizations (UNICEF and other groups linked to the Catholic Church and the 'social movement') devised a new way of assisting this street population, in opposition to the traditional approach of internment. It made it possible to recognize the value of a whole range of activities developed by poor children and adolescents from the 'streets' or from 'destitute communities'. A number of Brazilian cities now have outreach teams leading so-called 'alternative action' programmes and assisting a good many destitute minors and street children with 'educational' and 'liberating' techniques (often inspired by the work and writings of Paulo Freire). Street boys and girls being cared for by non-governmental groups (established as NGOs during the 1980s) object – occasionally with the support of the church – to the treatment meted out by the institutions belonging to the official system (represented by FUNABEM until its demise in 1990).

The official system is seen as repressive because it uses state homes as its chief form of both 'protection' and 'punishment'. Throughout the past ten years, all non-governmental action opposed to the educational methods deployed by FUNABEM since its inception in 1964 has come under the 'alternative' label.

THE CONSTRUCTION OF A SOCIAL PROBLEM   In view of the fact that the topic of street children has been part of the discourse of philanthropists, legal experts, the police and employers, and has occupied a growing place in the press and political debate as a poverty-related theme since the early 1900s, we may well wonder why it has recently become so topical. At the turn of the nineteenth century, people were already associating 'home' or 'factory' with 'the streets', and 'abandoned children' with 'broken homes'. But the various configurations differed according to the actors' interests: either the family should protect its children and prevent them from hanging about the streets which were places leading to criminality; or the factory should take over the protective role, replacing the family and also serving as a school, since regular schools have no place in the world of poor children and thus fail to provide a possible alternative to work and crime. (Alvim 1985).

Sociological thought on the theme of street children in Brazil must take account of how society has built this 'population' into a 'social problem' expressed in the various debates at various different points in Brazilian history; a social problem that has become all the more apparent since the early 1970s with the emergence of new specialists such as activists and educators working with the movements for the protection of 'children and adolescents' within new institutions (such as the NGOs), alongside more established actors such as lawyers, police officers, journalists and philanthropists. As for entrepreneurs, if many (directors of high-profile commercial companies, for example) now make donations to 'alternative' programmes rather than the traditional institutional homes, others (suburban shopkeepers and businessmen, for example) on the contrary stand accused of backing the 'extermination' campaigns that have marked the political struggles in this field since the late 1980s (Alvim and Ribeiro 1991).

Over the past ten years, a new approach to law-making has emerged, spurred by the UN Convention on the Rights of the Child. It has resulted in the Children and Adolescents Act passed in October 1990. It should be noted that a number of the above-mentioned social workers participated in the drafting of the Act with legal experts, politicians and activists (growing numbers of whom have now entered this field – a political problem since the 1980s). The new law abandoned the *menor* category and its supporters regard it as a law for the rights of the child and adolescent; from the legal standpoint, despite its apparent universality, the category of *menor* ended up stigmatizing the youngsters in question by generally referring to them as delinquents, paupers and blacks.

One of the purposes of this chapter is to point out the similarities and differences between each historical period in the construction of this 'social problem'.

1. *Early twentieth century.* Poor children become a social problem in the debates leading up to the 1927 Minors' Code. Working-class children and adolescents immediately found themselves torn between work and school – as indeed they still are today. Going hand in hand with the 1919 ILO Convention no. 5 which came into effect in 1921, the Minors' Code (decree 1794; 12 October 1927) set a minimum age of fourteen years for work in factories, shipyards, mines or any other underground activities, quarries, workshops and their outbuildings. When the Minors' Code came into force two years after the initial bill, however, it sparked a major debate between industrialists and the state. Representing the state was Mello Mattos, Brazil's first juvenile magistrate and one of the people responsible for the 1927 Minors' Code, otherwise known as the 'Mello Mattos Code'. The industrialists widely employing underage labour (in the textiles industry in particular) argued that work was the only source of education for working-class children. So the factory was regarded as a kind of school (Alvim 1985) where children could be taught discipline and be protected from marginality. Industrialists also said it gave children the opportunity to contribute to the family budget.

The main actors debating the legal category of *menores* included legal experts, police officers, doctors, journalists, industrialists and politicians. The legal experts, supported in the main by the doctors, declared that biological age should not be neglected in the interests of industry. Industrialists for their part argued that limiting the working age to fourteen and working hours to six a day would totally disrupt industry. Mello Mattos maintained that even if it did mean upsetting the organization of industry,[2] the Code would 'safeguard the race'. Along with the legal age at which a child could enter employment, penalties were defined for infringement, according to the interests and positions of the agents involved in the debate. Youth, to paraphrase Bourdieu, was therefore no more than a word. Among the most controversial points were the classifications marking inter-generational differences and the composition of certain social groups. Entrepreneurs wanted *menores* to be very young indeed: it would be better, they said, for organizing labour in their industries. Police officers agreed, as they wanted to be able to crack down on suspected juvenile offenders, bring them to justice and, hence, to rid the streets of individuals seen as unlawful passers-by.

As mentioned earlier, the issues of delinquency, universalized education and state control over families[3] were already talking points during this period; labour, however, was the topic dominating the dynamics of the debate.

2. *1930 to 1943.* This was the period of state action through the Minors' Code. Judges were the ones with the monopoly over dealing with juvenile delinquency and the monitoring of child labour. The Labour Law Consolidation (LLC) bill passed in 1943 incorporated the labour-specific passages from the Code. We have found (Alvim and Valladares 1988) that by doing so it ended up turning the LLC into a criminal code with poor children being the ones criminalized.

3. *From 1943 to 1964.* The Code came to be used mainly for cases of delinquency. It was the peak period for the institutional homes. The first criticisms of the system began surfacing towards the end of this period. In 1940, the Welfare for Minors Bureau (SAM) was founded to take charge of poor, 'abandoned' children in need of state support to feed themselves and go to school. Most of these children would actually be committed to the homes by their parents and remain there until they had come of age. From the late 1940s through the 1950s, and regardless of its educational projects, the SAM – an institution created by the magistrates, doctors and politicians in favour of the Code – was the target of press accusations that it was ill-treating its inmates. It came to be regarded as a school for crime. The press of the day pointed to several former SAM inmates who had subsequently become famous bandits. When the SAM was replaced by the FUNABEM, juvenile magistrates switched from the Mello Mattos approach, now viewed as too 'welfarist', to mediation between society and the institutions responsible for the 'protection' or 'punishment' of *menores*. They described themselves as '*menorists*'.

4. *From 1964 to 1990.* This was a period of modernization and reform

within the general framework of the military dictatorship (until 1985); delinquency was dealt with under the 'national security laws'. In the 1970s, institutional homes found themselves facing a groundswell of criticism from the movements for the rights of poor children who put forward proposals for alternative projects and programmes. Throughout the entire lifetime of the FUNABEM, whose professed role was to formulate welfare policy for *minors*, Brazilian states were developing a welfare system with detention centres for 'offenders' and homes for the 'destitute' – terms which now figure in the revised version of the Code. In Rio de Janeiro and Minas Gerais, however, FUNABEM inherited the jurisdiction of the SAM and had to govern previously existing homes and other forms of welfare support. FUNABEM policy was to foster a family atmosphere among its inmates and – especially in view of the fact that their problems were so serious – it stepped up supervision by social workers, psychologists and doctors, expanded accommodation facilities and ordered staff to participate in the rationalization and modernization processes advocated by the 'national security' policy. Contrary to Mello Mattos's eugenicist belief that disruptions to industry are acceptable 'for the good of the race', the new policy was that *menores* should be 'shut away' for the sake of public order.

5. *Post-1990*. Conflicting trends were observed in the 1990s. On the one hand, the new law stimulated the growth of new initiatives, NGO projects and programmes; on the other, in a climate of deepening social and economic crisis and with growing numbers of street children increasingly identified with delinquency and crime, the 'reformists'[4] – the 'right wingers' of the field – reacted against the supposedly 'liberating' fruits of the 1990 Act.

The new law attracted the support only of the few magistrates who fought to push it through and those activists who had been critical of the state's handling of the protection of *menores* since the 1980s. This created legal wrangling between supporters of the Act and those advocating a revised version of the old Code; the central issue being how much educational value there can be in depriving an individual of his/her liberty. Juvenile magistrates in favour of the new Act and striving to evade this type of camouflaged inprisonment often clashed with state prosecutors. The Act provides for short spells of detention for only the most serious cases. State prosecutors have tended to favour a much tougher approach, a view shared by large sections of society.

Meanwhile, the NGOs have been embroiled in power struggles of their own, with activists divided as to which of a wide range of alternative programmes offer the best forms of 'support' and for whom: street boys and girls or destitute boys and girls. The social work in these alternative NGO projects is largely carried out by street educators.[5]

A NEW PROFESSION 'Educators' in this field realized that strength in numbers would help them establish an identity. They formed a professional association whose first general meeting in Rio de Janeiro on 1 March 1993 was attended by more than ninety educators. Recently, a number of educator training courses have been held in the city: one at the private Catholic University; two staged by NGOs involved in developing alternative programmes; another run by an NGO pool and financed by a private multinational company with connections in the clothing industry.

In the early 1980s, the new professional group was composed only of a core of people who, though few in number, managed to coordinate the work of activists and volunteers throughout the whole of Brazil. More and more activists turned professional and more and more casual volunteers became activists. Some NGOs employ a permanent staff of lawyers, psychologists and social workers who are often the ones assuming the role of street educators. So we are talking about a new social group or, at least, the transformation of a class of activists and volunteers which, with the growth of the NGOs and awareness about the issue of poor children and adolescents on the part of certain sections of society, wants to be recognized as professional, with all the rights and technical know-how of a profession. It is a profession that involves dangers and difficulties *vis-à-vis* the boys and girls themselves and the police. Both children and educators alike, by the way, regard the latter as the chief perpetrators of gratuitous acts against children; and the police are the leading denigrators of state policy, for it allows them to imprison only minors they can catch in the act of wrongdoing. The existence of educators and lawyers gives the children someone they can count on to protect them from unlawful police conduct, even if the educators are having great difficulty developing their practices, as their objectives do not always chime with those of the institutions running their projects.

Because of the complexity of this situation,[6] the various actors involved are drawn into conflicts that set members of the judiciary against each other, the judiciary against the police, society against the NGOs and grassroots activists against the leaders of alternative NGO projects. There are also fights over which are the best methods of defending children and adolescents, with everyone trying to impose his or her own form of 'education' and disagreeing over the teaching project; and, as I say, the managers of the institution in charge of these projects are locked in a struggle with the educators in their employ. Among the groups working with street boys and girls, for example, some believe that they have to work with them in public, out on the streets; others, having started with that approach, now combine street work with indoor activities at a 'day centre';[7] others still go further with the added option of sleeping space at a 'night centre'.[8] There are also groups that avoid working with 'juvenile offenders' (thus causing rifts between magistrates and the managers of the NGOs linked to children and adolescents) and groups not specializing in this brand of support and only able to offer street boys and girls a partial service: the latter regard street children as difficult cases, almost beyond recall, and limit themselves to dispensing legal aid. The forms of outreach some of the groups are developing with children and adolescents from 'destitute communities' are often more effect- ive when they include vocational training in workshops, usually in association with companies which eventually hire the trained adolescents.

We should point out that the themes debated earlier in the twentieth century (up to 1927) tied in with different political and economic contexts. If the issue of labour created tension between entrepreneurs and magistrates, particularly from the late 1920s through to the mid-1940s, it is no longer such a highly conflictual subject. Since the Labour Laws Consolidation Act took charge of regulating labour for the under-eighteens, the Children and Adolescents Act has virtually been excluded; ironically, the activists exclude it too. However, if the debate is marked by internal differences over how best to educate and rehabilitate poor children, the overarching theme is that of delinquency, above all when the alternative movements are seeking the means to provide vocational training that will effectively introduce young boys and girls into the world of employment as a means of preventing them from falling into a life of crime. Work – a theme seemingly missing from the agenda, or relegated to a position of secondary importance behind marginality and education – is the solution the various educational projects in this field have come up with for either 'salvaging' the children or 'developing their individual potentialities'. If, at the turn of the nineteenth century, work replaced school for poor children as a means of protecting them from the dangers of the streets and criminality, nowadays (even though work is no longer the central talking point) there are vocational training schemes that provide a fast track into early employment, leaving formal education in second place. Despite the resistance of a handful of educators and projects, this seems to be becoming the dominant trend: for working-class children and adolescents, whether they come from the streets or not, the only way to escape a life of crime is to start work at an early age.

Child and Adolescent Labour

Brazilian literature analysing child and juvenile labour in the city over the past few years has done so from a primarily economic and statistical stand- point.[9] However, sociologists, social workers and psychologists have been examining the work of street children since the late 1970s when the theme first became a research topic using fieldwork as the primary means of gathering data – hence introducing the qualitative aspect (Alvim and Valladares 1989). This trend, observed in street minor surveys, has not been confirmed to the same degree as far as the urban labour of minors in general is concerned. It was on the basis of these surveys that, in the 1980s, inter- national agencies such as UNICEF began to differentiate 'children of the street' from 'children in the street': the former being those who live and sleep on the streets and the latter those who work there but return home to their families at night. It nevertheless remains that the process leading to a life on the streets can begin with informal work in the street.[10]

When we talk about labour of the under-eighteens, the age specification spurs comparison with adult labour. It is implicit recognition that in a sense this category of worker – as the very term *minor* suggests – has something incomplete or illegitimate about it. Actually, minors ought not to be in employment, for they are at a stage of life that society regards as a time of preparation for adulthood, for a future coming of age. The legislation governing their labour hinges on a body of rules establishing the conditions under which children and adolescents can work (age, working hours compatible with schooling), as well as on the banning of night work or any job deemed unhealthy because it puts the underage labourer's growth and health at risk. Such legislation also means that although this form of labour is necessary for poor working-class families and economic development itself, it nevertheless lacks legitimacy in the eyes of society at large.

In the vast majority of writing on the subject as well as in the justification given for passing child and adolescent labour laws, poverty emerges as the decisive factor behind the premature employment of so many youngsters. The term 'premature' suggests recognition of the fact that this situation is an anomaly; and that not only are the masses of working children in these poverty-stricken societies underage, but countless numbers of them are younger than fourteen years old – the limit set by the ILO (and ratified, to name but one, by Brazil).

I should like to draw the reader's attention to the influential role that economic and statistical research has played in establishing the profile of the underage Brazilian worker; and to stress how necessary it is to follow the pointers provided by these economic and statistical analyses in order to produce case studies that account for the various viewpoints of the social actors involved and shed light on still unresolved questions. These questions relate to the explanatory nature of the poverty variable which in my opinion has not yet been sufficiently put in perspective. This sort of variable may be regarded as a category constructed in economic terms, where the market is central to explanations for the frequent inconsistencies found in statistical analyses. By way of an example, take the findings of recent studies where the employment of children and adolescents is analysed on the basis of statistical comparisons: it has been observed that a larger percentage of adolescents belonging to families whose incomes exceed the national minimum wage[11] enter employment in São Paulo than in Pernambuco, where family incomes are lower. The reason for this would appear to be that São Paulo employment places greater emphasis on education and is more appealing in so far as it actually replaces school.[12] Similar comparisons have been made between São Paulo, Porto Alegre and Fortaleza. These studies have helped raise awareness of the importance of the poverty variable in explaining premature entry to employment and have enabled more in-depth work in at least three areas:

1. Observation of the different types of families according to family incomes and the internal hierarchy deciding that a young child should enter employment (with fathers playing an important role); in the majority of families, people are shown to start work in compliance with priorities established not only on the basis of the group's economic needs, but also in line with a hierarchy of gender, age and status: young boys of fourteen or older are the first to go, followed by adolescent girls and mothers. Children work only when their family's income is lower than the national minimum wage.

2. In comparing the various different regions of the country, we can relativize several affirmations (and recriminations) common to certain ideologies concerning underage labour, such as the equating of poverty with the Brazilian working classes.

3. Bringing out the subtler sides of education: premature labour cannot be viewed as the biggest and only factor hindering school attendance, which differs according to age and type of family. Family structures play their part too: whether the father is still head of the family or not, the numbers of people in the family group and so on. While we are on the subject, we should note the rise in the number of families headed by a woman. Silva and Sabòia observe that these families break with tradition in the hierarchical model governing entry into the world of work via an intensive use of children's labour and withdrawal from school. On the other hand, these authors also show how it is only in the families with a man at the head and an income well below the minimum wage that underage labour does not comply with this hierarchical model. Finally, premature labour is relativized as a means of reproducing the poverty cycle.

It would be necessary to analyse the family on the basis of its income level, taking into account the relationship between the labour of younger members – children and adolescents – and their standards of education. If the cultural side to the theme of labour and schooling in the working classes and poor underclasses is ignored, we would not be able to grasp the social and cultural characteristics that could perhaps take us beyond the picture presented by statistics and society. It is important to devise a way of differentiating poor people not just according to their income, but in cultural terms as well. The only solution is on-the-ground research taking the qualitative aspects into consideration.

To elucidate this point of view, I shall refer to work underlining the historical nature of the Brazilian debates on underage labour, as well as case studies of the industrial labour of minors in a company town in the state of Pernambuco (during the 1930s and 1940s) and in Rio de Janeiro (1989). Recent work by Felícia Madeira (1993) analyses the relationship between underage labour and education according to the cultural conceptions of certain sections of the poor population. In all the work I shall be referring to, the question of the labour and education of the under-eighteens is associated with the theme of violence. Even if the working classes and society as a whole do not regard work as 'good' for children, it appears alongside school as a means of protecting them from a life of crime. These studies also show that the actors at the heart of the matter (the workers, their families, the employer or his representative) value the formative role of work as a safeguard against marginality. So adolescent workers are not even thought of in terms of their future exploitation and unskilled status by their own social class.

Discussions on Underage Labour: Historical Reflections

If the history of industrial child labour in classic writing on the development of capitalism reveals its cruel side, it does not give grounds to claim it is the product of that economic system. According to E. P. Thompson (*The Making of the English Working Class*), capitalism did not invent child labour, but it did create the conditions under which children were turned into premature adults, into 'free' workers. They were also torn away from a tradition where work within the family unit enabled their social reproduction as children. Thompson supports his argument by referring to the games and music that were so much a part of working-class children's lives in the days before they were deprived of their way of life, their culture. Cast into factories and confronted with machinery, they found themselves under the supervision of strangers (even familiars, neighbours and relatives), forced to endure long hours of work without break for a lower wage than an adult. According to Marx, for (physical) capitalist anthropology, the child ceases being a child at ten, nine or even five years of age.

Historically speaking, the ideological grounds given by industrial sectors to justify their use of child labour are spectacularly uniform as much in the early days of capitalism, when it was widely utilized, as within other historical contexts, where it no longer represents the same degree of importance to industry. They are that poor children and adolescents have to work because work protects them from crime and marginality; the world of the factory is better than the disorganized and lawless world of the streets; and the under-eighteens' work helps to increase their family's income, while also acting as a school, a school for labour.

In Brazil, this discussion began at the turn of the nineteenth century and continued through to the 1930s.[13] During that period, 'underage workers' became a legal category structured through a raft of bills presented before the Chamber of Deputies. A succession of such bills during the 1910s and 1920s culminated in the drafting of the labour-specific section of the 1927 Minors' Code. The discussions praised the protective qualities of work: offering workers personal protection from marginality and protection for their families through higher family incomes. The importance of education was also discussed; minors must not be stopped from going to school because of work. Work would therefore conform to twin needs: those of the minors themselves and those of their families. It therefore made out that poor children were bound to become either workers or outcasts. Deputies only disagreed over the question of the age at which a child might work, the number of working hours per day and the compulsory nature of school.

Industrialists of the day, as well as their political representatives and ideologists in general, were all in favour of lowering the minimum age for admission to employment as established at the ILO conference in 1919 (and even earlier by a number of philanthropists or the legislation of a number of industrialized countries), i.e. fourteen years.

In 1915, the São Paulo industrialist Jorge Street reacted to a bill approved by the Rio de Janeiro city council on the industrial labour of underage children, which was eventually declared unconstitutional. In an article entitled 'In the Factories I Manage', published by the *Jornal do Comércio*, he spoke out against the minimum age of fourteen. His view was that there are children and there are minors: at fourteen, factory children become minors capable of working practically like adults; until that age, they are learning and therefore not ready for the same sorts of uses as older individuals. Meanwhile, he believed that school was important for every segment of society but that if the state neglected its duties, then the factory would take over the role of a school for working-class children and minors, delivering them from delinquency and crime and raising their family income into the bargain. It is also worth noting the case put forward by Rio de Janeiro industrialists when Mello Mattos produced his labour legislation for the 1927 Minors Code, a reaction that bore all the same hallmarks as the opposition in São Paulo to another magistrate with a similar approach to his Rio counterpart: namely that both the child and his or her family needed protection. Their case essentially boiled down to a forewarning of industrial disruption (because, they claimed, straight-faced, adults would never stand for having to do the sorts of humdrum work normally given to minors) and threats of mass redundancies of minors whose families would suffer as a result. Much influenced by the ideas of the eugenicists, Mello Mattos, as we saw earlier, said in response that he preferred to 'safeguard the race' rather than the interests of industry.

These polemics died down when industrialists no longer needed to count on the deferment of law enforcement orders: in 1932, the working day was set at eight hours for adults and the under-eighteens, whereas the Minors Code had restricted it to six hours. At the same time, the minimum age for industrial employment was set at fourteen years and twelve in the case of apprenticeship. Industrialists were also offered similar means of circumventing the earlier official ban on night-work for minors; the ban remained in place, but the starting time for night-shifts was raised from 7 to 10 p.m. It meant a considerable lengthening in the real working day. This legislation on working hours, age and apprenticeship is still in force today; the only departure came in 1979 when constitutional changes reduced the age to twelve. The changes were defended on the grounds of the economic needs of poor families. During the drafting of the 1988 constitution, amendments relating to underage labour brought the minimum working age back up to fourteen, yet kept that of apprenticeships at twelve. It offered the industrial sectors employing minors a whole range of possible loopholes: for example, using the apprenticeship laws to pay ridiculously low wages (the revised Children and Adolescents Act stipulates that minors of fourteen should be paid at least a minimum working wage even when indentured). Ana Isabel Aguiar,[14] a researcher at the Childhood Study and Research Centre (NEPI-UFRJ) shows how the amendment debates stem from what I myself have called the tedious monotony of the case relating the minors' and their families' need for, and interest in, work.

In 1943, underage labour legislation was extracted from the Minors' Code and integrated into the Labour Laws Consolidation Act (which in my opinion left underage workers even more vulnerable than before). With their rights now watered down under the Labour Code, they could no longer count on receiving justice specifically adapted to their situation as had been the wish of the philanthropists and magistrates of old. What is more, trade unions take little interest in these workers because they soon come of age and their work is of secondary economic importance to the family (only the family head really matters). The unions never regard minors as active players in the struggle, irrespective of the type of activity. Lumped together with all workers as a whole under the same legislation, their personal status has in fact been eclipsed, denied. From this point of view, they really are quite literally minor workers.

A Few Examples of Research Work and Qualitative Data

The conclusions of a number of pieces of research work whose data were gathered through first-hand, on-the-ground observation and open interviews allow one to approach child and juvenile labour from the standpoint of the workers and their families.

A study of the families of a group of textile-workers in the Companhia de Tecidos Paulista company town in the state of Pernambuco,[15] has shown that the heavy use of child labour in the 1930s and 1940s was regarded by underage workers' families as industry-driven, particularly in the case of fourteen-year-olds, yet also as educational and helpful for the family's reproduction of the working group. The families of the Paulista workers were financially better off than the majority of rural and coastal families – or those from the Nordeste *sertão* region – and now tend to rate education highly and retrospectively think that their children did not go to work at the factory before they were fourteen. We should note that these workers (interviewed in the 1970s and 1980s) regard child labour as part of their history, their life-course; not as something entirely negative. Labour is a part of their social identity. So underage labour is, and always has been, seen in a positive light.

In a recent article by Felícia Madeira, attention is drawn to the fact that truancy is not necessarily due to underage labour but to working-class views about an education system, universal since the 1980s, which does not offer the positive qualities that they themselves see in work. Such a glorification of work in the labouring classes explains why people in the company town of Paulista (which, when all is said and done, has no problems of violence or marginality) are still arguing along such lines at a time when legislation has been passed for a compulsory eight-hour day, a minimum age and wage. What is more, they stress that the legislation actually serves to penalize working families. Indeed, minors are going out to work in order to help their families and, with the majority of the other members working as well, the accumulation of low incomes only just provides an adequate living for the whole family. Workers used to appreciate the plentiful job opportunities, even for the disabled. There was work for everyone, even if it did not 'pay very well', which is no longer the case today. A 1988 research project conducted by Rosa Maria Ribeira and myself, on underage industrial labour in Rio de Janeiro, found a similar glorification of work among underage workers in the textiles industry. Adolescents and employers confessed that the work delivered them from marginality while at the same time making a significant contribution to the family income. What is more, the adolescents appreciated having pocket money to spend. They saw school as something desirable, but factory hours (8 a.m. to 6 p.m.) and travelling time did not leave them sufficiently rested to be able to benefit from the classes.[16]

So only the analyses that take account of the importance of culture for an understanding of the social facts can go beyond abstract and absolutist quantification which does not allow insight into the real movement of the socio-economic phenomena the subjects themselves experience. It is important to consider the differences *vis-à-vis* gender and family composition if we wish to grasp the complexity of child and juvenile labour. The cultural model placing the household head in the role of chief family breadwinner and the view that the labour of a young person, even a child, is a help to the family head permeate society and put young workers of both sexes (with girls, perhaps, being most at risk) in a position of invisibility as far as the civil rights of workers is concerned.

They find themselves prematurely cast into the world of employment, temporary minors and, as such, not regarded as fully-fledged workers. They are incomplete, onlookers; nobody owes them the slightest respect, not even of the kind they are granted in law. Socially invisible, they cannot even count on being protected and having their rights defended by trade unions.

Notes

1. FUNABEM (Foundation for the Welfare of Minors) was set up under the Department of National Health in 1964 as a replacement for the SAM (Minors' Welfare Bureau), a body attached to the Ministry of Justice since 1940; FUNABEM was itself replaced in 1990 by the FCBIA (Foundation for the Child and Adolescent) which is attached to the Ministry of Social Services.

2. With a six-hour maximum working day, a ban on night-work (from 1927 to 1932, night-shift began at 7 p.m.; then it was moved forward to 10 p.m.) and a minimum working age of fourteen years (the minimum age previously having been determined by industrialists themselves so that children as young as eight could be found working in the textile factories).

3. The 1927 Code made provisions for the Pátrio Poder question: allowing the juvenile magistrate to remove children from their parents' keeping and put them into state care.

4. Legal experts, politicians and entrepreneurs who agreed to a reform of the Code only when confronted with the alternative of a new one – the one ultimately adopted: the new 'Children and Adolescents Act'.

5. A recognized and comprehensive professional group which can include the social educators figuring in a number of preliminary documents acknowledging that street boys and girls have a childhood and adolescence, a condition they used to be denied. These agents have produced a series of texts which, in addition to their individual thematic titles, have been published under the general title, *Alternative Projects for Street Children*.

6. I have not sought to tackle the complexity of this field at the national level since my first-hand knowledge of the situation extends only to the municipality of Rio de Janeiro; my information on what is happening in the other states comes only indirectly from books, articles and the press.

7. Activities such as reading and writing, but sports too, and art and vocational training. 'Day centres' constitute the second stage of outreach work with street children; after a number of contacts with educators who develop similar activities in the street, the children are then invited to join in with the activities offered within an enclosed space. Not all the boys and girls stay at these centres overnight.

8. Some groups work with 'the street' and 'overnight centres' but do not use 'day centres'. However, there are several possible configurations and these projects often end up working with all three stages, either simultaneously or separately.

9. Cf. Cervini and Burger (1991: 17–46); Ribeiro and Sabòia (1993).

10. Oris de Oliveira (1994) talks about a PREALC study claiming that in 1990, the population of working Brazilian children and adolescents stood at 7,639,748 individuals, 1,456,748 of whom were aged between ten and fourteen, and 6,183,000 between fifteen and nineteen. The author also quotes an IBGE study (*Perfil Estatístico de Crianças e Mães no Brasil*, coordinated by Rosa Maria Ribeiro da Silva) including the figures for the ten sectors most often employing children aged between ten and seventeen:

Absolute figures:	7,020,623 jobs
Relative % figures	(100.0)
Agriculture	42.9
Processing industry	14.6
Construction industry	3.9
Commerce	10.3
Services	20.7
Others	7.6

11. According to R. Cervini and F. Burger (1991), the definition of the 'poor population' and its relations with child and adolescent labour are linked to per capita family income. The income which characterizes poverty is defined as being equal to half of Brazil's minimum wage. From the 1993 level of $US 100 it had fallen to $US 70 by October 1994.

12. Most of the data on child and adolescent labour come from the PNAD (National survey of sampled metropolitan area homes), an annual statistical survey conducted by the IBGE. In discussing the reasons for the premature appearance of children and adolescents on the labour market, Barros, Ricardo and Mendonça do not question the determining nature of poverty. They strive to show the important appeal of the labour market and job skills. Other researchers link premature entry to the labour market with per capita family income. This is because the majority of working children and adolescents are found to belong to families whose income has fallen to below half the national minimum wage.

13. I made a detailed analysis of the discussion in 'Child Labour': Chapter 5 of my PhD thesis 'Constitution of the Family and Industrial Labour: A Study of the Textile Industry Workers at a Factory with a Residential Area for Workers' (mimeo, PPGAS-Museu Nacional, UFRJ, 1985). In her recent dissertation under my direction entitled 'A Construção do Menor Trabalhador', Ana Beatriz Braga (1993) analyses the discussions at the Chamber of Deputies on the various projects concerning legislation on underage labour.

14. Ana Isabel Aguiar (1991), from the research work *O Trabalhor Carioca, Produçao da Classe Trabalhadora*, edited by Alice Rangel de Paiva Abreu (IFCS-UFRJ, 1989).

15. Alvim (1985).

16. Our research, which took in Rio de Janeiro's top industrial employers of underage labour, also confirmed that in 1986 (according to data from the RAIS: the Annual Statistical Data Report), the largest of the five was the clothing and shoe manufacturing industry (5951 adolescent girls, 1077 boys); 1332 boys and only 130 girls were working in the publishing sector; 820 young girls and 291 boys were working in the leather and hides sector; 580 boys and 227 girls in metallurgy. In the textiles sector the gender ratio was relatively more balanced: 388 boys and 327 girls.

Interviews were conducted only with adolescent males because the researcher was refused access to the factories employing youngsters of both sexes. From the statistical point of view, it is interesting to note the greater prevalence of young girls in trades, like dress-making, of relevance to the clothing and leather and hides industries, where apprenticeship in the home does not culminate in a recognized qualification.

References

Aguiar, A. I. (1991) 'Proteção ao Trabalho do Menor: Alterações na CLT', in R. Alvim and R. M. Ribeiro (eds), *O Trabalho industrial do Menor*, IFCS-UFRJ.

Alvim, R. (1985) *Constituição da Família e Trabalho industrial, um estudo sobre trabalhadores de uma fábrica com vila operária*, PPGAS-Museu Nacional, UFRJ.

Alvim, R. and L. P. Valladares (1988) 'Infância e Sociedade no Brasil, uma análise da literatura', *Boletim bibliográfico brasileiro*, 26, Rio de Janeiro, pp. 3–37.

Alvim, R. and R. M. Ribeiro (eds) (1991), *O Trabalho industrial do Menor*, IFCS-UFRJ.

Braga, A. B. (1993) 'A Construção do Menor Trabalhador', Programa de Pós-Graduação em Sociologia, IFCS-UFRJ.

Cervini, R. and F. Burger (1991) 'O menino trabalhador no Brasil', in A. Fausto and R. Cervini (eds), *O Trabalho e a Rua Crianças e adolescentes no Brasil Urbano dos anos 80*, São Paulo, Cortez Editora, pp. 17–46.

Madeira, F. (1993) 'Pobreza, Escola e Trabalho: convicções virtuosas', conexões viciosas, *São Paulo em Perspectiva*, 7, 1, January–March, São Paulo, SEADE.

Oliveira, Oris de (1994) *O trabalho da criança e do adolescente*, São Paulo, LTR.

Ribeiro, R. and A. L. Sabòia (1993) 'Crianças e adolescentes na década de 80: Condições de vida e perspectivas para o terceiro milênio', in I. Rizzini (ed.), *A criança no Brasil hoje: Desafio para o terceiro milênio*, Rio de Janeiro, Editora Universidade Santa Úrsula.

PART II

The Structure and Dynamics of Exploitation

CHAPTER 13

Introduction: Child Labour in the Light of Bonded Labour

Michel Bonnet

As an ILO expert with the International Programme for the Eradication of Child Labour (IPEC), I find myself tackling child labour from the viewpoint of the strategies adopted by the various different actors. Putting children to work, or withdrawing them from it, is a complex and difficult business because child labour has, at least since the 1970s, been an area where often antagonistic strategies meet and confront one another: from that of the young unemployed single mother forced to place her child as a domestic in exchange for a little food to that of the major powers seeking to manipulate international trade through the introduction of clauses concerning the employment of children.

What is new here is the emergence of a struggle to stamp out the phenomenon; an increasingly organized and methodical campaign with powerful means and involving an ever greater number and variety of actors. It has made its mark through the reworking of legislation under the influence, among others, of ILO Convention no. 138 (1973) and, above all, the ratification by virtually every member-state of the UN Convention on the Rights of the Child (1989). But the movement has reached beyond the tight-knit circle of legislators and become a major social issue: with each passing year since 1975, the United Nations Center for Human Rights, through its Working Group on Contemporary Forms of Slavery, has been keeping watch to ensure that international pressure does not run out of steam; policies have been put in place, national plans of action drawn up with support grants and NGOs have been specializing in action on behalf of working children and organizing themselves into networks; one final unmistakable sign is that the struggle to eradicate child labour has become a fertile niche for media interest and, when all is said and done, a lucrative market.

If child labour is always a meeting of two strategies – that of the family *vis-à-vis* its children and that of the employer *vis-à-vis* his company – it is absolutely essential to broaden its analysis to the environment and take on board the pressures brought to bear by society. Apart from the usual indicators

179

defining the child's working conditions, analysis material must therefore include observation of the forces present in the action; on the one hand the actors seeking to change the situation in favour of the children and, on the other, those upholding the established order. Even stronger emphasis needs to be placed upon the importance of this latter type of material because it is rarely taken into account in studies on child labour.

Without further ado, let us rule out the objection that such an approach might lead to confusion between analysis of the action to tackle the phenomenon and analysis of the phenomenon itself. From the ore mines through to the various workshops and foundries, child workers are not merely victims of the situation; they are first and foremost its actors, particularly in struggles to change it (and the fact that this struggle is constantly crushed, and hence remains relatively unknown, detracts nothing from its value). We should even go so far as to say that the militant, humanitarian and educational action undertaken actually represents no more than adult involvement in the children's struggle. For instance, the effectiveness of a programme of action really does depend on how active a role it offers or allows children. It is also worth remembering that just because we adults construct our case without giving the children the chance to speak, it does not mean they have nothing to say; similarly, adult organizations do not necessarily work harder for the welfare of working children than the children themselves.

Child labour is essentially a struggle. Childhood is like a ship tossed on a stormy sea; can we unravel a guideline from its tangled rigging? The line I propose to follow is that of bonded labour. I shall study its workings with a view to shedding light on the composition of child labour. The word *bondage* is employed in a technical sense with reference to bonded labour. Bonded labour is a very clearly defined category; it can be analysed. It involves many millions of children in a wide variety of industries and cultural environments; generalizations can be made.

My chief sources of material include findings from my own research on bonded child labour in the countries of southern Asia conducted between June 1988 and June 1989 for the Anti-Slavery Society of London, the annual meeting reports of the UN Working Group on Contemporary Forms of Slavery and the work of the International Seminar on Children in Bondage staged in Pakistan in 1992 by the ILO and the United Nations Center for Human Rights.

Bonded Labour

The United Nations has produced the following definition of bonded labour: 'the state or condition arising from a pledge by a debtor of his personal services or those of a person under his control as security for a debt, if the value of those services as reasonably assessed is not applied towards the liquidation of the debt or the length and nature of those services are not respectively limited and defined' (The Supplementary Convention on the Abolition of Slavery, the Slave Trade and Institutions and Practices Similar to Slavery, UNO, 1956. Article 1).

Bondage is not just a condition, it is a *mechanism* whose workings need to be observed. Two adults meet face to face and exchange a loan (usually a sum of money) for the labour of a child. This is not just any kind of loan; it is characterized by one term in particular, i.e. that it has to be repaid by an individual's physical labour. It has even reached the stage whereby many local languages have a specific word to differentiate it from regular loans. In Nepal, for instance, the latter are known as *sapati*, whereas bonded loans are *saunki*. Another characteristic feature of bondage is that the work done to repay the original debt generates new ones: every penny spent on the child's needs (a simple aspirin, say) is a penny extra on top of what is owed. And punishment is meted out not just in the shape of a beating, which is bad enough, but also in the shape of a fine. It is obviously impossible, even for an adult, to toil away in extremely difficult conditions for weeks or months on end without some slip-up, damage or infringement of the rules, if only due to a moment of inattentiveness. So the child incurs fresh debts which, when added to that of the parents, raises the amount of interest due, thus even further increasing the original debt.

Let us highlight some of the key features of bonded labour by observing three factors in the children's lives: the work they must accomplish, how they pass their days, and their overall careers as working children.

Children are not pledged to do a precise job. They must be ready to respond to the employer's every command and, in many domestic situations, particularly in the countryside, they are expected to remain available night and day to work in the fields or at the workshop, domestic service, running errands or working for a third party on the master's behalf etc. Children pledged as bonded labour at a company or workshop (e.g. for weaving carpets, making bricks or cigarettes) do of course tend to specialize in a particular task; but even then, they never have a say in matters regarding the post occupied and must be prepared to drop whatever they are doing as soon as they are called by the master; what is more, they have numerous other duties to fulfil outside the core activity: sweeping, carrying water, keeping watch at the workshop entrance etc. It should be stressed that bonded children are rarely as a rule assigned to production work as such; they accompany a worker or attend to a machine, they carry, clean, tidy up – in short, jobs regarded as typical of domestic labour.

Each day is exactly like the last for children in bondage: there are no calendars, no specific work or rest days; it all depends upon the decision of the employer. The same goes for working hours which can continue non-stop until the employer decides to call a break. Bedtime is the only time the children may have to themselves, and even then there is so little of that (four or five hours a night) that they are incapable of doing anything but sleep.

How are children pledged for labour at the age of, say, six or seven going to develop? What sort of a 'career' (if you can call it that) will they have? Tough working conditions and insufficient food and care cause their health to suffer and reduce their physical and mental abilities. Over the months and years, they discover the hopelessness of attempts to get out of bondage; at the slightest sign of independence they are beaten and fined, thus pushing the chance of freedom even further into an ever more distant future. Sometimes, when parents see their child's working conditions are too hard or hazardous, they will seek out another employer; but the latter then has to pay the original debt with the previous employer, so much so that any improvement there might be in the situation is only superficial and short-lived. Also, let us not forget that the children are not the only ones suffering. Wherever they look in their home environment, their village or the tribe, caste or ethnic minority group to which they belong, they see the same hardships; their only available models rarely allow them any other prospects than a repeat of their parents' and neighbours' experiences. They know that they must take up their position in the daily struggle to survive.

This brief look at the conditions imposed upon children in bondage allows us to shed light on two facets of child labour. On the one hand bondage deprives children of what they own – their physical and mental health, their relationship with the (especially social) environment – and on the other hand it locks them into a dependency on the present moment in time, putting their lives in suspended animation. Through bondage, the employer robs them of both their childhood and their future, whereas being in a phase of growth and preparation for the future is the very definition of childhood.

Impoverishment and paralysis – let us look at how these two characteristic features of bondage come together in child labour.

Bondage and Training

This is not an intellectual exercise of applying an analysis grid to a given situation. In real life, the bondage and labour of children are part and parcel of the same phenomenon. Before being pledged, they are already working or about to start; bondage just makes matters worse.

The decision to put a child to work is a complex and extremely painful one, an experience unique to each family, to each child. It is the family unit in the deepest sense of the term that reacts in the face of an unknown which may just as easily culminate in an opportunity for development as in a quasi-death sentence. In an environment marked by large numbers of young people out of work and an education system offering members of the poorest parts of society, particularly in the Third World, virtually no chance at all of finding work, hunger pangs go hand in hand with the fear that children are about to fall victim to the worst of all possible ills: unemployment. The most effective way of shielding them from that danger, the best solution (as it is the only one within reach) is to introduce them to the world of work at a very early age and even, if possible, set them up with an employer. From that point of view, the only way to establish a solid connection is often by incurring a debt and pledging a child as bonded labour in order to pay it off. Parents are tormented by worries for their children's future. All they want is to give their children the very best of what they have to offer – and what invaluable experience they have of the struggle to survive! – to equip them for life and, in short, help them develop, they hope, towards the longest possible future. That is what each and every parent has at heart; I am inclined to say it is visceral.

Hence, concealed beneath apparently erratic patterns of behaviour such as sending a child to work, lies a question crucial to all workers since their whole existence hangs on the answer, i.e. that of vocational skills. But if this is an issue of capital importance to the worker, it is every bit as important for the employer because of the influence it has on labour management, company structures and returns on capital. Vocational training for children emerges as one of the special areas where two institutions, two ways of thinking, confront one another: the family and enterprise. Let us examine the matter in how those institutions regard the elements fundamental to vocational training: the raw materials, the tools and the social actors.

TRAINING WITHIN THE FAMILY First of all, it should be said that a small child is indifferent to the materials: a log of wood becomes an animal taken to pasture or the watering hole. But in the poorest families, particularly in rural areas, children find that from a very early age (three to four years) their games come to include, or to be replaced by, a variety of different jobs: gathering wood, carrying water, sweeping out the house. That is when the materials have to be recognized as what they really are: a branch is no longer a knight's sword but firewood for cooking the rice and must take its rightful place beneath the cauldron. The more involved they become in their parents' work, children gradually discover that each material must be used according to its own specific nature. They learn that things are not slaves with which they can do what they like, nor enemies that need to be destroyed; they are assets; they have a role that calls for respect; they are partners.

The first tools children have are their hands. In game-playing, where they ape their parents at work, a hand will become a hammer, a saw or an axe. When eventually asked to help with the work, tools are rarely required for the jobs they are allotted within a familial context: they use their hands to pick things up, to gather, sort and clean. Any tools that might be needed are usually quite rudimentary, not far removed from the materials themselves: a piece of wood to pack clay into a brick mould, a stone to dam an irrigation canal. Real tools enter the frame at a somewhat later stage and – an obvious fact though not to be forgotten – are given to the child by the adult. They are the end result of generations of working experience during which time they have been honed into the perfect tool for the job. So to begin with, the child is made to spend a long time 'contemplating' them with respect, cleaning them, storing them away and, of course, watching how they are used by the adult who acts as the medium through which he 'communicates' with the raw material. As with the material, the child learns that the greater one's respect for the laws governing the use of the tool – laws dictated by the very nature of the tool itself – the greater is one's ability to enter a serious (i.e. adult) relationship with the material and, hence, become a skilled producer.

In the child's relations at work, the adult who decides to put him to work is the one who initiates the shift from the world of games to that of employment, from the company of playmates to that of workmates. The adult is the one who then ensures the cohesion between all the various elements involved: the materials, the tools, the workplace, the product, the customer etc. He has authority over the child and the right to decide when the work shall begin and when to call it a day; he knows what the family needs and what the child is capable of doing at each stage of the activity; and he himself is skilled in the tasks that the child is asked to undertake. In other words, he establishes the relationship between the child and his environment, between the past history of the materials and tools, the present action and the future, i.e. the end product. By putting the child to work in this way and giving him an opportunity to gain vocational skills, the adult is actually performing a social act, contributing towards the building of society; he teaches a child, whose understanding of the world around him is rooted in games and fantasy, to regard other entities (materials, tools, people) as partners and to regard himself as a partner too in the great adventure of existence on earth. Such is the true sense of vocational training, the ultimate aim of the family's approach as an institution: to bring a new partner into the world.

TRAINING WITHIN COMPANIES   By companies we are alluding to those countless production sites which child labour classification is in the habit of grouping under the banner 'sweatshop system'. Given the limits of this chapter, I hope we shall be forgiven for any oversimplification; the companies in question here are situated somewhere between artisans and modern big businesses, i.e. what might, in some parts of the world, be called small and medium-sized businesses.

The materials the child finds at a company appear drained of their identity. It is no longer they, the materials, that call the tune here but the end product, the merchandise. Raw materials reign supreme in other realms away from the production site, sometimes at great distance from the place where the child lives. On the factory floor, orders are given by the employer and are not open to discussion. Suddenly the importance is no longer that a child be able clearly to distinguish one material from the next by understanding its nature, but on the basis of the employer's orders. Merchandise has expelled raw materials from the child's field of relationships, thus robbing it, cutting from it the riches that a certain harmony with nature had deposited within him.

Children working for a company only rarely come into contact with tools: the tool has been replaced by machinery. If working with a machine may be rewarding for an adult worker, for a child it is enslavement. The machine does all the cutting, shaping, crushing. Unlike adults, children are not often allowed near the controls; instead they are used as auxiliaries for transporting raw materials and finished products or for cleaning and maintenance. What is more, motors keep machines running constantly at regular speed; there is no variety, nothing new. If a child finds anything in them that might be 'fun', it is regarded as a defect in need of repair. The mutation of tool into machinery gives the child a new relationship with time; time is no longer filled with opportunities for adventure, change and development so, to a child, the machine's rhythm is time without movement which puts history on ice.

Among the new faces the child will encounter at a company, newest of them all is the boss. The boss does not base his relationship with a child on the imparting of vocational skills; the greater the company's ties to the market, especially an export market, the more remote the boss will be from the child, for his sights are trained on where the orders are coming from rather than on the shop floor. Not only might the child never meet or have any personal contact with the boss, but the latter will no longer even serve as a role model; he does not encourage contact, he keeps his distance. Symptomatically, children and their bosses as a rule come from quite separate backgrounds (different birthplaces, ethnic origins, castes or religions). All in all, the child–boss relationship within the company framework is barren in terms of the former's training potential.

A Process of Enslavement

Appraisal of the phenomenon of bondage, as much as that of child labour, should not be built upon an analysis of the actual labour or bondage itself, but by focusing on the central fact that the subject in question is a child, a still-developing human being. Children are defined by potentialities: they are curious and like to listen, watch, imitate and try things out for themselves. They are ready for adventure, and it is through adventure that they learn.

Now there is nothing sudden about the way a company breaks down a child's spirit. Entering employment, in the sense of becoming a part of the world of work, is more like a long march than a parachute drop. The company approach summarized above never actually exists in a pure state; its physical and psychological effects on children only make themselves felt very slowly and the children themselves are only very rarely and partially aware of what is happening to them. And the loss of the materials' qualities and distinctive character is progressive too; even when artificially manufactured, they retain some of their appeal which serves to conceal their inner emptiness. A child does not have an experienced enough eye to be able to distinguish between an all-purpose saw capable of cutting through anything, and the wide range of subtly different saws adapted to a particular kind of wood or a specific operation. It takes time for the machine to lose its veneer of modernity. The same goes for human relations; and lord knows whether or not the employers have arrived at a mutual agreement to use a variety of interchangeable masks to disguise the inflexibility of their staff management. Children are defenceless when faced with this sort of enemy, unaware as to how their habits are being undermined and their ways of acting and thinking altered. The longer they stay in the job, the more depleted their physical and psychological capacities become. Emphatic evidence of this is available in studies produced by the WHO (World Health Organization). Their strength of resistance is worn down over a period of months; what suffers most is their vitality, that deep-seated energy driving each child forward, despite all opposition.

If all movement vanishes and there is no tomorrow to look forward to, what does it mean to be a child? Exploitation robs working children of their present and enslavement steals their future. The emptiness that exists in bonded labour belongs to the world of exploitation; opposition to progress belongs to that of enslavement. It is not exploitation – to which child and adult workers alike are subjected – that should be made the main focal point in the analysis of child labour, but enslavement. This is where the notion of struggle enters the frame.

Although an adult is in a position to fight – as seen in the workers' movement – the same cannot be said of a child. Adult society denies children any independence or right to organized opposition; when children quit their workshops and band together in order to survive through working on the streets, the process is usually described as 'delinquency' and they are hunted down, imprisoned, or even murdered (as is the case in Brazil). Children have to stay put wherever an adult has placed them and they must conform to the status quo. Child workers are acutely aware of this situation; their only option is to accept it and bottle up their inner energy. They interiorize their enslavement.

To be fair to working children, and in the interests of objectivity, we should recognize two particular findings from studies of bonded children which provide special insight into their silence and acceptance of their predicament. First, when bonded children are finally released and returned to a relatively normal life, above all by being given a suitable education, they are found to be much faster learners than ordinary schoolchildren; second, when, once released, they are asked what kind of a life they would like to lead if they had the choice, two main answers emerge: they dream either of a career which would enable them to penalize cruelty and injustice on the part of their employers, e.g. in the police or judiciary, or a career enabling them to assist children still in bondage, e.g. doctors, nurses, teachers. This speaks volumes about the wealth of humanity that they still have within them.

Current Trends

'Child labour' is a term that covers a wide variety of situations from the most qualifying work in terms of personal development and socialization, through to subservience and slavery. Since not a single agency today is able to provide a statistical evaluation of the various different groups in question, we have no real means of checking the direction in which the phenomenon is evolving. So we are left with estimates stemming from a theoretical approach. Greater emphasis needs to be placed on studying the influence on child labour of four main forces at work in our societies over the past twenty-five years: economic crisis, gangsterism, the media revolution and recognition of the rights of the child.

ECONOMIC CRISIS Reports by the World Bank, the UNDP and UNICEF as well as countless monographs on children's lives all deliver the same message, irrespective of the source: the situation of the poorest people has been steadily declining since the 1970s. It is true of the developing countries strangled by the mechanisms of their debt burden; it is true in other countries where growing numbers of families are sinking below the poverty line and where living conditions are going from bad to worse.

This affects child labour on many levels: that of the state cutting expenditure in areas of crucial importance to the most deprived people (the very sections of the population that also happen to have the largest numbers of children), i.e. welfare support, healthcare, education, public sector jobs; that of the companies moving production abroad to wherever labour is cheapest, preferring to outsource, offering no job security, paying wages according to output and thus forcing workers to enlist the help of children, when it is not the employers themselves hiring child labour; that of the struggling families resorting to strategies in an effort to survive that require the participation of each and every member, even the very youngest, no longer with a view to seeing them educated but in order to bring in urgently needed income. An working-class economy has emerged – the ILO released its first studies on the informal sector of Kenya in 1980 – one of whose mainstays is child labour.

There still exist a number of geographical or economic sectors with a highly dense concentration of child labour and where some workshops and factories are forcing children to work more than twelve hours a day; however, situations such as these – which smack of nineteenth-century industrial Europe – can be said to concern only a minority of the world's working children. For the use of child labour is actually extremely diffuse, spread across the entire surface of our planet: in Third World and industrialized countries alike, in both urban centres and rural areas and in the widest variety of different activities. Meanwhile, children's working time is diluted and, depending on the day and the circumstances, they have a blend of some schooling, idleness, helping the family and paid labour.

So for children and parents alike, labour is increasingly becoming a means not of learning a skill or establishing contact with a potential employer, but purely and simply of earning a little money; and, for the employer, a means of having access to a readily available labour supply whose chief quality is not its productivity, but its flexibility. Under pressure of needs and urgency, the work is being drained of its educational aspects and no longer represents a process of development for a child, much less the first step on the road to a career.

We should underline the fact that, with no apparent sign in sight of any meaningful economic recovery or improvement in the living standards of the very poor, in coming decades the problem of child labour can only grow still worse.

RISING GANGSTERISM   By gangsterism, I am alluding to the force creating social change through solidarity among actors whose ethics tend to be confused with the laws of financial gains. Banks are bursting at the seams with 'dirty' money from drug trafficking, corruption, the plundering of national wealth via tampered international trading agreements, siphoned-off development aid and so on. Beneath a humanitarian façade, built with the backing of so many principled declarations, lurks a power that is prepared to go to any lengths to thwart the least action threatening to disturb this vast one-way flow of money.

Anyone trying to tackle child labour with programmes designed to combat the phenomenon must come to terms with one obvious fact: it is a minefield, full of danger. Wrecked careers and reputations, lawsuits, confiscated passports, imprisonment, vandalized premises, violent assaults and even murders; such is the fate reserved for the activists and organizations committed to fighting for the rights of child workers.

If that is what organizations and individuals protected by a certain social status have to contend with, imagine the scale of pressure and violence that must be inflicted upon the poorest people to prevent them from speaking out about their children's working conditions, the sexual abuse to which they are made prey, the fiddled wages, bonded labour contracts; or even just to force parents to place or keep their children in work. Everybody knows how terrified many parents are at the mere thought of having to answer a researcher's questions, never mind play an active part in the fight against child labour.

When, while remaining attentive to the effects of gangsterism, we descend into the everyday life of the working child, we are rapidly plunged into an atmosphere of violence. With barely a word of explanation, the child is bombarded with usually screamed orders, all the more terrifying for the fact that the vocabulary used by a master or employer is alien to his or her own mother-dialect. Children are beaten and punished for the slightest error. A bonded child recaptured after running away faces serious battering or mutilation. In short, violence appears whenever a child steps out of line and breaks the code of silent obedience.

THE MEDIA REVOLUTION The marriage of computer technology and on-line data-processing has radically altered the world of communications. Let us take two of the trends that have a particular bearing on child labour: instant global data flows and the intrusiveness of picture images.

Nowadays, public opinion and policy-makers on the other side of the globe learn the content of a politician's speech, the findings of an inquiry, a court ruling, a company closure, a demonstration march of parents, a journalist's exposure of groups of child slaves and so on before the news has even reached the next village. Irrespective of the (far from solely geographical) distance, we can react to an event at the exact same time as the actors directly involved and for better or for worse we, in the industrialized countries at least, do not deprive ourselves of the chance to do so. Total outsiders to the geographical, economic and/or cultural context are able to influence its outcome. Take this recent example with a direct bearing on child labour: when, at the end of 1993, it emerged that the United States government was about to pass the Harkins bill as a means of regulating imported goods made with the use of child labour, within a few weeks Bangladeshi textile companies had laid off tens of thousands of youngsters, most of them girls.

Another factor which seems to be all the more effectively narrowing down the distance is the increasingly important place being given to picture images in the news. The progressive unravelling of facts as we develop our thoughts on a particular issue under debate – in short, the viewer's long road towards the heart of the matter – has been replaced by a picture that actually shows just a single side of the truth without allowing any of us a say in the criteria used to select it and, most of the time, depriving the actors themselves of a say with regard to the light in which they are shown. Returning to the example of Bangladesh, the pictures showing the children leaving the factories stopped short of telling us whether they were subsequently any better or worse off in terms of their living and working conditions. And it will probably not be long before virtual reality is introducing us to a situation without a single reporter having to set foot in the place!

The most serious outcome of this media revolution is that the actors directly involved in child labour, above all the children themselves and their parents, are less and less the masters of their own strategies. Their struggles are being undermined by factors entirely beyond their control and far more powerful than they. Policies and programmes of action are bedevilled, literally back-to-front, as they no longer stem from the needs and desires of the people concerned but from the ideas and feelings of actors totally alien to the community in question. Researchers, university academics or agency project managers, we have all had experience of programmes and research projects whose underlying principles and methods have not been established according to the subjects' needs but in line with the presuppositions of the authority supplying the funding.

THE RIGHTS OF THE CHILD   In 1989, the United Nations passed its international Convention for the Rights of the Child; within five years it had been ratified by virtually every member-state. It is certainly the most significant development in the field of childhood. As with the 1789 Declaration of Human Rights, whose fruit it is after two hundred years in gestation, the repercussions will be felt only in the long term; but whatever happens, it is a now an inescapable part of the world of childhood.

Even leaving aside the legislative measures provided for the purpose of tackling child labour and its corollaries, this Convention is of interest to our field on two counts: first, it represents a certain, let us say, modern conception of the child which, although certainly utopian when looked at alongside the present-day realities of the children's lives, now enjoys universal acceptance; second, considering the changes it has already prompted in the national legislation and policy-making of member-states, it is undeniably set to play an influential role in the future of the children concerned and our societies as a whole.

One of its chief contributions is that the child is now a recognized partner in social affairs. The consequences of this are enormous; and their analysis and management are a challenge to be met in the years ahead. Here and there around the world a number of questions are emerging that represent so many stimuli for research and action: the question, for instance, of the rights of working children, especially the right to associate, which calls for investigation as to how children can be actors within the labour movement; or the still more fundamental, yet at the same time much more disturbing, question of the child's right to work.

This is not a matter of purely theoretical problems but of already active forces: children are struggling with the established order for the right to work; they are proud to provide for their own needs and the needs of their families through their work; they are entering into dialogue with adult workers in order to gain from their experience and grasp their skills; they are organizing themselves in order to improve their working conditions and stand up for and protect their own rights; sometimes they are even forcing trade unions to allow them to participate at rallies and marches, especially on Labour Day. Our thinking on the subject has chiefly been fuelled by the data highlighting violations of the child's rights in the workplace and by the negative effects of labour on children; we shall have to ask ourselves whether the lack of data attesting to the value of work as part of their development stems from the reality of the situation or from the shortage of researchers in this field. There is no doubt that with so many NGOs having taken the Convention on board, we are about to see some rapid, drastic changes in our information and, hence, in the way in which we regard the child's relationship with work.

Conclusion

From the point of view of the family as much as that of the employer, economic reasoning does not appear to account fully for the root causes of child labour. It would seem as though the explanations are going to have to be sought more on the side of the training of future adults. For the parents, putting a child to work is a realistic way of preparing him or her for the future; for the employer, it is a matter of equipping himself with a labour force readily available to undertake any prospective work. The formative factor here has more to do with socialization than an effort to improve the child's abilities or provide an opportunity to acquire vocational skills; children are brought into employment and even, more explicitly, into contact with employers in order to increase their chances of a future job.

A view of child labour modelled on the pattern of a stable full-time job whose wages largely depend on professional qualifications cannot fully depict the realities of today. A truer picture would be one of job insecurity, where availability and adaptability are the key qualities, allowing children to switch easily from one job to another and pushing them more towards the services sector than that of production.

I already encounter the workers of tomorrow, emerging from the child labour of today, whenever I take a cheap flight from Bombay to Dubai and find myself in an aircraft packed with migrant Indian workers heading for the Gulf States; they ask me to help fill in their landing cards and, when I ask what I should put as their occupation, they do not know. 'Who cares?' they say. 'Just so long as it gets us into the country; we'll play the rest by ear.' They are ready for anything, open to any sort of work and all sorts of exploitation.

It is here, perhaps, in this transformation of a skilled worker into a subservient jack of all trades, that we should see the greatest threat posed by child labour and find our criteria for its assessment.

The Domination of Fathers as the Typical Social Relationship

Paternal Domination: The Typical Relationship Conditioning the Exploitation of Children

Alain Morice

Exploited child labour today (i.e. that which, in capitalist terms, is a source of commercial profit) has two characteristic features differentiating it from exploited labour in general. First, it is considered illicit and as such easily evades contractual rules; second, the social control taking the place of a contract is by and large paternalism, a more or less faithful reproduction of the governing authority within family units.

These two features have not always been so pronounced. In the past, European factory- and mine-owners had few misgivings about using children and it was not until the end of the nineteenth century that the law-makers – under pressure from trade unions in a changing economic and demographic climate – began showing concern for their protection from abuse. And it is only since then that child exploitation has tended to provoke feelings of shame in our planet's collective consciousness. Moreover, although the family model has often prevailed, history abounds with examples where people have treated children – be they sold, abandoned or torn from their kin – as independent adults while *a contrario* capitalizing on the physical and psychological assets that have always made them an attractive class of worker all the more coveted for being cheap to replace (their adaptability, vivacity and stamina, for example).

From Legal Insecurity to Economic Insecurity: Denial of Status as a Basis for Exploitation

The exploitation of children is now almost universally condemned in speeches and banned by law. Only a small number of countries remain steadfast in their refusal to sign the international conventions on the matter. And it is coming under ever closer scrutiny, as one can see in the growing number of publications released. Yet this tremendous leap forward in juridical and ideological terms, which must be gratifying for every defender of human rights, sadly has a downside: as long as certain economic realities endure, prohibition will largely remain at best an illusion, at worst a convenient tool in the hands of the exploiter.

Anyone requiring proof of the ambiguity of the laws meant to be protecting children from exploitation need look no further than their relatively feeble efficacy by comparison with their objectives, i.e. if not actually to eliminate the phenomenon, then at least to bring it under strict control. And what better undermines a law's credibility than for it to be seen to be incessantly flouted? Need we recall what seems to be the implicit conclusion of every writer in this book, from the most idealistic to the most sceptical: that child labour is an enduring fact of life despite all the efforts made, or claimed to be made, to counter it? Even though one cannot really talk without statistical evidence, for nobody really knows, about an increase in the use of children's work (more than is proportional to that of their importance on the age/population pyramid), all hope now seems lost of seeing a swift end to this epidemic through legal channels alone. From this starting point, each actor will, according to his or her own philosophy, plead the case for reforming attitudes or lobbying the authorities to bring more effective sanctions against the employers or boycott the countries judged to be overly lax on the matter. This body of concerns unquestionably makes a positive contribution to the crucial international pressure without which no progress would be possible. But there is something derisory, if not deceitful, in considering that all those good intentions have had no real impact at world level.

Let us return to the law. There is a whole series of potential workers throughout the world whom the legal establishment (or accepted customs) treats as inferior: illegal immigrants, prisoners and convicts, certain members of the clergy, military conscripts. It is above all the case of the majority of women and, of course, children. One aggravating factor is that individuals are sometimes said to belong to several such categories at one and the same time. None of them – a considerable number world-wide – finds the concept of a labour market, where workers freely compete for the attentions of an employer group, to be anything other than an illusion. Before tackling the issue of children themselves, it is worth taking a detour through the above-mentioned categories.

Women are a case apart yet symptomatic of the fundamental mechanism of exploitation through denial of status. In theory, the countries acknowledging modern constitutional principles and international anti-discrimination conventions recognize sexual equality. Yet women are still very often confined to inferior jobs. This stems from the patriarchal structure of the family where their waged labour is regarded as non-essential and, hence, of lesser value than that of men. So society, contrary to its own formal principles, sees the steering of women towards less stable, lower paid and low-grade employment as something quite normal, ultimately proper. That such an outlook is deceitful is apparent in the employer's partiality to a labour force whose lack of social status is supposed to keep them away from the labour market. So it is the 'natural' order that serves the interests of exploitation here, which obviously has a telling effect on the average rate of pay (men's included). The perversity of the patriarchal model is being exposed almost universally through the insurmountable obstacles engendered by its own contradictions: in one fell swoop, the growth in the number of female-dominated single-parent families plunges the families themselves into ever greater uncertainty and the men into deleterious marginality. Sadly, with the trend already underway we can foresee the children increasingly becoming the final links of this terrible chain. Those capitalists who instigate or benefit from the process would be well advised to prepare themselves, for it is not necessarily going to go on reproducing for ever.

Meanwhile, society 'tailors' laws, so to speak, to specific categories of workers. We know for example about the unrestrained use of convicts from the times of the French Empire through to present-day China via the former USSR. These people represent an ever-ready supply of labour used in return for nothing but bed and board on the grounds that that is the penalty paid for wrong-doing. A similar variation exists in religious communities or sects except that their members, in theory at least, are not working under duress but out of benevolence or the ideals of abnegation. Non-professional soldiers could also be placed in this category. Forced labour in all these cases is argued to be a way of paying a more or less imaginary debt to society. So whole sections of society find themselves in the singular position of being denied the benefits of common law and deprived of status. They constitute a sort of parallel pseudo-wage-earning class without the foundations of the regular wage-earning class (the contractual relationship between capital and labour) which nevertheless serves as the model for the former as far as the extortion of surplus labour is concerned.

There are, however, other cases where the legal insecurity is more complete and it is the labour itself which flouts the law. This phenomenon can be observed among illegal immigrants (or people possessing a residence permit not allowing them the right to work). War, persecution, famine or quite simply hopeless economic situations all add to the increasing numbers of displaced persons around the world; it has now been established that national security measures actually do nothing to stem the 'invasion of foreigners'. Restrictions on the employment of those foreigners then becomes a lever for exploitation in that they force such people underground where they introduce themselves to their employers with the balance of power firmly weighted against them. Denial of citizenship also helps to enhance the 'flexibility' so dear to the hearts of capitalists who, in 'rendering a service to needy foreigners', feel this gives them the right to every possible form of abuse as regards wages and job security. With no legal grounds to make any demands whatsoever, illegally employed immigrant labour (and it is no coincidence that this is so often found to include large numbers of children) generally proliferates in sectors such as seasonal agricultural work, the garments trade, tourism or public works, that is to say 'just-in-time' work in sporadic bursts throughout the year, which needs to be able to exploit unregulated labour. Though this might not be their intention, immigration laws are most accommodating. If such laws did not exist, it would be in the employers' interests to invent them.

For anybody wishing to exploit them, children constitute a synthesis of all the above-mentioned cases and, hence, a positive godsend. Let us not forget that childhood is a temporary condition, not a social class. Like their mothers, they have no 'natural' place on the labour market; so one is 'doing them a favour' by granting them access to it, and that favour is in itself already something of a payment. The young children breaking rocks in Asia today have taken over from the Cayenne convicts; the only difference being that they are cynically refused worker status because there are laws that are supposed to be protecting them from exploitation. Finally, from the point of view of labour law, they and illegal immigrants share the plight of being non-persons.

Child labour is now an acknowledged reality publicly condemned by the international community. But it is up to us as researchers to present a theoretical interpretation of it to lend weight to that condemnation which, there is no point denying, sometimes seems to come to nothing and even, in the very worst cases, needlessly sets the parties involved at each other's throats. This reality creates a harmonious blend (albeit not without friction) of a legal order (not always consciously) aiming at the negation of the worker and an economic order pressing for a depreciation of the work. Convincing evidence of this emerges from an examination of the concerns of the various parties on the ground, i.e. the children themselves, their parents, their employers and the authorities.

The State

Honour to whom honour is due, let us begin with the state which makes the laws, applies its decisions (if it so wishes and is able to, that is) via administrative and legal channels and, perhaps first and foremost, integrates itself into international ways of thinking. It is worth dwelling on this leading actor which – especially when seen from the outside as being 'strong' or 'authoritarian' – so rarely prioritizes children's education and sometimes (when it is not its own agents who are the perpetrators) obligingly turns a blind eye to the trafficking revolving round their usage. Laws almost everywhere condemn the basic principles of such practices, but that, remember, scarcely hinders their global proliferation. Naturally it would be wrong to make generalizations about government policies given how different the pressures are from one country to the next. A few have managed to clamp down more or less effectively on the exploitation of children; but they deserve little credit for that. They are generally the ones whose privileged position on the world market and irreversibly reinforced legal structures enable them to dispense with the need to put their youngsters to work. At the same time we cannot help but notice an outbreak of the phenomenon in such countries due to unemployment. Children there may well enjoy some degree of protection from the exploiter, but let that not disguise the fact that the problem is offloaded on to countries still locked into a state of dependency and weakened by the finance and trading rules imposed upon them.

Unable to offer their labouring populations an honourable means of survival, the latter countries inevitably become soft on illegal labour in general and on child labour in particular. But as soon as they are integrated into the world market those self-same countries do not always stop at merely tolerating so-called 'informal' activities when distributing their national product. Without necessarily needing to be pressured into it, the state can go still further on what appear to be the following grounds: 'Our country is in debt. If you want us to purge those debts, then you have to work for the export market.' In promoting an ambition over which they have but partial control – for its success depends largely upon the purchasing nations – the powers that be ironically end up using their authority more in favour of a growth in child labour than its abolition. 'Let's supply gold, carpets, services etc. at lower prices than our neighbours,' they say, 'then the problem of underdevelopment will be resolved'; an argument which even makes some governments feel they can justifiably complain as much about being attacked for their use of child labour as about the plots they say neighbouring competitor nations are hatching against them. Those with the political will to quit this path will run the risk of finding themselves stranded in a commercial and monetary wilderness.

Employers and Principals

State arguments about international competitiveness are plainly echoed in the language of the entrepreneurs and employers hiring this type of labour force. And while we are on the subject, let us dispense with some of the illusions surrounding the benefits of the 'informal sector', supposedly the realm of resourcefulness where people can find the means to compensate for the shortcomings of the state by resorting to a lot of parallel work and earnings. A misnomer, the 'informal sector' is the realm where the most insecure sections of the population, above all children, are exposed to exploitation. Many informal activities do of course appear to be a mere extension of the domestic economy and geared to the needs of the domestic market. Some people try to portray it as a harmless, if not morally just, phenomenon where the family unit faced with poverty calls on each member to contribute towards the group's survival; and, it is often added, children have been participating in agricultural work, for instance, since the beginning of time. Depicting it as an everyday phenomenon in this way, however, is dubious on two counts: first because the basic arguments are drawn from precisely the same ideology as that of the exploiters of juvenile labour who have every interest in seeing their practices portrayed as belonging to an age-old, therefore natural, order; and second because on the whole times have changed and change very fast for a given working child. Experienced investigators know how quickly children sucked into work tend to become subject to the laws of profit. With shortages and proletarianization dominating the lives of (particularly urban) populations, mercantilist use of child labour power is always just around the corner. Imagine a small boy helping his father in the workshop or a little girl helping her mother with the housework; as soon as the parents find themselves confronted with a market, they almost automatically begin to think of their child's labour power in terms of its profitability. Predators outside the family unit are meanwhile on the scent. Among others, the example of young girls sent to work in other houses as all-purpose maids is all too familiar. Yet we are equally well aware that what at first glance appear to be the most autonomous or familial forms of activity often conceal an irrepressible network where the child never sees the principals and can thus go under the illusion that s/he is being kept safely out of the clutches of the profiteers. Such is the power of ideology to transform an exploitative social relationship into a simple strategy of resourcefulness.

The end buyers' interest in these chains of exploitation is patent. They need never know a thing about the conditions under which a product is supplied to them. Child labour, remember, does not exist in law and is situated at the other end of the chain: it can therefore be ignored. They can remain at peace with their consciences and the law, shielded from the truth by the very intermediaries responsible for hiring illicit child labour. At once both the exploiters and the exploited, these intermediaries argue that they are forced to recruit children because of the one-sided conditions imposed by the principals. This mechanism operates the world over, particularly in the carpet-weaving and lapidary industries, the cottage clothing industry, not to mention street-trading and scavenging on city dumps. It should also be noted that the intermediaries in these chains are sometimes none other than the parents themselves: the outcome of a common strategy among employers wherever production can be paid by the piece or per yield. Whole family units are made to work in this way, especially on large plantations where the planter officially (by law) only hires adult members, or even just the headman alone, yet sets their wages at levels so far below the bread-line that they have to make up the difference by putting their children to work as well.

The children harnessed by these networks – be they placed in work, cast out onto the streets following the break-up of the family or hired to supplement their own seniors' labour – are all largely ignored by the law, except when some obscure conflict of interests prompts it to act (generally against the children themselves more than against child labour). This is where we see the clearest manifestation of the de facto collusion uniting employers with the makers and enforcers of the law.

With the exception of the very special case of apprentices, which we shall go into later, the law immediately and by definition excludes exploited children from any statutory regime: one cannot apply labour laws to persons not officially allowed the right to work, for that would strip the universal principles underlying the latter of their legitimacy. Like their procurer counterparts in the prostitution industry (child prostitution included), employers of children are masters at the art of playing on that ambiguity; since it is not recognized, exploitation cannot exist. This contradiction has in truth given rise to a number of legal safeguards providing for a sort of special transitional status (generally from twelve or fourteen through to eighteen years) designed to protect underage workers from abuse and risks to their health and equilibrium. Underage worker status is loaded with far-reaching symbolic significance, for it both recognizes it as an established fact and addresses a solemn warning to exploiters not to overstep the mark laid down by law. But apart from its extremely vague wording – at least in the international conventions that are incapable of drawing a strict line between 'employment' and 'exploitation' – such a status remains at odds with its own objectives, for it combats neither the legal powerlessness of minors *vis-à-vis* their employers nor the barriers to their unionization. The underlying logic of this special status, prioritizing 'protection' rather than citizenship, is notoriously weak in practical scope. It may, albeit unintentionally, increase the risks to children in so far as it encourages employers to conceal their abuses and coerce their juvenile labour force to toe the line or face the wrath of the law and unemployment.

Hence, while adding to the children's confused feeling that they are 'doing something wrong', employers naturally seek to secure all the right conditions to shield child labour, physically as much as morally, from social sanctions in order unrestrainedly to maintain the prevailing tandem of legal insecurity–economic insecurity. They do this in numerous ways which all essentially boil down to a conscious effort to twist the meaning of the word 'outlaw'. First is the real or imaginary extra-territoriality that results from the existence of 'rights-free' zones whose geographical remoteness or customary practices basically enable them to operate beyond the jurisdiction of central government. Apart from the circumstances of civil war, when the absence of state control obviously leaves local tyrants free to round up child labour to their hearts' content (for military purposes included), fate has it that the earth's mineral and vegetal riches are located in places where climatic and geological conditions often make them relatively inaccessible and where the isolated agents in charge of state outposts can hardly be said to occupy a position of great strength. This combines with a second, highly compatible, process whereby those public servants are drawn into the local customs and generally end up being corrupted. Usually underpaid, they work under the constant pressure of their own personal needs and the threats imposed upon them by a hostile environment, until they (those that survive at least) are swiftly enrolled into the very order they had been assigned to combat. Such is the modus operandi of many remote mines and plantations which, being way beyond the reach of any legitimate control, are known to have children to thank for a large share of their profits. The right blend of these two compatible processes – mafia-controlled territories and, more generally, the jungle of towns and shanty-towns with their own parallel laws – offers fertile ground for the unrestricted growth of forced child labour far from the eyes of the law.

In a certain manner of speaking, that extra-territoriality is mirrored by western consumers buying goods produced by exploited juvenile labour in those uncontrolled areas because of the market, their tastes and, at times, blindness. In the light of the devastating effects of 'offshore production' policies, we cannot fail to make the following connection: an ever-growing volume of the goods consumed by rich countries is produced at lower cost in these vast lawless tracts of underdevelopment, so it is worth their while to offload the guilt on to the producer countries. This attitude is an extension of that of local employers of juvenile labour, who artfully point out how they are sandwiched between the pressures brought to bear by the market and the families. By a strange reversal of the causes and effects, as seen in the recurring success of the theme that 'it's all a matter of education (or awareness-raising)', public opinion actually holds the families to blame and the employers, safe in the knowledge that they are echoing accepted wisdom, rarely miss an opportunity to point the finger at parental neglect. Or else they talk about the favour they are doing families 'who don't know what to do with their children' by consenting to take them into their 'protection'.

Before returning to the parents, let us take a brief look at a third procedure known to provide a harbour from the law: tapping the resources 'stashed away' within the family unit. In anticipation of what will be said about the paternalist mechanism, it might be said that we would be well on our way to resolving the issue of child labour were it not for that fundamental obstructer of civil rights, the family. Unless there is some sort of conflict, what labour inspector, judge or police officer has the right to penetrate a domestic environment universally regarded by both traditional customs and the law alike as a private space? The principals are only too well aware of that; whenever production requirements permit it, the best employers of a child are his/her parents and, of course, uncles, grandfathers, elder sisters etc. This, as we shall see, is not only because they have ascendancy over the child, but because the law cannot easily enter the home, above all for matters to do with labour. Hence the success – and this is where the circle closes – of the above-mentioned chains of exploitation, whose ultimate agent is the child's parent.

From Economic Insecurity to Social Insecurity

'It's all a matter of awareness-raising', 'priority must be given to the education system', 'the real problem is that families are too fatalistic', 'what's missing are tough penalties for exploiters', 'everyone's an accomplice because everyone has an interest in it' – and on it goes, an endless list of fine words which sadly seem as reproducible as the exploitation of children itself. The most commonly levelled criticisms of parental authority in that battery of stereo-typed views – each of which, it must be said, has a measure of truth to it – warrant further investigation, for that is where the social crux of the matter undoubtedly lies.

PARENTAL LOVE AND INTEREST: THE PATERNAL METAPHOR   As far as their children are concerned, parents (as well as seniors and tutors) are faced with a choice: school work or professional work. Only rarely do the two remain lastingly compatible, except (with great reservation) in the case of apprenticeship. Contemporary history has imposed the model of school education, but if every country subscribes to its basic principles only a minority conform to them. Without going into the validity of this now universal option here, let us measure how the gap between values and practices affects parental strategies.

There are usually three, often mutually conflicting, categories of concerns underlying those strategies. The first pertains solely to physical reproduction needs: the group's daily survival. The second concerns the group's social reproduction, entailing a wide variety of commercial, matrimonial and symbolic exchanges; whether this form of reproduction responds to a logic of expansion (in terms of dependants, wealth or power) or merely maintenance, it represents extra costs on top of those of physical reproduction alone, but the latter comes to depend on it in the long run. The third, which stems from the second, involves lump-sum or deferred spending as the group invests in its children in order to perpetuate itself as a group.

These strategies, which might just as easily have been called 'constraints', clash with one another and affect the children's fate in a way that is even further complicated by the fact that it occurs within the framework of an unequal social relationship (based on the pretext of age): domination. Domination is exerted all the more easily within the family unit because no other authority such as, above all, the state is in a position to fulfil similar functions. Whenever the family finds itself faced with serious financial difficulties, the above three categories converge and the children are prematurely pushed to start work; in order to finance a marriage or settle a debt, for example. Clearly, though, the countries where households suffer the greatest degree of economic insecurity are the very ones whose school education system is most deficient, as much in terms of quality and quantity of schools as the poor careers prospects it has to offer.

If there is one clinical observation on which all observers unanimously agree, it is this: flaws in the education system and child labour are closely inter-related. From that point onwards the analyses diverge. We often hear it said that the parents are sacrificing their children upon the altar of exploitation rather than themselves making sacrifices to offer them a good education and that such selfish short-termism creates far more serious problems in later life. Others, on the contrary, conclude that it is pointless sending a child to school when it offers no real openings: it would mean two-fold losses as a household would be deprived of the use of its younger members' labour power while also having to splash out on a costly education with no sure-fire results at the end. But one thing is certain: family reproduction needs converge here with the appetites of employers of children. When the domestic unit and production unit are one and the same, the collusion of all parties involved is plainly masked by a guilt-relieving ideological device: it will be frequently said that the children are put to work 'to stop them hanging about the streets', 'so they can learn a trade', 'earn themselves a little pocket money', or simply 'because there's no school'. The ensuing exploitative relationship henceforward assumes the appearance of a protective relationship.

This is where the second characteristic feature of child labour enters the frame. Generally speaking, and despite an undoubtedly growing number of exceptions (e.g. in the mines or factories subject to the rule of the crudest form of capitalism), labour relations resemble the paternalism prevailing within the home environment. It sits very well with working children's lack of rights: because of their age, they are denied access to any form of contractual status and are instead subordinated to the traditional-style author-ity of a 'tough but caring' paternalist. Paternalism describes itself as a relationship of authority which associates force and protection and is (or claims to be) essentially more interested in the child's long-term welfare than contractual concerns. The way this works is plain to see in the case of apprentices, including those who have come of age: the employer is not an 'employer' but a 'master'; he must treat his 'employees' as if they were his own children; and the sacrifices he demands of them, the punishment he metes out, in short, all the oppression he brings to bear, is for their own good. It is the family model with its all-powerful father adapted to the workplace, as if it were a straightforward extension of a natural law.

The matter of wages illustrates and confirms the omnipresence of paternal-ism. Exploited children's wages are generally in keeping with this singular form of social relationship. First, any wages they might receive are less than enough to cover their basic vital needs; so they are therefore placed in a position of being dependent upon either their family or their employer to stay alive, which serves to block their road to emancipation. Second, whenever the social context allows it, children will consequently tend to be paid almost entirely in kind (lodgings, food, gifts) rather than in cash, with small sums distilled in dribs and drabs in such a way as to prevent them from accumulating savings; or else the master will manage a savings scheme on their behalf, making deductions from their wages. Third, pay is arbitrary, linked to the activity's financial gains and, above all, unstable: uncertainty as to how much they will earn makes the children increasingly dependent while at the same time forcing them into a wait-and-see policy, competition with others, fear of slip-ups and a desire to overexert themselves. In the child's mind, this brand of paternalism also transforms wages into rewards and, hence, class consciousness into gratitude. The stranglehold is even more perverse in that, by assuming the role of a 'father', the employer can make the child feel duty-bound to obey him as he would his own father; protection and exploitation work hand in glove, reinforcing one another and defusing the slightest urge on the part of the child to flee the system. It is a situation which seems to hark back to the bonds linking masters and their slaves: once freed, the latter would find themselves incapable of coming to terms with their new-found independence; in the same way, children who spend too long trapped in the ruthless logic of paternalism are like birds with amputated wings. The ultimate perversity of it is that if those wings ever grow back to give them some degree of autonomy, they will carry with them into adulthood the awesome legacy of an apprenticeship in servitude and perhaps use the same techniques in turn on their juniors. Some of the toughest exploiters – the ones belonging to the above-mentioned class of exploitation chain intermediaries at least – are recruited from the ranks of those who have themselves born the brunt of such a system.

THE CONTRADICTIONS OF PATERNALIST SUBORDINATION The model presented here finds its most accomplished form in traditional (i.e. non-institutional) apprenticeship and appears to function as a universal social reference for the exploitation of children. In practice, it rarely exists in its pure state because it undergoes many changes, partly due to the reactions and behaviour of the children themselves. As soon as it starts from the basis of a denial of status, and whenever there is no customary contractual bond between the children and their protectors, paternalism of this kind operates in a contradictory ideological field. It therefore has within it the seeds of its own potential breakdown and manages to keep up the illusion only when the employers and parents are one and the same. However, children placed outside the family unit often regard their parents as failing in their duties towards them; furthermore, they have plenty of opportunity to see the brutal reality of exploitation for what it really is (even if their perceptions of it may be muddled).

As human beings endowed with thoughts and feelings, as people with something to say and more generally as individuals, working children are the chief absentees from the campaigns and studies concerning them. Apart from a few splendid, praiseworthy exceptions, the paternalism stemming from the above-mentioned symbiosis between parents and employers is reflected in the essentially protective action and thinking of which they are the subjects – if not victims. With their call for abolition, the people championing their cause often unwittingly help exploiters by enhancing the insecurity and dependence of those they claim to be defending. Moreover, mentors taking up the children's plight for the good of their own personal reputations only create additional paternalism, alas, which thus leads to even further infantilizing the child. The intentions are not being called into question here, merely the fact that they may, because of an inability truly to modify the international rules pushing children into exploitation, end up creating another form of confinement. The international vendors of child-made goods know something about this, as do the financial institutions systematically bleeding the planet, for their well-intentioned paternalist action enables them to set the producers against one another, much to the advantage of the buyers.

It is therefore worth taking a look at what is emerging in terms of solutions and the obstacles created by the children themselves. We would be fooling ourselves if we thought we could avoid the pitfalls highlighted above and, what is more, it would be unfair to level criticism at the people devoting their time and energy to saving children from exploitation. But the researcher, for whom it is both a privilege and a weakness not to be engaged in any action, can help to clear the path.

In my view, exploited children regardless of their situation all demand four things: first, to be released from all servitude; second, to be paid the wages they deserve; third, to be left in peace; and finally, to top it all, respect. According to everything ever written about them, these demands appear to cover the best part of their desires. But they are full of ambiguity because the children have, as a rule, voiced them within a political, economic and social environment essentially geared towards subordination. What is more, they come from a wide variety of different workplaces. So we had best examine both the contradictions and specific features, while always bearing the omnipotence of paternalism in mind. As it is impossible to examine every single case, let us pick out a few typical common denominators from the nature of their bonds with their parents and employers.

A point about the typology below: not one of the cases presented exhausts the empirical reality and none is mutually exclusive. Having said that, we must always remember that the children's reactions to such situations are largely determined by the fact that one day they will no longer be children. Finally, there is no such thing as a generalized 'child'. But the complexity of the facts and practices must not stop us from seeking theoretically plausible configurations which might be used as a framework to interpret individual situations.

CHILDREN IN THE MIDST OF THEIR FAMILIES Certainly the most widespread case is where the children are either working for their families or with their families for an employer or outside principals – a whole range of other possibilities exists between the two depending on the extent of their attachment to the market. The overriding concern here is survival and sharing. Paternalism thrives because the child believes s/he is supplying his or her labour power in return for the upkeep of the group giving him or her its protection: in the child's mind, the principles of solidarity and dependence are one and the same thing. This system can continue reproducing for as long as the customary rules of the game remain unbroken by capitalist behaviour on the part of seniors. But if, when market openings offer opportunities to accumulate wealth (even when it is appropriated by those financing the operation), parents become exploiters, the moral contract is broken and the child begins to feel robbed. Paternalism in such cases will have unwittingly sparked the child's desire for independence, as s/he will then want to enjoy the fruits of his or her labour. This in turn leads to a fight for freedom and a fall in the number of productive family units; there is nothing subversive about the process itself, because the issue here is where the earnings go rather than a challenge to the principle of subordination. It is even more likely to happen if their earnings are diverted for ends whose usefulness is not immediately apparent, e.g. for throwing a party to boost the family's social standing. Spending of this sort will seem even less justified if the child is made to work additional hours and hence is left with shorter daily rest periods – what might be called the Cinderella syndrome. Yet this major flaw in the paternalist system only very rarely leads to rupture, for its strength here is above all that it instils in children the desire one day to reverse the situation of dependency; they are living in wait, bottling up their rebelliousness until the time or circumstances arrive for them to take over as the heads of the households into which they were born. Or else their vague desires for freedom are neutralized by the fatalism underpinning the paternalist solution and reinforced by religion; to add to which they are for ever hearing their seniors saying, 'I had a hard time of it too, you know', as if to stress the 'natural' side of exploitation.

Children accompanying their parents to an outside work site belong to this category too. Here, though, confrontation with the market or principals who are continually driving down his purchase price is replaced by direct contact between an employer and an employed family. As a result, first of all the market ceases to act as a screen concealing exploitation, and second of all the children (even those under the wing of the family head) are confronted with an employer as visible as he is powerful, and sometimes even end up automatically courting exploitation. Such is the case on the large plantations. Paternalism acts in a similar way as the authority within the self-employed family: it is hard to see how a child can refuse to follow his/ her father and mother to harvest if his/her daily bread is at stake. But once outside the domestic environment where they encounter entrepreneurs who fix wage levels for the labour of the group as a whole – made all the more necessary by the regular cuts in job prices – children find themselves in a new situation where uncertainties about their future are flung in their faces. What used to be hidden from them when the family was managing its own resources is made plainly visible by the presence of an employer; they have to push themselves to the limits and make the most of their labour power both to bolster their family's earnings (paid, of course, according to the yield) and above all to secure their own future. The children 'lay it on thick', for ever improving on their work rate in an attempt to show that their family deserves the work and, at the same time, to demonstrate their personal potential as future employees. If they do not do so of their own accord, the parents will find a way of coercing their child(ren) to comply with the ruthless order of this system of delegated exploitation, especially when the employers also own the shops where the family needs to purchase its provisions. Also found in workshops and, more generally, wherever workers are forced to compete with one another, this sort of competitive behaviour (with its obviously harmful effects on the health) is typical of the forms of domination that exist where a collective labour supply finds itself facing a single employer. Paternalism here takes over the management of the family and assumes the omnipotence of the boss – and the more benevolent he can make it look the better. It gives him the advantage of being able to capitalize on all the resources of domestic authority. But it also has the corollary defect of failing to detect effectively any potentially explosive situations: indeed, as the many outbreaks of unrest and revolt have shown, exploitation can easily exceed the limits of tolerability because the exploiters, in the belief that there is nothing to prevent them from fully satisfying their appetites, tend to forget what is by nature the delicate balance of paternalism. Yet there are points beyond which family solidarity may turn from faithful service to dissent, e.g. if the employer ceases to offer guaranteed job security or if he is seen to be misappropriating money that he ought to be paying in wages. Once he has run the gamut of classic intimidation techniques (religion, police etc.), he will then find himself facing family groups, often with the children on the front line, whose internal bonding he will have ironically helped to weld through his paternalist policy.

CHILDREN PLACED OUTSIDE THE HOME   Children who have been placed away from home or, worse still, sold are to some extent dispossessed of the degree of bargaining power they used to enjoy within the family through age-related defence mechanisms such as tantrums, sickness, emotional blackmail, ganging up with other young siblings, running away from home, premature marriage and so on. Forcibly plunged into an alien environment (or pushed, out of interest, to move in with relations by marriage), they find themselves physically and emotionally isolated and become withdrawn and silent, bottling up an accumulation of grudges and ambitions. Anyone who has come into contact with the victims of bonded child labour, for example, will have remarked upon their astonishing blend of precocious maturity and an inability to speak freely. In their employers' adaptations of domestic paternalism, discipline and scare tactics prevail over care and protection, particularly in the case of children forced into prostitution. If and when they gain their freedom and embark upon adult professional and domestic life, such solely oppressive versions of paternalism will prove not to have been a positive system for them. They often end up either becoming outcasts or repeating the brutality, inflicting it just as mercilessly on others because it is the only form of social relations they have ever known; as far as girls are concerned, a similar, just as 'natural', mechanism can be seen when, after a childhood spent working as an all-purpose maidservant, they go on to deliver themselves into another form of dependency: married life. On the whole, albeit to undoubtedly varying degrees, this type of working child is kept in a position of prolonged lack of responsibility.

Digressing slightly, this category also includes child apprentices even though they theoretically have some compensation: learning the skills of a trade and hence, presumably, acquiring an advantage for adult life. It has to be said, with all the force necessary to measure up to the powerful argument in favour of paternalism, that many surveys prove apprenticeship is often a façade dressing up exploitation with the merits of training – a depressing fact which also holds true in the rich nations. Craftsmen naturally need to pass on their skills if only to be sure of having someone qualified to take over from them when they retire. But the opportunity to acquire those skills is often restricted to younger members of their own families; and standardized production techniques have taken the variety out of an overwhelming proportion of workshop activities, leaving them in need of very little sophisticated know-how. Genuine and effective apprenticeship does not chime with current market laws which, under the severe pressure of falling prices, prioritize levels of output over training. And paternalism provides an awesome degree of leverage for the exploitation of apprentices. Because it is so arbitrary and, in many cases, never-ending, vocational training becomes something of an impossible dream in the children's imagination and encourages their subordination. Far from being seen as the 'master's' source of profit, in their minds the labour they supply assumes the appearance of a payment in return for his instruction. Ultimately, the boss seeks to maintain his authority by keeping his young protégés in a state of ignorance; it serves to justify both the lack of wages and the threats of punishment which are so much a part of life in apprenticeship workshops. Some surveys show that apprentices are far from always fooled by the device, but their only means of escape is to run away. This is a very serious step to take for it basically means breaking the contract between the family and employer, thus leaving them either isolated or, if caught, open to tough disciplinary action.

CHILD WAGE-EARNERS   The children cast on to a more anonymous labour market when the adults of the family are short of resources constitute a somewhat different ensemble. Whether employed in mining (where they are highly in demand due to their size) and factories or as seasonal farm-hands, they all come into direct contact with bosses and foremen, competitive workmates and wage bargaining. Gone are the anaesthetizing effects of a paternalist ideology which masks the unfairness of their earnings – under-payment, remember, being a universal feature of child labour – the tough working conditions and the long hours. Here they are exposed to the stark reality of capitalism. Unlike children placed in other houses, they are often not torn from the family unit; on the contrary, they remain with their family and directly contribute to its upkeep. But in many cases, their active role in the reproduction of the family is likely to undermine normal relations within the group, removing the traditional authority of the parents. Domestic paternalism is still further undermined if the family head is out of work (or has gone missing) and the children become the chief breadwinners. Without suggesting that families in circumstances such as these are right to send their children to work or into the clutches of exploitation, the children themselves may be presumed to be acting out of a sense of responsibility, precisely because their childhood has been taken away from them and they cannot count on any protection. Having said that, they come up against a powerful obstacle to full citizenship: the law does not recognize them as workers.

Although we have already dealt with this at some length, further comments are required here from the point of view of the children in question *vis-à-vis* the difficulties stemming from such a denial of justice. Declared inferior by society on the (theoretically fair) grounds that their age entitles them to be kept away from any form of exploitation, those of them that are subjected to it have no other option but to learn the codes and reflexes of the underground economy. Their bosses can easily coerce them to do so with the threat of exposure or redundancy. Sometimes those bosses receive the assistance of corrupt local authorities striving to turn a campaign against child labour into a campaign against the labouring child.

Such oppression follows the most tortuous routes according to a variety of factors: among others, the competition between employers (sometimes resulting in cases of whistle-blowing), initiatives on the part of certain state officials (who can often earn a backhander in return for their silence), the government's desire to boost its country's international standing. As the children need the work, the threat of the law paradoxically cements their bonds with the employers and creates general collusion in the face of a common enemy: the state. Here again exploitation feeds off the power of the imagination – very few countries really do crack down on child labour. The fact that the children involved are the ones defending themselves and their right to work due to the lack of any other solutions forthcoming from the state places charitable bodies fighting for the eradication of underage labour in an extremely awkward position. Indeed, these bodies find themselves torn between two extremes: the struggle to abolish child labour and the struggle to establish recognized rights and wages for working children – with the ever-present danger that the former might place the children at greater risk while the latter legitimizes the very thing they have set out to condemn.

STREET CHILDREN: A SITUATION THAT SAYS IT ALL   Finally, there are the street children. The first impression casual visitors and natives, not to mention journalists, sometimes share is that in a tough environment where resourcefulness mixes with delinquency, it is 'every man [child] for himself'. Such exotic imaginings are fortunately losing their potency thanks to an ever-increasing number of studies and reports; we now know that these children frequently belong to a network. At the other extreme, there is a temptation to put it all down to organized crime and clear the collective conscience by arguing that people in poor countries are exploiting each other. What precisely is the situation and, more particularly, does the paternalist pattern of social relations operate on the streets?

Let us first of all recall that one at least has to draw the distinction between the children working in the street but not living there and those for whom it is both workplace and home. The latter are the only ones who will have witnessed the crumbling of the familial fabric. The former, whether working for their families or a street boss, are expected to take home their earnings. Even if they are not working for parents, however, they face far greater risks than the above-described 'children working in the midst of their families', for their place of work exposes them to parallel systems of subordination, if not racketeering. Generally speaking, such systems (in the shape of gangs or hierarchized networks) tend to surface and take control spontaneously as the only possible response to a hostile environment marked by a threatening police force, the ill-will of shopkeepers and passers-by and inter-gang rivalry. Gangs grouping together out of necessity essentially bear all the outward traits of mutual solidarity which, depending on the case, replaces or complements the role of the family. Under the influence of collectively shared risks and competing for customers, these communities naturally end up staking their own territories where the leaders' protection of younger, newer or weaker members can itself easily spill over into violence. In this sense, then, there really is body of paternalist-type social relations on the streets, often acting as the basis upon which the distribution of revenue is carried out. But this form of paternalism is fundamentally unsound, with the respective positions of the children for ever being redefined through the use of force and the influx of new arrivals. It can end up competing with the cradle-to-grave type of domestic paternalism when a child is called upon to obey conflicting orders or when his/her labour is solicited by both groups to which s/he simultaneously belongs. This competition in turn tips the balance towards the 'force' side of the paternalistic binomial of 'force and protection'. Even when a child's 'protector' submits him or her to pure and simple racketeering, paternalism will not necessarily vanish if only because this extreme mechanism

of extortion thrives on its subjects' (conscious or otherwise) acceptance of a
position of servility or, at least, submission towards their protectors.

The street children's insecurity combined with the existence of these
parallel control systems makes them attractive and easy targets for the
principals on the outside of the child's world. Although the details of this
phenomenon may largely remain unknown, the networks of children certainly
do seem to be structures that frequently open on to a chain of exploitation,
irrespective of whether the profits are productive or commercial. An analogy
may be made with the case of the carpet children working for an artisan
who is himself working for a manufacturer in turn acting on a principal's
orders. Selling manufactured articles on the streets (especially stolen or
contraband goods), scavenging or even small-scale crafts production inevitably
lead back to the so-called 'formal' economy, i.e. factories, wholesalers, supermarkets, mechanical repair shops (not to mention drug traffickers), in short
to the people holding the means of production and distribution.

Here we have the key to that proliferation of street children so typical of
struggling economies and which is in itself evidence of the general condition
of exploited children. It is not solely because the free-market diktat of the
international finance organizations directly leads to the impoverishment or
even break-up of the family and, at the same time, the failure of state
education, it is not just as a result of that mean-spirited logic that so many
children are cast into the world of work or, as a last resort, on to the streets.
From the point of view of the interests stealthily progressing beneath the
banner of free enterprise, it is a positive mechanism, i.e. profitable; doubly
profitable since on the one hand it liberates a tremendous mass of weakened
labour power under conditions that are particularly favourable for no-holds-
barred exploitation, while at the same time those interests can devolve the
disciplinarian authority necessary for extracting surplus value to their victims.
Street children represent an extreme yet telling example: although they may
be working in violation of the law or on its fringes, such children are not
unemployed. With the help of structures modelled on domestic subordination,
which the ultimate beneficiaries of street-child labour would have had to
cultivate widespread slavery to match, street children are far more profitable
to use than if they were recognized workers. I believe this to be true, albeit
to varying degrees, of all exploited children. And whenever he can manage
it, the capitalist prefers to tap the resources of paternalism rather than resort
to the legal, yet impersonal, contract.

That is why, at risk of offending the abolitionists, I ask myself in conclusion
whether the first stage in the battle to bring an end to the exploitation of
children might not be to secure them statutory recognition as fully-fledged
workers alongside a concomitant struggle to release them from the stranglehold of all kinds of paternalism. What would really unsettle the exploiters
of children far more than international directives would be the prospect of
no longer being able to sit back and let the oh so miraculous formula of

domestic domination do their work for them. The truth of the matter is that the way things stand at the moment on our planet, this option is bound to be just as utopian as any other.

Note

This chapter is longer than originally intended because I felt it important to set out clearly the terms of such a complex issue in full. I therefore decided not to include explicit author references and apologize to those authors without whom this article would obviously not have been possible.

CHAPTER 15

Child Employment in a Capitalist Labour Market: The British Case

Michaël Lavalette

In Britain 'child labour' is usually viewed as either a purely historical phenom-enon or as something which happens in the 'Third World'. Yet in the last few years there has been a steady stream of reports which all suggest that employment remains a significant feature of children's lives during their school years. Explanations as to the causes of this phenomenon, however, remain undertheorized. In Britain the dominant explanations are framed in economic terms, but this fails to locate child labour in its wider social and political context. A recognition of the socio-political factors does exist in the writings on child labour in the newly industrializing countries (NICs) and in the underdeveloped countries (UDCs) but the relevance of this research to British circumstances has not always been recognized. Here it will be suggested that theorizing over child labour in the 'advanced' economies needs to engage more fully with the writings from the NICs and UDCs. This chapter, then, intends to look at the British research and the common explanations offered by these researchers for the continuance of child labour. The theoretical paradigms offered will be criticized and, instead, it will be suggested that a more critical reading of the investigations from the NICs and UDCs allows us to view child labour as a structural feature of modern capitalist economies, the precise form of which will vary historically and cross-culturally.

Defining Terms

What do we mean by 'child labour'? For many in Western Europe this is a phrase which applies to labour practices which have been abolished by 'historical progress' or, alternatively, it is something which is pervasive in the NICs and UDCs and indicative of their economic 'backwardness'. In Britain it is generally assumed that when children work they do so in light, healthy jobs which are compatible with schooling and aid the transition to adulthood. This perspective has been incorporated into the writing of some researchers who, as a result, have tried to draw a distinction between 'child work', which is viewed positively, and 'child labour' which is viewed negatively.

Such a distinction is explicit in the work of Fyfe (1989) and Whittaker (1986). For Whittaker the healthy western teenager delivering newspapers before going to school is a 'child worker'. This is because there is no economic compulsion forcing the child into employment; rather the child 'keeps his wages and spends them on such peer group *necessities* as the latest style jeans, records or, increasingly, videos and home computers [...] He simply wants to augment his pocket money' (Whittaker 1986: 20). 'Child labour' is defined as work which does not take place in such relatively idyllic conditions. It is assumed to have a degree of economic compulsion associated with it and, according to Fyfe, involves a time and energy commitment which affects children's abilities to participate in leisure, play and educational activities. Finally, child labour is 'work which impairs the health and development of children' (Fyfe 1989: 4)

Yet this distinction is not particularly useful. Clearly Fyfe and Whittaker are right to suggest that child labour can be either good or bad depending on the social context in which it takes place, but merely to give the two assumed types of practice different labels does not advance our understanding in any way. Indeed it may lead us to assume that we are in a position to distinguish clearly between acceptable and unacceptable work for children. Yet given the present state of knowledge in the area this is not feasible. It makes the strong distinction between 'work' and 'labour' illegitimate. Indeed, such a distinction can become tautological. The only way in which a job can be classified as 'child work' as opposed to 'child labour' is because we assume *a priori* that the task will not affect the child's play, leisure or educational activities.

In this chapter, the following definitions will be utilized. First, 'child' refers to anyone up until the end of compulsory schooling. Second, 'work', 'labour' and 'employment' will be used interchangeably. They are defined as paid activities carried on outside the family, that is when the activity takes place on the market and becomes a commodity. This definition excludes school-based work experience programmes and two other important areas of work experience: children's domestic labour activities and those children who work for their parents in the family businesses. Whether writers are discussing the 'advanced' economies, NICs or UDCs, there is a general agreement that employment is qualitatively different when it is taken outside direct familial control (Challis and Elliman 1979; Rodgers and Standing 1981; Greenberger and Steinberg 1986; Bequele and Boyden 1988a and 1988b).

Thus, 'child labour' refers to naturally occurring jobs performed outside direct family control by school students who have not reached their minimum statutory school-leaving age.

The Extent of the Problem

Research produced by a number of groups over the last ten years has emphasized that the exploitation of children at work is unfortunately alive and well in the British labour market and 'part-time out of school work' remains a significant feature of children's lives (Lavalette 1994; McKechnie et al. 1993, 1994; Balding 199; Hobbs et al. 1991; Pond and Searle 1991; Lavalette et al. 1991; Finn 1987; Moorehead 1987; MacLennan et al. 1985). The consensus of this research suggests that at any given time somewhere between a third and a half of school students in their last two years of compulsory schooling will be working and, among the same cohort, approximately two-thirds will be either working or will have worked in the recent past (cf. Lavalette 1994; McKechnie et al. 1993, 1994; Balding 1991). Further, the evidence suggests that the children's employment is a clear cause for concern on a number of counts.

1. The types of jobs they perform. The commonsense picture in Britain is that children perform a limited range of light tasks. Yet all studies undertaken have pointed to the fact that while the main sectors employing children coincide with those normally viewed as 'children's jobs' (e.g. delivery work), children can be found working in a wide range of activities, often competing with adult workers for jobs (e.g. in shop work and in restaurants) and occasionally in tasks which the majority of the population consider inappropriate for children (e.g. factory and warehouse work) (Lavalette 1994; McKechnie et al. 1994; Balding 1991; Lavalette et al. 1991; Pond and Searle 1991; MacLennan et al. 1985);

2. The age at which they start employment. With the exception of a limited range of agricultural tasks carried out under direct parental supervision, children in Britain are not allowed to work before their thirteenth birthday. Nevertheless, studies which have looked at full school populations have found that children as young as eleven can be employed in various tasks (Hobbs et al. 1994; Pond and Searle 1991; Balding 1991; MacLennan et al. 1985).

3. Their hours of work. The laws in Britain regarding children's hours at work are very confusing, covering times during the day when they are prohibited from working and including both daily and weekly maxima (both of which are affected by the age of the child). Nevertheless, while relatively few children work more than the weekly maximum, significant numbers start their jobs earlier in the morning and finish later in the evening than they are legally allowed to – some starting work as early as 3 or 4 a.m. while others can finish at 11 p.m. or midnight (Lavalette 1994; McKechnie et al. 1993, 1994; Hobbs et al. 1992; Pond and Searle 1991; Lavalette et al. 1991).

4. The lack of legal control. Legal controls are uneven throughout the country, being made up of a mixture of national statutes and local authority by-laws. Thus, employers taking on children in two different areas of London will be faced with different sets of regulations. Further policing of child labour is covered by three agencies: the police, the Factory Inspectorate and the Educational Welfare Service (EWS). On the whole the EWS is left to police this area, but this is only one minor activity they are expected to cover in a hybrid job (Moorehead 1987).

5. The failure of the work permit system. All children who work in Britain should obtain a 'work permit' from their local authority, signed by an educationalist and a doctor. The permit should ensure that the child's work will not detrimentally affect their education or their health. It represents the main regulatory device available to local authorities to control child employment in their area. However, repeated evidence has shown that the permit is completely inadequate for the task. In most studies approximately 90 per cent of the working children did not have or had not heard of the work permit (Lavalette 1994).

6. The wage rates given to children. Although some children can earn substantial hourly sums, the majority of children earn very poor rates of pay (Lavalette 1994; Lavalette et al. 1991; Pond and Searle 1991; MacLennan et al. 1985).

7. Health and safety issues. Children are repeatedly shown to be in danger due to the weights they are expected to carry, the times they start and finish work, the unhealthy conditions of work they find themselves in or due to the fact that they are expected to operate machines designed for an adult (Murray 1991; Pond and Searle 1991; Landrigan 1993).

Given this consensus it is clear that child employment is, or at least should be, an 'issue of concern'. Nevertheless, child labour remains a relatively understudied topic with little concern given to addressing why it should remain such a persistent phenomenon in the 'advanced' capitalist societies.

Existing Explanations of Child Labour and Their Application in Britain

The vast majority of the writing on child labour is concerned with the NICs and UDCs. Writings on these regions are substantial and often at an advanced theoretical level (Rodgers and Standing, 1981; Bequel and Boyden, 1988a and b). In this literature it is common to locate the differences in child labour in diverse societies where children are often subject to different relations of production in various social settings. Local political, cultural, ideological and social aspects are often stressed to account for the particularity of child labour in various societies. However, given the restrictions on time and space it is not possible to address all the arguments presented by the writers and researchers of child labour in these regions. Instead it is intended to identify the factors from this research which have been adopted to explain the continuance of child labour in Britain. While the literature from the NICs/UDCs is rich in identifying an array of factors which shape the specificity of child labour, it could be suggested that for the majority of the writers the core factor is an economic one: the restrictions and poverty which families find themselves facing force them to utilize all their various sources of labour power, including their children. This is occasionally combined with a perspective which suggests that local employers themselves are constrained by the circumstances in which they operate; their subordinate position with regard to multinational capital forces small local employers to employ children if they are to compete with more efficient units of capital. Nevertheless, both accounts stress the wider socio-economic features which constrain economic development and force families into poverty.

Rather simplistically, it can be suggested that the literature on child labour in the NICs and UDCs promotes four general conclusions. First, most writers in the field assume that child labour is qualitatively different when it takes place outside direct familial control. The main problem, then, is where children have to sell their labour power on the market. Second, there is a common agreement that children are employed because they are a source of cheap labour power. Third, children are more likely to be employed by small undercapitalized units of capital. Finally, child labourers and the people they work with are unlikely to be unionized to any significant extent (see generally Challis and Elliman 1979; Mendelievich 1979; Rodgers and Standing 1981; Bequele and Boyden 1988a and b).

There is not uniform agreement about the relative importance of all the various factors identified and even within the general parameters of the 'economic debate' there are ongoing controversies, such as whether child labour is 'efficient' for those sections of capital which employ it. Mehata et al. (1985: 107), for example, suggest that child labour involves 'the use of labour at its point of lowest productivity and is, therefore, an inefficient utilization of labour power'. Here child labour is portrayed as an anachronism and barrier to economic development. The maintenance of child labour is due to their 'vulnerability and dependence [which means] they can be exploited, ill treated and directed into undesirable channels by *unscrupulous elements* in the community' (Mehata et al., 1985: 107–8, emphasis added; see also Mendelievich 1979). Here, the continuance of child labour is due to the activities of rogue employers who grossly exploit children, and the solution to the problem rests in establishing an adequate legislative framework and policing mechanisms to restrict their opportunities to employ children. For other writers (for example Challis and Elliman 1979 and Bequele and Boyden 1988a and 1988b) the use of child labour by sections of capital, far from being inefficient for their immediate needs, offers a plentiful, cheap and relatively docile workforce easily amenable to the requirements of surplus value extraction. Here, of course, the solution is rather more complex as the problem is essentially bound up with the dominant relations of production in society.

Nevertheless, for all the writers child labour is essentially caused by poverty and the problems associated with this form of labour arise from children's inferior position within the 'age-hierarchy' which restricts them to certain types of jobs, in certain specific locations and for low, 'children's' wages.

Not surprisingly these writings have informed many of the recent writings on child labour in Europe (MacLennan et al. 1985; Fyfe 1989; Valcarenghi 1981). However, when applied to the 'advanced' economies much of the focus on social, cultural and ideological factors is omitted. Instead child labour is reduced to a purely economic category and can be assessed by adopting a simplistic economic axis. High unemployment and low wages, it is suggested, force families to utilize the labour of their children to supplement the family income. Fyfe (1989: 42–3), for example, suggests that, 'where parents are unemployed or on low incomes there may be added incentive for their children to work', and Forrester (1979: 259), writing about Birmingham, has claimed that 'economic decline in the Midlands has led to a massive increase in child employment [...] The pressure on living standards and unemployment in the home has forced large numbers of children to take part-time jobs.' The essential cause of child labour, therefore, is poverty.

Alternatively, some writers have utilized the economic axis to suggest that in 'advanced' economies children will exist as an example of a 'reserve army of labour'. Children, it is suggested, have been marginalized in the production process and will be drawn into employment only when there is an excessive demand for labour. Equally they will be among the first to be expelled when the market becomes overstocked. Moorehead (1987: 47) suggests that this is the case. She has claimed that in Glasgow 'high local unemployment, the fact that small businesses are trying to cut costs and do without part time help and the introduction of [...] Government [...] Training Schemes have driven most young people out of work'. Here the essential cause of child labour is not poverty but rapid economic expansion.

Following the work of most writers on the NICs and UDCs, therefore, the two explanations of child labour in Britain both stress economic factors. But they do so to the exclusion of the other factors identified by the NIC/UDC writers (social, political, ideological and cultural) and produce an overly and overtly economic reductionist paradigm. It also produces two dominant explanations which are in contradiction with each other.

Evaluation of the Existing Paradigms

Having identified the two dominant paradigms utilized by child labour writers in Britain, we can assess their validity by applying them to British conditions. First, for Fyfe (1989), Forrester (1979) and MacLennan et al. (1985) child labour is caused by poverty. If this is correct we would expect more children to be employed in declining regions of the economy, where unemployment is highest, low wages more prevalent and family poverty more overt.

Second, if children are a reserve army of labour then the suggestion is that child employment will be lowest in depressed regions where unemployment is prevalent and highest in expanding regions. Moorehead (1987: 47) suggests that the conclusion that 'there is a dwindling child labour force' will not be replicated 'in more prosperous parts of the country'. If this is correct, we would expect more children to be working in expanding regions of the economy.

To test these conflicting hypotheses it is necessary to look at research from contrasting regions of Britain. MacLennan et al. (1985) focused on London, Luton and Bedford. At the time of their study, this was an expanding economic region with low levels of unemployment and relatively low indicators of poverty. Lavalette et al. (1991) focused on Clydeside in Scotland, an area of high structural unemployment and significant levels of poverty (see Lavalette 1994). By contrasting this research it should be easier to assess which, if either, of the two economic explanations is more suitable. If children are a reserve army of labour one would expect more children to be working in London, Luton and Bedford. If child labour is caused by poverty one would expect more children to be working in Clydeside. If either paradigm is correct we would expect the range and type of job performed by children to be significantly different in each area.

Again there is not time and space to reproduce all the findings of each study. The key findings suggest that the level of employment was not significantly different in the two areas nor were the types of jobs they were performing (Lavalette 1994). Further, as noted earlier, research from other regions of Britain suggest that in their last two years of study there is at minimum one in three children working at any given point and that the jobs they perform will be relatively similar. Increases in the number of working children will reflect local factors and local job availability, but here it is not that children are a labour reserve; the evidence would rather suggest that children will take any job that becomes available. Thus the evidence suggests children work throughout Britain, that some children may work because of poverty but many child workers come from affluent families and that while local employment factors are important in shaping some of the tasks children perform, the majority of children are employed in tasks which are viewed as 'children's jobs', such as delivery work which can be easily combined with schooling.

This suggests that neither of the two hypotheses identified is fully adequate to explain the causes of child labour in Britain.

An Alternative Perspective: Child Labour as a Structural Phenomenon of Capitalist Societies

To offer a more comprehensive explanation of child labour it is necessary to return to the debate in the NICs and UDCs. As Rodgers and Standing (1981) note, to comprehend fully the significance of child labour in any particular society we must locate it in its 'relational aspects', that is as it is affected by and, in turn, affects an array of political, ideological, cultural and socio-economic features. This conclusion is equally valid for Britain.

Thus, in trying to understand and determine the social position of the child labourer in modern Britain, the 'relational aspect' must be recognized. Essentially, when children enter the labour market in the advanced economies, they do so from a disadvantaged position within the age hierarchy. The age hierarchy is a socially constructed phenomenon: 'a system of seniority in which those in junior positions are unable to achieve full social status in their own right' (Elson 1982: 491). The ideological construction of childhood and the age hierarchy are based on a number of assumptions. Among the most important are that children are

- incapable of supporting themselves and must be protected by individuals further advanced in the age hierarchy
- members of a family unit, one of whose members will be earning a 'family wage' capable of supporting the entire family
- primarily involved in social activities deemed suitable for children, such as gaining an education
- protected by state legislation and government agencies from abuse, oppression and exploitation, including protection from harmful labour activities

It is worth emphasizing that these are ideological assumptions and do not necessarily match the reality of children's lives.

The majority of children work at jobs which are commonly viewed as 'children's'. They are jobs which require little training and hence are assumed to be particularly suitable activities for them to perform. These tasks are also normally temporally suitable for children, being 'out of school' work which can be combined with education and performed before or after the school day, at weekends or during holidays. Further, existing research suggests: 'children gain their work experience through filling in certain economic niches left empty by the adult world' (James 1984: 11). Partially as a result of these features, and due to the assumption that children do not have to support themselves financially, their jobs tend to be poorly paid and are often characterized as a form of 'pocket money'. These features are mutually reinforcing with the result that even when children are employed in other sectors of the economy, performing illegitimate 'adult' jobs, their inferior position within the age hierarchy will affect their pay and conditions of employment. Thus the labour activities of children are devalued and cheapened. This has little to do with the actual economic activities performed by children, but instead reflects social phenomena and assumptions and the effects these have in structuring the labour market.

Within social analysis, similar issues have been addressed by feminism and Marxism. Both these bodies of theory potentially offer insights which may be fruitfully applied to the analysis of child labour. 'Feminist economics' (Phillips and Taylor 1980) has analysed the position of women in the paid labour market. This literature has stressed that 'economic' phenomena, such as the skill classification attached to certain jobs and the variation in wage levels between 'gendered' tasks, are not determined by purely economic factors. As Elson (1982: 488) notes, these phenomena are: 'structured systematically by the hierarchy of gender, a hierarchy in which women as a

gender are subordinate to men as a gender. Gender differentiation is constructed socially and though it relies on biological differentiation, it is not
reducible to the latter.'

Feminist analysis of this form is multi-variant, stressing the wide variety
of features and power sources which are co-equal in shaping the subordinate
position of women in the labour market.

Such a perspective has been adopted by Elson to explain the position of
child workers. She suggests that the dominant form of child labour must be
understood as resulting from the influence and interaction of a number of
'authority sources' such as the authority of adults within the family, the
demands of the education system and the needs of capital. As a result, she
suggests the analysis of child labour could be fruitfully elaborated by accepting
the concept of the 'social construction of an age hierarchy; of a system of
seniority in which those in junior positions are unable to achieve full social
status in their own right' (Elson 1982: 491). Lack of 'seniority' does not
reflect or suggest any 'lack of personal capacity for autonomous behaviour'
(p. 492); rather, such capacities are not socially recognized. Capitalist economic
relations, therefore, although not in and of themselves ascriptive of seniority,
do reflect and become the bearers of this ideological category. A similar
conclusion has led Qvortrup (1985: 141–2) to claim that 'children's objective
position in the social division of labour would justify, on theoretical grounds,
the childgroup being assigned a distinct status or class'. However, such a
proposition undermines the economic basis to the theory of class and replaces
it with one which gives primacy to ideological and political criteria. While the
importation of ideological and political criteria are important, they are not
co-equal with economic criteria which remain the principal determinants of
class (Wright 1978).

Within Marxist theory, the concept of class is anchored in production
relations, which is clearly a structural feature of societies. Miles (1982: 156)
identifies the process adopted by Marxists in analysing class positions and
structures. He suggests that one proceeds 'by first identifying its dominant
mode of production because this constitutes the foundation for the subsequent identification of the primary classes'. Any dependent modes will
delineate the existence of additional classes. This structural identification of
the primary antagonistic classes is, however, only a first step in the division
of any society. In itself this does not reveal anything about the particular
economic, political and ideological content of those classes or 'the way in
which they are fractionalised' (p. 156). All that is established, he claims, is the
sites or structures of class positions. He proceeds: 'Thereafter, historical
analysis of the economic, political and ideological relations of that social
formation entails consideration of the persons who occupy those positions,
their political consciousness and the strategies that they actively pursue (that
is in the class struggle) within the structural constraints established at the
outset' (pp. 156–7).

Here, Miles introduces the concept of 'class fractions' to explain ideological differences within classes and raises the possibility that this may usefully be adopted to explain the position of discriminated groups within the working class. The specific example Miles is discussing is the black population in modern Britain, but the concept of a class fraction can also be applied to the study of child labour, by recognizing that the ideological differentiation of children and the development of the concept of childhood have located children in a disadvantaged position within the seniority system. Thus the 'simple' analysis of class positions and the allocation of particular agents to set class sites takes no account of differences by age. However, it is clear that age differences exist and are legitimized by the socially constructed age hierarchy and the ideology of childhood. Such an ideology is based within, and reproduced by, familial relations which provide social significance and meaning to the oppression faced by children in the social world. The ideology of childhood acts in such a way as adversely to affect the activities of children in all aspects of their lives within particular societies including their labour market activities. Such features allow us to view children as a 'fraction' of their particular social class. Such a conception allows a recognition to be made of the ideological differentiation between adults and children and the importance of the seniority system in delineating children's tasks, but it also emphasizes the importance of their class location in determining their life experiences and overall position in the social structure.

Of course children form very peculiar class fractions. For working-class children this results in them being ideologically differentiated and, in the advanced core of the world system, economically marginalized and expected to spend the majority of their time in educational institutions. They are also only temporary members of this particular group within their class. These features are mutually reinforcing. Thus, their presence in educational institutions affects their ability to enter waged labour and reinforces their 'immaturity' in the age hierarchy. Their perceived immaturity and the conception of their waged labour activity as a 'spare time' activity has been important in their economic marginalization and an important feature affecting their remuneration at work and general conditions of employment. Thus, as James notes, 'the major structuring principle governing such work experience is the marginal social position of the school child to the main labour force' (James 1984: 12).

In modern Britain the labour activities that children perform are significantly different from those undertaken by children in the past. Historically, the form of children's labour has altered radically. Such change is the result of complex historical processes which affect all society and not just children; but the changes represent an 'advance' or victory for working-class children and are, therefore, something to be defended.

Children have always worked. Generally there has been a recognition that they are incapable of fully undertaking an adult workload. Of course their work was often exceptionally hard but, at the very least, they were usually introduced to work gradually, under the supervision of their parents (Pinch-beck 1969). The obvious exception to this pattern occurred during the industrial revolution. Here children were increasingly employed in factory production as individual proletarians. Not only were their jobs controlled by overseers and managers, whose aim was to maximize output, but their tasks were paced by the relentless drive of the machines (Thompson 1968; Thomis 1974). Although they often still performed 'children's jobs', as scavengers and piecers for example, little acknowledgement was made of their special needs and requirements and the children were often driven to the limits of their physical abilities. Further, because they were children, they were paid less and, where possible, this was used to undermine the wage rates of adult men and women.

Yet it was not simply the location of this work in the factory which increased the exploitation of children. In family cottage industries in the period of 'proto-industrialization', and when children worked as part of a family labour unit, down the mines for example, the abuse of child labour was severe (Pinchbeck 1969). The hidden nature of much of this employment has obscured the fact that the pressure to exploit child labour fully and ruthlessly grew with the development of a more complex market economy: when child labour became commodified. The development of capitalist competition within the market and the logic of surplus value extraction forced employers to utilize the cheapest available labour resources (Levine 1977). In the mining and cottage industries the direct 'employer' was often the skilled worker who acted as a sub-contractor. He would get a set amount of money for the work that he undertook and it was up to him to hire his own helpers. The sub-contractor primarily did this by utilizing his family's labour resources but, when needed, he would supplement this by hiring waged labour. In such a system, the skilled worker was constrained by the market to internalize the logic of surplus value extraction on to himself and his family. Thus the extreme exploitation of child labour can be identified as a feature associated with the growth of a fully-fledged capitalist market economy.

Yet although the levels of child labour exploitation found in the early factories was excessive it is important to recognize that this is an exception to the general picture. Even during the industrial revolution it was a minority experience (Tranter 1981; Cunningham 1990). Indeed, many children were employed in specifically 'children's jobs', for example as trappers in the mines and as chimney sweepers. This is not to underestimate the harmful and exceptionally exploitative circumstances in which children found themselves; rather, the aim is to redirect the debate towards the general issue of child labour and exploitation under class societies and away from an overbearing focus on child labour in factory production. Such a redirection allows two general conclusions to be emphasized. First, that the development of pro-tective child labour legislation has not stopped children from working, though it has been significant in altering the form of that work. Children's work activities have been primarily marginalized to 'out of school' work, which is viewed as a legitimate arena of experience, though it is one where there is still a significant level of exploitation. Second, the worst manifestations of child labour occur where children are employed in 'adult' jobs. Here, children are employed because of their cheapness. Instances of this type of child labour exploitation tend to occur in undercapitalized sectors where the extreme level of exploitation allows the employing unit of capital to compete with more efficient, capital-intensive outlets. These undercapitalized units tend to be small and employ an unorganized workforce. This conclusion can be applied to underdeveloped, industrializing and advanced sectors of the world economy, and hence is far from being of only historical interest.

The marginalization of child labour in Britain in the late nineteenth century cannot be isolated from other features and changes in Britain at that time (Hall 1984; Hall and Schwarz 1985). Thus, although 'child labour' is on one level a purely 'economic' phenomenon, the process of marginalization was affected by, and in turn affected, other 'ideological' and 'political' phenomena. Hence, the re-emergence of the working-class family (German 1989) and the acceptance of the ideology of childhood (Davin 1982) by the working class were crucial to the process. These developments were aided by, and reflected, changes in social policy formation, and the changes which in turn demanded further social policy initiatives (Lewis 1986). Equally, at the turn of the nineteenth century there were significant developments in the economic structure (Stedman Jones 1976) and an increasing realization of the need to educate the future workforce (Simon 1960, 1965). In this context, education became identified as the most suitable activity for children to perform. Yet the changing form of child labour was not simply imposed on the working class by bourgeois society but matched particular needs and goals held by the working class itself. Hence, the working class, and working-class children in particular, were instrumental in shaping the process of marginalization (Davin 1982; Humphries 1981).

Thus, in considering and analysing child labour in Britain, it is necessary to tackle a number of interrelated issues. Not only must the existence and marginalization of child labour itself be explained, but also why the existence of child labour should clash with the dominant ideology of childhood and the perceived role of children within the family.

In essence there were four interrelated elements involved in the process of marginalization. First, the re-emergence of the working-class family from the middle of the nineteenth century. There is some evidence that the working-class family was breaking down in urban areas as a result of the pressures of factory production. However, by the middle of the nineteenth century, problems associated with both daily and inter-generational reproduction meant that increasingly the working class defended the family as the best available means of maintaining its standard of living. One demand that was raised at this time was for a 'family wage', a wage earned by the male head of the household but large enough to support the family without the need for his wife and children to enter the labour market. Although the demand was by and large unsuccessful, it did reinforce the working-class family and the sexual division of labour that predominates within it. This emphasized the female role as provider of domestic labour, as carer and as child-rearer. An offshoot of this process, however, was the reinforcement of the ideology of childhood within the working class. In this sense the family wage demand was partially successful. The aim of the demand was to reduce the supply of labour on the labour market by withdrawing women and children and increasing the wage paid to men. The demand has often been assessed in terms of its effect on working-class women and has been regarded as unsuccessful since many women still had to perform whatever tasks they could to earn money (Barrett and McIntosh 1980; Humphries 1977; German 1989). However, in terms of its effect on child labour it was relatively successful. The change in the form and activity of child workers in the late nineteenth century partially reflected this. Thus, the second element was the acceptance of the ideology of childhood by working-class families (Davin 1982, 1990).

The third element was the growth of family- and child-related social policy at the turn of the century. The realization of the horrendous living conditions forced upon the working class in Britain and the perceived danger that this would have on British industry, the country and its ability to defend the empire, prompted a move by the British state in the direction of basic welfare provision. This provision was informed by the ideal of a 'normal' (i.e. bourgeois) family form and by a view of the needs of working-class children similarly shaped by an idealized conception of bourgeois childhood. Such policy intervention had the effect of further strengthening the family as an institution in society, of limiting the labour activities of children that could be regarded as legitimate, and of establishing an activity that was thought of as particularly suitable for children, that is, gaining a useful education. The significance of the developing education system was that it firmly established an activity that was quickly accepted as necessary and useful by the majority of bourgeois commentators. Gradually this discouraged firms from breaking the statutes and employing children, a practice which previously they had been willing to engage in (Lewis 1986; Carr and Jamieson 1990).

Finally, underlying each of the above was the whole issue of child employment, and child underemployment and unemployment. As the nineteenth century developed, both child labour and the problem of order that child unemployment was thought to create, were instrumental in promoting legislation to restrict children's labour activities and encourage and eventually enforce children's attendance in educational institutions (Cunningham 1990).

Thus, as a result of the interaction of specific economic, ideological and politico-legal phenomena, there was a marginalization of child workers to a particular type of job activity, broadly characterized as 'out of school' work. This process occurred in the period *circa* 1870–1914. This did not stop children from working, but it did deproblematize their labour activities. 'Out of school' work increasingly became viewed as a healthy pastime and an embodiment of the work ethic. Equally important was the fact that education occupied children during the working day. This removed the 'problem of order' presented by under- and unemployed children. Thus, importantly, work and education could coexist.

Children's labour activities were increasingly restricted to those jobs which could be combined with schooling and these jobs quickly became identified as 'children's jobs'. As James (1984: 11) notes, the historical processes 'which, during the last century, have gradually separated children off from the adult world of work – through the introduction of schooling, the provision of welfare and social legislation for the protection of children – have made their very peripherality from the work sphere a condition of their entry into it'. As such, the issue of child labour was gradually deproblematized and ignored. From around the turn of the nineteenth century the child worker disappeared from social research as concern focused on the whole question of the 'youth labour market' and the transition from school to work.

The result was that, until fairly recently, the labour activities of school-children were left uninvestigated. The interest that was occasionally shown focused on the most extreme manifestations of child labour exploitation; for example, in June and July of 1994 most British newspapers covered the story of children employed in a textile factory in Preston, Lancashire. This story led to a short-lived 'moral panic' about child labour but, in keeping with such exposure, after the initial burst of outrage the issue quickly disappeared from the pages of the press.

This example deals with children working in small undercapitalized sectors, where they were employed to do jobs that took no account of their special needs or requirements. They were employed, therefore, as individual prolet-arians, but paid according to their status as children. This and other similar examples are important. They represent one form of child labour exploitation in modern Britain. Where the employing unit of capital is small, the number of employees small and unorganized and the employer pushed by the com-petition of larger and more efficient units of capital, one way the employer has to make profits is to exploit cheap, sweated labour. This might mean paying low wages to migrants, to married women or to children. In other words, the employer will exploit whatever source is available; all that is required is people desperate enough to work for the money on offer.

However, a focus on such examples can skew an understanding of the majority experience of child workers. Most children do not work in factories. Most are employed delivering milk and newspapers, selling in shops and icecream vans and waiting and serving in restaurants and cafés. These are jobs which people think of as particularly suitable for children, but, as the evidence suggests, these jobs are far removed from the idealistic conception often portrayed.

The perspective outlined above not only provides a new theoretical starting point for explaining the present form of child labour in Britain but also allows an analysis of both the historical continuity and change in children's labouring activities throughout the period of capitalist development. It also emphasizes the complexities and contradictions of socio-economic processes and developments – they are not unilinear and monocausal – a point that sits rather uneasily with simple developmentalist perspectives which some contributors to the conference seem to share. Finally, at the conference there was considerable discussion of the 'globalization issue', that child labour has become a global phenomenon. Yet there are potential problems with such a formulation. First, given the examples which were discussed over the four days it was not clear, to me at least, what is 'new' about child labour; it has always been with us but its form and intensity have changed in line with changing socio-economic processes. Secondly, the use of 'globalization' in this context can oversimplify and give the impression that children's labour is the same throughout the world, which it clearly is not. Rather, a reformulation is required: what we are talking about is the globalization of capitalism and the effects and consequences this has on child workers in different sectors of the world economy.

References

Balding, J. (1991) 'A Study of Working Children in 1990', *Education and Health* 9, 1.

Barrett, M. and M. Mcintosh (1980) 'The "Family Wage": Some Problems for Socialists and Feminists', *Capital and Class*, 11.

Bequele, A. and J. Boyden (eds) (1988a) *Combating Child Labour*, Geneva, ILO.

— (1988b) 'Working Children: Current Trends and Policy Responses', *International Labour Review*, 127.

Carr, H. and L. Jamieson (eds) (1990) *The Politics of Everyday Life*, Basingstoke, Macmillan.

Challis, J. and D. Elliman (1979) *Child Workers Today*, Sunbury, Quartermaine House.

Cunningham, H. (1990) 'The Employment and Unemployment of Children in England, 1680–1851', *Past and Present*, 126.

Davin, A. (1982) 'Child Labour, the Working-class Family and Domestic Ideology in Nineteenth-century Britain', *Development and Change*, 13.

— (1990) 'When is a Child Not a Child?' in H. Carr and L. Jamieson, *The Politics of Everyday Life*.

Elson, D. (1982) 'The Differentiation of Children's Labour in the Capitalist Labour Market', *Development and Change*, 13.

Finn, D. (1987) *Training without Jobs: New Deals and Broken Promises*, Basingstoke, Macmillan.

Forrester, T. (1979) 'Children at Work', *New Society*, 1 November.

Fyfe, A. (1989) *Child Labour*, Cambridge, Polity Press.

German, L. (1989) *Sex, Class and Socialism*, London, Bookmarks.

Greenberger, E. and L. D. Steinberg (1986) *When Teenagers Work: The Psychological and Social Costs of Adolescent Employment*, New York, Basic Books.

Hall, S. (1984) 'The Rise of the Representative/Interventionist State', in G. McLennan, D. Held and S. Hall, *State and Society in Contemporary Britain*, Cambridge, Polity Press.

Hall, S. and B. Schwarz (1985) 'State and Society, 1830–1930', in M. Langan and B. Schwarz (eds), *Crises in the British State, 1880–1930*, London, Hutchinson.

Hobbs, S., M. Lavalette and J. McKechnie (1992) 'The Emerging Problem of Child Labour', *Critical Social Policy*, 34.

Hobbs, S., S. Lindsay and J. McKechnie (1993) 'Part-time Employment and Schooling', *Scottish Education Review*, 25.

— (1994), 'Le travail des enfants au Royaume-Uni: idéologie et réalité', in Bernard Schlemmer (ed.), *L'enfant exploité, oppression, mise au travail, prolétarisation*, Paris, Karthala-ORSTOM, pp. 215–22.

Humphries, J. (1977) 'Class Struggle and the Persistance of the Working Class Family', *Cambridge Journal of Economics*.

— (1981) 'Protective Legislation, the Capitalist State and Working-class Men: The Case of the 1842 Mines Regulation Act', *Feminist Review*, 8.

James, A. (1984) 'Children's Experience of Work', *ESRC Newsletter*, 51.

Landrigan, P. J. (1993) 'Child Labor: A Re-emergent Threat', *American Journal of Industrial Medicine*, 24.

Lavalette, M. (1994) *Child Employment in the Capitalist Labour Market*, Basingstoke, Avebury.

Lavalette, M., J. McKechnie and S. Hobbs (1991) *The Forgotten Workforce: Scottish Children at Work*, Glasgow, SLPU.

Levine, D. (1977) *Family Formation in an Age of Nascent Capitalism*, New York, Academic Press.

Lewis, J. (ed.) (1986) *Labour and Love: Women's Experience of Home and Family 1850–1940*, Oxford, Basil Blackwell.

McKechnie, J., S. Lindsay and S. Hobbs (1993) 'Child Employment in Cumbria: A Report to Cumbria County Council University of Paisley', Paisley.

— (1994) *Still Forgotten: Child Employment in Rural Scotland*, Glasgow, SLPU.

MacLennan, E., J. Fitz and J. Sullivan (1985) *Working Children*, London, LPU.

Mehta, M. N., S. V. Prabhu and H. N. Mistry (1985) 'Child Labour in Bombay', *Child Abuse and Neglect*, 9.

Mendelievich, E. (ed.) (1979) *Children at Work*, Geneva, ILO.

Miles, R. (1982) *Racism and Migrant Labour*, London, Routledge and Kegan Paul.

Moorehead, C. (1987) *School Age Workers in Britain Today*, London, Anti-Slavery Society.

Murray, J. (1991) 'Working Children', in M. Lavalette et al., *The Forgotten Workforce*.

Phillips, A. and B. Taylor (1980) 'Sex and Skill: Notes Towards a Feminist Economics', *Feminist Review*, 6.

Pinchbeck, I. (1969) *Women Workers and the Industrial Revolution, 1750–1850*, London, Virago.

Pond, C. and A. Searle (1991) *The Hidden Army: Children at Work in the 1990s*, London, LPU.

Qvortrup, J. (1985) 'Placing Children in the Division of Labour', in P. Close and R. Collins (eds), *Family and Economy in Modern Society*, Basingstoke, Macmillan.

Rodgers, G. and G. Standing (eds) (1981) *Child Work, Poverty and Underdevelopment*, Geneva, ILO.

Simon, B. (1960) *Studies in the History of Education, 1780–1870*, London, Lawrence and Wishart.

— (1965) *Education and the Labour Movement, 1870–1920*, London, Lawrence and Wishart.

Stedman Jones, G. (1976) *Outcast London*, London, Penguin.

Thomis, M. I. (1974) *The Town Labourer and the Industrial Revolution*, London, Batsford.

Thompson, E. P. (1968) *The Making of the English Working Class*, London, Penguin.

Tranter, N. (1981) 'The Labour Supply, 1780–1860', in R. Floud and D. McCloskey (eds), *The Economic History of Britain*, Cambridge, Cambridge University Press.

Valcarenghi, M. (1981) *Child Labour in Italy*, London, Anti-Slavery Society.

Whittaker, A. (1986) 'Child Labour and Its Causes', *Third World Now*, Spring.

Wright, E. O. (1978) *Class, Crisis and the State*, London, Verso.

CHAPTER 16

Coffee Beans and the Seeds of Labour: Child Labour on Guatemalan Plantations

Charles-Édouard de Suremain

Until now, literature on the economic and social life of Guatemala has barely touched on child labour. Rather than hold a general discussion on that theme, however, we have chosen to begin with an observation of the country's large coffee plantations, a field covered by an ethnographical survey of ours. First we shall analyse what the actors living and working there understand by the term 'child'. Then, after a description of 'child' labour, we shall look into what the phenomenon means to the 'children' involved, their parents and, above all, the place it occupies within the broader context of the big plantation.

Child labour has become an unavoidable reality in various areas of Guatemalan economic life, in the urban informal and rural agricultural sectors in particular. The youngest children consistently play a crucial role in the daily work cycle of the highland farming economy. That role is certainly more ad hoc and of secondary importance in the large Pacific coast coffee, sugar and cotton plantations to the south, where working conditions generally comply with the child labour laws and the division of labour sees the heaviest duties of the agricultural calendar assigned to adult men. Yet there are still times of the year when, if only because of the sheer size of the plantations and the large numbers of families living there, hordes of children can be found at work in the fields, pastures and coffee estates.

Guatemala is one of the world's top ten producers of arabica. Coffee-growing alone accounts for over half of the country's GDP and brings in the bulk of its foreign currency. Guatemalan plantations (or *fincas*) are especially large in comparison to their counterparts in other parts of Latin America. Indeed, each covers an average of between 100 and 200 hectares, compared to 50 to 100 hectares in neighbouring countries (El Salvador, Costa Rica).[1]

Finally, we should bear in mind that the coffee shrubs, on the modernized plantations at least, require a great deal of attention all year round. The fact that they grow on steep wooded slopes makes mechanized farming out of the question and an abundant supply of labour a necessity.

The Large Coffee Plantations and Their Workers

These basic characteristic features create quite specific living and working conditions for coffee-workers. Indeed, the *fincas* accommodate a great many families, each of whom inhabits a small shack within the confines of an encampment. Some encampments are known to house no fewer than one hundred families. As a rule, each household has an adult male as the 'head of the family' and he is the only one benefiting from a permanent employment contract. This contract guarantees a wage, accommodation, social security, school for the children and a few advantages such as the right to use the river and gather dead wood around the plantation.

There are about 50,000 'permanent workers' on the *fincas* of Guatemala. But the figure has been steadily declining since the 1950s and the shift towards the employment with little job security of temporary workers (now numbering somewhere in the region of 300,000). They are sometimes referred to as 'satellites' or 'volunteers' and live on the outskirts of the plantation where they are given short-term work in return for a starvation wage. Many factors lie at the root of this situation, among them the considerable population growth on the coast and the one-way exodus of natives from the highlands to these supposedly 'wealthy' regions.[2] Generally speaking, the labouring populations currently inhabiting the *fincas* have very few family and property ties remaining with the highlands. They feel more at home in coastal society and more comfortable among people of mixed race (Ladinos or non-Indians) than the Indian farmers whom they largely tend to regard with disdain. It is true that Guatemala's piedmont regions were cultivated for coffee-growing between 1850 and 1880. Since then, though, the Indians have left their homelands to re-create a unique social and cultural environment within the relatively closed confines of the *fincas*.[3]

Division of Labour on the *Fincas*

Permanent jobs are theoretically an adult male preserve, with the women supposedly left in charge of domestic tasks. Officially, then, the only workers on the coffee plantation and, hence, the only wage-earners, are men. In actual fact, women are doing the work too, but their work is sporadic, often part-time and relatively less well paid with little scope for self-betterment. The plantation owners (*finqueros*) who lay down the *finca* labour policies justify these disparities on the grounds that 'coffee is masculine in nature' and that women are incapable of doing 'steady and attentive work'.

Meanwhile, the sons of full-time workers often compete with one another for their fathers' jobs. Boys begin taking an interest in coffee plantation work from a very early age and do their level best to play a role. Out of touch with their farming roots and penniless, most *fincas* children rarely harbour ambitions of setting themselves up as small-scale independent producers. The work is organized such that young adolescents and older single men sometimes form teams known as 'reserves', a term describing temporary labourers living with their parents in the plantation encampment. An average family is comprised of five members, which means there are large numbers of 'reserves' providing the *finquero* with an appreciable reserve labour force.

The 'reserves' still like to distinguish themselves from the other groups of casual labourers who come to work on the *fincas* at certain periods of the year. Indeed, 'reserves' present themselves as the plantation 'natives' and look upon the others as 'foreigners' who are out to steal their jobs and, although they rarely say so openly, their women. The casual workers originating from outside the *fincas* have their own hierarchies too. The *finquero* and full-time workers differentiate 'seasonals' from 'day labourers': of Indian extraction, the former are recruited in groups and stay on the *finca* for a few months, while the latter are employed individually and leave the *finca* at the end of the day.

So despite its apparent homogeneity, the plantation is riddled with socio-economic and cultural divisions. Far from being a world apart, the *finca* often reproduces, in an albeit original form, the particularly strained social relations characterizing Guatemala as a whole.[4]

Coffee-picking and Child Labour

THE WORK-DAY   At harvest time, *fincas* are a positive hive of activity. In the west of the country where we conducted our survey, harvest stretches from mid-August through to mid-December with phases of greater and lesser intensity. Not all the coffee fields are located at the same altitude, so the beans are not all ripe and ready to pick at the same moment and the same areas need going over several times at intervals of some weeks. A successful harvest therefore requires a large work force: on an 'average' 100-hectare plantation employing a permanent force of fifty workers, the wage-earning population can grow to around 300 people. This figure varies from year to year and includes the permanent workers, most of their wives and elder children (the 'reserves') as well as the 'seasonals' and 'day labourers'.

During the four-month harvest period, women are paid, like men, according to the quantity picked. Ripe beans are picked off the shrubs and dropped into wicker baskets hanging at waist height on a cord passed around the back of the picker's neck. Once filled, the baskets are emptied into large nylon sacks. A full sack holds about 50 kg of beans. At the end of the work-day, i.e. towards 3 or 4 p.m. when the rainfall becomes too heavy, the workers carry their sacks down to the *finca* coffee-processing plant on their backs. Each worker harvests an average of two to three sackfuls a day unless, that is, the plantation-owner has decided to impose a limit.[5]

At harvest time, the work-day can begin as early as 5 a.m., although the women will have begun preparing the meals at 3. Generally speaking, the men are first out of the house. They are progressively joined by the rest of the family. The young girls of the house bring them a breakfast of corn cakes and a glass of coffee. Then, at around 11 a.m., those same girls return home to fetch the lunch, occasionally in the company of their mothers. This is tough work given the topography and sheer expanse of the plantations. The journey between the coffee fields and the encampment sometimes takes three-quarters of an hour each way.

THE WORK OF THE WOMEN AND CHILDREN For women, the coffee harvest means additional work on top of their usual domestic duties. Recruited as 'reserves', they are accompanied in the coffee fields by their 'children' – those not themselves employed as 'reserves'. In actual fact, the women regard children as belonging to one of two categories: 'infants' or 'youths'. The former include babies and toddlers, while the latter are able to pick beans without damaging the shrubs. This is a major responsibility because if they do cause any damage their parents have a heavy fine to pay to the plantation-owner. It should be said that this family-based division of labour is not subject to any rules laid down by the *finquero*. The women are the sole judges of, and the only ones responsible for, their offspring. Another point to note is that during the harvest season, the children abandon their schooling. And not long after that are the national school holidays: from mid-October to mid-December when the coffee crops are at their best.

It is difficult to say how much of an economic contribution is made by the 'infants'. On the one hand, they constitute an unquestionable burden for their mothers, slowing them down. On the other hand, however, the toddlers pick the scattered fallen coffee beans up off the ground. Naturally, when all is said and done, this activity does not count for very much in economic terms; but it does mark a start to a small child's technical training in coffee-farming. As for the 'youths', their contribution is much more easily discernible: not only do adolescents of both sexes do the picking, but the girls also take charge of emptying the wicker baskets into the sacks while the boys drag the sacks along the rows of coffee shrubs, keeping up with the main body of pickers.

Young boys, by the way, go for this punishing work with gusto in order to show that they have the qualities required to become good workers. Each gesture is in fact a perfect imitation of their seniors. To prove just how hard they have been working, they roll their shirts up to the chest to let the air get to their bellies; they tilt back their straw hats and wipe their brows with the back of a hand; they noisily clear their nostrils between forefinger and thumb. Frequently, the 'youths' also race one another for the title of the fastest coffee-sack dragger on site. They do this in the hope of attracting the attention of the plantation supervisors. Even though it mostly takes the form of game-playing, young boys have already learnt what to do to become good coffee-workers. Notwithstanding their tender age, they are thus clearly showing their keenness and social ambitions.

The Child's Status on the Plantations

WHAT DO THE PARENTS DO ABOUT IT? Legally, a 'child' is considered to be any individual under the age of fifteen years, but the law in fact forbids only paid employment for the under-twelves. So it is not entirely illegal for children aged between twelve and fifteen to be earning money, especially in agricultural regions. On the majority of *fincas*, however, the under-fifteens are paid nothing at all for the labour they supply. And, as we shall see, this is a situation encouraged not just by the *finqueros*, but also by the men, women and children whose position on the plantations is one of insecurity and dependency.

Naturally, *finqueros* fully capitalize on the ambiguities in Guatemalan legislation, for they are perfectly aware of the importance of 'youth' labour. They know full well that women could never gather as much coffee as they do without the assistance of 'youths'. They also know that the 'youths' are in no stronger a position than women as regards pay demands. Under such circumstances, the planters knowingly use Guatemalan legislation to justify their recruitment policies. In some cases, they even manage to pass it off as a matter of doing people a favour, since it enables youngsters to become familiar with 'the ways of coffee' irrespective of whether or not it is against the law.

Women for their part are only too happy to be able to work 'full-time' and earn a 'proper worker's wage'. For once, they have a recognized economic role on the *finca*. And they know that if they were to petition the planter with wage demands, he would regard it as a sign of profound ingratitude. Equally, such demands might implicitly be taken to mean that they are unable to work without another person's assistance. Then the planters would feel right to have assumed women to be neither 'steady, confident nor attentive' enough in their work. So mothers are unable to demand wages for their children without putting their own jobs at risk.

As for the men, they largely stay out of it. They are well aware of how sought-after their permanent worker status is and have no intention whatsoever of jeopardizing it for the sake of an extra few pennies. It is equally likely that the men regard the difficult phase of childhood as a period of initiation that is necessary to become a fully-fledged picker. To some extent, they are of the opinion that since they themselves had to undergo a similar trial, there is no reason why their own sons should not follow their example.

Besides, there is little guarantee that young people, especially boys, would support their parents should they eventually decide to put in a claim for an additional wage. For they are not blind to the fact that permanent worker posts on the plantations are scarce and that they have to demonstrate their obedience if they wish to stay in with a chance. In other words, competition for jobs on the *fincas* is such that the children assimilate the essential qualities of a 'good worker' as soon as they can – obedience, stamina, loyalty – without worrying about their working conditions of the moment.

Finally, beyond these socio-economic and cultural particularities, we cannot help but notice that there is not much of a tradition of trade unionism, or even plain protest, in the world of the coffee-worker. Contrary to the huge coastal sugar plantations, relations between *finca* workers and bosses remain personal, even if they are rarely described as such by the actors themselves. Hence, whenever work-related tensions and conflicts erupt they are more likely to be settled via an informal face-to-face arrangement rather than through stereotyped written rulings. To put it another way, each individual seeks individual protection from the boss to the detriment of the community, which does not necessarily mean to say that they do not feel a sense of belonging to, or solidarity with, the community in other areas of social life.[6]

DOMINATION, INTERNALIZING DOMINATION, SOCIAL ADVANCE-MENT Within the context of the large Guatemalan coffee plantations, we see clearly that the problem of hiring children during harvest represents an overlap of very distinctive fields: it reveals the importance of the areas of legality and economics while at the same time stressing the strength of the actors' social representations and aspirations.

On the one hand, the laws currently in force in Guatemala obviously provide the planters with the legal grounds they need to justify their employ-ment of children without pay. Yet in the minds of lawyers, economists, politicians and, hence, planters, there is nothing unfair about these laws and nothing abusive about applying them. On the contrary, they even see them as serving to shore up a long tradition of farming without which the Indians, farmers and workers would be lost. Beneath this sort of legislation and reasoning, we recognize the utilitarian and idealistic thinking of the repres-entatives of the Guatemalan economic elite which includes the planters.

The planters do not see it as a matter of surreptitiously scooping up a few coffee beans for free via the intermediary of children. They actually believe they are giving those children the opportunity to prove themselves and, hence, become socialized within the confines of the plantation. *Finqueros*, in other words, are convinced that they have a bona fide mission to civilize children from a humble background. Sometimes the *finquero* and a worker's son are even united in a tutelage style of relationship. To the parents of the protégé, such a relationship means social recognition for the whole family and the near certainty that their offspring will have secured a firm footing for their future career.

Coffee plantation-workers hardly put the problem of child labour in terms of exploitation.[7] If they did so, it would be akin to opposing the social system and established order of the plantation, which would seriously jeopard-ize their position there. They would then lose their jobs and accommodation to become sub-proletarians after the fashion of the numerous families crowding the surrounding hamlets on the outskirts of the *fincas*.

We should also remember that the insecurity of their situation places coffee-workers in a position of great emotional dependency towards the plantation and the planter. So the workers do not express any particular anti-*finquero* sentiment as regards their children's labour. As mentioned above, parents view the participation of younger members of the family in the work as a kind of initiation into adulthood. Finally, the children themselves for their part set the (often game-like) rules for that initiation which raises their hopes of achieving the dream of social advancement. Games here unquestionably help the very young to internalize the domination.

The nature of the laws in force and the economic insecurity and emotional dependence of the workers are among the most decisive factors contibuting to the form, function and direction taken by child labour on the coffee *fincas*. When all is said and done, *fincas* children are the victims of an unbending, hierarchical, competitive and precarious established legal, economic and social order; what is more, they are the main agents responsible for the reproduction of that order. Their complex legal, economic and social status makes them the actors of a comprehensive system with which they identify and which, in the absence of other prospects, they help to perpetuate.

Within this context, it is understandably going to take a lot more than merely amending the labour laws to alter the system as a whole. And changing mentalities is not a measure that can just be taken and steered through at will. Child labour is part of a complex body of interrelated dynamics, none of which can be looked at in isolation from the others. Instead of adopting a moral or ethical stance, we really ought to be asking ourselves how the various different actors participating in a given established order might work together to change it thoroughly and without producing the sort of perverse side-effects which would have a negative and irreversible impact on the children's affectivity and socialization.

Notes

1. For more on the coffee economy in general, see Daviron and Lerin (1990); on the various Latin American and African societies and coffee farming communities, see Tulet et al. (1994).

2. For more on the various types of migration in Guatemala and their socio-demographic importance, see Bataillon and Le Bot (1975).

3. Their highly unusual social organization is studied in depth in our ethnological thesis (Suremain 1994).

4. Le Bot (1992) offers the most complete study of the conflicting and violent dynamics that have been structuring Guatemalan society for the last thirty years.

5. Some *finqueros* demand that 'seasonals' and 'day labourers' gather no more than two sackfuls of coffee a day so that more might be left for the plantation's 'native' workers.

6. Methods of resolving plantation labour disputes are complex. For an illustration of a case where an incidence of food poisoning sparked off a mass protest of permanent women workers, see Suremain (1992).

7. The same cannot be said with such certainty of the highland Indian populations migrating to the plantations on a seasonal basis. Indian farmers are actually very often critical about life on the *fincas*. However, they let their views be known only once they have returned to the home community. On the living and working conditions of Indians on sugar and coffee plantations of Guatemala, see respectively Caldera (1979), Schmid (1973) and de Suremain (1993).

References

Bataillon, C. and Y. Le Bot (1975) 'Migration intérieure et emploi agricole temporaire au Guatemala', *Cahiers des Amériques latines*, 11, pp. 117–47.

Caldera, J. R. (1979) 'Las fuerzas de la cuadrilla indígena', *Alero*, 2, pp. 73–92.

Daviron, B. and F. Lerin (1990) *Le café*, Paris, Economica.

Le Bot, Y. (1992) *La guerre en terre maya. Communauté, violence et modernité au Guatemala (1970–1992)*, Paris, Karthala.

Schmid, L. (1973) *Trabajadores migratorios y desarrollo económico. El papel de la mano de obra migratoria en el desarollo económico de Guatemala*, Guatemala, Univ. San Carlos de Guatemala, Instituto de Investigaciones Económicas y Sociales.

Suremain, C. É. de (1992) 'L'opposition planteur–cueilleur. Ethnographie de la contestation dans une grande plantation de café guatémaltèque', *L'Ethnographie*, 88, 2, pp. 7–20.

— (1993) 'Le rendez-vous annuel du caféiculteur et de l'Indien. Culture du café et identités culturelles dans une grande plantation du Guatemala', *Caravelle* (numéro spécial sur les cultures du café en hispanoamérique), 61, pp. 103–11.

— (1994) 'Dans l'ombre du café. Ethnologie d'une grande plantation caféière au Guatemala', thèse d'ethnologie, University of Tours.

Tulet, J. C., B. Charlery, F. Bart et al. (eds) (1994) – *Paysanneries du café des hautes terres tropicales. Afrique et Amérique latine*, Paris, Karthala.

CHAPTER 17

The Exploitation of Apprentices in Togo

Yves Marguerat

The 1981 census found that the cities of Togo had 22,750 apprentices (30 per cent of them girls) working in the informal sectors of production, commerce and services, 11,500 of them in Lomé (32 per cent girls). The boys (5 per cent aged less than fifteen years; 76 per cent between fifteen and twenty-four) were scattered over a wide range of sectors: 4500 in transport, 4300 in various services, 4000 in construction, 2000 apprentice tailors, 1800 carpenters, 600 mechanics. The girls (7 per cent younger than fifteen; 80 per cent between fifteen and twenty-four) were overwhelmingly employed as apprentice seamstresses (86 per cent), the next largest category being hair-dressers (5 per cent).

It is hard to say exactly how the figures have developed since then, but one thing is for sure: very large percentages of the youngsters dropping out of school have gone into apprenticeships in the informal sector where, as we shall see, there are a good many available openings. The Kodjoviakopé-Nyékonakpoè[1] division of the Tailors' and Dress-makers' Union recorded 300 indentures for the year 1986 alone (90 per cent girls), in a district which already had a garment workshop on every street corner. The clothing market may not be growing at that same rate, of course, but the 'bosses' are no less generous in offering opportunities because, in Togo, having apprentices means profits.

In a paper produced with a social services working group,[2] we estimated that there were 25,000 apprentices in Lomé and 10,000 in the rest of the country in 1987, not counting all those who wished to become an apprentice but lacked the necessary means. These figures certainly must have grown since then.

The Establishment of Apprenticeship Practices

Apprenticeship first emerged in Togo when modern manual occupations were introduced at the turn of the nineteenth century (baroque-style construction techniques having been brought into the country earlier in the century by repatriated settlers from Brazil). Most of today's practising tailors, carpenters, mechanics and typographers are the direct descendants of those who learned their trade from 1912 onwards at the remarkable 'Brotherhomé' School of Professional Studies run by the Lomé Catholic Mission.[3] The handful of craftsmen working during the colonial period were regarded as prominent citizens, not as wealthy as the shopkeepers and coconut plantation-owners but well-off nevertheless and highly esteemed. Lomé people still talk about the tailors Comlan 'Télagan'[4] and Gaspar Noudekor, not to mention Aboki 'Gbèdè' the blacksmith, Gbadoé the carpenter and the photographer Alex Acolatsé.[5]

Apprenticeship became codified remarkably early. In 1924, the French governors of Togo in their annual report to the League of Nations described it thus:

> The craftsman agreeing to teach a child his trade may demand no payment in return. It is understood that on completing his apprenticeship, a young man shall remain with his employer for a certain period of time – two years as a rule. During such time, he is employed as a worker without fixed wages but receives, in addition to his bed and board, a share of the sum his employer takes in earnings from the produce of his labour. Sometimes, in more progressive establishments, a privately settled contract stipulates that the employer be paid compensation should the apprentice quit prior to the agreed date.

This paternalistic-type system (where the employer treats his apprentice like his own son and the latter 'shows his gratitude' by working free of charge) still prevails in countries such as Burkina, Zaire or the Niger. In Togo, as in the Ivory Coast or Cameroon, apprenticeship is no longer free.

Lomé 'bosses' began demanding payment in 1945 and quite hefty sums at that, even more expensive than today's prices given the depreciation of the currency: in 1950, a four-year training course could cost an apprentice tailor between 8000 and 10,000 CFA francs[6] (i.e. more than half the price of a Singer sewing machine)[7] plus five or six bottles of what they call 'the hard stuff' (whisky, brandy, rum or gin – quality labels only!).

Written contracts first appeared as early as 1924 and soon became systematized, usually with a compensation clause included to cover the artisan in case the apprentice gave up before having paid for his/her release. Normal procedure is currently as follows:

1. The apprentice reports to a workshop once a verbal agreement has been made between the workshop-owner and the parent or legal guardian. An entry fee is paid in cash (between 1000 and 5000 CFA francs) in addition to one or two bottles of 'hard stuff' and a few of 'soft'. This is to help 'see to the rules'.

2. At the end of a three-month trial period, if all parties are in favour, a contract is signed and the first half of the agreed fees is paid along with the drinks (full details of which will have been laid down in writing). Most

contracts last for a term of three years (apart from hairdressers, for whom six months suffice). Shorter ones (two years) are more expensive, longer ones (four years) less so;[8] employers are keen to keep hold of an apprentice for as long as they can.

3. When the contract ends, the apprentice is 'released'. Outstanding fees are settled along with the same number of bottles as before plus, in most cases, the ingredients for a celebratory feast (the most expensive rice, yams, oil and biscuits possible; a roasting fowl, goat or sheep; chairs; a sound system) at which the apprentice is officially 'released' before an assembly of invited guests – parents, colleagues, union representatives – and presented with a printed and calligraphed 'certificate'; despite having no real value in the eyes of the law, this document is regarded with the same quasi-religious reverence as if it were an academic degree.

4. It is very common to find that an employer still expects his apprentice to show his 'gratitude' by supplementing the various 'gifts' with three to six months' extra work, free of charge; only then will he give the 'blessing' which is seen as essential for later success in professional life. The young person can then finally set himself up in business[9] and, on the strength of his certificate, in turn recruit apprentices of his own.

The Logic of the System

Informal sector economics operate on the basis of small sums of money rapidly changing hands between large numbers of people of very modest means within a regime of limitless competition. As a rule, the customers are more interested in rock-bottom prices than top quality when purchasing goods or having them repaired; apart from actively encouraging mediocrity, this forces craftsmen to work virtually at cost price in order to keep their customers.

Profits are therefore extremely low, allowing craftsmen virtually no chance of being able to afford to pay a journeyman's wages (as much as 800 CFA francs a day, when the employer himself is only taking in 1200).[10]

Apprentices thus serve a double purpose: (1) to supply free, relatively unskilled labour (skills being of scarcely any consequence here) which actually bears fruit very quickly – by the end of the first few months, apprentices have already learnt the basic essentials for their future careers with some having even mastered the finer points of the trade; and (2) to renew workshop capital, for apprenticeship fees mean a fresh injection of money that the employer can use to cover his living and equipment costs.[11]

It is easy to see why, during an economic recession when there are too many people after too few jobs, employers tend not only to hire apprentices but also to raise indenture prices.

Apprenticeship is therefore extremely important to the development – if not the very existence – of the small-scale production sector which is in turn a key part of everyday life in urban areas for the masses of people earning barely enough to meet their needs. So the employer therefore needs appren-tices, lots of apprentices; meanwhile, each apprentice 'released' becomes an additional competitor for his former master: not as proficient perhaps, but certainly more flexible in his prices.

Although the system is coherent enough, certain aspects of it are, or become, far too unfavourable to the most disadvantaged young people, who find themselves increasingly excluded from it.

Soaring Costs and the Official Riposte

Stagnating business and the influx of young people into the workshops have together produced a very strong rise in indenture prices: from between 15,000 and 30,000 CFA francs in the early 1980s, to 40, 60 or even 80,000 by 1987–88, with certain profitable sectors such as hairdressing or electronic repairs asking 100,000 CFA francs.[12]

Some employers may well tend to ask for fewer bottles (whose unit price has also risen sharply) as more ready cash is seen as fair enough compensation for less drink. But others continue making exorbitant demands.[13]

These (albeit not very old) traditions may well have some cultural and religious aspects about them, which everybody – employers, apprentices and parents alike – regards as some sort of proof of credibility: metal-workers, for example, have to make a sacrificial offering to Gu, the guardian spirit of blacksmiths, and the tools of a future craftsman must be drenched in the blood of a chicken, otherwise they will be liable to injure him. But there is a great deal of abuse with regard to the compulsory expenses.

More and more employers are ordering novice apprentices to waste no time acquiring their own tools (or the tools that they themselves might need): until they have done so, they will have to settle for merely watching while the others work. Imported tools from Europe are very pricey; although less expensive, those coming from Nigeria or China are of mediocre quality and not as long-lasting. For carpenters or mechanics, a 50,000-CFA-franc outlay on equipment is practically the bare minimum: 100,000 would be required for a more operational range. Naturally, a graduating apprentice needs his own tools to start up a business; but buying them all in the early stages of an apprenticeship – rather than spreading the costs over the full three years – puts an overwhelming strain on the parents' finances. In some cases, the apprentice is not even allowed to keep tools – e.g. a set of spanners – that he will have put to all manner of uses over the years. The same goes for the often very costly uniforms that many workshops (especially in tailoring) demand should be worn either for everyday work or else – an even greater luxury – for the release-day celebrations.

Costs such as these can be crippling for less well-off families and many apprentices are forced either to drop out or to remain at their workshops for years and years without the prospect of release.

In 1989, the Ministry of Technical Education and Vocational Training (METFP) issued three decrees[14] laying down precise rules governing apprenticeship conditions (a forty-hour week, one day off per week, thirty days off a year), the term of indentures (from one to four years, according to the seven professional categories regrouping the seventy listed trades) and above all, fees (according to the trade: 18,000 CFA francs in the food trade, 30,000 in hairdressing; such sums being inclusive of 'all ceremony-related charges and other fees called for during the course of the indenture's lifetime'; and employers lost the right to demand drinks of any kind).

If the stipulations regarding working conditions were always bound to go unheeded (how many inspectors would it take to check up on the 8000 or so workshops in the city of Lomé alone?), the war on costs was certainly worth a try. Indeed, the Togo Tailors' and Dress-makers' Union (for unstructured bodies can sometimes undertake their own structuring) has managed to keep the cost of a dress-making course stable at 24,000 CFA francs for several years, with union delegates officially present at the signing of an indenture and an apprentice's 'release' ceremony. For one or two years, the employers seemed to have been brought to heel thanks to the robust authority of a then unchallenged state; and they more or less complied with the restrictions laid down in the decrees of 1989.[15] But it was not long before control slackened and prices have apparently returned to previous levels. Having said that, the current recession makes it impossible to carry out thoroughgoing research or to extrapolate.[16]

Use and Abuse of Apprentices

The logic of the system allows some bosses to take on an unbelievable number of apprentices: dozens of them (as many as eighty have been found at a cabinet-maker's; twenty working on two sewing machines at a tailor's). What can anyone actually learn under such conditions? How can sixteen people manage with a single refrigerator?

Notwithstanding the Togolese legislator's calls for compulsory schooling, there are still children under the age of fifteen in the workshops. They are generally not there to learn, but to be used as dogsbodies for the chores: the shopping, the laundry, the dishes. If they are actually 'released' at seventeen or eighteen years of age, what chance will they ever have of being hired for waged work, or being able to set themselves up in business and find customers? Such children as these will therefore remain limitlessly exploitable labourers way beyond the customary three years and three months.

Before the official formulation of a standard model indenture (which we cannot safely say has really been generalized) each employer had his own forms, written in very rough French and with a generally suspicious and one-sidedly demanding attitude towards the apprentice. Many of these contracts make a point of stipulating that the apprentice shall remain entirely at the disposal of his boss and 'seniors', that is those who have been at the workshop longer. It offers numerous opportunities for abuse, where apprentices, especially the youngest, are used for all sorts of chores that have nothing to do with the trade they are supposed to be learning: cultivating the boss's fields or making breeze-blocks for the house he is building. Breaches of discipline are often punished with overly severe blows (particularly to the hands) and genuinely cruel humiliation.[17]

Equally deplorable is the practice of making apprentices keep watch overnight at the workshop, be it by rota or because they are living on the premises for want of a home of their own. Beyond the attendant hygiene problems, these night duties can leave them in potentially risky situations (e.g. initiation into drug-taking).

What is more, the quality of workshop training is in many cases far from satisfactory. There are, of course, employers who take the time and trouble to explain to their apprentices what they are doing, making them strip down and reassemble a given piece of equipment as many times as is necessary for them to assimilate it. But there are others who, out of fear or jealousy of potential competitors, would appear to go so far as carefully to keep certain techniques hidden from their apprentices. In any event, not everybody is gifted with the talents of a teacher; just because someone has a thorough working knowledge of his or her trade does not necessarily mean he or she knows how to impart it.

The apprentice's 'release' is a mark of success only in that it proves he or she has managed to last the course, been obedient and met all the necessary expenses; it is not confirmation of his or her abilities. Once again tailors (along with typists) are the pioneers, as they make their prospective 'releasees' take an examination to show what they are capable of doing. By the way, 'releasees' may in turn recruit apprentices who know even less than they do. This can send a trade spinning into a downwards spiral of deteriorating technical quality, with ever-increasing numbers of workers of limited ability: people who know how to repair the engine of a Renault but not a Peugeot, are bewildered by a two-way switch or can do nothing but endlessly reproduce the same pieces of furniture or shirts.

To tell the truth, making apprentices take an end-of-apprenticeship examination may also turn out to be something of a trap. It is very easy to withhold the certificate and force them to return to the workshop for another six months or a year.

So the large numbers of candidates applying should not deflect our attention from how hard life is for an apprentice in Lomé. In any case, being young is in itself already enough of a handicap, for youngsters are exposed to systematic bullying by anyone dressed in a uniform or carrying a firearm. In these days of crisis, with no clear paths to the future, it is to their credit that they are still, in spite of it all, striving to grow into adult men and women.

Sample Indentures Offered to Apprentice Joiners in 1993

SAMPLE I

We, the undersigned, Mr [Parent], on the one hand, and Mr [Employer] on the other, have agreed that [Apprentice] shall be submitted for apprenticeship under the following terms:
The duration of the apprenticeship shall be: 3 years, 4 years or 5 years, from [date] to [date]

- Three (3) years: Thirty-five thousand CFA francs (35,000 CFA francs)
- Four (4) years: Twenty-five thousand CFA francs (25,000 CFA francs)
- Five (5) years: Fifteen thousand CFA francs (15,000 CFA francs)

ON ENTRY: 6 bottles of 'hard liquor' + a down payment of half the agreed sum
ON RELEASE: 1 flagon of palm wine – 1 case of beer – 12 yams – 6 bottles of hard liquor – 1 case of soft drinks – 1 ram – the remaining half of the agreed sum

ARTICLES

- Article 1 – Each apprentice shall undergo a trial period of three (3) months' duration.
- Article 2 – During his apprenticeship, the apprentice shall obey and put himself at the mercy of his employer. He must promptly execute every task he is given.
- Article 3 – He shall be responsible for every tool placed in his keeping.
- Article 4 – The father or legal guardian shall pay for any acts of sabotage he might commit.
- Article 5 – If he should terminate his apprenticeship prior to the agreed date, the father or legal guardian shall pay his employer the sum of 25,000 CFA francs.
- Article 6 – The father or legal guardian shall request permission in advance for any leave of absence.
- Article 7 – Each day of absence without leave shall not be counted as a completed day of apprenticeship and shall thus extend the agreed finishing date by one day.
- Article 8 – At the workshop, the apprentice shall comply with all instructions issued by the shop foreman.

Date
Signed

1. Legal Guardian
2. Employer
3. Apprentice
4. Witness

SAMPLE 2

Apprentice's family name:
given name(s):
date of birth:
place:

DURATION OF INDENTURE

- 3 years: 1st payment 30,000 CFA francs + Rum, J.B., Martini, Gordon's Gin
  2nd payment 30,000 CFA francs + Rum, J.B., Martini, Gordon's Gin
- 4 years: 1st payment 25,000 CFA francs + Rum, J.B., Martini, Gordon's Gin
  2nd payment 25,000 CFA francs + Rum, J.B., Martini, Gordon's Gin

- The apprentice must work steadily and shall never leave his place of work without prior permission. Costs of keep and food shall be charged to the parents.
- If ever the apprentice is disobedient or impolite enough to quit the workshop without his employer's knowledge, his parents shall pay us a sum of 100,000 CFA francs; but the employer does not have the right to dismiss his apprentice without the knowledge of the parents.
- The apprentice is under obligation to work overtime (including nights) with his employer 'free of charge' should the need rise [...]
- The workshop opening hours are from 06:30 until 12:30 mornings and from 14:30 until 18:30 afternoons.
- When the apprentice returns to his lodgings, he may not rightfully take from the workshop anything (such as tools) belonging to his employer; should he do so he shall be dismissed forthwith.
- The apprentice's parents shall equip their child with his own tools.

Two copies of this contract shall be signed, one to be given to the parents and the other to be kept by the employer.
Witnesses on behalf of the apprentice

Director:
1:
2:

Notes

1. Districts of south-west Lomé, close to the frontier with Ghana (pop. 40,000).
2. 'General Discussion Document on the Problems of Young Apprentices in Urban Areas', Lomé, General Direction of the Social Services, Department of Youth Protection and Advancement, 1987 (9 pages), a number of whose elements have been used in this article.
3. *Brotherhomé* literally means 'with the brothers'.
4. Lit. 'Big Tailor', from the pidgin English: *Taylor-gan* (*gan* = big).

5. See, in particular, Y. Marguerat and T. Péleï, 'Si Lomé m'était conté', 2 vols (1992–94), Lomé, University of Bènin Press.

6. Multiply by 10 for the 1993 rates (1500 CFA francs = ± US$ 1). All figures given here are from before the January 1994 devaluation of the CFA franc.

7. Today, a Singer costs between 60,000 and 80,000 CFA francs, although there are high quality Chinese copies selling for about 35,000 CFA francs.

8. For instance: 2 years = 40,000 CFA francs; 3 years = 30,000 CFA francs; 4 years = 20,000 CFA francs (e.g. for an apprentice plumber in the Nyékonakpoè district of Lomé).

9. Often taking with him a share of his employer's clientele; all the more reason why the latter tends to delay the parting of the ways for a maximum length of time.

10. A few journeymen may be found working at the most highly skilled garages and joinery shops.

11. Which accounts for the employers' generally hostile attitude towards contracts allowing payment on a monthly basis, an arrangement a lot of parents would prefer. Only a few haute couture dress-makers operate a monthly payment system (e.g. 3500 CFA francs a month over a period of one year or a year and a half).

12. Many such examples have been observed in various occupations and various districts of Lomé.

13. A case observed in 1987 at a cabinet-maker's shop on the road to the airport: on top of the basic 30,000 CFA francs for the contract itself, one apprentice had to bring with him twenty bottles of 'the hard stuff', fifty-six bottles of beer or lemonade (costing a total of 45,000 CFA francs) plus 35,000 CFA francs' worth of food and other sundry items for a large banquet and a further 2,500 to pay for printing the certificate – in short, the monthly salary of a high school teacher.

14. 89.013, 89.014 and 89.015: METFP, 25 April 1989.

15. It was naturally far easier for a social services official or an expatriate like myself to demand adherence to the official 1989 indenture than it would be for a humble father in a position of inferiority vis-à-vis his son's future employer.

16. Observed in early 1995: a 50,000-CFA-franc indenture had become the strict minimum in all trades right across the board – and not without some hard bargaining – and the bosses had started demanding their bottles again (with drinks prices having doubled since devaluation); meanwhile, the economic and political crisis has left families high and dry and the decrees of 1989 are now a thing of the past.

17. Running away from this is one of the reasons why there are so many young outcasts on the streets.

CHAPTER 18

Apprenticeship in France: A Parallel Case in an Industrialized Society

Bernard Garet

When I began teaching at the Angers city Chambre des métiers (Chamber of Trade) training centre (CFA), I noticed frequent signs of fatigue in my 670 students (some of whom even fell fast asleep). Fellow members of staff, accustomed to such a state of affairs, told me that there was nothing unusual about that. Once I had gained their trust, the students began confiding in me and I soon learnt why they were so tired: overwork. In September 1989 I decided to quantify the problems and issued a ten-point questionnaire to each of the students on my register with the assurance that their answers would remain strictly confidential. Two further questions were added the following January on account of the increased level of fatigue observed following the Christmas and New Year holidays.

The apprentices were subdivided into four trade-specific groups: 210 butchers, 146 *charcutiers* (cooked meats), 106 bakers and 205 pastry chefs. Incomplete results owing to absenteeism during either or both of the two questionnaire periods (when apprentices were out working for their employers) were excluded. A total of 618 completed questionnaires were returned, allowing a safe degree of statistical representativeness.[1]

Every member of the survey population was enrolled on a sandwich course including two weeks at a company for every week in class; each had signed an indenture (under Labour Code regulations) for the 1988–89 or 1989–90 academic year; each was studying for a vocational training certificate at the CFA and with regional artisans.

The findings were far worse than had previously been imagined, the majority of cases showing a disregard for the law over working hours and rest days, holidays or rates of pay, if not all three. They were not, as the Chambre des métiers tried to make out, isolated cases but the 'norm'. Unwilling to collude in this situation, I refused to bend to CFA management threats when, on 21 March 1990, I was asked to 'desist from any action aimed at setting up a working group in the establishment without prior permission'. Following my dismissal for 'inaptitude', my determination to continue to work on behalf of the apprentices sparked off a national movement in support of the survey; the story received media coverage and 10,000 people around France signed a petition. In May 1990, the press published a number of the findings and the Angers city Chambre des métiers immediately hit back, branding it as unreliable, lacking in credibility, pure fantasy, even though the final report itself had not yet been written in full and published. It was released in May 1991. The 'Garet Case', actually a defence of the apprentices, was then brought before the administrative court which ruled in June 1991 that the authorities were to provide me with another job and launch a full review of apprentices' working conditions.

The results are there for all to see today, with the legal pre-apprenticeship age now lowered to fourteen years and a national campaign underway to promote apprenticeship. The five-year employment law that came into effect in January 1994 curtailed meetings of the only remaining regulatory body, the 'apprenticeship masters' review board' (which includes union representatives), and put paid to the last few scruples of opportunistic masters. The solitary bodies still exercising any form of control here are the Labour Inspectorate and the Apprenticeship Inspectorate; the limited means they have at their disposal leave no doubt as to how far the authorities are prepared to accept violations of law, as long as other political priorities having nothing to do with respect for the working conditions of apprentices are satisfied.

The Survey Questionnaire

Each student group was asked to answer the questionnaire verbally during a half-hour period prior to classes, with a number (hours, days, percentage of statutory minimum working wage), a 'yes' or a 'no'. Here are the questions:

1. Age (over or under 18)?
2. How many hours do you work on average per day?
3. How many hours do you work on the busiest day of the week?
4. How many days do you work per week (a half-day counts as one full day)?
5. What is the total average number of hours you work per week?
6. How many paid weeks' holiday have you had over the past year?
7. What percentage of the statutory minimum wage do you receive?
9. Have you worked on a Saturday, Sunday or both following a week of classes?
10. Has your apprenticeship master ever resorted to violence?
11. How much overtime do you reckon you worked per day during the Christmas and New Year holidays: 1 hour? 1½ hours? 2 hours?
12. Did you work from 15 December to 1 January without a full day off?

The survey results revealed that:

- there was almost never any distinction between day work and night work
- 85 per cent of apprentices had done more than the maximum legal hours per day
- the same was true of 97 per cent of them on the busiest day of the week
- 82 per cent had worked longer than the maximum legal working week
- 62 per cent had worked during class weeks
- 39 per cent had not taken all their legal paid holidays
- 16 per cent had worked fifteen days without a break
- 20 apprentices had been paid less than the legal percentage of the statutory minimum wage
- some apprentices were working seven days a week
- 4 apprentices had officially been recognized as victims of employer violence

AGE Leaving aside the indentures for apprentices who had already passed a vocational training certificate and who had opted to specialize in a second (e.g. baker/pastry chef), the percentage of legal adults (eighteen years) studying for their first vocational training certificate was close to 5 per cent. In all, 8.74 per cent of the 618 sample population were aged eighteen years or over. So more than 91 per cent of the apprentices were minors and thus belonged to the category of 'children' as understood by the UN Convention on the Rights of the Child.[2]

AVERAGE HOURS WORKED PER DAY The general mean is 8 hours 40 minutes. This, plus the narrow difference between the extremes (41 minutes), conceals some quite considerable variations and a data distribution far in excess of the maximum legal 8-hour working day. A total of 84.8 per cent of the apprentices were found to be working over and above the 8 hours and more than 16 per cent of them were on more than 10 hours a day.

NUMBER OF HOURS WORKED ON THE BUSIEST DAY OF THE WEEK There is always one day each week when the workload is heavier than the others because of the employer's need to fill orders with the weekend approaching. The aim here was to discover just how far some masters were prepared to push their apprentices on a day not necessarily followed by a rest day. Apprentices across the board were found to be working an average of 10 hours 12 minutes: way beyond the 8-hour limit stipulated by the Labour Code.[3]

NUMBER OF FULL DAYS OFF In pointing out to the apprentices that a half-day's work during the week counted as a whole day (the goal being to distinguish the number of full rest days), it emerged that 6- to 8-hour 'half-days' were standard practice among artisans in every trade. What is more, some such days fell on a weekend (once every two or three weeks or once a month); agreements between apprenticeship masters and apprentices *vis-à-vis* working at the weekend generally tended to vanish as working weekends became the norm.

The average number of days worked per week across the board was found to be 5.52. The decimals correspond to a sixth, partial, workday meaning that a single rest day would appear on average to be the norm. Furthermore, if we look at the distribution by half-day shifts rather than the general average, it would appear that the law stipulating a minimum full day off per week is not always observed. Fifteen apprentices were working over six days a week and three (delicatessen) were on a full seven-day week. Given the number of hours they put in, however, two rest days a week could hardly be said to be too much.

Meanwhile, the apprentices working five and a half days a week were all found to be starting the sixth day in the morning (some as early as 2 or 2.30 a.m.). They often continued working for far longer than 4 hours. Having finished by noon, some of them felt that they had done only half a day, regardless of how long the morning had been. Young apprentices are seen to be submissive to their masters and unable to refuse a 'request' to 'help out' on a Sunday morning.

AVERAGE HOURS WORKED PER WEEK The Labour Code clearly states that apprentices in the food trade should not work more than 39 hours per week. Yet the general norm here was 47 hours and 31 minutes, i.e. equal to a whole extra day's work. So the weekly rest day is all the more vital, especially in view of the fact that they also have their studies to consider. A total of 505 apprentices (i.e. 81.7 per cent) were found to be working more than 39 hours a week (151 of them doing over 50 hours, twenty-seven over 60 and five doing more than 70). Some apprentices had worked longer in fifteen days than a regular wage-earner would in a month. The press at the time highlighted a record which makes particularly grim reading: one sixteen-year-old apprentice baker had worked 92 hours in a single week.

NUMBER OF PAID WEEKS OFF IN PAST YEAR This question could be analysed only in the cases of second-year apprentices, because not all of those enrolled in the first year after having completed pre-apprenticeship classes or fourth-year secondary school had ever had first-hand experience of a paid holiday. Among the resulting 331 answers, the average number of paid weeks off over the preceding year came to 4.54. According to the law, 'an apprentice has the right to two and a half days off for every month worked, i.e. thirty working days per year not counting class weeks at the Apprentice Training Centre (CFA)'. This latter detail may appear self-evident, but it must have escaped the attention of the many employers who had given their apprentices a paid holiday during class week. Many apprentices saw no distinction between working days and public holidays because they regarded Sundays and public holidays as work days too. Nearly 40 per cent of them had not taken all their legally allowed paid rest days.

PERCENTAGE OF MINIMUM WAGE RECEIVED The 1990 apprenticeship indenture states that an apprentice should earn 15 per cent of the minimum wage during the first six months, 25 per cent during the second six, 35 per cent during the third, 45 per cent the fourth and 60 per cent the fifth and sixth, with 10 per cent extra for anyone over the age of eighteen years.[4] Many apprentices had no idea of the percentage they were earning; just the amount of money in their pockets at the end of the month.

The average was 29.8 per cent. They could hardly hope for more than the minimum rate dictated by the law, no matter how long the hours (and it is strange to note how, apart from odd instances of generosity, the masters stick so rigidly to the rules when it comes to the matter of remuneration; and how conveniently some of them 'forget' that a 10 per cent raise is in order when an apprentice turns eighteen or the next six-month period begins).

WHETHER OVERTIME IS PAID This question had to be put because many apprentices consider a 100-franc note for a weekend's work or a cake to take home to the family to be a fair reward for 'favours rendered'. Pay slips make no mention of 'overtime', for the law forbids it under apprenticeship – apart from exceptional cases where a dispensation is granted by the Labour Inspectorate on submission of a detailed application.

Approximately 12 per cent of the apprentices reckoned they had been paid for their extra hours in cash (although the sum did not appear on their pay slips). Another 12 per cent or so said that their boss had offered them some token of his appreciation. None specified an hourly rate: it is left to the employer's better judgement. Pastry chefs, the apprentices working the longest hours per week, received the least overtime pay: only 9.7 per cent of them had anything at all, compared to 11.5 per cent of delicatessen workers, 12.1 per cent of butchers and 15.2 per cent of bakers. Yet 80 per cent of all apprentices right across the board were found to be working well beyond the legal 39 hours. Masters use the overtime ban to avoid having to pay in full for the amount of labour supplied.

WEEKEND WORK FOLLOWING A WEEK OF CLASSES A total of 62 per cent of apprentices worked the Saturday following a class week, 39.5 per cent the Sunday and 35.1 per cent both the Saturday and Sunday. Figures vary far more per trade for working Sundays than Saturdays: 12 per cent for butchers, 29 per cent for delicatessen workers, 49 per cent for pastry chefs, 51 per cent for bakers (the pattern being the same *vis-à-vis* apprentices working the whole weekend). These facts demonstrate further disregard of the apprenticeship laws, and not just in a 'few isolated cases'.

VIOLENCE PERPETRATED BY THE MASTER This question did not come to mind when I devised my original survey. It was only on hearing the stories a number of apprentices had to tell that I felt it needed to be added. It is a sensitive subject. The first step is to pinpoint what apprentices perceive 'violence' to be. Certainly not all the teasing, harassment and humiliation that constitute their daily lot. The issue here is deliberate and malevolent acts intended to inflict physical pain and make them potential entries on the register of 'blows and wounds'. However, apprentices suffering violence at the hands of an employer are not necessarily going to own up to it in a questionnaire. Inextricably trapped in an unfair balance of power where the stronger party resorts to increasingly severe corporal punishment, victims are fearful of retaliation. Nor is it easy for them to confess to having been beaten up by an employer in front of their classmates. They wonder whether they might not have done something to provoke the boss; to some extent, their own guilt would serve to justify it in their eyes. Many apprentices would therefore prefer to hold their tongues rather than sow the seeds of doubt.

Four apprentices claimed to have been the victims of violence within the framework of the survey (a delicatessen boy who had been 'beaten up'; an apprentice baker struck with a bread platter; one butcher's boy punched and kicked and another smacked in the face). A good many other hair-raising cases have come to my attention since then; some have been brought before the industrial tribunal. Take, for instance, the delicatessen's apprentice who narrowly escaped serious injury when he slammed a door shut and only just cut the trajectory of a knife thrown at him by his boss. Or the complaint lodged by a parent that an employer had forced his son to drop his trousers in front of the rest of the staff to prove he had 'got one'. Another document accuses a baker/pastry chef of sexually harassing his sixteen-year-old apprentice girl and continuing to abuse her in his car whenever they met in town. Fear plays a paramount role in such cases, few of which ever reach the official complaints stage, even when parents become aware of what is going on. The apprentice suffers alone and in silence hoping that time will soon change things for the better.

Violence seems to be one of the 'rules of the game' in employer–apprentice relations. Humiliation is regarded as a healthy means of teaching youngsters how to stand up for themselves; and this brand of 'initiation' into the workings of hierarchical relationships can often include physical aggression as a means of 'making a man of them'. There is only ever any dialogue when the apprentice answers back: does that 'make a man of him'? It is not just the bosses but the other workers too who are the perpetrators, for each level of the hierarchy has the 'right to intimidate' those on the next level down. I have heard several reports of apprentices being pushed around by another worker while the boss looks on in amusement.

Since few complaints about such acts of violence ever reach the courts, fifteen-year-old children continue being downtrodden in this way, constantly branded as 'incompetent' or 'temporarily useless'. It would seem to suggest that there is nothing wrong about using aggression as a proper means of training an apprentice.

ESTIMATED EXTRA DAILY WORKLOAD DURING THE CHRISTMAS HOLIDAYS This question was added to the questionnaire in view of how much more tired the apprentices were when they returned to classes in January 1990. It set out to make a quantitative measurement of the extra daily workload from 15 to 31 December 1989 to within the nearest half-hour.

The 618 apprentices questioned had on average worked almost 2 extra hours per day (1 hour 58 minutes). The daily average rose to 10 hours 38 minutes and the weekly mean to 58 hours 40 minutes, i.e. almost 150 per cent of the legal working week. In the fifteen days between 15 to 31 December 1989, the apprentices had done the equivalent of three weeks' work. How many adult wage-earners would be willing to accept such conditions without recompense?

WORK FROM 15–31 DECEMBER WITHOUT A FULL DAY'S REST One hundred and six apprentices had worked fifteen successive days without a day off, i.e. 16.4 per cent of the total (25 per cent of the pastry chefs and 28.3 per cent of delicatessen workers). This seemingly quite common practice shows how companies rate their economic and commercial interests far higher than the apprentices' health and quality of life, many of whom received nothing but a pat on the back for having 'lasted the course' or, at best, a couple of 100-franc bills masquerading as a Christmas bonus. And an apprentice who is for ever striving to gain recognition and reassurance regards an 'initiation' like this as having raised his standing in the eyes of his fellows, simply because he had responded to the boss's call – or, rather, order – and managed to 'last the course'.

CONCLUSION The survey did not set out to call in question the apprenticeship system itself as a means of vocational training, but the ways in which it is applied in practice with the existing laws flouted daily by apprenticeship 'masters'.

Iy may be tempting to believe that although apprentices do endure very long working hours, it is made up to them in the pay packet or with extra rest days. Nothing of the sort. They face long hours, low pay and no rest with the sole consolation being that they are learning a trade sometimes by mowing the employer's lawn or painting the shutters of his house; and they have to keep their mouths shut if they want to continue putting petrol in the moped and 'living a normal life'.

What of the contract governing relations between 'master' and apprentice? As the document signed by the two parties (or a parent if the latter is a minor) puts it, the employer undertakes to 'respect the legal and contractual provisions regarding apprentices' working conditions and pay'. It is surprising to see the ease with which the 'masters' openly ride roughshod over the law and how submissive the apprentices are. The whole affair is cloaked in silence. 'Keep your eyes open and your mouth shut' is one of the system's guiding principles; if nobody is saying anything, everybody must have found their proper place.

Within the space of a single year, 618 apprentices between them supplied a cumulative total of close to 300,000 hours of labour which, apart from infringing the legal limits, could have provided 160 unemployed people with a whole year's worth of work. Little wonder the Chambre des métiers was so determined to discredit the survey and distance itself from a teacher deemed 'unfit for the duties entrusted to him'. And one can understand the embarrassment of a government faced with the publication of such results just as its pro-apprenticeship campaign was being launched in the media.

The Actors and Their Interests

I was saying that everybody must have found their place; let us now analyse the actors and their interests. I hope I shall be excused for my perhaps immoderate tone which is far from sociological (for I am no sociologist): real life is often harder when experienced first-hand.

THE APPRENTICESHIP MASTER Apprenticeship stems from the ancestral tradition of a master passing his craft on to an apprentice. Yet masters very soon become aware of the opportunities and dangers involved in imparting their skills.

The apprenticeship master is regarded as the epitome of social success: a proud possessor of know-how, honourably entrusted with the task of transmitting it. Experienced at using his authority and abusing his power, he finds in the apprentice a compliant and low-cost source of labour. He is the latest in a long line of traditional paternalism, capitalizing on the image he has in the eyes of the apprentice while at the same time representing certain reassuring values. By setting an example alone, he is passing on the essence of social patterns: man works to 'succeed', woman looks after the house and the children (the unemployment level for female ex-apprentices is 8 per cent higher than for males). And nothing worthwhile can be learnt at school; experience is the only thing that really counts.

The National Apprenticeship Drive brochure clearly states that 'as far as the company is concerned, apprenticeship rhymes with benefits': a FFr 7000 subsidy per indenture, a FFr 7000 deduction in taxes, exemption from apprenticeship tax and company and employee social security contributions. An employer can take on at least two apprentices so as to cover himself when one of them has to take time out for class weeks.

A master's top priority is not necessarily to train a young person eventually to take over from him (he may fear the potential competition). Few craftsmen seriously set out to dispense that sort of training; as is recommended by law in liaison with the Apprentice Training Centre. Only 20 per cent of the 'apprentice logbooks' designed to harmonize relations between apprenticeship masters and teaching staff are actually filled; and only a few of these show any evidence of progress or true communication between the two sides. The craftsmen themselves have had no specific training to become apprenticeship masters: five years' experience or a vocational qualification is enough to hire an apprentice and 58 per cent of masters do not hold certificates.

The Apprentice Training Centre (CFA)

The CFA exists under the all-pervasive scrutiny of the employers. The employers' federation plays a highly influential role in managing its funds which in turn come from public sources (regional council subsidies and apprenticeship taxes from the education offices). Often, CFA presidents also preside over the commercial courts. Their directors confess to being 'administrators, not educationalists'. The complaints they record rarely ever make it to the desks of the labour and apprenticeship inspectorates, the employer's voice is heard more often than is that of the apprentice.

According to the law of 1971, supervision of apprentices on company premises should be carried out in person by members of the CFA teaching staff. Visits, however, have dwindled on account of a lack of funds for travel expenses. Technical instructors – former professionals who have maintained good relations with craftsmen – are the only ones actually keeping up the visits, although generally these tend to be more of an opportunity to meet old friends rather than an occasion to write up a training report or check working conditions.

Vocational training certificate candidates are often claimed to yield 50 to 60 per cent success rates. These figures, however, are based purely on the students actually sitting their exams. A personal investigation of mine has shown that a declared rate of just over 50 per cent would actually fall to below 30 per cent if the number of youngsters who did not turn up for all their exams were taken in account. The majority of teachers have undergone inspection only once, even some of those who have been working for twenty years.

Instruction at the CFA is reduced to a face-to-face encounter in the classroom, away from the reality of daily life. The term 'working conditions' corresponds solely to the equipment and technical criteria of work. Meanwhile, apprenticeship masters are very much opposed to apprentices learning labour legislation. Artisans often regard apprentices' week-long attendance at the CFA once every three weeks as an obligation they must tolerate. They often entertain a negative view of school: they see it as a waste of time, a rest period. What a way to improve the apprentices' perception of theoretical training, or their respect for teachers of French or exact sciences!

THE PARENTS Apprentices' families for the most part belong to the socio-professional classes of the primary and secondary sectors; it is rare to find a banker's son becoming an apprentice butcher, or a lawyer's daughter an apprentice greengrocer. The parents of children who have failed at school are tempted to criticize their offspring's intellectual weaknesses, branding them as incompetents. The only positive features to be valued are 'having guts' and 'knowing how to work' – the passport to social integration.

Once the indenture has been signed, many parents put their children entirely into the hands of the institution, placing their trust in the artisans and turning a blind eye to any problems encountered. If a child complains, they make him or her wait until they are eighteen years old, at which point they will have 'done all they can' and be within their rights to relinquish responsibility for them.

Parents live in trepidation of problems arising with the artisans for they would then have to start all over again, seeking another accommodating employer willing to take their child after all the trouble they have already gone to the first time round. The pressure is such that exploited children are forced to accept their fate and put themselves at the mercy of anybody other than their parents.

Finally, it is regrettable to note that many families frown upon any use of the intellect, for they do not want their children becoming 'useless white-collar workers'. So apprentices can hardly be said to receive much encouragement from their parents to take their studies to heart; the family either hinders or saps the self-confidence they need to blossom. Only 5 per cent of parents bother attending the 'open days' designed to foster parent–teacher contact. The whole thing is tainted by resignation, neglected responsibility and even cowardice.

THE CHILDREN Pre-apprentices can now legally be aged as young as fourteen years. They are given neither work contract nor pay. Of schoolchild status, they none the less spend half their time (fifteen days a month) at a company.

As the survey did not take these youngsters on board, I shall not venture to extrapolate. However, the signs are that their situation is no better than that of apprentices. Pre-apprenticeship is actually a means of keeping under-achieving school pupils in the education system. The children in question have one foot in school – look hard and you will see them in the prefab at the far end of the courtyard – and the other already in the world of work. Their future is all mapped out for them: apprenticeship in how to be meek and obedient.

Apprentices are no longer small children, but neither are they adults. They are what the law calls 'workers-in-training'. In addition to the usual personal development problems every adolescent has to contend with, they also face a monolithic and relatively unscrupulous hierarchy which they join at the very lowest level. They want to avoid failure and, aware of their inferiority, will do anything they can to resemble their boss – who takes the place of a father – and to 'make good just like he did'.

Guilt-ridden at having failed at school, they enter a sort of purgatory. Their apprentice status may well represent independence and some degree of recognition, but the meagre amount they stand to earn puts them in the category of underpaid workers. They are submissive, obedient, constantly stretched to the limits and prepared to suffer in silence, since it is all just a 'bad phase to get through'.

In an editorial for *L'artisan* magazine, the president of the Maine-et-Loire Chambre des métiers spoke of 'moulding the human clay of young apprentices'. These apprentices are often gripped with fear: fear of causing disappointment, fear of losing their place, of not doing as well as their fellows, of being teased and punished. Once out of the system and proud at having lasted the course, the ex-apprentice inexorably helps to carry such forms of initiation from one generation to the next on the pretext that 'there ain't no success without pain'. Naturally, nothing can be gained without effort. But why the collective neurosis (expressed in the demands adults make on children) that, imbued with the spirit of competition, makes out that the chances of 'succeeding in life', of not being 'excluded from the system', are proportional to the pain apprentices put themselves through in order to 'make it'?

Despite the fact that apprentices have the right to join a trade union as soon as they sign an indenture, attempts at unionization have until now been doomed to failure. How many fifteen-year-old apprentices are capable of single-handedly forcing their way into the labour exchange; and how many trade unions have shown concern for the fate of apprentices? The only bodies to react are the highly ideologically-driven associations such as the Young Christian Workers' Movement and the Young Communists.

THE AUTHORITIES Abuses are subject to fines following an investigation by the Labour Inspectorate. When questioned recently, however, a local government official in charge of labour affairs pointed to staff shortages and said that more urgent matters needed to be attended to first. The only thing they could do would be to return the employer's recruitment applications which, remember, have not been subject to review since 1994. Inspections for their part are rather rare these days and when one apprentice is officially withdrawn from a company, there is nothing to prevent the employer from taking on another eight days later and, if it escapes the inspectorate's attention, earning himself another FFr 7000 subsidy. Computer follow-up of law suits has become impractical for there is simply not enough time. It takes so long for a case to come before an industrial tribunal that it is a hopeless course of action for an urgent appeal.

Any society which does not equip itself with powerful enough legal means to enforce its legislation and hence merely resorts to hushing up transgressions, is irresponsible and lacking in credibility.

Although increasing amounts of money may have been poured into the apprenticeship system since the law of 1971, no accompanying demands are made for better quality training. What might well have been perceived as a sign of progress (i.e. fixed pay and an established standard indenture) is in fact a step backwards: inspections are rare, sanctions even more so. We are left with the distinct impression that these measures stem from a policy allowing the exploitation of apprentices to be swept under the carpet; as long as there are sandwich courses available to continue absorbing the bulk of school failures, the authorities can fudge the visible unemployment figures while at the same time taking pride in a mission to offer training, if not an education. It is nevertheless a particularly onerous policy: FFr 7000 subsidies for 200,000 apprentices amounting to a hefty bill of FFr 1.4 billion.

In fact there is only one word to describe the situation: 'exploitation'. Apprentices are often individuals who have turned their backs on the schooling system in order to seek recognition as people capable of being productive and financially independent of their families. Yet they have too little self-confidence to be able to stand on their own two feet and resist the enticing offers from profiteers interested in tapping their cheap labour power. 'Apprenticeship masters' grasp the opportunity, shielding themselves with the formative aspects and the virtues of their craft. With a relative disregard for the legislation, they are first and foremost masters of their own premises where the labour laws are held well at bay: they take the liberty of observing not a single point of apprenticeship legislation, be it at the level of working hours, rest days, pay and holidays or the dispensations for which they are meant to apply to the Labour Inspectorate.

Notes

1. Editor's note: For the sake of brevity, the author has not presented his findings per study year (first year, second year). Similarly we have had to cut most of the specific results relating to trade and course length presented in the original manuscript. Please contact the author for full details of the survey (data per year, frequency charts, standard deviations and so on).

2. Editor's note: Beyond its declaration of principles, the Convention's wording actually sets a more flexible framework; and this survey of apprenticeship in France only corresponds to the normally accepted age criteria for the employment of children (cf., supra, Gendreau) vis-à-vis a limited number of apprentices. We nevertheless thought it perfectly justifiable to publish it on account of the wealth of information it offers and the outstanding illustration it provides of one of the world's seven richest nations. Because of

the conditions imposed upon them by both their apprenticeship masters and training centres, the majority of adolescent French apprentices are prey to the same confinement and exploitation as very young children. We see here the process of worker infantilization described in Chapter 1 (General Introduction) to this book.

3. Six apprentice bakers claimed to have worked over 15 hours on their heaviest workday of the week. Taking all trades together, 97.4 per cent of the apprentices were found to be working more than 8 hours on that particular day; 62.3 per cent of them were doing more than 10 hours; 18 per cent more than 12.

4. Some apprentices on what is known as a 'parallel contract' (2nd City and Guilds), and thus in their fifth six-month period, were receiving 60 per cent plus 10 per cent for being over eighteen, i.e. 70 per cent of the minimum wage.

From Socialization through Work to Exploitation for a Profit

CHAPTER 19

Family versus the Logic of the Market

Robert Cabanes

Are there any societies or social formations left today whose articulation with the market economy remains settled enough not to have deprived them of control over their own reproduction processes? Or any societies with a specific social organization keeping the goods and labour market in check and – albeit each with its own methods and procedures – allowing every man more or less fair access to land and production, marriage and reproduction? Societies where, even if inequalities exist between families, groups, castes or lineages and correspond to the degrees of social hierarchization, age-related inequalities continue to operate according to the principle and cycle of inter-generational investment: children supplying their labour today being repaid by other children's labour in the future as a sort of advance payment redeemable once they themselves become parents (Mbaye, Ngueyap), an exchange deferred from one generation to the next and one of a number of different forms of socialization (gender inequalities being different as they are fixed and unbending: young girls are regarded in terms of gender rather than age)?

As long as access to land is unrestricted, any growth in the labour force will be warmly welcomed by societies such as these for it comes with the promise of both higher levels of production and enlarged or more sophisticated family and/or social organization. The child-as-benefit or child-as-wealth (Ravololomanga) belongs to an order of social reproduction where the concept of exploitation is alien to that of socialization through work. It is only in the event of a break in the inter-generational cycle and lack (or uncertainty) of accession to land and women that the problem of free, non-recouped labour arises, beginning within the domestic group.

That is when 'child labour' comes into its own as a specific term denoting a form of labour inextricably linked to the notion of exploitation, which is what I mean by the term when it is used in the text that follows.

The Household within the Framework of the Market

Upheavals created by joining the market economy are generally regarded as the root causes of child labour. The market economy undermines the very foundations of original social formations by initiating a direct relationship between households and the goods and labour markets. It destroys the organic interrelations between households both vertically (balanced reproduction of access to land) and horizontally (exchanging women; human reproduction). This direct relationship creates inequalities between households that crystallize and grow over generations and lead to the emergence of social classes. It is equally responsible for the changing nature of divisions of labour within the domestic group as the goods and labour markets exert pressure on it to adapt its organization of work and to create new forms of labour and new inequalities.

These upheavals first appeared in agricultural production in the shape of cash crops introduced within the framework of the family farm; it can safely be said that not a single rural society today has remained untouched by the process. But the deepest-seated upheavals have occurred in urban societies whose economies are non-agricultural and therefore not governed by the inter-generational cycles of exchange; urban exchange cycles are shorter, more fragile, making the least productive act into an act of vital necessity. Lest we forget it, the urban population as a percentage of the total population now ranges between 30 per cent (India, China) and 80 per cent (Latin America); with 35 per cent in Africa and 43 per cent in other parts of Asia.

Child Labour and the Disadvantaged Social Classes

Child labour spreads most in the least advantaged social classes to whose weakened or crisis-hit households it begins as a means of subsistence: the child is put to work 'in the midst of the family', 'outside the home' or employed as a 'wage-earner' (Morice); when the domestic group loses control over it, the work then proceeds 'independently'; as it does in the case of underage wage-earners, street-workers and children working and living rough on the streets (Mérienne, Taracena). Most prominent of the very varied forms of household crises is that of the general spread of child labour and deteriorating working conditions. We shall take just one example, first of all because its brutality is so commonplace and second because it is apparently already rather widespread: households keeping only one or two children while placing the others into the care of a distant relative or even a friend. So only one or two 'heirs' will be able to go to school and have the opportunity to make a better life for themselves than those 'placed' with families where their status is lower, and they are inevitably steered straight into work and excluded from school (Labazée, Poirier).

Exploitation does exist within the household (Nieuwenhuys) and easily borrows from the language and ideology of family relations (Verlet). The opportunities and means for this kind of exploitation depend upon the household's structural position within the social system as a whole, i.e. its isolation in the face of an omnipresent market which can drive it into a universal and cumulative form of dependency: bonded labour (M. Bonnet), whose cycles are adaptable to every situation. It is in order to keep its position on the market that a household exploits its own young; it is in order to maintain the access of adults to paid work outside the domestic group that the labour of the young is confined to within the domestic group (Nieuwenhuys). It is in order to guarantee the physical upkeep of the domestic group alone that children are made to pay their parents rent for a place to sleep (Ravololomanga). There are countless examples of exploitation within the household that are just as hard and violent as anything found outside. When the debt factor is added – as is often the case after years of being ground down and dominated – the circle closes and the household finds itself completely in the grip of the market economy. Some regard international debt between nations as a mere extension of the original debt, a further link in the chain (in both senses of the term). At any rate, the umbrella of a universal moral duty – paying one's debts – paradoxically harbours the most shameless forms of exploitation, outside the domestic group as much as (at times) within, between nations as within each nation.

Exclusion and Public Order

In his broad historical tableau, Alessandro Stella shows how a sort of natural reproduction of outcasts, exclusion and marginality is established over generations and perfectly integrated into every society. He observes that even in the Middle Ages the periods when the use of child labour was proliferating in urban areas coincided with a simultaneous rise in delinquency and greater vigilance on the part of the authorities concerning issues of public order. Another outbreak occurred during the period of industrialization in the nineteenth century. For the children 'entering service' or an 'apprenticeship' had generally been deprived of any social status, abandoned or orphaned and there was every chance of them spawning a generation that would reproduce their own predicament. There is all the more reason to stress the link between child labour and 'public order' because it is being consolidated and aggravated by the interdependency of nations which in turn increases the exploitation of the dominated nations.

For its radically original and indisputably modern feature is the accompanying, massive-scale expansion of a form of work parallel to the (legal and illegal) work done within a climate of exploitation or violence, but which does not as a rule destroy children or prevent them from continuing on their albeit uncertain road to adulthood. The form in question is explicitly rooted in violence and employs children as the actors and stakes in what amounts to a form of urban warfare: that which stems from the drugs trade, and which in turn relies upon the existence of outrageous inequalities; that perpetrated by organized guerrilla groups using overwhelming numbers of children (Uribe); but, more often than not, that between gangs, between gangs and the police, and between the different police forces backing different gangs – with drugs relieving the misery like a noose to a hanged man. The consumption and dealing of drugs by the children and the political use made of it by the police and leaders enable the physical as much statistical elimination of a good many young and adolescent children via a varied range of almost ritualized incidents (denunciation, traps, gangland killings, acts of intimidation).

Given the future inequalities the world seems to have in store, this warfare is a far cry from a passing epiphenomenon. It could well assume some quite unexpected forms if the police continue playing sorcerer's apprentice by sparking gangland killings in the hope that the 'misfits' and 'bandits' will wipe each other out. Several articles (Alvim, Fukui, Lange) highlight the perverse device used to obscure child labour: the sense of propriety gained from recognizing its existence combined with silence on the matter of children's rights. This device is even further reinforced here as it is still more difficult to accept that the world is ravaged by urban warfare and that underage children are marked out as the actors and frontline victims (be it just the single monthly death in France or the dozens daily in Brazil); hence, the exploitation of child labour – which we can always manage, notwithstanding the difficulty, to discuss – will be presented as a phenomenon that is separate from 'delinquency', which is very easy to talk about as long as it is disassociated from questions relating to work, and solely for the purposes of condemning it (Fukui). Or else it is poverty which, contrary to all the evidence yet with stubborn perseverance down the years, will be stigmatized as leading to crime while work is endlessly presented as an alternative to crime (Alvim).

In fact they all come from the same discriminatory mould and each really does boil down to a matter of labour and survival. Reproduced here, in this street work, which is far more illicit and violent than ordinary forms, is an old pattern of division of labour: in a war, far more boys pay with their lives than girls. And if received wisdom immediately associates delinquency with poverty, making the association appear natural, working-class families are so well aware that poverty can easily lead to delinquency that they are just as likely to stigmatize it in front of their children as middle-class families; even if they do not, of course, actually manage to believe it themselves.

Continuing Exclusion

Many chapters underline the fact that household crises are aggravated by the free-market policies of structural adjustment: growing numbers of single-parent families and, moreover, female-dominated families, children 'of the street' or children 'in the street'. If the official and legitimated prospects of globalization and the single market can only sustain and intensify urban warfare, there is just as much of a commitment to paving the way towards a more rationalized (from the point of view of exploitation) use of child labour. What has until now been but a trend – strong, though at times contested by organized social forces – is in danger of becoming a self-enforcing rule: the deskilling, underpayment and overexploitation of any labour force which may, for any reason, be weakened.

This has already come to our attention when observing how child labour is used at every level from the household to the multinational company (Temgoua) and in any economic climate, growth or recession (Banpasirichote, Bigou, Liao). The deskilled group should include so-called 'international' migrants, newly urbanized country people, women; it is also, broadly speaking, the case of any other labour group which may, under local or individual circumstances, be weakened. In the context of an increasingly flexible global labour market and a growing upwards or downwards diversification of labour groups, it seems perfectly clear that the weakest groups will continue to be more easily crushed than others, regardless even of each country's position in the world economy: 'newly industrialized countries' or 'least developed countries', but developed countries as well. Their weakened position can only encourage the development of exploitative relations within the households concerned that will eventually cause many of them, as in the past, to fall apart. In the current world 'order' enforced by the rich countries and 'their' international institutions, we see hardly a hint of any fundamental change on the horizon (Meillassoux). And the odds are that, in the decades to come, India and the Far East are where urban populations will grow to 80 per cent of the total while the level in Latin America looks likely to fall to 30 per cent.

So, if it is theoretically true that paternalistic exploitative relations work best within the privacy of the family home where no law has the right to enter uninvited and, more often than not, as the final link in a chain of exploitation, we must not lose sight of the fact that this process is initiated from above and that it will splinter family groups prematurely as young children leave home early and, very often, die young. When, however, this process reaches its conclusion through a more normal split at the child's coming of age, it starts all over again at a macro-economic level by 'force of circumstances' rather by than a sort of spontaneous self-sufficiency which sustains itself within the domestic sphere.

Hence, knowing the dangers of decline and developing forms of slavery brought on by child labour, we must now and in the future tackle the very roots of the evil – i.e. the ruling economic system and market logic – not the resulting social effects as far as patterns of family behaviour in the milieux affected are concerned. Otherwise, social measures aiming at re-inforcing the family unit and legislative measures aiming at regulating child labour can only ever act as a certainly useful but, in the long run, feeble stop-gap.

CHAPTER 20

The Demand for Labour within the Household: Child Labour in Togo

Marie-France Lange

Child labour in rural areas is often regarded as something so natural that few people are angered by it, few studies are made, few questions asked. With the help of surveys carried out in Togo between 1984 and 1989, we wish to show that there is nothing 'natural' about the use of children's work, but that it belongs to a frame of relations specifically geared towards production and domination. It is alive and thriving thanks to a combination of the development of monetarist economics, the ever increasing demands of state officials occupying posts in rural areas and state cuts in social spending which shift the burden of infrastructure building and maintenance on to rural communities.

Recognizing Child Labour

If child labour is often ignored or underrated in rural areas, it is because it is so deeply entrenched in local customs and regarded by rural communities and state-controlled authorities alike as a natural and legitimate practice; it is also because of the common belief that it is relatively rare and has no real impact on labour management, nor even on a child's development. It may be said that children from a farming background have always been involved in production work and that this is to some extent a functional part of their education, their socialization.

In actual fact, the socializing aspect of work is something of a smoke-screen, concealing the reality of the children's working conditions and their economic role. It makes one wonder what lies behind representations depicting child labour first in a negative light – as exploitation – and then in a more positive (or neutral) light – as a factor of socialization and apprenticeship. Children's farming or domestic work should be considered as stemming not from a 'natural', but an established social order.[1] In rural societies, such work can range from light, relatively undemanding jobs through to heavier labour incorporating the very youngest of children into the production system. Here is where the first distinguishing feature appears; for if boys may be excused from work, every single community studied imposes domestic chores on girls from a very early age. Indeed, the child's role is viewed in terms not just of the notion of childhood itself,[2] but also of social representations regarding age and gender. The notion of 'labour' for its part arrived with the birth of capitalism when, to begin with, it referred exclusively to waged labour.

These notions and representations are used to conceal the existence of child labour as a social fact; notwithstanding the increasing degree of recognition conventional economic analysis may be granting domestic labour,[3] it almost always takes account of productive labour alone and continues to ignore the drudgery children are forced to endure. Clearly, the non-recognition of child labour means children are more and more in demand. Unless it is seen for what it really is (and stops being passed off as a form of assistance, training, initiation, or even a child's duty towards an adult, a sign of respect), it will remain hidden. Then, the labour power of children will cease to be considered as belonging to their parents and other groups will be free to step into their shoes and assume the duty of training them or the right to their respect.

The first major distinction with regard to how various activities are hived off to children hinges on whether or not they are attending school. Children not going to school are above all used by the family group, while those that are find adults competing for the use of their spare time after school: members of the family, functionaries (teachers, customs officials, soldiers) or rural development firms looking to assemble a large force of obedient and well-managed labourers (numbers of whom vary according to school sizes). The second distinction resides in the child's gender: girls supply a larger, and more underrated, amount of labour than boys (references to training for future mothers, to duty and helping other female members of the family are omnipresent).

By pinpointing the main activities children are compelled to perform at the behest of their families, prominent members of the community or functionaries, we should be able to measure the amount of work time extorted from them, identify the beneficiaries and, finally, shed light on the 'invisible' work concealed by the façade of pseudo-socialization.[4] The struggle to gain control of their labour power gives rise to often bitter fighting, which seems to suggest just how important children's work is to the various groups involved as well as how specific and irreplaceable it is within the current socio-economic and political climate.

Work within the Family

As mentioned, childpower is used in a wide variety of different ways. Children may be required to perform domestic tasks (fetching water from the well, cleaning the house, preparing meals) or productive work (farming, sales, services).

In order to measure the workload of children within the family, we spent five years observing thirty farms in the southern Togo region of Moyen-Mono. Our qualitative and longitudinal approach enabled us to highlight the family strategies governing child labour and measure the children's workload in productive and domestic labour alike; in polygamous households with large numbers of offspring, the head of the family derives his wealth from the work of his children and the surface area of farmed land varies according to the number of wives and (unschooled) children fit and able to work the fields.

In the years 1985–90, Moyen-Mono underwent remarkable economic changes: farm sizes grew thanks, on the one hand, to the appropriation of new lands and, on the other, to the increase in available hands. Although partly due to the return of youths from Nigeria and numbers of wage-earners and unemployed people from Lomé, undeniably the biggest factor behind the growth in the work force was the large-scale withdrawal or withholding of children and adolescents from school (Lange 1987). Moyen-Mono was the region worst hit by falling Togolese school attendance rates (Lange 1991a and b, 1993).[5] The huge number of children joining the work force has played a major role in expanding the areas being cultivated, thus contributing to a significant rise in farmers' earnings.

Division of labour adheres to a few basic rules. Boys must remain confined to working their fathers' fields and require his permission to assist their mothers. Girls must work with their mothers. Women, by the way, are given free rein to manage the female work force; hence, small girls are 'passed around' between the women of a family as a means of offsetting demographic fluctuations so that no woman might find herself working her farm alone. Husbands must never farm their wives' fields. The only allowable exceptions are when a woman needs her husband's help to build a corn loft or plough the land, both of which are regarded as men's work; elderly men abstain from this as a 'point of honour', delegating it to their sons, while young married men often work their land together with their wives. Women are duty-bound to assist their husbands in just two specific activities: sowing (though they actually just drop the seeds into holes dug by the men) and harvesting. The latter can be heavy work, especially when the crop in question is cotton. Finally, the women, aided by their daughters, are in charge of collecting water and firewood and preparing the meals.

Since the rules governing the division of labour are relatively securely fixed, household tension chiefly arises over the work allotted to the young girls within the family. Their versatility means they are in far greater demand than boys. And city-based relatives add to this by requesting their services as baby-sitters and home helps. If it is in the fathers' interests to lend out their daughters (and accumulate favours owed), mothers – being, as seen, highly dependent upon young girls – are generally opposed to it. The schooling of children in polygamous households, another cause of often bitter domestic wrangling, highlights the contradictions in the arguments and representations revolving around child labour, not to mention the economic stakes. If one of the wives manages to enroll her child at a school, the others want the same for their children and polygamous husbands often end up refusing to allow any of their children access to the education system. So beyond all the talk about how positive it is for children to work in the fields, we see that partially escaping it by going to school is actually a hotly contested privilege.

Similarly, the rules regarding inheritance provide a telling statement on the value of child labour since they distinguish between children who have been to school and those who have not and who have therefore worked from a very early age in the fathers' fields. Indeed, the latter are regarded in a preferential light when it comes to distributing possessions, in recognition for their contribution to building up the paternal estate. The most violent conflicts flare up over the use of income earned from perennial crops[6] (with annual crop-related earnings going without question to those who have worked the particular plot). Cutting palm trees to make *sodabi* (distilled palm wine) guarantees the farmer a stable income, for *sodabi* is always highly in demand; as this usually represents a good deal of money (often half the farm's financial yield), the stakes are high in the struggle for control over the palms.[7]

This raises questions as to whether or not child labour within the framework of the family farm corresponds to exploitation. Child farm labourers are directly responsible for increasing the wealth of the family head (they seed over 50 per cent of the land), but since this is eventually left to them in their father's will, it is something of a 'return on investment' for the work put in during childhood or adolescence. Meanwhile, farmers offer incentives to encourage children to work in the fields or to dissuade them from going to school;[8] if the production and sale of cotton, for example, has gone well, the best producers will be given a bicycle. It would therefore seem difficult to talk of exploitation within the family in cases such as these. Nowadays, however, the production and sale of agricultural commodities are never sufficient to meet a family's most basic needs without the contribution of child labour. Far from a matter of merely lending a hand or being a training/socializing tool, child labour is an absolute necessity for survival in rural areas. And this is where we find all the ambiguity of school reforms which, in imposing compulsory education for every child,[9] repudiate the vital contribution child labour makes to the country's economy, leaving us to suppose that parents' resistance to school must be motivated on grounds of a strictly cultural or religious order. The economic reasons for rejecting school have much more to do with loss of earnings (due to the loss of children's labour power) than the extra expenses incurred by sending a child to school.[10]

Labour Extorted by Functionaries: Domestic and Productive Chores

In a practice harking back to colonial times, functionaries occupying posts in rural areas systematically call on young schoolchildren to work for them.

Teachers tend to be the main beneficiaries of their labour because they have more immediate access to them; but all functionaries as a whole 'cash in' on this 'captive' work force.

Teachers in rural areas often send their pupils to fetch water and wood for their own personal use or, if they are lodging with a pupil's family, make them clean out their rooms. (In such cases, by the way, rent arrears can be become something of a problem as the father hardly dares ask for settlement for fear of the repercussions on his child's marks at school.) However, few people object to these practices, particularly when the teachers are believed to be capable and examination results are satisfactory. But other practices, such as teachers capitalizing on the mix-up between school fields and private fields and putting their pupils to work in their own fields, create discontent. The management of earnings from the school field is unclear. Moreover, farming tasks have increased since the development of cotton crops, which offer teachers good extra earnings as they do not have to pay for the labour used.[11] If working the teacher's field in some sense belongs to the prevailing customs as long as its purpose is to supply him with the produce he needs for food, it is often felt to be unacceptable as soon as he attempts to sell any of the yield from child labour.

The other functionaries in question mainly include soldiers, customs officials, forestry wardens or even farming supervisors. In fact, virtually every civil servant occupying a rural post assumes the right to do what he wishes with the children's time. Generally it involves domestic chores, for these types of functionaries do not stay in the same job long enough to be able to cultivate land. And groups of functionaries with no wives, children or servants of their own at hand call on the nearest child to run and fetch them water, wood and sometimes even food, tasks that no self-respecting well-to-do man would condescend to perform for himself.

The chores rural schoolchildren are forced to undertake correspond to the domination state officials maintain over farmers. The ongoing process of democratization in Africa may well be bringing increasing pressure to bear to curtail such practices, but a good deal of inertia remains because they are not seen for what they really are: child labour. They are regarded as favours that young people are duty-bound to do for their elders, or that rural communities have to do for functionaries.

'Political' Duties

In Togo, as in any country governed by an authoritarian regime, the political role of school is asserted at several levels: nation-state building, coercion and control of schoolchildren, personality cult. Playing on patriotism, the conditioning occurs on a day-to-day basis: ceremonial respect for the national flag, recitals and songs to the glory of the president or party ... (Lange 1991b). There are also regular pro-government rallies, guards of honour along the roadside to greet the president, a prefect or visiting dignitary; group activities, a wide variety of political events (women's day, green revolution day, tree day). If children not attending school sometimes manage to escape such duties, those in the classroom are practically held hostage and may be expelled at the least sign of a lack of enthusiasm. Political activities in Togo are sometimes more time-consuming than regular school work. During the 1986–87 academic year, for example, four whole months were lost to preparations for the festivities surrounding a Franco-African summit held in Lomé, followed by celebrations to mark the regime's twentieth year in power; primary and secondary school pupils and university students were requisitioned from September 1986 through to February 1987. Although it may well have been an unusually eventful year, schoolchildren are regularly called up for a succession of official visits (the pope, various heads of state).

Referring to the views of the teaching body and parents, E. Floriani (1987) considers that such activities 'disrupt school life and significantly diminish the time devoted to studies [...] They are partly to blame for falling education standards.' In the course of 1986–87, discontent among schoolchildren, teachers and parents alike (although not voiced openly) was such that when the usual methods of restraint had failed to achieve their desired ends, the authorities were forced to resort to handing out cash: examination pass rates that year were the best of the decade, which caused much disturbance among the very young.[12]

The children, however, did not take this lying down. Rebellious acts, though covert, became frequent. From the stolen rope preventing a school flag from being raised through to the adulterated lyrics of official slogans (Toulabor 1986) via the ransacked school field, resistance grew increasingly bolder, culminating in the 'explosion' of the 1990s.

School, in fact, is actually where children are treated to a foretaste of the techniques of economic exploitation and political submissiveness. Be it economic, political or simply pedagogical, violence in schools (Toulabor 1982; Lange 1991b) is just a pale reflection of army or police tactics (Toulabor 1986; Merlet 1987) and the embezzlement of public funds by high-ranking government officials; the fate reserved for children is not detached from that of their parents – it is a direct sequel. School, like training within the family in the name of socialization, can only reproduce the prevailing societal patterns even if it does, at times, also offer the means to go beyond alienation.

Community Labour: From 'Traditions' to Modern Forms of Exploitation

State disengagement, as prescribed by the structural adjustment programmes, compels rural communities to take on the burden of local infrastructures (building and maintenance of schools, clinics, roads); being closer to the public domain, urban communities manage to avoid these constraints. The same cannot be said for the countryside. For it is often only by resorting to the (meeker and more manageable) labour of children that village communities can complete such tasks.

Children and young people living in the countryside are therefore called upon to undertake a whole range of public works: repairing paths after the rainy season, building and maintaining wells, schools, clinics. Schoolchildren are responsible for building new shelters to serve as classrooms when the old ones have been destroyed by the rains. As it takes them about three weeks to put up a straw hut, the entire first month of the academic year may need to be devoted to preparing the school facilities. Furthermore, shortages of materials (benches, desks, blackboards, chalk, books) and generally dilapidated conditions oblige teachers to use earnings from the produce of the school fields in order to ensure they have the strict minimum necessary for running the school. Again, however, state spending cuts have forced schools wishing to remain open to transform themselves into production sites, to the detriment of the basic education that a primary school is meant to provide (reading, writing, arithmetic). Underlying country people's refusal of school is their refusal to see schools turned into production sites and ceasing to be places where their children are supposed to learn recorded knowledge.

Village community labour stems from a long tradition and was first harnessed by NGOs as a means of promoting local, or 'self-centred', development while at the same time 'raising the awareness' of the population. Despite the fact that they have very often been based on a mythical vision of a sort of African community egalitarianism, some projects underpinned by principles such as these have managed to bear fruit in certain areas.

Next came the turn of the international agencies which recommended these practices within the framework of structural adjustment as an effective means of easing the financial burden on the state. After starting out as a matter of building and maintaining social infrastructures, the ban imposed by structural adjustment on public sector recruitment very soon led to rural communities themselves having to hire and pay their own teachers; and, in the majority of cases, children have once again had to be put to work in the school fields in order to pay supply teachers' wages.[13]

Conclusion

In these times of economic hardship, competition between the various different prescribers is growing, often at the expense of the children. State officials use children within the framework of a dominatory relationship that they themselves have established. Akin to racketeering or plunder, their confiscation of the children's time for their own ends is among the methods used to control and exploit rural communities. The fall in school attendance rates affects rural areas in particular (Lange 1991a, 1993) and is both cause and effect of the premature employment of country children. This process of withdrawing children from school is serving to widen the gap between city children, who continue to enjoy the benefits of state and family investment (being sent to the best public sector or private schools, even in Europe), and country children, who remain confined to the educational sphere of the family or religion.

Far from being a mere training or socializing tool, child labour within the framework of family farms is first and foremost a vital necessity for the family's very survival. Economic pressures represent the real reason why children cannot be released from work. The role of cash crops shows the impact of commodity market prices on their schooling. Whereas the coffee- and cocoa-producing regions have managed to keep the vast majority of children out of productive labour and in the classroom, the opposite is true of the cotton-growing regions where children have had to be taken from school in order to keep the production system going.[14]

On a more general level, this chapter sets out the problem of the links between employment, exploitation and proletarianization. The title of this book may seem to suggest that the three conditions are interdependent. But as we have just seen, children who are put to work are not necessarily exploited; and if they are, it does not necessarily mean that they are proletarianized. In addition to productive labour, the concept of extorted labour must also cover the domestic chores forced upon them (fetching water, wood, etc.) as well as how they are used politically, because even if the time thus confiscated does not correspond with economic exploitation, all these practices are part and parcel of the domination-based relations imposed upon rural communities by the representatives of the state. This is at any rate true of the time extorted from children at the expense of their training, their future integration into society.

Child labour should therefore be defined as the extortion by clearly identified beneficiaries of a child's time to the detriment of his or her study and leisure-time activities. The sometimes brutal responses with which the children oppose practices that they consider abusive suggests that the labour demanded of them may, or may not, be perceived as legitimate. Analysis of the various ways in which parents and children alike regard the work may thus help to produce a sharper definition of the concept of labour and exploitation.

Notes

1. According to Durkheim's basic rule suggesting that a social fact may not be explained by recourse to 'nature' or psychology.

2. The notion of childhood or adolescence varies according to the times and civilization; see Ariès (1973).

3. See Marcoux (1994).

4. This notion has not escaped the notice of researchers and the example of some of the conference papers that link work within the family almost entirely to its socializing

role shows the enduring nature of the approach involving the opposition between 'positive' labour within the family and 'negative' labour in other social spheres.

5. Prefecture of Haho: primary schoolchildren 1980–81 = 15,302; 1984–85 = 11,985; secondary school 1980–81 = 3,857; 1984–85 = 1776.

6. Oil palms are among the chief perennial crops in the region. Perennial crops in general are regarded by farmers as a kind of safety net to protect the family from life's ups and downs. It should be noted that in other coffee- and cocoa-producing regions the question of sharing out inherited perennial crop commodities also opposes former school-children with those excluded from school.

7. As we have found (Lange 1987), the safety net can be assured in one of two ways: either the farmer cuts the palm, distils and sells the *sodabi*, putting money aside as he goes along, or he sells the palm trees whole for a modest lump sum. The second solution, while enabling him quickly to receive a not inconsiderable amount of money, often brings him into conflict with his brothers, because those working as wage-earners in the city often need a lot of money to survive there, and also because it gives the seller control over the proceeds from the sale of the trees.

8. That, at least, is what we were told by the schoolteachers interviewed at the height of the school attendance crisis when classrooms were becoming deserted before their very eyes. When the cotton had been sold, farmers would give presents to the most productive children; among them the famous bicycles which the teachers cited as being the reason why their former pupils had dropped out.

9. See the 1975 reform of the Togo education system which, as in most other African nations, called for universal schooling.

10. In the regions opposed to school, bearing in mind that coercive measures do not remain very effective for very long, the only incentive for sending children to school which has always produced positive results, in every region and country concerned, is free school dinners. The fact that the child is given a daily meal is enough to ease pressure on the family purse and, indeed, allows him or her to be released from productive labour.

11. One schools inspector, noticing how some of these teachers were becoming wealthy by growing cotton, decided to borrow a plot of land in the hope of making substantial profits. In fact, he managed only to break even because, unlike the teachers, he did not have access to free labour and ended up having to take on hired hands. He came to the conclusion that, given the production and marketing conditions, growing cotton can only ever be financially worthwhile if one has 'a pack of slaves' at one's disposal.

12. A 76 per cent pass rate. But this had negative repercussions in that it tarnished the schools' image, earning them the reputation of being as 'corrupt' as any other state institution. Moreover, such a huge wave of primary pupils then swept into secondary education that, in order to regain control over student flows, the authorities were obliged to sanction those taking examinations the following year; success rates subsequently fell to their lowest level ever: 26 per cent.

13. Around 15 per cent of schoolteachers in Togo are now paid by the parents; in Chad, this percentage stands at around 50 per cent and concerns only the most deprived rural areas; although no figures are available for Mali, we do know that more and more primary teachers are being paid by parents. 'Community' schools – set up and financed by parents – are in rapid expansion in most of the French-speaking countries of Africa as a response to the withdrawal of state funding.

14. In the hilly coffee- and cocoa-producing plateau region, around 90 per cent of indigenous rural six- to fourteen-year-olds are attending school – a higher percentage than

in the majority of the Togolese cities; migrants' children are generally less well educated than indigenous children, albeit better so than children from the same ethnic groups that have not migrated. In this region, therefore, the children of even the most deprived groups have managed to leave the sphere of production, contrary to those in the cotton-growing belt drafted in to ensure the development of cotton production (Lange 1987).

References

Ariès, P. (1973) *L'enfant et la vie familiale sous l'Ancien Régime*, Paris, Seuil.

Floriani, E. (1987) 'Qui a peur de la philosophie?' *Politique africaine*, 27, September–October, pp. 67–72.

Lange, M. F. (1987) 'Dynamisme économique et reviviscence sociale et culturelle chez les Adja-Ehoué du Moyen-Mono (Togo). Quel projet de société?', in P. Geshiere and B. Schlemmer (eds), *Terrains et perspectives. Actes du colloque international sur l'anthropologie face aux transformations des sociétés rurales, aux politiques et aux idéologies de développement*, Paris, ORSTOM, pp. 143–59.

— (1991a) *Cent cinquante ans de scolarisation au Togo. Bilan et perspectives*, Lomé, Collection 'Les dossiers de l'URD', Université du Bénin, Unité de recherche démographique.

— (1991b) 'Systèmes scolaires et développement: discours et pratiques', *Politique africaine*, 43, October, pp. 105–21.

— (1993) 'Déscolarisation et crise scolaire au Togo', in R. Chaudenson, R. Clignet, M. Egly and M. F. Lange, *L'École du Sud*, ACCT, Diffusion, Didier Édition.

Marcoux, R. (1994) *Le travail ou l'école. L'activité des enfants et les caractéristiques des ménages en milieu urbain au Mali*, Bamako, Collection 'Études et travaux du CERPOD', CERPOD.

Merlet, L. (1987) 'Domaine réservé: la protection de la faune', *Politique africaine*, 27, September–October, pp. 55–66.

Toulabor, C. M. (1982) 'La violence à l'école: le cas d'un village au Togo', *Politique africaine*, 7, September, pp. 43–9.

— (1986) *Le Togo sous Eyadéma*, Paris, Karthala.

CHAPTER 21

The Household Economy and the Commercial Exploitation of Children's Work: The Case of Kerala

Olga Nieuwenhuys

For some years now, Indian newspapers have regularly exposed the sorry stories of crude profiteering to which migrant girls from the southern state of Kerala who work thousands of kilometres away from home in the prawn-curing factories of Gujarat and Maharashtra are exposed. Their cruel fate has caught the imagination of social scientists and journalists and this has generated a number of influential articles and reports (see Anonymous 1984; Saradamoni 1989). Having read that many of these girls hailed from fishing villages near a village that I knew quite well, I was naturally curious to know more about them. What awakened my curiosity was the fact that a rural society that I had known to be extremely disinclined to have girls working away from the immediate vicinity of the home would so suddenly turn out to be willing to release them to such distant and unknown employers.

This was indeed not so, as a few of the girls to whom I spoke in their homes during a study trip in July–August 1992 asserted.[1] The girls, many of whom had started work by their early teens, explained that they had had to go to quite some trouble to convince their fathers to let them join the company of female neighbours and friends who journeyed yearly to the curing yards in northern India. Most of the fathers had only reluctantly agreed to what they felt entailed a loss of status and this only because they felt themselves to be too old or ill to work and had no grown-up sons who could help maintain the family.

The girls had been attracted by the stories of neighbours and friends whose work in the curing yards had not only helped to support their families but also to earn, both for themselves and their sisters, that crucially important source of female wealth, a dowry. The girls' stories contrasted sharply with the image that newspapers and reports conveyed. Rather than squalor and exploitation, they spoke vividly of the pleasure of working alongside their peers, of journeying across India, of watching video shows on Sundays, and above all of having gained respectability in their own homes.

When, somewhat surprised, I inquired about the long nightly working hours mentioned by the reports, some girls explained that they undertook the trip to make as much money as possible and, since they were being paid a piece-rate, did not object to long working hours. One girl even described the dormitory – depicted by the reports as a single hall without beds in which the girls were locked up at night – as a very convenient and safe place to stay.

Sitting with them in their father's house, I indeed wondered whether the journalists and social scientists who wrote so graphically about their plight were at all familiar with the village life of these girls. Most girls would spend their time making coir by their mother's side, or drying fish, and they had hardly any possibility at all of obtaining nutritious food or earning money of their own. On the whole, their homes were quite rudimentary and lacked running water, sanitation and even simple furniture. With rising dowries, these girls could not help but feel gloomy about their future chances of marrying a man who would be able to take care of them and their children. Abiding by the customary ideals of girlish demeanour was certainly no guarantee that they would fare better than the girls who broke the rules by working far away from home.

This brought me to question the underlying reasons for the outrage engendered in the media by the labour migration of girls from Kerala. Why did the media remain indifferent to the silent suffering of village girls and expose as exploitation the situation of the few who sought to break out of their hopeless situation? As I will discuss in this chapter, the search for an answer brought me to question the very assumptions that underlie common wisdom on the exploitation of children. This wisdom is based on the belief that anyone employing a child is an exploiter; only the family is thought to be equipped with the means to put children to work without exploiting them. Even under conditions of extreme indigence, the family would, as sole social institution, be capable of protecting children from excessive drudgery and provide them with a space for harmonious growth. It is my contention that this belief ignores the impact of working conditions on individual children, be they in employment or working under parental supervision, and is therefore simply false. The way common wisdom conceptualizes the exploitation of children betrays a greater concern with the threat posed to society by deviations from what are seen as acceptable forms of socialization than with the welfare of working children.

In the study of children's work, it is common to make a distinction between work performed in the context of the family and work performed on the labour market. This distinction, however obvious it may appear, has far-reaching consequences, for it is critically connected to the notion of the exploitation of children's work. It is only when a child is directly engaged as cheap labour by the market and is paid a wage, however nominal, that both labour experts and the lay public concur in feeling that s/he is exploited. The child who works alongside his/her parents is unlikely to be considered exploited, for the main preoccupation of parents would be their children's welfare and successful socialization. It is considered natural for parents to protect the children who work with them from excessive drudgery and to allow them sufficient scope for education and leisure. The multitude of daily tasks performed by children to help their parents are perceived as the expression of an essential obligation that ensures the stability of family life and the continuity of society.

To acknowledge this distinction between non-exploitative and exploitative work, it has become common practice to use two notions: that of children's work and that of child labour, with the understanding that only the latter is 'work which impairs the health and development of children' (Fyfe 1989: 4). The borderline between salutary work that is part of children's normal upbringing on the one hand and, on the other, exploitative child labour is then of a moral nature: it pertains essentially to the quality of parent–child relations and bears no relation to the modalities of work in the adult world.

The most remarkable aspect of this divide is that while in the adult world the notion of exploitation is essentially of an economic nature, in the world of childhood it is first and foremost a moral category. While an adult may claim to be exploited when his/her work contributes to excessive gains or is carried out under inhuman working conditions, a child can do so only when his/her work is not mitigated by parental devotion. This chapter challenges the theoretical soundness of describing children's exploitation in purely moral terms. In support of my argument, I will show that, when applied to real situations, the moral distinction between exploitative child labour and non-exploitative child work is untenable. Elaborating on my fieldwork experience in a village in Kerala (India), I argue that the popularity of the distinction is basically inspired by a preoccupation with child labour's potential threat to the harmonious insertion of poor children in a life of indigence and hard work. In the final part, I examine the difficulty of applying the concept of economic exploitation to children's work and propose a notion of their exploitation that allows for understanding its dimensions, not only in the sphere of production, but in that of the reproduction of labour and of the continuity of society as a whole as well. I conclude by contending that the modalities of children's exploitation in the contemporary world can be fully understood only if these three levels of exploitation are taken into account.

The Moral Economy of Children's Work

The literature on child labour is suffused with an unquestioned faith in the family as an ideal space for children to grow up in and be trained for their future working lives. For the sake of my argument it will suffice to criticize two aspects of the family that are of direct relevance in the way children's work is conceptualized: its economic rationality, and the laws of seniority and gender that govern it.

Chayanov has undoubtedly made the strongest case for understanding the family as an economic unit governed by other principles than, for example, the capitalist firm. Though he was primarily concerned with the economic rationality of the Russian peasantry at the beginning of the twentieth century, many of his ideas have found fertile ground in the way family economics have been conceptualized. For Chayanov, the peasant family would make intensive use of the labour of all its members, produce use rather than exchange value and aim primarily at the satisfaction of consumption needs rather than profit (Chayanov 1966: 89ff). This assumed harmony between production and consumption has very much dominated the way children's work in the family has been perceived particularly in peasant societies. It helps explain why economists still perceive the growing numbers of children in peasant societies as a liability rather than as a source of wealth. It also helps us understand why anthropologists have been so slow in acknowledging the work performed by children in peasant societies (cf. also Hull 1981: 49).

The peasant family being, in Chayanov's view, governed by emotional considerations, more specifically parental love and filial devotion, the question of parents exploiting their own children simply did not arise. The past decades have, however, seen scattered attempts at a more in-depth understanding of the nature of children's work within the peasant family. A number of studies have disclosed that the emotional considerations that dominate the way peasant parents perceive their children's work are not divorced from the realm of economic circulation. These studies have pointed out that these parents value their children not merely as objects of emotional satisfaction, but because they represent, within peasant society, real economic assets. The economy of the peasant household simply requires a large number of unpaid workers and helpers to be able to satisfy the demands of the market and survive expanding capitalism (see also Mamdani 1981; Schildkrout 1980). This is a point to which I will return in the next paragraph. Children's labour is also an important asset in gaining access to resources of wealthier kin, and there is a modest body of literature that describes how children are sent to work as servants and assistants to service the circle of kin or pseudo-kin; are given in adoption in exchange for credit or in repayment of debts; are used as purveyors of services and political support; and represent very tangible sources of status, power and prestige (see for instance Caldwell 1982; Reynolds 1991; Salazar 1991; Schildkrout 1980).

So, in spite of the romantic renderings of peasant life, there is no doubt that peasant families are often governed by sharp inequality, particularly, as now amply documented by feminist studies, between the sexes. Feminists have criticized approaches that treat the family and the household as a purely altruistic unit. Although from the perspective of older males, women's domestic work may appear as inspired by love and dedication to the well-being of the family, a closer analysis reveals that this work is grounded in unequal power relations both inside and outside the domestic arena. Kinship systems and legal and political institutions together lend adult males considerable leverage in obtaining a position of privilege *vis-à-vis* women in the economic sphere (Folbre 1986). A large number of agrarian societies, for instance, deny women the right to inherit land and/or to avail themselves of social security benefits, while world-wide the labour market puts women at a disadvantage, too (Folbre 1994).

The dedication of women to domestic work can therefore hardly be seen as merely the result of their natural inclination, being indisputably also born out of sheer economic necessity. The role of child-care is interesting in this respect, and feminists have stressed that the association of women's work roles with their mandatory tasks as mothers, which society portrays as being biologically determined, is the most powerful instrument of patriarchal domination.

The analogy with children's role is striking, both children and women being tied to their biological roles as a legitimation for their lack of economic and political power. Analysing the analogy between women's and children's work roles, Elson has proposed to view the subordination of children from the perspective of the seniority system. Seniority she defines as a hierarchical system by which those in junior positions are unable to achieve full social status in their own right (Elson 1982: 491ff). Seniority would explain why children's work is by and large considered inferior; an inferiority that is not attached to the nature of the work but to the status of those who perform it. Seniority also makes for children being allotted the tasks that are viewed to be less economically valuable, that is those that are linked rather to 'reproductive' activities than to direct 'production'. The most pervasive effect of seniority is that children, regardless of the amount of work they do, are not perceived as workers in their own right because what they do is sub-merged in the low-status realm of the domestic to which women too are relegated.

The distinction between domestic, or reproductive, work and productive work, however, is – and this is crucial – as much the result of the perceived inferiority of women's and children's work roles as of actual differences in the creation of economic value. There is no intrinsic reason why reproduction, that is the production of life and human energy which is the task of the domestic domain, should be economically less valuable than production, which is essentially the extraction of material resources from the physical and social environment (see also Wadel 1979: 379). Particularly in peasant societies, production and reproduction are necessary and complementary aspects of the same economic cycle, their separation being in fact significant only for labour performed in the market economy. The predominance of the domestic in children's work does not necessarily signify, as I will now show, that they are protected from excessive drudgery or, to use Fyfe's words, protected from work that impairs their health and development.

Working Children in a Kerala Village

The work of children in Poomkara, a coastal village of central Kerala, in which I have periodically been doing fieldwork since the late 1970s, illustrates my argument.[2] The village depends largely on two main economic sectors: the manufacture of coir yarn with manually-operated spinning wheels and fishing with country crafts. These are also gender-specific sectors, women and girls making coir, while men and boys engage in fishing and fish-vending. The crafts used for fishing are large ones, and they are manned by a crew of hired labourers. There is a clear hierarchy of work based on seniority, the most rewarding work, fishing at sea, being the preserve of adult men. Boys are hired only seasonally to fish with shore-seines and are paid only half a man's wage or less.

What these boys do, however lowly valued, is in village society by no means the most inferior work a boy can do. There are numbers of tasks a younger boy must perform with no reward other than a few fish, before he can be included in a shore crew. Work in a crew is at the top of a hierarchy of work ordered by age; by the age of seven or eight, a boy starts to forage for fallen fish from the beach for subsistence, then gradually goes on to engage in small-scale fish-vending and, finally, in providing help and assistance to the crew during beach operations before he can be included, in his early teens, as the youngest worker in a shore-seine crew. So a long process of socialization marks a boy's entry into the male world of fishing, and he has to comply, during a laborious period to a subordinate position, accepting what the men feel is inferior work.

The point, however, is that this foraging and servicing work, though lowly valued and remunerated only in kind, can hardly be said to be economically less necessary than the work of boys who are hired by the crew. A boy's earliest task of picking up fallen fish from the beach provides his family with daily food, which is later supplemented with a little cash earned by selling the fish obtained as a reward for petty services. In this way, even young boys' activities help the household to survive in periods in which the men are either out of work or migrate to better fishing grounds.

There is a second aspect of the activities of boys that has a clearer bearing upon the fishing economy, and these are connected to the marked imbalances in labour demand at the various stages of operation that are typical of artisanal fishing. The petty services rendered by the boys are important to the adult fishermen enabling them to carry on their activities. The bunch of boys lured by the prospect of receiving a little fish can, during the short-lived but critical stages in which labour demand suddenly rises, easily be brought into action. The marked seasonality of the equipment is another source of imbalance in terms of labour demand. The boys who are hired to work the shore-seine are included in the crew only in the less productive periods, in the weeks just before and after the peak season when the harvest is uncertain. If successful, the owner of the equipment is assured of a higher income from his investment. If the returns are disappointing, the whole operation costs him a trifle anyway. Without the presence of the boys, however, artisanal fishermen would not only be handicapped in carrying out their activities; they would also probably not be well-equipped enough to compete with the motorized fishing of today.

The combined effect of foraging, petty trade and hired labour has, thirdly, an important bearing upon labour costs in the sense that they relieve the owners of fishing equipment from the responsibility of paying the men enough to feed their families and particularly to maintain them in periods of unemployment and crisis. Hiring his sons on the shore-seine crew and allowing the younger ones to forage for fallen fish is, in addition to rare ceremonial payments, the only kind of assistance a fisherman can expect from his boss to help him feed his family and support him in times of need. Boys' activities on the beach are therefore attuned to their fathers' lack of security in times of crisis and their inability to maintain their families by their own endeavour. Boys' activities alone, however, are insufficient to provide this basic security and it is therefore important to turn now to the work of women and girls.

As said, coir yarn manufacture is a typically feminine craft, and among the coastal poor is carried out in conjunction with fishing. The activity is undertaken all year round by women and girls in the immediate vicinity of their homes. About half of the workers engaged in the cottage industry work on their own account, while hiring additional labour from neighbouring houses if necessary. For both family workers and hired labourers, remuneration is just as depressingly low. The hierarchical ordering of the work, though less pronounced than in fishing, is nevertheless there. Grown-up women mostly engage in the less tiresome and better-paid spinning of the yarn, while girls are allotted a variety of preparatory and menial tasks: peeling and beating of coconut husks to make fibre, winnowing and turning the spinning wheel. These tasks, however, demand a high labour input, one spinner requiring the assistance of two helpers, by and large girls from the age of seven, to make fibre and help in spinning.

Being, as it is, carried out in and between other domestic tasks, girls' work is even more markedly viewed as inconspicuous than boys'. Their primary responsibility, ideally at least, is the welfare of the family and they are brought up in the belief that income-earning is not their concern. The alternation between highly valued domestic chores with the lowly valued making of coir yarn heightens parents' conviction that their daughters' work, however crucial for production, is not economically relevant. This holds even when girls are hired to work for neighbours, their wages being generally not directly paid to them, but either reduced from debt incurred by the parents or added to their mother's wage.

Girls' work is nevertheless part of a production process that relies heavily on the need of poor women to feed their families, the family relying in times of crisis mainly upon these earnings and those of boys to make ends meet. Few girls are aware that they actually contribute, either as family helper or hired worker, between 60 to 70 per cent of the labour necessary to make the finished product. The sector's very survival in the face of dwindling demand for coir products in the world market does indeed depend on extremely low levels of pay and this in turn makes a heavy input of family child work mandatory.

If one were to visualize the ranking applying within the household as based on how each member's contribution relates to income generation, his or her economic value would closely reflect their positions in the hierarchy of seniority and gender. It is a man's duty, but also privilege, to earn most of the income of the family in cash, women's and boys' to provision the family with food and girls to do the servicing work. Boys, by gender, never find themselves at the lowest levels of the hierarchy of work, though they spend quite a length of time subordinated to men. Girls' position at the bottom of the social order is sanctioned by their being denied access to income, in cash or kind, and by their depending upon the other members of the household for the satisfaction of their most immediate needs.

If we now look at the huge input of cheap labour that the village economy needs, it becomes questionable whether the hierarchy of seniority and gender, though finding its legitimacy in their perceived biological limitations, can protect children from excessive drudgery or provide them with a safe space in which to grow up. Most village adults would indeed admit that children's work is often more trying than that of adults, and this they feel is justified in so far as their adult status exempts them from performing certain demeaning tasks, such as beating husks, peddling fish on foot or pulling the shore-seine. These tasks, in spite of their being rather taxing, are economically so inconspicuous that they are felt best suited to children. Children's lack of access to the economically more rewarding tasks is reinforced by the belief that their needs are also fewer: children are indeed more often inadequately dressed, malnourished and affected by disease than adults. Nor do children enjoy more leisure time than adults, as they combine their domestic tasks with income-earning and schooling (Nieuwenhuys 1994: 67ff).

It is clear, then, as the Kerala case shows, that the family of the rural poor is not, and cannot be, the safe haven where children grow up shielded from hard work and drudgery. This makes the assumption that children's exploitation would be of another order than the economic exploitation of adults, untenable. However, creating the myth that it is, does serve a purpose. Children's work under parental supervision or for the subsistence needs of the household, and thus their virtual exclusion from valued waged work, is directly linked to the payment of wages to adults upon which the family cannot survive. The economy of the village can clearly not cope without the insertion of children at the lowest levels of the work hierarchy. This insertion is supported by an authoritarian family structure that makes it very tough, if not, as in the case of the migrant girls, entirely impossible for children to enter the labour market. The case also shows that girls can do so only when the weakening of paternal authority, in this specific case caused by the absence of a male with earning capacity, provides them with a space to negotiate the nature of their work. Having argued against viewing children's exploitation in purely moral terms, the question now is as to the nature of the economic exploitation to which working children are subjected. In the following section I will therefore critically assess the relevance of the concept of economic exploitation in understanding the modalities of children's work both within and outside the family.

The Economic Exploitation of Children

As said, social scientists have recurrently pointed at the extra-economic value of work undertaken within the ambit of the peasant household. The fact that much work is undertaken for subsistence, even when, as in the case of fisheries, it is linked to the market, indeed poses serious obstacles to conceptualizing and measuring economic exploitation (Firth 1979: 81ff) This is, as said, also the reason why anthropologists have generally shied away from studying children's work in the domestic arena and why only work that is directly associated with the labour market has hitherto been considered as exploitative.

Morice, working from the idea of exploitation as the extraction of surplus value by the appropriation of all or part of the product of labour, has provided the most elaborate attempt at associating exploitation with work performed by children outside the labour market. He remarks that this work is characterized by the convergence of inherited social relations and an exploitation of which the ultimate gains – whatever the intermediate processes – serve the dominant mode of capitalist production.

There are, according to Morice, four types of non-capitalist labour in which children are engaged and that can lead to exploitation:

1. *Work in the domestic unit*: because this work does not result in a clear product, there cannot be extraction of surplus value and hence exploitation is bound to be only indirect.
2. *Work in a situation of quasi-slavery*: this situation involves not only the appropriation of the product of the child's labour but also of the child him/herself.
3. *Work in a quasi-feudal situation*: this situation is based on a dependent personal relationship between the child and his/her employer. The child supplies labour to an employer, who could be a relative, the product of which is appropriated in exchange for protection, lodging and food.
4. *Commercial activities*, such as street-vending and peddling, in which the surplus value is made through the pricing mechanism, customers being

inclined to pay for a child's merchandise less than if s/he were an adult seller. (Morice 1981: 147–8).

The problem with Morice's approach, however valuable, is that it is too narrowly linked to production and therefore tacitly assumes that work in the domestic sphere would in itself be economically less valuable. The approach also fails to explain why women and children are not only more likely to be engaged in subsistence activities for the home than men but also stand at a disadvantage when competing for jobs or for profits in the market. Considering the low cost of female and child labour, it is indeed astonishing that the market is unable to avail itself on a larger scale of this phenomenal source of profit than it does today, and that waged employment is still so much male-dominated. I have suggested above that children's work within the ambit of the peasant family is valued less than work carried out in the realm of material production rather for ideological than for economical reasons. Morice's typology, in short, does not help explain the interlinkage of production and reproduction in the realization of surplus value.

It may prove useful, in this respect, to return to my Poomkara case, and dwell on how both productive and reproductive work are part of one and the same system of economic exploitation. The totality of the work, irrespective of pay, is what allows for the very sizeable profits that are made by the village power-holders on the one hand and, on the other, by distant wholesale merchants and exporters. The appropriation of surplus value from children's work takes place at three distinct levels.

1. The first level is obviously at play in the case of *goods produced directly with child work*, and this happens by including boys in a crew and having them help during beach operations; alternatively by having girls prepare the fibre for spinning and turn the wheel. As said, this work contributes directly to keeping the total costs of labour so abysmally low.

2. There is, however, another level at which surplus value is being appropriated, and it pertains to the *savings being made on the cost of adult labour* when children are able to contribute substantially to their own upkeep. These savings are not only made by involving children in the productive process, but also by their being engaged in such cost-saving activities as foraging and domestic work. The latter contribute to reducing the wage paid to the male earners and freeing adult women for productive work, a woman's capacity to make yarn depending as much on the direct assistance of her daughter at work as on her domestic help. Some authors have called this level, which denies poor parents the ability to maintain their children, that of 'super-exploitation'.

3. There is also a more elusive level at which surplus value is appropriated from children's work. By this I mean the savings that society at large makes on *the social costs of bringing up new generations of workers*. These are costs that are generally not borne by individual employers but are met by a variety of redistributive systems that guarantee the continuity of society. This third,

social, level is, I feel, what distinguishes children's exploitation from that of adults; society as a whole clearly has a stake in children's work for the simple reason that a true elimination of child exploitation would imply significantly higher costs in raising new generations. In the case of a market economy, we could think of the costs of family benefits, paid leave for child-care, child labour inspection, free education and scholarships, health services and nursery schools, supervised play and sports grounds – costs that deeply affect the levels of taxes to be paid collectively by the earning section of society.

These three levels of exploitation illuminate the crucial importance of incorporating children's work within the ambit of the family into the notion of exploitation. Some clues as to how this could be done, by bypassing an undue preoccupation with production for the market, may be derived from the way Rey has conceptualized the articulation between pre-capitalist modes of production and capitalism. Central to the theory is the concept of specific class alliances based in different modes of exploitation. The concept of class alliances is particularly interesting for my purposes. Only the capitalist class can appropriate the products of labour through the ownership of the means of production. It is the control over land, by contrast, that enables the feudal class to extract surplus from the tiller and his family in the form of rent and forced labour. Meanwhile seniority in the lineage structures power relations, and neither production means nor land are economically very valuable. Economic wealth, as analysed by both Rey and Meillassoux for parts of Western Africa, is amassed through the control of women and juniors. The control over women determines the flow of wealth, juniors being able to marry only after payment of a bride-price to the lineage elders (Meillassoux 1977). From this perspective, colonial domination has been perceived by Rey (1973) as an alliance between the colonial powers and ruling elites which were able to retain a great deal of their power, e.g. over the flow of bride-wealth (West Africa) or over access to land (Asia), in exchange for their cooperation in producing colonial revenue.

In Rey's view, the economies of developing societies are still largely shaped by the overbearing role played by class alliances although, in the post-colonial setting, it is no longer based on revenue but on unequal terms of trade between agricultural and industrial goods (Rey 1973: 49ff). Class alliances rather than the moral economy of the peasant as believed by Chayanov, I feel, can also help explain the interplay of production and reproduction in the exploitation of children's work in today's countries of the South. The idea of modes of exploitation corresponding to different power structures has the advantage of de-linking the exploitation of children from the capitalist sense of work, and allowing for its analysis in the broader context of post-colonial societies. It particularly evidences that children do not necessarily have to engage in activities directly adding to the marketable surplus for their work to be transformed into economic value; nor does their work need to be performed for that express purpose.

Returning briefly to the Poomkara case, we can visualize different dimensions of exploitation as being borne by the shared interests of at least three groups of identifiable power-holders: first of all, the merchant-exporters who hold key positions in the long-distance trade of the produce of the village; second, the local landowners who control the supply of husks to the women and own the main fishing equipment; and finally, the senior males who control, through their privileged access to cash, the lives of the women and children in their households. The very fact of family labour being performed as part of non-monetized familial obligations, provides the labour-intensive sectors of the village economy with their competitive edge and allows for the high profits made by both the landed power-holders at the local level and the merchant exporters. So it is precisely because they are submitted to the authority of the family – more exactly to paternal authority – and do not dispose of a legitimate economic arena outside the domestic one, that lies at the core of children's exploitation. This subordinate position – children not being acknowledged as workers in their own right – while allowing for their insertion in the least valued tasks of village economy, also explains children's vulnerability in the face of exploitation by the market.

Conclusions

I have argued in this chapter that the notion of children's work has been unduly clouded by moral considerations and that this has prevented its analysis in terms of economic exploitation. I have sought to explain this moral preoccupation by linking it to a pervasive seniority system that subordinates juniors in society on the basis of biological immaturity. The prominence of the biological translates in a perceived lack of competence and a need for protection against the adult male world of the market. Seniority, however, while claiming to protect children against the non-family sphere of labour, does impose upon them a range of activities that are indirectly articulated to this market and are essential to the cheap labour rationality of the economy.

The economic being based on the seniority system, the preserve of adult males, explains why the entrance of children into the labour market is accompanied by a feeling of shame and grave concern. It is not only widely felt by individual men as a loss of paternal power and prestige but also by society at large as an indisputable manifestation of social disruption. As remarked by White, children are indeed the only group of workers 'whose exploitation is generally addressed by attempts to remove them completely from the labour market rather than by efforts to improve the terms and conditions under which they work' (White 1994: 1).

De-linking adult exploitation from that of children means children's work cannot be measured with the same yardstick used for adult work: it submerges the waged work of the entire age group between five and fifteen under the heading of exploitation irrespective of wage levels and conditions of work.

The notion of child labour in its purest form condemns all work by those who are socially 'children', irrespective of individual inclinations, interests and talent. Nor does the notion allow for any serious appraisal of the nature of the relationship between the working child and his/her employer: the only work relations that children can legitimately entertain are those sanctioned by kinship obligations. This leaves very little scope for children to negotiate their conditions of work, any attempt at doing so coming dangerously near to questioning, if not challenging, the very moral assumptions of their entitlement to protection and nurturing. Many of their entitlements are, however, as I have tried to show, a myth and there is a serious need to understand how the articulation of different levels in the exploitation of children is instrumental in making children particularly vulnerable when operating in the market. This poses a serious dilemma, for if children do need special laws and regulations that address their special status in society, child labour legislation has also proven to be heavily permeated by patriarchal values. Discriminatory labour practices that are based on seniority can clearly not be removed by seeking to strengthen the very system of subordination that causes them in the first place.

Notes

1. The study trip was generously supported by the Netherlands Foundation for the Advancement of Tropical Research (WOTRO), The Hague.

2. The results of the research are discussed in detail in Nieuwenhuys 1994. To protect the integrity of the inhabitants of the village I have given it a fictitious name.

References

Anonymous (1984) Summary of Proceedings, Employment of Women from Kerala in the Fish-processing Units of Gujarat, Round Table held at the Institute of Management in Government, Thiruvananthapuram (Kerala), 2 January 1984 (unpubl.).

Caldwell, J. C. (1982) *Theory of Fertility Decline*, London, Academic Press.

Chayanov, A. V. (1966) *The Theory of Peasant Economy*, Illinois, American Economic Association (1st edn, 1925).

Elson, D. (1982) 'The Differentiation of Children's Labour in the Capitalist Labour Market', *Development and Change*, 13, 4, pp. 479–97.

Firth, R. (1979) 'Work and Value, Reflections on Ideas of Marx', in S. Wallman (ed.), *Social Anthropology of Work*, London, Academic Press, pp. 177–206.

Folbre, N. (1986) 'Hearts and Spades: Paradigms of Household Economics', *World Development*, 14, 2, pp. 245–55.

— (1994) *Who Pays for the Kids?*, London and New York, Routledge.

Fyfe, A. (1989) *Child Labour*, Cambridge, Polity Press.

Hull, T. (1981), 'Perspectives and Data Requirements for the Study of Children's Work', in G. Rodgers and G. Standing (eds), *Child Work, Poverty and Underdevelopment*, Geneva, International Labour Office, pp. 47–80.

Mamdani, M. (1981) *The Ideology of Population Control*, in: K. L. Michaelson (ed.), *And the Poor Get Children: Radical Perspectives on Population Dynamics*, New York, Monthly Review Press.

Meillassoux, C. (1977) *Femmes, greniers et capitaux*, Paris, Maspéro.

Morice, A. (1981) 'The Exploitation of Children in the "Informal Sector": Proposals for Research', in G. Rodgers and G. Standing (eds), *Child Work, Poverty and Underdevelopment*, Geneva, ILO.

Nieuwenhuys, O. (1994) *Children's Lifeworlds, Gender, Welfare and Labour in the Developing World*, London and New York, Routledge.

Rey, P. P. (1971) *Colonialisme, néo-colonialisme et transition au capitalisme, L'exemple de la 'Camilog' au Congo-Brazzaville*, Paris, Maspéro.

— (1973) *Les alliances de classe*, Paris, Maspéro.

Reynolds, P. (1991) *Dance Civet Cat, Child Labour in the Zambezi Valley*, London, Zed Books.

Salazar, M. C. (1991) 'Young Workers in Latin America: Protection of Self-determination?', *Child Welfare*, 70, 2, pp. 269–83.

Saradamoni, K. (1989) 'Crisis in the Fishery Industry and Women's Migration', in *Women and Seasonal Labour Migration in Rural India*, research report, Amsterdam, Anthropological Sociological Centre (unpubl.).

Schildkrout, E. (1980) 'Children's Work Reconsidered', *International Social Sciences Journal*, 32, 3, pp. 479–90.

Wadel, C. (1979) 'The Hidden Work of Everyday Life', in S. Wallman (ed.), *Social Anthropology of Work*, London, Academic Press, pp. 177–206.

White, B. (1994), 'Children, Work and "Child Labour": Changing Responses to the Employment of Children', The Hague, Institute of Social Studies (inaugural address).

CHAPTER 22

The Disintegrating Social Fabric: Child Labour and Socialization in Senegal

Serigne Mor Mbaye and Abdou Salam Fall

In traditional African societies, the socialization and protection of children used to be the responsibility of the community; a child was regarded as belonging to the kinship group as a whole rather than to the parents alone. Nowadays, however, the cash economy and urbanization are among the factors that have combined to undermine family structures and the representations, rites and myths relating to children; socialization is no longer a community affair but the private business of the family unit.

Yet a succession of crises has stripped many a Senegalese family of the ability to remain self-sufficient; the economic system no longer allows for domestic production geared towards self-sufficiency and the impact on children born into households whose very survival is in doubt is dramatic. Talk of crisis here inevitably conjures up images of those very young country children on the road with their parents or marabous, heading for cities where dreams of *el dorado* end in the harsh reality of slums and the constant threat of a traumatic eviction.

Added to that, another crisis of certainly even greater consequence to a young child's harmonious development is the breakdown of the family. It can turn children into outcasts, force them to join informal communities of 'street children' and live in the company of youngsters of all ages without the protective presence of an adult. The physical and social dangers for children growing up unprotected are enormous. This world, with its lack of opportunities for social integration, has no facilities specifically designed for children.

The Source of the Problem

Socialization in traditional Senegalese society is, as said, a collective affair where the child's cultural, cognitive, psycho-motor and psycho-affective development are the responsibility of the whole social group: maternal and paternal sides of the family alike. The father, mother, uncle or aunt each has a specific role to play in a scheme planned to manage the child's education and welfare and prepare him or her for life in the adult world.

Socialization mapped out within the family group and clan and apprenticeships designed to ensure the continuity of the group's trades help to create a high degree of affective security and a clear sense of one's own destiny. Children are first introduced to the work through imitative games encouraged and developed by group members. This initiation forms part of the division of labour, although the children's (albeit not inconsiderable) share remains restricted to educationally-oriented support work, rarely direct production. One common traditional practice consists of placing them in the care of qualified professional outside tutors. These tutors provide placed children with virtually the same education as their own children. The practice therefore corresponds to the collective project. Indeed, an education project is designed not just for an individual, but for an entire age group.

Wolof people have a saying which systematizes the notion as follows: 'It's how your father jumps that can break your back.' One cannot escape one's father's professional and material life path. Destiny is mapped out; if undermined, one's whole future life will become uncertain and hazardous.

This ideology plainly stands in the way of innovation and creativity. It has been the cause of maladjustment in an increasingly unstable and agitated world. In the past, stable values and social identity models reigned supreme. Agriculture was the only mode of production and professional activity centred entirely on farming. The professional classes were inward-looking and self-reproducing. Society was gerontocratic and hence extremely hierarchized. Duties and responsibilities were a function of status, age and gender. Decision-making powers belonged to the elders; and the individual long remained confined within a collective project from which the only possible exit was a change of status.

Islam has introduced a new dimension to a child's socialization by requiring them to attend an institution of Koranic studies for their religious education. Although these institutions are often located some distance away from the home, they have successfully managed to incorporate traditional values.

The Individualization of the Social Project for the Child

The current social context is marked by rampant population growth and a high proportion of young people: 70 per cent aged under twenty. New family units have broken away from bedrock communities, the old ideologies are under threat and there is nothing to take their place. Each family has to seek to readjust according to its own invidividual interpretations and represensions of reality. The urban masses are primarily socialized through schooling and apprenticeship in new careers, largely in the so-called 'informal' sector. School education tends to reverse the model of social advancement. It has added another dimension to the socialization process by contributing to the individualization of the project. Schools offer a means of advancement which no longer accounts for genealogical status, thus undermining both the system of social organization and group management of an individual's progress. Rather than calling in question this development, the crisis in education is consolidating it.

Waged labour and the emergence of new trades mark a departure from a form of socialization whose goals used to have to embrace collective as well as individual aspirations. The transition is felt in the shift from *wootal* to *nawtal*, that is to say from the caring approach of nurturing and patiently guiding a child through growth and education, to the free-market approach of withdrawal and the premature autonomy of children left to the un-structured schools of the streets.

The family has become increasingly destabilized by high divorce rates and the mobility (migration) of its members, causing a rise in the numbers of lone parents. Prospects for social integration remain vague because family units lack the ability to come up with valid individual projects tailored to present-day needs. Children who fail at school are left to fend for themselves; and drop-out rates among the very young have soared. At best they will be taken in by *daara* (Koranic houses), 'SOS villages' or orphanages. Infanticide is commonplace.

So another model of social success is emerging based on strategies of survival and resourcefulness. Indeed, in these times of endemic economic crisis, the groups developing within the informal sector have shown them-selves to be better able to adapt; and theirs are the values that count.

At this point, let us recall the social, moral and economic conditions that society has to offer children, and consider the extent to which they prepare them for future life.

From the Traditional Situation to Modern Society

What opportunities do children have to prepare for such a transition? Is the existing education system fulfilling its mission? What doors to the future does it open up for an adolescent? Does school pave the way to a career and individual responsibilities in a rapidly changing society?

We have to return to the analysis of traditional society here in order fully to understand its evolution. The social role of the child is extremely import-ant. Children not only represent the future, but present strengths too. From the time a child is weaned, it is taken from its mother to be cared for by other members of its community and enjoys the general affection of the group as a whole. Children find their place very quickly through the special relationships they have with each of their 'parents': grandparents, uncles, aunts, brothers and sisters. Until the age of fourteen or fifteen, they are taught how to 'behave properly' towards both family and strangers; they are imbued with the prevailing moral rules and learn to conform to them. In addition to this moral education, they learn to handle objects and use their senses. They then go on to perform various domestic tasks and join in with work in the fields. They have already been introduced to the scope of the network of external relations revolving round the family; not to mention their role, depending on whether they are boys or girls, and relationships with the opposite sex.

Although coming somewhat later, the child's economic and socio-political integration is just as important. Children are established as active members of their community at about the age of fifteen years old, from which time they will be counted as *bona fide* economic producers and contribute to the accumulation of the family head's material possessions.

Alliances are formed between the direct family and neighbouring groups through marriage: giving one's daughter's hand in marriage used to be regarded as a means of allying oneself with another group and acquiring goods, material or otherwise, in the shape of a bride-price. The husband or wife, depending on the mode of matrimony, allows new productive or reproductive forces to be brought into the community.

The chief characteristic of traditional education is its authoritarian nature: it is delivered not in writing but through the experience gained through contact with one's elders; relations between educators and educated are marked by the authority of the former over the latter; a variety of coercive techniques are frequently employed. By and large, the intended aims of the education are achieved. The child willingly yields to the existing order because it applies to everybody else and refusal to do so would mean exclusion from the community. In return, traditional society is duty-bound to prepare the child's future.

Traditional society considers it improper practice to leave children with the means or tools to carve out their own social advancement or allow them to choose their own functions and social roles. For it would lead to individual competitiveness which, if allowed to spread, could cause serious and unforeseen problems within the community. Determining a child's place and function is regarded as a collective responsibility. In an education system of this sort, personal aspirations go unrecognized or are at least kept well in society's control. If individuals are unable to express such aspirations, they are compensated with the guarantee of never having to experience failure.

Today, children live in the parental home. They are no longer surrounded by a compact and coherent domestic or tribal society, but by an urban society characterized by ethnic or tribal heterogeneity. The child finds it hard to fit into an environment marked by two opposing trends: the urban intermixing of populations and withdrawal into idiosyncrasies.

Children here find themselves powerless to resolve the conflict created by the very nature of their new surroundings; they have to struggle to maintain their balance and feel a strong sense of isolation. Competition occurs between individuals, not family groups: it is the individual that matters not the family, no matter how large or well off it might be. Individual interests dissociate themselves from those of the family and, what is more, the two are often mutually antagonistic. This new society features a differential valuation of occupations, a social hierarchy by and large based on wealth: the highest stake, the most legitimate criterion for classification, being economic power, access to financial capital.

The child acquires new needs that develop its individualism. It learns values that have nothing to do with assuring the group's continuity or safeguarding the established order. Within the framework of present-day urban society, the child is offered a variety of personal projects with a whole range of means for carrying them through, but with an uneven chance of success: those choosing to follow such paths are given no assurance that they will not end their lives among the discarded wrecks of society.

Very few children enjoy acceptable living conditions today: cases of delinquency – markedly rising in number with each passing year – are partly related to the general situation where children finds themselves exposed to nothing but conflicting values, competitive relationships, injustice and a feeling of the emptiness of daily life and prospects for the future.

Child Labour

We take child labour to refer to any economic activity contributing to the production of goods and services. A survey carried out in July 1993 by the Statistical Forecasting body of Senegal shows that over a twelve-month observation period, one in ten Senegalese children had a regular paid or lucrative job. More than three-quarters (78 per cent) of the children in question are classed as 'home helps', 9 per cent as waged workers, 6 per cent apprentices and some 5 per cent freelance workers. Girls outnumber boys among the waged workers. It is important to note that child labour, concerning both girls and boys, is as much in evidence in rural areas as in the city.

Numbers of 'home helps' have grown with the slump in agriculture; many children move from rural and suburban areas to the city to work as 'home helps' for middle-class and, increasingly, low-income families. The seasonal type of economic activities children perform in their own homes is replaced by a full-time job in other houses where they become indispensable. When they finish work at the end of the day, some of them join the dozens sharing single bedrooms in the slums of Dakar. Because of both the work and the accommodation, these children are profoundly marginalized. But, as Abdoulaye Sadio concludes from the above survey, 'the majority of working Senegalese children remain within the framework of the family'.

The survey shows that '40% of the girls are employed as domestics and 42% are farm hands'. There is greater diversity among boys, who are primarily used in trades such as dress-making, mechanics and carpentry. A new phenomenon has appeared on the various marketplaces of Dakar and even in smaller towns: the employment of very young girls in retail and redistribution businesses.

In everyday life and on the marketplaces money and street culture have become the overriding social values.

It may be said that premature employment stems from the rise of non-school attendance as a model. A 1989 IFAN/ORSTOM study on urban integration in Dakar found that the economy was already becoming more tertiary-oriented. If that trend continues, as all the indicators currently suggest is more than likely, then the massive use of young girls on the markets will continue to grow, irrespective of the legislation condemning the practice.

We must also consider the city children forced to work as apprentices or employees in the informal sector, for these are the categories of workers most at risk. As a rule, apprentices are not paid: the above study showed 84 per cent of them receiving not a penny from their employers. And there is much evidence to show that an apprenticeship can last up to ten or even fifteen years before the master craftsman recognizes his pupil's skills or mastery. That hardly makes apprenticeship very appealing to children, and many end up opting for the streets.

Meanwhile, the economic crisis has also exacerbated family tensions. With the absence of a group relay within the household and the lack or inefficiency of the social services, children are at great risk of being thrown out on to the streets when their choices conflict with those of their parents. The growth of the street-child phenomenon is relentless, in spite of a growing campaign to raise awareness. A report published in 1993 by the government of Senegal and UNICEF estimated that the city of Dakar had a population of between 2000 and 3000 street children.

The *Talibés*

In the eyes of the Senegalese government and UNICEF 'the spectacle of these scruffy children wandering the streets and public places of the large cities of Senegal, holding out their bowls in the hope of a bite to eat or some money for their own survival as much as to support their marabous, is becoming a social epidemic'. Indeed, the most disturbing and most visible situation of all is that of the young beggars known as *talibés*.

A UNICEF survey carried out in 1992 reveals a strong correlation between the migration and begging activities of the *talibé*. There are two strands to this. First and foremost is the seasonal migration of marabous arriving in the city with their *talibés* during the dry season. Second is the placing of children by their parents with marabous living in urban areas. So it is a matter of internal migration – the survey confirms that only 8 per cent of the migrant *talibé* beggars identified at the time had entered Senegal from neighbouring countries.

Talibés come from low-income families. Fifty-five per cent of them have parents in farming, livestock or fishing. Thirty per cent are travelling salesmen, merchants, low-ranking marabous, Arabic-language teachers, employees, labourers or artisans.

These observations suggest a steady decline in Islamic education in urban areas of Senegal. In place of the once sacred duty of teaching the Koran, marabous now use *talibé* children as their instruments, their means of earning a living. According to the 1992 survey mentioned above, nearly 58 per cent of *talibés* give their marabous an average of 100 CFA francs a day (min.: 50 CFA francs; max.: 500). To raise that sort of money takes a *talibé* an average of five hours' solid begging; which leaves only 30 per cent of their time remaining for religious education. So the original social contract is not being respected. The government/UNICEF report found that 'the ideology of seeking charity formerly sanctioned apprenticeship in asceticism and humility [...]; now [it serves] unscrupulous marabous in their abusive utilization of young *talibés*'.

Conclusion

Children's behaviour is increasingly conforming to the new norms of a changing society. In the past, the domestic community used to have direct control over them, teaching them respect for its traditions, retaining the way they thought and acted within a well-defined framework. A child's only possible path in life was that which led towards its predetermined status, functions and roles. The choices formed beneath the illusory models of urban society, however, are uncertain, the means of action unexplored. Nowadays, a clear rift has opened up between traditional communities and urban society. Without proper assistance – not really forthcoming from the state – children will rarely manage to cross it safely.

References

BDA and UNICEF (1993) 'Mesure de l'impact de la convention sur les Droits de l'enfant (Région de DAKAR)', Dakar.

Bonnet, M. (1992) 'Le Travail des enfants en Afrique, OIT', *Revue Internationale du travail*, 132, 3.

Cornia, G. A., R. Jolly and F. Stewart (1987) *L'ajustement à visage humain. Protéger les groupes vulnérables et favoriser la croissance*, Economica, UNICEF.

Ene, S. (1993) 'Le travail des enfants au Sénégal, cas des apprentis', BIT.

Government of Senegal and UNICEF (1993) 'Analyse de la situation de l'enfant et de la femme au Sénégal', Dakar.

Houle, G. and H. Roch (1991) 'Parler de faire des enfants, une question vitale', *Recherches sociographiques*, XXXII, 3, pp. 385–414.

OUA/UNICEF (1992) 'L'avenir de l'Afrique: ses enfants', *Études sectorielles*, Dakar, 25–27 November.

PANOS (1989) *Quand les pauvres du Sud s'autofinancent*, Paris, l'Harmattan.

Sadio, A. (1993) *Le travail des enfants au Sénégal: enquête méthodologique, du ministère de l'Économie, des Finances et du Plan*, Dakar, Direction de la Prévision et de la Statistique.

UNICEF (1990) 'Étude sur la situation éducationnelle des enfants déplacés de Mauritanie', Dakar.

CHAPTER 23

'Unexploited' Labour: Social Transition in Madagascar

Bodo Ravololomanga and Bernard Schlemmer

From the Child as Wealth ...

It is no exaggeration to say that ancestor worship occupies a crucial place in the lives, preoccupations and decision-making of Madagascan people, the like of which is found in few other societies. Madagascans might even be said to regard securing their succession as a matter of supreme importance. It is not so much in order to have someone to care for them when they grow old (albeit not an unimportant goal), but above all to ensure that there will be somebody there to take proper charge of performing their burial ceremony: the rites of passage allowing the deceased access to the ranks of their forebears. They therefore depend upon their children for their very survival or, in other words, the quality of their ancestral afterlife. Sterility, being heirless, is the greatest fear of men and women alike. Orally transmitted folklore frequently employs the notions of fertility and sterility in an extremely eloquent system of binary opposition. Fertility is seen as a blessing, a gift from the gods and ancestors, bestowed only upon those who have managed to earn their generosity. Fertility incarnates happiness, life. Sterility, on the other hand, is regarded as among the worst of all possible curses and translates into a feeling of anxiety, fear.[1] It is associated with the image of death. So it is common to find the family at a wedding wishing future husbands and wives 'seven sons and seven daughters' (on such occasions, the figure seven, which is sometimes believed to be dangerous, signifies plenitude).

These days, however, perceptions are somewhat different. Making these sorts of wishes is now liable to be taken badly: as an ironic barb or even a curse. The fact is that the devastating economic crisis has affected the ideal of fertility, although it nevertheless remains deeply rooted in Madagascan culture and has doubtlessly helped people to cushion the potential impact of the recession.

... to the Child as a Burden

In rural and urban areas alike, households are now anxious to have as few children as possible so that they can be sure to provide them with medical care in the event of illness and to feed them and find them work, if at all possible, when they reach adulthood. But a large number of families can no longer even feed their children, never mind clothe them. If households cannot, as once they could, count on relatives to adopt or lodge one or more of their children, their last resort now is to place offspring in friends' or acquaintances' homes where they will be put to work. According to a Malagasy saying, 'children are wealth': yet these former gifts from heaven are now becoming a burden, and a burden that is sometimes far too heavy to bear.

> My name's Theo and I'm fourteen years old. I am the second of my parents' six children; the oldest boy. Dad died three years ago. Mum sells yams and peanuts on the roadside in Fianarantsoa. My big sister has gone to work as a housemaid in Antananarivo; because mum couldn't look after my younger brothers and sisters and I any more, she sent me to my grandmother's house in this small town so I could go to school and carry on studying. I had to stop school in fourth year primary. It was too expensive for my grandmother (textbooks, exercise books, pens). She's old and can't afford to buy clothes and food for both of us any more. So she's asked Mamy's mum and dad (Mamy's a one-year-old baby) to employ me. I've been working for six months.

So in 1991 Theo became a domestic at the couple's house in his grandmother's town.[2] Only they do not have a lot of money coming in either. Mamy's mother is a seamstress but she has too few customers. She makes barely ten dresses a month selling at 2000 Malagasy francs apiece.[3] Her husband owns a broken-down old van given to him by his father, and he uses the little money he earns to buy new or second-hand spare parts to repair it for eventual sale in the hope that it will fetch him enough to be able to open a small shopkeeping business. He keeps the family alive with his carpentry work. Even then, not many of the townsfolk ever place an order and he only just manages to sell two chairs, a couple of footstools and a table per month. But because Theo's grandmother (seventy years) came and begged them to take on her grandson (in return for food, lodgings, clothes or, better still, a wage), the couple took pity and agreed, despite already having enough trouble of their own.

Theo does odd jobs around the house, looks after Mamy when the mother is sewing or preparing meals. If the opportunity arises, he helps the father planing wood for the furniture. That is where he works most. But his biggest dream is to become a driver. Every time Mamy's father goes to work on the van, he does his best to advertise his availability. He is especially keen to learn mechanics: drivers in Madagascar need to know how to repair their own vehicles because there are not that many garages there. And since Theo likes cars so much, he says he offered to join Ravony (a fifteen-year-old who also works as a domestic for Mamy's grandparents) sleeping in the van at night. In winter as in summer, the boys act as night watchmen guarding the van from burglars.

As for Ravony, he is the second oldest boy in a five-child family. His elder brother (sixteen years) is a hired hand working for a town shopkeeper. Ravony's parents sent him out to look for work when they found themselves no longer able to feed all their children. Dressed in rags, he did not dare approach anybody to ask for a job. And since his younger brothers and sisters had hardly a thing to eat, he preferred to rummage through the bins instead of begging. In 1989, he had been scouring the streets for days, when Mamy's grandmother[4] saw him and took him some food. She kept this up for a week before eventually offering him a job. Ravony has been her domestic ever since.

Theo and Ravony both earn 5000 Malagasy francs a month. Their employers buy them new clothes twice a year and they receive family cast-offs at other times. They eat at their employers' house. As for their pay, almost all of it goes to their families: Ravony's to his parents and Theo's to his grandmother who forwards the money to her daughter, now living in Fianarantsoa.

A Disastrous Economic Situation

The economic crisis which has hit the whole world, above all the weakest countries, has been particularly devastating in Madagascar (see Schlemmer 1995). Up until 1971, Madagascar was producing enough food to satisfy local consumption needs and even exporting premium rice. Today, it is counted as one of the world's 'least advanced countries', unable to afford to import all of its required foodstuffs. The whole country has become greatly impoverished: if one relates GNP to population growth, at national level Madagascans lost more than 50 per cent of their earnings between 1972 and 1992. The very poorest parts of the population – around 40 per cent of the total – also saw their share of national income shrink by half, meaning they now receive only 10 per cent compared to the previous 20 per cent and have slipped well below the 'poverty line'.

Another indicator of this erosion: certain endemic diseases linked to extreme poverty have resurfaced. Meanwhile, 'the structural adjustment policies [...] are [without doubt] the chief cause of cutbacks in social spending. In real terms, per capita social expenditure in Madagascar has been reduced by about half (with a 40 percent fall between 1980 and 1984)' (Chasteland et al.: 131). There is an abundance of evidence we could mention, but for the purposes of this discussion, let us settle for the point that

> the situation in the education sector is characterized by widespread decline in qualitative and quantitative terms. Children, boys and girls, are now becoming the main family wage-earners. Their work, in cities and rural areas alike, is

necessary, not to say vital, for the family's material stability. In the survival strategies that have become essential during this period of growing impoverishment, school has been relegated to second place in the priorities of young Madagascans who need to contribute the family budget before all else. (UNICEF 1993: 6)

As the rot sets in, the decay of the state and the corruption and 'deregulation' carried in its wake to the benefit of the few combined with the accelerated impoverishment of the rest of the population, have together given rise to the development of economic activities which are increasingly evading state control. There has been a proliferation of various forms of undeclared labour, small businesses, more or less clandestine and illicit activities: so many 'forms of cut-and-run social practices adopted by, or imposed upon, an increasing number of young boys and girls' (UNICEF 1993: 187). The poor population bear the brunt of this, but it offers the poorest people – the unemployed, the dispossessed countryfolk, the displaced new arrivals in the city – their only possible solution.

To be Cared for – but by Whom?

If the case of children like Ravony scavenging for food in refuse bins is still rather exceptional in small provincial Malagasy towns, that of Theo is more common.[5] Recently, village children have been going from door to door asking for food, a situation which always used to seem unacceptable, unthinkable, in this agriculture-based society, particularly in what is regarded as the rice loft of the Betsileo region. Nowadays, however, when parents have no rice, corn or manioc to give their children, they beseech their slightly better off neighbours or acquaintances to lodge one of them in their homes, mostly the eldest boy or girl. This is how children from the age of twelve come to be placed in various different homes with the town's traders and functionaries.

Some parents have told us that if they had to choose, they would put their children into the home of a teacher (primary school, secondary school or college), but many teachers with two or three children to take care of, which is usually the case, have trouble enough of their own making ends meet. In placing their children with teachers, parents hope that while performing their domestic duties, their offspring will be well educated and instructed. They believe contact with teachers offers prospects of a good education and advancement for their children. The manager of the 'ATD-quart monde' NGO also stresses the huge demand for children to attend school, adolescents included. Madagascan education standards are relatively well developed compared to those of other countries of comparable or even higher income; the majority of parents have been school-educated and regard illiteracy as a form of degeneration. Naturally, they can send their children to school only if there is guaranteed free education, but we should not underestimate the fact that allowing a child to go to school is already something of a sacrifice, given the lower earnings stemming from the loss of extra income, no matter how minimal, generated by that child's labour.

Meanwhile, there has been a discernible change in the relationship between the employer and placed child over the past few years. Host families do not call placed children *mpiasa* or 'workers' but *mpanampy*, 'assistants'. For their part, the children in question do not call their 'employers' 'Madam' or 'Sir' as would be the case with bosses with whom they should keep a respectful distance. They always use the structure 'so-and-so's father' or 'so-and-so's mother', sometimes even calling them 'Father' or 'Mother' if their 'employers' have children of about their own age. So there seems to be a sense of understanding and affectivity between the host family and placed child worker. Can we take this development to be a conscious effort to tone down the difference in status between employer and employed, and has it been initiated in order to respond to the need for mutual aid in a society which, despite its hardships, still wishes to maintain cohesion? Or does it suggest the already ongoing transition towards a paternalist type relationship which will provide the basis for a specific exploitation of this new labour force with its urgent need to work?

Perhaps we can find the makings of an answer by comparing the situations from traditional rural areas with the large conurbations (Antananarivo, Antsirabe) via the small provincial town. Indeed, there really is an evolution taking place whereby people whose roots in the village are now threatened have been sucked into an accelerated migration towards the big cities where social ties no longer correspond to the intimate logic of the family. The big city, despite the crisis, effectively remains a place that offers a wide range of incomes and apparently more ample possibilities and opportunities to earn a living, if not to 'strike it rich'; it has, incidentally, had the chance to prove it, and that (along with the growing and justified fear of rampaging gangs of looters in the countryside) explains why it has remained a centre of attraction for migrants, even when there is scarcely any more work there for the displaced. The city outskirts are overflowing with such people who arrived in the vain hope of finding success as they know others have succeeded before them, only to end up living in abject poverty.

Children in Rural Areas

Many stockbreeders and farmers living in isolated hamlets (who have sometimes had their cattle rustled and crops stolen by armed gangs with no qualms about killing villagers) want to move to the city. Those who stay in the village to farm their fields cannot always afford to pay hired farm hands and day labourers to help them. It used to be customary practice in the Betsileo region to call in relatives, neighbours and villagers to participate in the various stages of the rice-growing cycle.[6] If adult members of the extended family do not respond to this call for solidarity, which is still issued yet increasingly less frequently, child workers are used. They find themselves having to take time out from school for the paddy work period, or even give up their studies altogether to assist their parents full-time.

For their part, families with neither the financial nor human resources rent out their land on three- to five-year leases for a lump-sum payment paid at the time of signing. If landowners ask for an advance on forthcoming leases, they fall into debt and end up having to sign their fields or rice paddies over to their tenants. Thus dispossessed of their wealth, they resign themselves to packing their eldest children off to the city as soon as they are old enough (about twelve), so that they might work and give them some or all of their earnings to help them survive and feed younger brothers and sisters.

But in village society, even the slackest solidarity networks still continue to secure a certain degree of redistribution; while in the city the family-type networks are giving up and hardly fulfil the role any longer and the specifically urbanization-linked (endogenous or NGO) networks are as yet unable to cope.

Children Placed in the City ...

If, in their exodus to the towns, adults do not find enough work to feed their families, it is once again up to the children to replace them, primarily as daytime car attendants on the streets or parking lots.

The most common form of employment – the only one not seen as a serious setback – is placement in private homes where the children perform various domestic duties. Their condition can be either advantageous or tragic, depending on the family. The majority, though, are at least fed and housed, generally just as well, or badly, as in their own homes; meanwhile, they are more often than not expected to work far harder. As a rule, the parents are given a sum of money when the child leaves home, after which neither child nor employer is under any further obligation towards them. On average, children are paid 5 to 7000 Malagasy francs a month in the country and up to twice that in the capital (where the cost of living is far higher); yet there are cases where they receive no wages at all.

There do not seem to be any existing placement networks as such;[7] generally speaking, an exchange takes place between families who know one another and (as in the case of Theo) the families taking charge of a child do not necessarily feel happy about capitalizing on cheap labour; it really could be a matter of somebody doing somebody else a favour, which can end up costing more than it yields. Particularly orphans – girls or boys, for both can work as domestics, even if it is a more common feature among girls – are in many cases taken care of by the extended family. Sometimes, in the capital at least, girls seek to be placed of their own accord at the suggestion of a friend already working as a maid.

We also occasionally find more comfortably-off employers who go out in search of children ready to be placed and, of course, they take full advantage of it. In the majority of cases, however, exploitation is held at bay by the fact that the families know one another or, if they have gone through an 'intermediary' family, that the latter acts as a moral guarantor. Once again, we heard no mention of any placement 'channels'; all the field-workers we questioned were adamant on this point. However, wages are not always paid, the work is sometimes too hard for such young children and girls are often sent packing without notice as soon as they reach an age where their employers fear they might become pregnant. But we think it important to stress the following: there are adult maids too and their living conditions, and above all pay, are not necessarily any better; children are paid as well, or as badly, as adults, a point quite rightly made by the manager of the WFP (the UN World Food Program); which means to say – and this is worth underlining, for it is quite peculiar to the case of Madagascar[8] – that it is the work itself that is being exploited and not specifically the vulnerable under-aged worker.

... and the Others

Most of the children who remain in the small towns and are unable to find domestic work, peddle home-made foodstuffs (yogurts, doughnuts, biscuits or other cooked dishes). From the early hours of the morning, they walk the streets carrying huge trays of cakes on their heads or ice-boxes full of yogurt pots. Since these children do not generally have enough money to buy meat, flour, oil, milk and sugar, every day they must therefore find suppliers to give them ready-to-eat food to consume. Each evening, the employer gives them 5 Malagasy francs per doughnut sold and 10 Malagasy francs per pot of yogurt (a tenth of the retail price). So at the end of the day, anyone who has managed to sell fifty cakes and fifty pots will receive 750 Malagasy francs, i.e. the equivalent of a kilo of rice at harvest time or 750 grammes during periods when supplies are low: at any rate, not enough for the daily ration needed to feed a family of three, and this in a country where rice is sacred, the main staple of people's diet. What is more, being able to sell fifty cakes and fifty yogurts a day can be regarded as quite a feat, for there are at least twenty children in the town doing this kind of work. Children with nobody to supply them with such merchandise sell fruit, vegetables and cooked foods of rather mediocre quality on pavement stalls, taking only a very meagre sum home with them in the evenings, and sometimes even ending up having to feed themselves with left-over spoiled merchandise.

Apart from peddling food, some children also hawk *fandrehitra* (lit.: lighting stuffs), going from door to door selling the kindling households use to save on petrol for lighting charcoal or firewood. Some of these children have told us that they can sell up to twenty small bundles a day at 50 Malagasy francs a bundle. This sort of work causes problems because the children, and their families, who hack away at the trunks of upright pine trees are regarded as forest despoilers and thus risk the penalties stipulated by the new environ-mental protection laws.

To add to that, there are also young boys of between twelve and fourteen years old hauling sacks of rice, sugar, flour and so on across town in carts (*baramba*) loaded with merchandise weighing as much as 300kgs. Working in teams of four, they end up with about 2000 Malagasy francs to share out between them on regular weekdays and from 4000 to 5000 Malagasy francs on market days. This exhausting and occasionally hazardous work has the children making up for the absence of small-town taxi services. They tend to be overly keen, overstretching themselves in their efforts to attract customers and prove that they are the strongest. And in view of their age, they are not always in full control of their vehicles, which thus leads to accidents. Whenever a fight breaks out, adults have to intervene to sort them out and restore order.

Working Conditions in the Big City

The kinds of work on offer to children here are similar to those in the small provincial towns (or the countryside), although begging is far more prevalent, second only to being placed with a foster family. We find as many girl beggars as boys aged from three or four; girls of twelve and over are largely looking for domestic work. Most of these children still have parents to whom they hand over a share of their earnings. They are relatively well organized, with well-defined territories. Yet racketeering has not become customary practice, even if it is true that, among those who sleep rough, the younger ones often have their money confiscated by their elders. This, though, has more to do with a form of initiation: the manager of 'NRJ', an NGO which has become particularly well established among young Antananarivo marginals, explained that the 'elders' take care of those whose money they have taken if the latter fail to make any earnings during the day. And, in cahoots with secondhand goods dealers, they sometimes find them occasional earnings by teaching them how to steal. Meanwhile, the NRJ adds that parents push their children to work because the income represents a much appreciated supplement. In the poorest circles (especially in the case of adopted children) it is now even accepted practice for the child to pay for the right to sleep in their parents' – i.e. their own – home.

Notwithstanding that, UNICEF points out that

> all [these] children support their families even if they are no longer living with them, or have been rejected by one of their parents. In the latter case, they will hand a share of their earnings over to a single parent, generally the father, or the remarried mother whose partner refuses to have them in the house.

The child is aware of the family's difficulties and the *fihavanana* (feeling of solidarity) is very much present. (UNICEF 1993: 194)

In less dramatically disadvantaged circles, the children are at least working in a proper job. In the provinces, for instance, they work as water-bearers (paid 50 Malagasy francs per 20-litre bucket, thus earning 500 to 1000 Malagasy francs a day); or brick carriers (the youngest being six to eight years old; the wages being about 5 Malagasy francs per brick, depending on the distance covered with a load of six to eight bricks a trip); or else shop or car attendants; or even 'carry your bags, ma'am?', etc. They see themselves in a far less degrading light. To these children, having been brought up in a society where the notion of 'failure' is omnipresent, this is particularly important.

On average, they all earn between 500 and 1000 Malagasy francs a day and have to go out and find work each and every day. Whereas the children placed with families for their part earn only between 5000 and 10,000 Malagasy francs a month, albeit including bed and board.

What about the Future?

Even if they manage to resolve the matter of material survival, the children who have migrated to the capital have other problems hanging over them. Devoid of family ties, and sometimes even friends, the young worker is often subject to a lack of affection. And if they offset this emptiness in the various types of entertainment on offer in every capital city, they will be tempted to take the initiative of cutting all contact with their family back in the village. They may even come to regard their financial contribution to the family as a burden, a shackle. When that happens, the young worker will cease to see the point of family cohesion.

What is more, if the child counting on returning to the home region at some later stage has not managed to make any savings and if, on top of that, he or she has not gained a training during his or her early working life, it will be hard to pluck up the courage to re-establish contact with the family. In such cases, boys might slip into a shifty life of wheeling and dealing on the city streets, while the girls might deliver themselves into prostitution. Situations like these remain rather rare, because the majority of young workers coming to the city stay in touch with their parents. Their time away from the family can be experienced as a temporary expatriation rather than being uprooted from their place of birth. Hence, at the age of twenty or twenty-five, those who have managed to help their families and save some money will return to set up home in the midst of their loved ones. And those who have managed to buy themselves a few head of cattle,[9] some land and rice paddies to farm will have made the biggest successes of their lives. They will be held in high esteem by their families.

Faced with the economic hardships of his or her elders, the working child thus assumes responsibility as an active member of the household from a very early age. Before the parents have reached old age, adolescents find themselves obliged to ease their family's difficulties through the fruits of their labour. Still youngsters, their behaviour is that of real adults, especially when they have to come to the assistance of parents and young collaterals. But what will become of these children when they actually do enter adulthood? How will they flower if they for ever remain unskilled labourers? And if, miraculously, they are given an apprenticeship, will they one day be able to turn their training to their advantage? Will they still have the option of returning to the land to raise livestock and cultivate crops?

Child Labour, a Vital Necessity; not yet a Specific System of Exploitation

Many families have no choice but to arrange for their children to contribute to family income simply to survive, or else to provide for their own subsistence; the sheer scale and speed of the deterioration in living standards for the majority of the population has, of course, gone hand in hand with worse conditions at work and on the labour market.

Also, it is hardly surprising that so many passing observers are struck by the desperate circumstances of some of these children: the three- or four-year-old beggars; the swarms of kids competing for the privilege of carrying your shopping bags for you or watching your car; the small children knee-high to a grasshopper carrying piles of bricks on their heads or breaking stones on building sites for days on end; not to mention the sickening spectacle of children scavenging through dustbins and refuse tips and devouring foul-looking scraps for which they sometimes have to fight with adults.

For all that, when we put the issue to more in-depth analysis, we are on the contrary struck by the fact that, despite the truly catastrophic scale of the economic situation and the speed at which it has deteriorated, child labour is actually not worse than it is; i.e. that it is still more or less spontaneous and not yet organized, rationalized or cultivated by adults who might have been expected to capitalize on these children's real need for cash and maximize economic exploitation of their labour power.

This analysis might well cause offence; rightly shocked by the desperate living conditions of children who are basically forced to work instead of going to school, to support their families instead of being supported by them, our duty as observers is of course to denounce this scandalous wrong. We could, here as elsewhere, analyse the machinery whose central explanatory role is known (see Meillassoux 1993: 69–70) and be satisfied. By going the other way and bringing subtle shading into the analysis of the situation, we might be in danger of appearing to lend it support. We should therefore provide some clear explanation.

1. As seen, the type of work most commonly undertaken by children is domestic employment in other families' homes. What we wanted to underline, however, was that at the time of our survey there was still no organized recruitment network whose economic activity might have been geared towards exploiting this 'market' for its own financial gains. This obviously does not mean to say that there is no one capitalizing on the situation (one of the managers of the 'Sentinelles'[10] NGO, whose aim it is to reintegrate child prisoners into society, explains how the gaols are overpopulated with 'little maids' sentenced for theft, most of whom would have otherwise found it impossible to survive had they not 'stolen' food from their employers; and there are some people who have acted as middlemen between parents and employers on so many occasions that they have made a name for themselves and are now in a position to demand a percentage on the transaction). But nobody is actually making a career of it or helping to maintain and consolidate the system, as is the case in certain other countries in a comparable economic position.

2. Similarly, despite the fact that many children are making a living as beggars, there is (to our knowledge) no racketeering here; and if, as the same Sentinelles manager claims, parents with disabled children refuse to have them fitted with artificial limbs free of charge because handicapped beggars bring in higher earnings, we did not see any cases of self-mutilation; there are children employed as assistants, usually by parents who could not otherwise cope, but they are paid at the 'going rate', i.e. the same as an adult doing the same tasks (on the other hand, they are for ever doing the same elementary work, with no apprenticeship and, if they are in an envious position in terms of having secure jobs and income, their future still remains just as uncertain; the new ILO manager for Madagascar is, we feel, quite right to have put the issue in the following terms: it is not a matter of *eradicating* child labour, but of ensuring that it remains consistent with their physical and mental age and gives them a training.

2. A final example: there are underage prostitutes (young girls, as reported by a Médecins Sans Frontières volunteer, agree to sleep with people without asking for money, in order to have a bed for the night free of charge; for, as we mentioned earlier, the most disadvantaged children are made to pay for a place to sleep), but there is no 'child prostitution' as such. ASA was the only NGO to talk about procurers, but there is nothing to suggest that very much organized procurement goes on, or that a child prostitution ring exists to service the sex-tourism industry.[11]

Compared to the worst of what we know about other places – and what we might have expected here too – this situation remains relatively favourable. Can it continue or is it heading relentlessly towards the kinds of models being developed in the countries of the Third World where industrialization is more advanced and capitalism more deeply rooted? Those countries have developed a market-driven logic which, in a situation of sustained economic tension, tends ever more systematically to override the protective duty that every society undoubtedly feels *vis-à-vis* its children, but which, in Madagascar, still seems to prevail.

The problem is all the more apparent when we see how economic needs have already come to transform Malagasy mentalities in the city, the picture they hold of the child. Children here still remain sufficiently highly valued to have so far contained any spread in the temptation to exploit their labour. But the fact remains that the idea of making children pay for the right to sleep at home already exists in the milieux worst hit by the recession, which is proof enough that no ideological barrier can remain standing for ever when faced with the ordeal of a reality with which it has become far too incompatible.

For the time being, the temptation of a rational exploitation of this potential source of income remains confined to the realms of fantasy: there is talk of stolen children whose vital organs are sold to private French clinics, of foreign networks purchasing children for adoption-hungry couples, of child-sex-tourism via Nossy-be for the benefit of wealthy Réunion people and so on. But notice how foreigners are involved in every one of these rumours. They are also the ones often found spreading them. Does that mean to say that the danger comes from them alone? Obviously not, alas.

The future of Malagasy children is no longer any better protected than that of other exploited children in the Third World. But we think it is important to stress the following: throughout the whole world, aggravated poverty naturally leads to deteriorating working and living conditions which tends to lead to a call for the participation of every available hand, including children; but no matter what its scale, via who knows what rational thinking within the 'Economy', economic crisis alone is not enough to result in child labour being exploited *any differently* than is the case with adults. We are not questioning 'economic rationality' here; it is just that the perverse effects of market logic (or that of profits, which amounts to the same) are developed all the more thanks to the fact that this logic can supplant any other form of reasoning and impose itself upon any other wills – as it seems to be able to do whenever the vital interests of capitalism are at stake.

Such is the case of Madagascar, which is of scarcely any real interest to international capitalism. By the same token, we see that when free-market economics do not totally dominate the collective representation of a social system or the day-to-day activities of its members, the alleged 'inevitability' disappears. As anywhere else, minority status opens Malagasy children to domination-based relations in addition to the production- and exploitation-based relationships linking the labourers of the dominated classes to their employers. However, it is free-market economics alone that compel employers to cash in on it. So it is not *economically* impossible to suppress child labour, but that would require quite another economic world order.

Notes

1. For more on the comparison between fertility and sterility as well as the child's place in Madagascan society, see Ravololomanga (1992).

2. Most of our study (B.R.) was undertaken between 1992 and 1993 in the Fivondranana district of Ambohimahasoa, a small town of 9000 inhabitants, about 50km from Fianarantsoa and 450km from Antananarivo.

3. 1000 Malagasy francs = more or less US$ 0.50 (1994 rates).

4. Mamy's grandmother (fifty-four years) and grandfather (a retired middle-ranking civil servant) still have three of their own children living at home. Apart from Ravony, they also lodge two other children whose respective parents had been seeking to find them a place to work.

5. At least one in three homes in that small town is lodging one or two children placed there for work.

6. Ploughing, sowing, bedding rice plants, weeding, harvesting and transporting sheaves to the threshing area. Whoever receives the *haono* (lit.: 'call' or 'request') must either come (or at least send a replacement) or supply rice, salt or meat. Generally, they are not paid cash, but offered the *tamby*, the biggest sheaf of rice they can carry unaided on their head or back (this is just a one-off when the work is over). Whoever calls for help should also feed whoever comes to work (this can sometimes be very expensive because, on top of the rice, they have to kill a pig for the meal). And they in turn should answer a call from those who came to their assistance, this duty being called *valin-tanana* (lit.: 'the answer of the hands').

7. None, at least, that was visible at the time of the survey – conducted in Antananarivo in 1994 – and this was a point which I was particularly keen on investigating (B.S.).

8. At the time of our study which, it should be remembered, dates back to 1992–93 for rural areas (B.R.) and to 1994 for the capital (B.S.); if we were able to draw these sorts of conclusions, they are plainly dated; anyone wishing to use them today should have them carefully checked via another survey.

9. The *zebu*, the chief element of family wealth, is equally vested with symbolic value. It is the sacrificial beast *par excellence* in traditional ceremonies, also representing strength and virility.

10. Lit.: Sentries.

11. In 1994, I have to insist (see note 8, above), since the situation has worsened, according to Nasseem Ackbarally, a journalist quoted in *Courrier international*, 430, 28 January–3 February 1999, p. 29.

References

Camacho, M. (1986) *Les poubelles de la survie – la décharge municipale de Tananarive*, Paris, Harmattan.

Chasteland, J. C., J. Véron and M. Barbiéri (eds) (1993) *Politiques de développement et croissance démographique rapide en Afrique*, Paris, PUF/INED/CEPED, Congrès et colloques, 13.

Meillassoux, C. (1993) 'Troubles de croissance: la perspective d'un anthropologue', in J. C. Chasteland et al. (eds), *Politiques de développement*.

Raharijaona, H. (1993) 'Rapport sur l'application de la convention relative aux droits de l'enfant à Madagascar', Antananarivo, UNICEF/Ministère de la Population (Comité de suivi de l'application de la convention des Nations-Unies sur les droits de l'enfant à Madagascar).

Raharinarivonirina, A. (1992) 'Étude sur la législation en matière de protection de l'enfant à Madagascar', Antananarivo.

Ratsimbazafy, E. (1990) 'Rapport sur les enquêtes entreprises à Antananarivo, Antsirabe, Fianarantsoa, Moramanga', Antananarivo, Ministère de la Population, de la condition sociale, de la jeunesse et des sports/UNICEF, Projet Services urbains de base pour la protection des enfants en situation difficile.

Ravololomanga, B. (1992) *Être femme et mère à Madagascar – Tanala d'Ifanadiana*, Paris, Harmattan.

Schlemmer, B. (1995) 'Crise et recomposition des identités à Madagascar', *Revue Tiers Monde*, XXXVI, 141, January–March, pp. 129–44.

Sentenac, E. (1991) 'Enfants des rues', Antananarivo (in consultation with Médecins Sans Frontières).

UNICEF/République de Madagascar (1993) 'Analyse de la situation des enfants et des femmes à Madagascar', Antananarivo (document de travail).

CHAPTER 24

Looking Ahead: A General Conclusion

Claude Meillassoux

Not all children are exploited. The exploitation of child labour corresponds to a social class which, wherever it may be, suffers all the century's ills: malnutrition, disease, illiteracy, drugs, delinquency, accidents, even natural and industrial disasters. The vast majority of the children exploited are found in the economically dominated regions; and throughout the world in the most dispossessed social strata. Underage labour helps perpetuate the existence of an illiterate, overexploited, prolific and delinquency-generating sub-proletariat. It stocks and replenishes an abundant reserve of deskilled, hard-working and insecure labourers who, unaware of their rights, are cheap and easy to exploit. Within the framework of a deregulated system of competition, the exploitation of children produces some immediate gains. For the populations suffering the consequences, its social cost is prohibitive. Its moral cost is incalculable.

The Family Working against Itself

When southern countries are deliberately placed in a position of economic and political dependency and, because of the accompanying growing poverty,[1] a socio-economic mechanism is set in motion which leads to the breakdown of family structures and the exploitation of children.

In the words of Usha Ramanathan, 'poverty is sustained by inadequate attention to the wages of the adult population'. The lower the earnings of the family head, the more income the household needs to find to survive. However, this simple equation is frustrated by the workings of the market economy: the fact that families need to send more of their members out to work in order to multiply their sources of income contributes to the un-employment of adult men, then women.

When the men are receiving overly low wages, their wives and children are compelled to seek paid work. But the influx of extra labour on to the market helps to bring wages down even further, thus favouring the cheapest labour. As women (according to an ancient cultural model) are reputed to be materially dependent upon their husbands, employers have always considered that their earnings, not to mention those of children, represent *secondary income*. It follows that women's and children's wages are always pegged lower than those of adult men. Branding groups of workers as inferior by nature, and hence available at a better price (due to gender and age here as elsewhere due to nationality, skin colour, etc.) leads, wherever feasible, to the cheaper groups tending to replace the others and, hence, a general trend of falling average wages. As a result, three competing categories of labour emerge within a single family: adult men, adult women and children. Many employers prefer cheaper female labour to male. Similarly, child workers, who are known to be paid ten times less, will be preferred to adult men and women.

At this point, family solidarity is turned against itself. Instead of increasing family income, the employment of the (conventionally less well paid) woman or children contributes to the exclusion of the family head.

The spread of child employment conforms to the logic of competition between entrepreneurs, each of whom is compelled to make use of the least costly labour. One thing leading to another, many children find themselves in the position of being the only breadwinners in the family. In many companies or activities, child employees are not there merely to assist the adults, but to replace them. They sometimes even constitute the entire work force.

For the family supplying this labour, the earlier the children can go out to work the sooner they cease to be a burden on their parents. A child who is put to work moves directly from a non-productive state to the position of provider. Furthermore, while the unemployment of adults means that the children have to work longer hours in order to earn more, it is to the employers' advantage to prolong the working hours of these cheap labourers as much as they can.[2] Families facing the increasing substitution of children for adults find themselves having to produce ever larger numbers of offspring in order to increase their chances of securing an income. So the employment of children may stimulate a population explosion suited to this type of labour market. These new circumstances may give fresh impetus to the high birth rates in peasant societies (vulnerable to the random nature of food production) which should have been easing off with a view to improving living standards (Meillassoux 1991). In the societies experiencing population growth, the youngest age groups are actually the most populated and rapidly replenished. Children constitute a quick-turnover pool of flexible, readily available labour that is well suited to unskilled manual work. Because of their vast numbers and short-term renewability, they become so cheap as to be disposable, if not ruthlessly destructible (Meillassoux 1993).

Breakdown and Perversion of the Family

In the traditional, formerly self-sufficient, domestic family, 'each child belongs not just to a couple – its parents – but to the whole family group' (Mbaye).

Its socialization takes place within a parenting circle extended to include both paternal and maternal branches of the family. The children are in a 'situation of social indivisibility' (Alvim). They are encouraged, according to their means, to participate in the tasks within their reach. They learn the work performed by the adults around them through observation and imitation. Once adolescent, they join in with collective work which hinges on emulation and where they make a positive contribution to production by devoting great yet gratifying physical efforts. Even if it is not strictly egalitarian, the inter-generational and differed mode of redistribution between productive and non-productive generations excludes the systematic exploitation of a class of individuals in general, or of children in particular. To see a continuity between child labour in the domestic community and in the peasant economy or proletarianized urban families is to disregard everything that contributes to the 'civilization' and culture of the individual in the former, and all that is disappearing from the latter. In the rural domestic environment, families are primarily concerned with giving their descendants a training and equipping them with the means to take over not just the immediate economic tasks, but also the moral obligations associated with the group's reproduction. A large amount of time is devoted to the transmission, acquisition and practice of the knowledge and arts that go to make up the social personality. 'Child labour within the family enabled their reproduction as children' (Alvim).

This form of family organization, however, is not purely harmonious. It is also rooted in a notion of seniority that may act as a framework for the exploitation of the very young when the family is engaged in the production of marketable produce (Nieuwenhuys, Amin). Even in the mercantile peasant economy, the family often still remains the only institution able to offer its members material security[3] and, in competition with schools, provide structure for the moral education of its children (Tran Kiem). But the introduction of cash crops in the countryside contributes increasingly to the altering of rural norms. A family can continue to protect individual rights only if it remains large enough for each member to be able to resort to the arbitration of several relatives. Families reduced to the size of a household become enclosed spaces where, unless they can become part of an urban neighbourhood that offers a potential sphere of arbitration,[4] children are more prone to ill-treatment.

Although the family may well be the only institution to create and train a labour force, and although that labour force may well be subject, like any commodity, to the 'laws of the market', the family is not recognized as a company and familial relations are not based on wages. Unlike a company, relatives are bound to one another by non-monetized, inter-generational bonds, and not by contract. We do not pay our children wages; we take care of their needs and expect their help and assistance in return.[5] The family provides for its non-producing members: the young and the elderly. It cannot simply 'sack' people if their yield is low or if times are hard. Unlike the company chief who recruits employees on the market of 'ready-made' labourers and pays them exclusively for the work they do, the head of the family employs offspring fed and brought up within that family from birth, or wives who stay and work in the home. Finally, only rarely do families ever enjoy the benefits of the provisions made available to companies by commercial legislation. It is harder for them to be awarded a grant to purchase production equipment, for example. Family workers are therefore less productive and more 'costly' in real terms than company employees. As a result, and despite appearances, mercantile peasant economy families are often less competitive than commercial companies, hence condemned to making greater efforts and contending with greater tensions. Olga Nieuwenhuys's analysis looks at the mercantile peasant economy families struggling to 'satisfy the demands of the market and survive expanding capitalism'. Such families are tortured by the demands of the market economy or, in other words, made submissive, under variable economic conditions, to the 'cheap labour market rationality of the modern-day economy in developing countries' (Nieuwenhuys). 'Abuse of paternal authority is not what creates the exploitation of children; quite the opposite, it is capitalist exploitation which makes that authority degenerate into abuse,' said Karl Marx. We cannot analyse the domestic economy geared towards self-sufficiency in the same way as we would the mercantile peasant economy. In another piece of work (Meillassoux 1975), I have attempted to show how the market keeps itself supplied with goods and cheap labour by withholding investments from the domestic economy, a situation that has a negative effect on everybody working there. Nevertheless, Olga Nieuwenhuys describes a condition which seems somewhat less restricting than that found in the wage-paying firm, for the young girls she talks about have successfully managed to escape the constraints of their family employers in order to work thousands of kilometres away from home.

The way family workers are treated depends upon the economic climate and commodity prices on the market. Family ties are just as liable to alleviate the exploitation of children, as is still the case in Madagascar (Ravololomanga), as to make it worse. Marie Anderfuhren believes that 'working in rural areas within the framework of the family unit is worse than being an urban maidservant'. Because of the development of commercial agriculture in northern Togo, for example, parents have withdrawn their children from schools in order to increase family labour power on the plantations. But according to Marie-France Lange, Togo families are not always found to be exploiting their children, as the latter are not only provided for but sometimes receive material rewards into the bargain.

The proletarianization of rural families happens in a more or less brutal fashion. Without the means to produce agricultural export commodities, the only way a family can earn a living is to sell their labour. This is the case, for example, of the families hiring themselves out to the coffee plantations of Guatemala (Suremain). The parents are the only ones receiving any pay, even though they make their children help them with the work. The potential for competition between a child and its parents is kept in check by a unanimous refusal by all concerned, parents and children alike, to acknowledge and pay for the young person's labour.

Many families of rural origins living in country towns and even cities (50 per cent in Korhogo, Ivory Coast, according to Pascal Labazée) try to retain access to surrounding lands in order to cultivate subsistence crops and avoid succumbing to total proletarianization. The marketing of a share of their mini-harvests is part of what Labazée calls domestic 'polyactivity', which mobilizes the children and generates competition among older members of the household over the use of their services.

When separated from the land and dispossessed of all means of production, newly urbanized and proletarianized families soon find themselves downsized to households; from which point their role as pockets of solidarity and spaces for forming responsible members of society begins to diminish. Left with no other option but to join the market economy, they then have to procure all their basic necessities there and acquire the cash allowing them the access. They are subjected to rising consumer goods prices, inflation, depression, unemployment and taxation. The more submissive they are to the 'labour market', the more compelled they will be to adapt to it by abandoning their purely 'family-minded' functions and reorganizing their short-term existence with a view to securing a place as producers of the only commodity they have: labour power.

These badly crippled families can no longer afford to accommodate non-producing individuals if they want to remain 'profitable'. Elderly people unfit for economic service become too costly for society to keep, and they die before their time. With them disappears their erstwhile role of transmitting social and civilizing values. The most impoverished families become incapable of feeding new-born children for the five or six years it takes for them to become 'profitable'; hence the spread of infanticide.[6] Then it is father's turn to feel his position threatened. 'The erosion of the man's place [...] is a critical sign of the times', Martin Verlet rightly observes. When working, the man is exposed to dangerous or disabling conditions. When sick or unemployed, he becomes an unwelcome parasite within the family. Many go into exile for years on end, searching far and wide for usually badly paid work. They do not always return. The notion of 'father' associated with that of 'provider' and hence 'authority' vanishes when the man is out of work and he is often driven to abandoning the home. Absentee fathers are becoming a commonplace phenomenon (Verlet), paving the way for the abandonment of the children. The married woman loses her social role as a wife (assuring the continuity of the family group) and tends to become a purely economic agent restricted to the role of begetting and bringing up exploitable little workers as fast as she can for the sake of rapid turnover. As more and more men succumb to financial ruin and disappear, there are growing numbers of single-parent families. Even when they do manage to perform the domestic tasks of reproduction and economic tasks of production, women uphold their position as 'mothers' only at the cost of total exhaustion, which prevents them from fulfilling their role as educators.

Children forced to endure heavy and prolonged labouring quickly wear themselves out. They cease to represent the seeds of the future either for their families or for themselves. They cease to be regarded as security for elderly relatives in their old age, but as an immediate resource available to their natural parents alone. They need to be put to work at an ever younger age. And the children themselves rarely have enough time or energy left to devote to their studies and prepare for the future. 'The social values linked to the role and rights of the child are being replaced by a purely economic rationality' (Banpasirichote) and by the here and now. They are 'ruthlessly serviceable' (Verlet).

Here, then, we see the so-called 'market' economy revealing its true colours: neutralizing the most able-bodied labour – adult men, then women – in favour of the most delicate and vulnerable. And because it prioritizes the short term, it destroys anything given to the future.[7]

What do these children represent to that mercantile economy if not a labour force – or, failing that, organs – poor items of merchandise subjected to the material laws of direct competition, exposed to uncompromising exploitation at the hands of the least scrupulous, if not the most villainous (M. Bonnet)?

The Social Cost of Child Labour

Today's monetarist agencies argue that child labour is none of their business, that there are specialized institutions to deal with it; but that to suppress it would mean the ruin of the underdeveloped countries. However, as Chantana Banpasirichote remarks, there is little mention of the social (and economic) cost of child labour. The extent of that cost can be estimated by its precedents: the broken homes, the physical, intellectual and moral crippling of millions of children, the growth of juvenile delinquency and the obsolescence of productive machinery due to their employment. Above all, more than the backwardness of youth education, the overwhelming and onerous prospect of a coming generation of ignorant and ailing adults will weigh heavily for at least twenty years.[8] While claiming to be contributing to the country's wealth, companies resorting to the use of child labour are in actual fact draining it of its very substance.

One of the most serious pretexts for child labour is linked to education. Rosilene Alvim's study of history shows how the same arguments about the formative nature of work for children have been repeatedly used by employers and refuted by the facts time and again since the beginnings of industrialization. For the Brazilian industrialists of 1927, 'work is the only possible means of educating working class children'. This line was taken up more recently in the United Kingdom: in 1993, a health minister proclaimed that 'work can bestow a greater sense of responsibility' (Hobbs et al.). Moral and civic considerations have been put forward in favour of sending children to work for the sake of their education, as a means of avoiding juvenile delinquency or simply because children are better off in factories and work-shops than out on the streets, even if it means arranging it so that they have time for study and recreation (Mathur, Taracena et al.). The education angle sometimes causes confusion between child labour and apprenticeship so that one is used to justify the other (Alvim). But several papers describe and analyse how the abuse of apprenticeship acts as an efficient and cost-effective means of exploiting young workers.[9]

These grounds for justifying child labour penetrate the working classes: 'work forms part of their social identity' (Alvim). The children themselves express a desire to 'earn some cash' observes Yacouba Yaro; and Marie Anderfuhren notes how the young maidservants of Recife have 'interiorized the image of the untrained – and migrant – woman who can never be herself'. As Martin Verlet puts it: 'We are looking at a whole generation of children that has grown up under (structural) adjustment with no vision of the future other than that which is mapped out and obscured by international macro-economic constraints.' It is also true that some young people see the urban experience and the workshop pay packet as giving them a certain degree of freedom *vis-à-vis* family structures hardened by need. But does culture really have to shape itself according to the demands of the labour market and lead people to regard child labour as a fact of nature in working-class life?

Against this alienating drift, all the authors unanimously note the 'negative effect work has on school attendance rates' (Iyidiker). 'Although school activities do not exclude children from employment, employment can exclude them from school' (Fukui). Marie Anderfuhren remarks upon the low level of schooling among the young maidservants of Recife, yet also how they see school as an exceptional place for socialization which allows them, among other things, to put their working conditions in perspective; so it represents a place for civic training too. But in many cases school is seen by children and parents alike as standing in the way of paid work (Alvim), a waste of time, especially in view of the unsuitable hours and inadequate curricula. For Djilali Sari, the choice between educated child and exploited child is put in a dramatic nutshell in the slogans chanted by Algerian demonstrators: 'Give me a child and I'll make him a genius or a monster.'

However, this debate sometimes rests on a confusion between juvenile labour and child exploitation. The involvement of young people in working life unquestionably has its virtues. But such an involvement takes an unhealthy turn when the child's work is primarily intended for financial gain. If those directly or indirectly profiting from his/her labour do not regard him/her as given to the future, then s/he is at great risk of being exterminated. Exploitation stems from lucrative considerations which are not only bad for the child's development, but dangerous for his/her physical and intellectual integrity. The chapter describing the small-scale traditional coal mines of Columbia depicts the situation regarding the children's health as follows: 'the child workers' state of health in these regions is marked by parasites, calorie and protein deficiencies, anaemia, avitaminosis and rotting teeth. Working down the mines causes infectious diseases: pharyngitis, tonsillitis, sinusitis, influenza, pulmonary ailments and silicosis. Skin diseases and injuries to hands and the face are a permanent feature. Bone deformations are common in those who have been working for a number of years' (Céspedes et al.).

It remains that child labour is *not necessary* to an economy that can and should operate on the use of adult labour. By replacing the latter, child labour contributes, as we have seen, to the unemployment of the children's parents, the breakdown of the family and increases the burden of the social cost to society. This situation must be tackled with the whole picture firmly in mind.

The remaining question which seems to be at the root of the problem ties in with the incongruousness of child employment. How is it that physically weak, inexperienced beings, widely known for their unruly, inattentive nature and still limited in understanding, are liable to be chosen to work in place of able and responsible adults?[10] How come labour of this kind is the preferred choice of economies whose low labour productivity is their major obstacle to development? Contrary to what is generally maintained by the employers, not one of the posts currently filled by a child could not be taken over by an adult.

This extraordinary paradox stems from another: *the welfare of the individual is not the first purpose of the economy.* Conversely, human beings are the ones who have to adapt to the competitive climate of the economy and are shaped, if not crushed, by market costs and prices.

From that point of view, the shortcomings of a child labour force become virtues. Taken together, they serve to justify the low prices paid for such a labour force. Separately, each has its own advantages on the social plane: physical weakness makes children easy to dominate; inexperience deprives them of professional guarantees; their indiscipline exposes them to the terror of constant punishment; their naïvety prevents them from being able to clearly assess their position, resist abuse or oppose it through organized action. Furthermore, their family upbringing has trained them to respect their elders against whom any rebellion would be sacrilegious. The authority of the adult is accepted as natural. The boss or mistress ordering them about or beating them belongs to this skewed extension of family discipline. Paternalism imposes itself in all its guises, even the most perverted (Morice). 'It is not exploitation – to which child and adult workers alike are subjected – that should be made the main focal point of an analysis of child labour, but enslavement,' writes Michel Bonnet. The sum total of all these 'qualities' bestows upon the boss a number of other benefits and amenities including that of being able to make the child work longer hours, to submit him/her to a multitude of tasks or to sexual abuse (Verlet). Many papers make the point: the children are 'ruthlessly serviceable'.

Those childish traits that are so much to the advantage of the employer are not lasting, however; they vanish with age. If the child loses his job as soon as he has grown into a stronger and more aware adolescent, it is because he had been employed as a child and not as a person and is being replaced by another, submissive, child. Child labour is reproduced in this way, without a thought for the necessary transition into adulthood. In working life, ageing child workers acquire neither seniority nor prestige. 'The longer they stay in the job, the more depleted their physical and psychological capacities become. [...] If there is no tomorrow to look forward to, what does it mean to be a child?' (M. Bonnet). Few authors ponder the question asked by Ravololomanga: what will become of them once they have grown out of their labouring 'childhood', if and when, stronger and more aware, they become unfit for 'ruthless service'? What are their life-chances, if not their chance of a life? With what disabilities or diseases, psychological or social, will they be afflicted?

Does the answer not lie in the streets? That is where many of them spend their adolescence. Several authors recall the distinction between 'children in the street' and 'children of the street'. The former are the ones performing a paid activity there during the day while continuing to live in their parents' home;[11] whereas the latter no longer have any regular contact with their families. This also suggests that they are no longer the family providers either; that they are working for themselves, outside any family or social control. They are living permanently on the streets, surviving at best on odd jobs, at worst on the proceeds of crime. They are potential recruits for the mafia-style groups dominating the poorer parts of certain cities. *Is it not above all a case of adolescents no longer submissive enough to be 'ruthlessly serviceable'?* To what extent does 'child labour' help to form such a population, one that people everywhere describe as delinquent and dangerous and even go so far as to make a target for the death squads?

Solutions at National Level

Usha Ramanathan goes some way towards explaining why the problems of child labour are not fully apparent: as it is against the law for children to be employed, they do not attain 'personhood'; they are mere hands, legal non-people. This effacing of the exploited child casts a veil over the employer's responsibility and evinces the dehumanization caused by the realism of the law.

As shown in the debate on education, the solutions on offer stem from a basic choice: should child labour be abolished or should it be modified, regulated? In this respect, Usha Ramanathan sees three possible approaches that the law-maker may adopt: realism, pragmatism and idealism.

Realism. The law aims solely to codify an existing situation; all it does is draw up a list of prohibited types of employment. But its responsibility is aggravated by the legitimacy it offers.

Pragmatism. The law takes the situation for what it is but at least seeks to improve conditions. Stemming from the 'humanitarian' approach to social problems, it is hard to criticize this in so far as it is an attempt to alleviate an intolerable situation as quickly as possible. However, it has also been shown to sustain the very situations it is setting out to correct, giving them an appearance of legitimacy instead of eradicating them and, by prolonging them, offering their initiators the justification they need to continue exploiting children. In order to avoid coming to grief, a policy like this can remain only an emergency measure and regard abolition as a long-term goal.

The fact that the problem of child labour has received attention from the United Nations, and that a charter on the rights of the child was passed in 1989, is certainly something to be pleased about. And a look at public policies shows that nearly every country has since brought in laws to crack down on child labour. It also shows that in nearly every case their application goes by the board. The legal provisions for dealing with the problem boil down to the sanctioning of a common labour law violation. Whereas the exploitation of children affects the most dispossessed social strata, i.e. those on the borderline of survival, these sections of society are terrified that if the Labour Inspectorate takes action, they will be deprived of a vital resource. Under the circumstances, we cannot expect to see the victims lodging a formal complaint or resorting to legal action; on the contrary, they enter into a de facto collusion. It is therefore left to the authorities to engage legal proceedings which, in view of the current development of juvenile labour, represents an undertaking of a scale and expense regarded by all too many states as off-putting, if not inappropriate. Without detracting from the importance of the benefits gained in a number of countries from having UN agencies and Labour Inspectorates up and running there, it remains that actions like these, even when best applied, do nothing to change the economic circumstances giving rise to the employment of children.

Legal action is equally problematic when it comes to identifying those responsible. Bring action, sure, but against whom? At what level of the chain of exploitation? Should the parents be punished? But if the parents' wages are too low for the family to survive, if they themselves are unemployed, if there is nothing else they can do, should they be blamed for the recession that has forced them to send their children out to work? Are the employers guilty for preferring youthful, cheap labour to that of adults? Of course they are! But they will object on the grounds that because of competition they cannot afford to employ more costly labour without being forced out of business and, hence, further worsen the conditions of the people who depend on them; are they not acting more like benefactors by having consented to employ those children? Moving along the chain, we find the bulk buyers of goods manufactured by child labour, the local exporters, the consumer country importers, retail outlets and so on, all of them claiming that the stranglehold of competition forces them to push producers to sell at rock-bottom prices. At every level, the argument of 'competitiveness' is advanced to explain how the least wage rise will only drive companies to ruin, create worse unemployment and, consequently, even worse standards of living. So what about the shopkeepers and consumers of the importing countries who purchase goods with barely a thought for where they came from – might they be the ones responsible for buying at the lowest price? In which case, the labour laws, if applied only to the producing countries, are inoperative.

Idealism. This, finally, is Usha Ramanathan's suggested approach, since the so-called realistic and pragmatic measures have proved unreal and unworkable: it involves striving for an ideal, *the abolition of child labour*, without allowing oneself to become a slave to the status quo. 'The law may, perhaps, have to confine itself to taking an uncompromising moral stance [...] and consider the possibility of advocating abolition.' But there is no discussion about abolition. 'The right to a childhood could be the motivating force' (Ramanathan), so that children can regain their childhood: their time of preparation for adult life.

Action at International Level

Another way would be to act at international level radically to change the economic policies leading to child labour.

The countries of the North recommend two possible methods, sometimes inspired by entrepreneurs or trade unions: boycott and 'social taxation'.

We know how some of the work done in overexploited countries is severely undercutting whole branches of industry in the wealthy countries: textiles, sports shoes, even computers. Their unemployment is growing in proportion to the numbers of companies relocating abroad. Opinion among entrepreneurs in the North is therefore divided as regards such a strategy depending on whether or not they are the ones gaining from relocation. Some sectors have launched a campaign to boycott the countries where children are made to work. This moral stand is somewhat surprising in view of the fact that, as we have seen, the employment of children in the Third World stems from economic conditions created by international trading policies and, in good measure, by western investments. The campaign has not unreasonably been denounced as a manifestation of protectionism on the part of the great powers. One viewpoint which is gaining ground in the countries most affected by these practices is that 'the uncompromising application of international standards *vis-à-vis* labour laws is a form of protectionism designed to undermine the competitiveness of the developing countries'.[12] This is also used locally as a pretext to justify the employment of children. There is now a debate underway on the possibilities of introducing a labour law in the southern countries subjected to the overwhelmingly strong competition of the major powers. It is music to the ears of today's 'realists' who contend that child labour being, under the circumstances, 'unavoidable', all that can be done is make it tolerable. This naturally leads on to the claim that the 'competition' imposed by the market economy is the primary and fundamental cause of child labour. Be it dressed in the robes of morality or cynicism, the logic of the market economy likes to think of itself as inevitable. It is a drift that can work to the advantage only of the exploiters of every shape and form.

Another solution suggests taxing imported goods produced by children-employing companies and channelling these taxes back into the countries concerned for the purposes of funding education. But should this measure be taken by the importing countries rather than by the countries of origin? Does it not give the former another means of imposing themselves on the latter? Furthermore, such a tax could only ever be applied to the companies identified by the tax department and, hence, operating more within the law than their shadowy sub-contractors.

A New Assignment for the Monetarist Agencies

Neither of these solutions strikes at the root of the problem by questioning the validity of the modern free-market postulate of competition which underlies the choices defined and applied by the World Bank and the IMF.

Yet despite being among the most powerful international policy-making institutions with the largest reserves of funding at their disposal and influence second to none, these monetary and finance agencies do not come under the authority of the United Nations. They operate on the basis of an archaic system whereby voting strength is proportional to the states' financial contributions. This reduces the participation of the poorest countries practically to zero, meaning that they do not enjoy at world level the benefits of the democratic rules that they are being urged to apply at home!

The managers of the Bretton Woods agencies justify their existence by setting themselves up as the international arbiters of large-scale monetary financial interests. When structural adjustment measures are being advocated, everyone is well aware of the degrading, if not fatal, effects they will have on certain social strata while other groups suffer little or not at all and others still are raking in the profits. The 'arbitration' of these agencies does not go so far; for rather than redress the widening gap between rich and poor and the social and demographic effects inherent to monetarist economics, the World Bank and the IMF have, on the contrary, made matters worse with economic policies forced upon economically weaker countries. Their logic goes hand in glove with an elitist educational policy that definitively anchors in the social fabric the constituent economic inequalities of antagonistic classes. Blind to the material and moral condition of adult workers and children alike, these 'programmes' logically operate with the collusion of governments that are in turn blind to human rights. Note the scarcely veiled indulgence of the worst dictatorships and the aid supplied to the most warlike states.[13] As long as these programmes – regardless of their vague (genuine or hypocritical) desire to promote local enrichment – continue to hold sway, the condition of working children can never change. On the other hand, international bodies of this scale, with all their means for effective economic action at international level, could well be reassigned to reform international natural resource management so that those resources might be distributed according to need. They could work towards the equalization of living conditions from above; the establishment of a protocol for the world-wide circulation and distribution of international investments so that the most deprived countries might be removed from sustained de facto domination. With this new perspective in mind, a few basic measures could be recommended for eliminating the competitive use of child labour: a minimum working age established for every country right across the board and, above all, an education system in every country to provide compulsory, free and secular schooling up until that age, tailored to each country's individual customs and financed at international level by harmonizing countries' resources according to their respective budgets. In short(!), the goal would be to eliminate illiteracy as a loathsome source of international profiteering and allow all the world's children to grow into educated, free and responsible adults.

There are a number of United Nations agencies (UNDP, UNICEF, ILO) dealing with the fall-out of the so-called adjustment policies. Working on a more representative basis than the Bretton Woods bodies, these agencies are more aware of the social problems and are trying to bring to prominence a less obtuse range of development criteria than monetarist figurings. However, they have no say in the decision-making at the World Bank and the IMF. And yet the modern free-market doctrine clearly proved itself incapable of managing the unprecedented growth in labour productivity of the 1980s: which, instead of being deployed to improve general living standards, led to spreading unemployment and growing social inequality throughout the world (via the unchecked profiteering of the few on the back of all-powerful financial capitalism), and paved the way for the bloom of mafia-style businesses that have contaminated economies and governments world-wide with their villainy.

In matters such as that of child exploitation, where the future of the human species is threatened at its most precious and vulnerable point, we must avoid falling into the traps of the utilitarianism or realism that lead to the reification of human beings. We must start out from the principle that production should be geared towards the welfare of the human being:

that human beings are not (even 'the most precious kind' of) 'capital', or (human!) resource, or 'means' of production; but the lucid, independent and informed agents of that production whose goal ought not to be profits in themselves, but to allow human individuality to blossom.

We must reaffirm that *any policy which reverses this proposition by subordinating the welfare of the individual to production is an affront to the rights of humankind.* Only by demanding justice and applying these rights can we bring a halt to the slow killing off of children through the enforcement of strict laws of profit.

For the last resort is to act by restoring a code of ethics to a field where it is most likely to make an impression on the conscience. This moral crisis is what is revealed by the generalized perversity of economics, and it is in the name of the most fundamental rights that we must subject to radical review the powers and 'teachings' that are leading to the ultimate horror of all horrors: the exploiting to death of our children.

Notes

1. See my presentation in Chapter 3: 'The Economy and Child Labour: An Overview'.

2. Rosilene Alvim notes that, in Brazil, an official report from 1932 explained how the working hours for minors were raised from the previous five hours a day to eight hours because of poor families' economic needs.

3. As with any insurance scheme, family solidarity at this level allows the urban and rural branches to pull together to help balance overall family income; but it is small-scale, which makes it vulnerable. If the rural branch has land to cultivate, penniless members of the urban branch are offered a place to which they can retreat. When urban employment is healthy, the city branch transfers a share of its earnings to the rural.

4. These neighbourhoods also feature the practice of parental transfers: cf. Fonseca (1985).

5. There are exceptions: children working as hired hands for their father's businesses (Temgoua), children required to pay rent to sleep in the parental home (Ravololomanga). Such cases illustrate the extremes to which people are driven by the deteriorating social bonds eroded by economic circumstances that have become far too difficult.

6. Far from resolving the problem of overpopulation, growing mortality due to poverty actually makes matters worse, as undernourishment also goes hand in hand – and proportionally so – with the physical and mental invalidation of children who then become a burden on their own generation and other generations to come.

7. Basing herself on Pires, Lia Fukui maintains that 'child labour is not inherent to capitalism, but the outcome of specific, concrete forms of that mode of production'. Yet the context gives us to understand that if child labour is no longer technically 'necessary' to industry (irrespective of what the employers often claim), it economically suits the capitalist principles of competition. When not held in check by adequate legislation, capitalistic free competition serves to propagate child labour. On the pretext of the competitiveness of underdeveloped countries, a European Community directive (enacted in 1994) authorizes children to work from the age of thirteen 'within the framework of a system of sandwich courses' already in force in France (Garet). In Great Britain, they may undertake farm work from the age of ten if accompanied by their parents: 'The existence of economic forces which treat children as a source of cheap labour is clear' (Hobbs et al.).

8. Speaking on the informal sector and its social effects, the director of the São Paulo consultancy firm CLA stressed that: 'the current model of production is cutting back employment in industry. The problem of unemployment cannot be solved by growth. But Brazil has an additional handicap: education. Even if one were to take measures to improve education right now, it would still take another twenty years to resolve the problem' (*Courrier International*, 25–29 March 1995).

9. I refer here to the texts by Alessandro Stella, Bernard Garet, Yves Marguerat, Michaël Lavalette, as well as Alain Morice's presentation.

10. A question tackled by Michaël Lavalette.

11. As opposed to the child sent to work at a company, a workshop or as a domestic, the 'child in the street' is working sometimes for an 'employer', who may also be a blood relative, sometimes freelance. This type of activity is described in many of the papers.

12. Statement by Mrs Nieves Roldan-Confesor, president of the board of directors of the ILO, interviewed in an issue of *Asiaweek* (November 1994) whose cover bore the banner headline: 'Can Asia afford Workers' RIGHTS?' (It should be said that she did not intend these to be taken as the official views of the ILO.)

13. The president of the IMF, Mr Camdessus, granted a loan of unprecedented proportions to Mr Yeltsin while his CIS army was massacring Chechens (through the winter of 1994 and spring of 1995); the self-same IMF regarded General Pinochet as a model head of state; there are countless other such examples we could mention.

References

Chasteland, J. C., J. Véron and M. Barbiéri (eds) (1993) *Politiques de développement et croissance démographique rapide en Afrique*, Paris, INED.

Fonseca, C. (1985) 'Market Value, Maternal Love and Survival: Aspects of the Circulation of Children in a Brazilian Shanty Town', *Annales ESC*, 5; cited in A. Cadoret (1995) *Parenté plurielle*, Paris, Harmattan, p. 10.

Gendreau, F., C. Meillassoux, B. Schlemmer and M. Verlet (eds) (1991) *Les spectres de Malthus*, Paris, EDI-ORSTOM-CEPED.

Meillassoux, C. (1975) *Femmes, greniers et capitaux*, Paris, Maspero (new edn, Paris, Harmattan, 1992).

— (1991) 'La leçon de Malthus: le contrôle démographique par la faim', in F. Gendreau et al. (eds), *Les spectres de Malthus*, pp. 15–32.

— (1993) 'Troubled Growth', in J. C. Chasteland et al., *Politiques de développement*, pp. 61–80.

Index

abandoned children, 8, 28, 29, 31, 163, 319; child labour of, 27

abolition of child labour *see* child labour, abolition of

Acolatsé, Alex, 240

action against child labour, at international level, 325–6

activists on child labour issues, treatment of, 188

Adorno, Theodor, 126

age: minimum, of apprentices, 249; of child labour, 95, 120, 250 (minimum, 109, 110, 111, 119, 128, 142, 143, 146, 163, 167, 170, 172, 216)

agriculture, child labour in, 23, 84, 115, 121, 137, 198, 231, 268, 271, 296

Aguiar, Ana Isabel, 171

Alberti, Leon Battista, 34

All India Carpet Manufacturers' Association (AICMA), 59, 61

Alves, A., 123

Alvim, Rosilene, 114, 320

ancestor worship in Madagascar, 300

Anderfuhren, Marie, 7, 318, 321

Anti-Slavery Society, 180

apprentices, 12, 25–7, 31, 146, 297; ages of, 26; boys as, 27; Genoa silk-spinners, 25; humiliation of, 253; logbooks of, 256; maximum numbers, 27, 29; release of, 244; running away by, 29–30; supervision of, 256; use and abuse of, 243–5; wages of, 27; workloads of, 254

Apprentices Training Centre (CFA) (Angers), 248, 256–9

apprenticeships, 58, 77, 78, 119, 127, 128, 129, 171, 201, 205, 209, 265, 293, 298, 309; cost of, 240, 242; establishment of, 239–41; grants for, 127; in France, 248–60; in Ghana, 74; in Togo, 239–47; rules governing, 243

Ariès, Philippe, 25, 125

Aristotle, *Politics*, 21

armed struggle, children in, 8

Bachpen Bacoa Andolan, 56

Bangladesh, layoffs in textile industry, 189

Banpasirichote, Chantana, 320

Baranwal, Kailash Nath, 59

Barros, R., 124

begging, 28, 297, 302, 303, 307, 309, 310

Bogota, child labour in brickworks, 23

bonded labour, 13, 57, 179–91, 265; and training, 182–5; definition of, 180–2

Bonnet, Michel, 13, 15, 115, 323

Bourdieu, P., 102

boycotts of produce of child labour *see* import bans

boys: employment of, 268, 287 (in coffee-growing industry, 232, 234–5; in fishing industry, 283–4); labour of, 268; used in war, 266

Brazil, 10, 114; child labour in, 118–34; poor children in, debate about, 160–75

Bretton Woods institutions, 326

brick carriers, children as, 308, 309

brokers *see* child-brokers

Brotherhomé School of Professional Studies (Togo), 240

Burma, 136

Cairo, children in tannery works, 23

Calsing, E., 120

car attendants, children as, 305, 309

care lease, 28–30

Carpet Export Promotion Corporation (CEPC) (India), 55, 56

carpet industry: child labour in, 200, 212; in India, 51–66 (competitiveness of, 58–63; statistics for, 55–8; structure of, 60–1); international market for, 54; production process in, 57, 60

Casa Alianza, 93

cash crops, growing of, 275

cash economy, 292

Cerrejo mining complex (Colombia), 83, 85

charities, and exploitation of child labour, 27